SIR DOUGLAS HAIG'S DESPATCHES

SIR DOUGLAS HAIG'S DESPATCHES

(December 1915 — April 1919)

EDITED BY LIEUT.-COLONEL
J. H. BORASTON, O.B.E.
(Private Secretary to Earl Haig)

WITH SPECIALLY PREPARED
MAPS, SKETCH PLANS
& PORTRAITS

The Naval & Military Press Ltd

Published by

The Naval & Military Press Ltd
Unit 5 Riverside, Brambleside
Bellbrook Industrial Estate
Uckfield, East Sussex
TN22 1QQ England

Tel: +44 (0)1825 749494

www.naval-military-press.com
www.nmarchive.com

In reprinting in facsimile from the original, any imperfections are inevitably reproduced and the quality may fall short of modern type and cartographic standards.

PREFACE

THESE Despatches are republished as a tribute to the valour of the British soldier and the character of the British nation.

They were written in the first instance with the object of telling, in plain and straightforward language, all that it was possible to make public at that time; with the knowledge then available and without either lowering or exalting unduly the splendid spirit of the nation, or giving assistance to our enemies. By their means, I sought to convey to my countrymen in all parts of the Empire the information it was their right to possess concerning the progress and prospects of the war; to make those at home understand the full nature of the difficulties with which our Armies in the field had to contend, and the magnificent spirit and determination by which all difficulties were overcome.

That the account given in these Despatches is so frank and full speaks very highly for the steadfast patriotism, good sense, and equanimity of all classes of the people of our Empire, to whom at all times the truth could be told. The long series of glorious actions related all too briefly in their pages bear equal testimony to the courage and devotion of all ranks of the British Armies, and therefore cannot be too widely known.

The general accuracy of the narratives, and the not inconsiderable amount of detail which it was possible to incorporate in them, reflects credit upon the staff arrangements for the collection of reliable reports and for their rapid transmission from the lower to the higher formations. In normal times operation reports from Armies reached General Headquarters by wire twice daily, in the early morning and late evening. These "Army wires" were based upon a complete chain of reports extending through Corps, divisions, brigades and battalions to the companies in the line. Each link in the chain acted as a report centre, where the information reaching it was collated and summarised and the material portions forwarded in the form of a brief and precise statement to the formation above it. To ensure accuracy, to make certain that the reports sent on contained only what it was material that the higher formation should know, that nothing of consequence was omitted, and that a minimum of time was lost in the actual process of transmission, entailed a high degree of organisation and training in all formations.

During the periods of battle fighting, these diurnal statements were supplemented by many others, as well as by telephone, wireless or aeroplane messages sent whenever there was anything of moment to report. These additional messages might be the result of the immediate observation of liaison officers, whether of Armies, Corps or divisions; they might be amplified, confirmed or at times even forestalled by aeroplane reports received direct from the Headquarters, Royal Air Force, or by the reports of Intelligence Officers.

A further and most important source of information was supplied by the liaison officers sent out direct from General Headquarters. These were all specially selected officers, young, but of proved ability, experience and tact. Their duties took them frequently to all parts of the zone of the British Armies and into the actual fighting line. Their reports were often of high value.

The senior officers of my Staff also made numerous visits to lower formations. The information they were able to obtain formed an important addition to the results of my own personal observation.

There was present, therefore, at General Headquarters a very ample source of current information from which the framework of the Despatches could be built up. This was again supplemented and checked by weekly Operation Reports from Armies, by Army Diaries, Intelligence Sum-

PREFACE

maries and at times by special reports obtained from Armies, Corps and divisions relative to particular actions or battle periods. The other Branches of my General Staff also kept records of their activities and these were available as material for such portions of my Despatches as it was possible to devote to their work.

Compiled, however, during the actual process of the events they describe, the Despatches do not pretend to be a complete and final account of the three momentous years of crowded incident and stupendous happenings with which they deal. Yet because they were put together under the immediate strain of battle, while the results of the decisions and actions they recount were still undetermined, and were issued for the information of a nation whose fate still hung in the uncertain balance of war, they possess an atmosphere of their own which gives them a definite historical importance. Moreover, they are at the moment the only available official account of a most splendid and most critical period in our national existence.

For these reasons, I thought it desirable to bring together under the same cover all the different Despatches sent by me from France and to arrange for their publication as a single book, accompanied by a complete series of maps with the aid of which the reader may follow every turn of the great struggle. The text of the book is throughout substantially the same as that which appeared in the Gazettes. It has been possible, however, to insert the names of divisions which in the earlier Despatches were omitted for reasons of secrecy; to correct one or two minor errors, and to add a few explanatory notes and sketches. The large maps are copies of, or based directly upon, those which actually accompanied my original Despatches to the Secretary of State.

Being intended primarily for the eyes of British subjects and dealing with the operations of the British Armies, the Despatches necessarily refer but briefly to the actions of our Allies. It must be left to future historians to write the book in which the exploits of the different Allied Armies shall appear in their true proportion and perspective. For me, it is enough to acknowledge here, as I have done more than once in the Despatches themselves, the inestimable debt we owe to our Allies, and especially to the French. I would emphasize also once more the cordial relations which throughout the whole period of the war prevailed both between the officers and men of the different Allied Armies in the field and between British soldiers of all ranks and the civil population of France and Belgium. To the general interchange of courtesy between the French and ourselves, Marshal Foch has lately added an example personal to myself by writing his admirable introduction to the French edition of this book.

I am indebted to His Majesty's Government for permission to republish my Despatches in book form.

Douglas Haig, F.M.

HORSE GUARDS,
    2nd September, 1919.

INTRODUCTION
BY
FIELD-MARSHAL FOCH[1]

IT has always been the custom for the Commander-in-Chief of the British Forces in the field to forward to his Government Despatches summarizing the principal periods of a campaign. Field-Marshal Sir Douglas Haig has conformed to this practice. Twice a year on an average, he has prepared a brief account of the most important features of the British operations on the Western front. His Despatches cover the period during which he was Commander-in-Chief, from the end of 1915 to the first days of April, 1919.

Written with the strictest regard for the truth and scrupulously exact to the smallest details, these Reports are distinguished by their unquestionable loftiness and breadth of view. The information that they give, not only on the operations themselves, but also on the condition of the troops—on the changes made in their training and their formation during the course of the war—constitutes them historical documents of the highest order. They throw into relief the special character of each contingent that the Empire provided, the unremitting labours of the Staffs, and define their respective merits. They are a record, in fact, of the work thanks to which all ranks rapidly improved their fighting experience and professional skill, and adapted them to a struggle full of surprises. They give a picture of the enormous task devolving upon the various services charged with supplying the ever-growing needs of a modern army.

If the facts are sometimes set forth with a light touch, which does not take us down to the underlying causes and some of their results, it is because these Reports, written during the course of the war, and addressed to the British Government, were destined eventually for the eyes of the whole Nation, whose feelings must be considered,

[1] This Introduction was written by Marshal Foch for the French Edition of the Despatches, and is reproduced here in English with his permission and approval. The French version will be found at the end of this volume—see page 358.

just as the enemy must be kept from gathering information of value. None the less, to read them is to discover how remarkable was the unswerving purpose which fashioned the British Army from 1917 onwards into a magnificent instrument of war. Its effect can be seen in the training of the troops, in the creation of special services to deal with the increasing number and variety of engines of modern warfare, in the production and transport of munitions to satisfy a demand hitherto unknown, and in the construction or repairing of the lines of communication.

No instrument, however, can produce of itself; there must always be the hand which knows how to use it. When, therefore, the Despatches are content with telling us that the period of attrition was followed in the natural course of events by the period of decision, that the German armies, exhausted and worn out by the fighting of 1914, 1915, 1916 and 1917, were to be defeated in 1918, they do not say why the former period was so long and the latter so short. Still less do they explain the change in the decisive period when the Allies advanced to victory at the double, only to be stopped by German capitulation at the Armistice. The results are briefly set forth, their causes are not explained. All mention of the hand which guided the instrument is omitted. We may be allowed to make good this deficiency, in which the all-important part played by the British Higher Command is lost to sight.

The period of attrition coincided, in fact, with a period of weakness for the Allies, which was the result of their incomplete preparation for war. To the battlefields of 1914 the Entente had not brought more than a British Army of six divisions and a French Army lacking in the artillery and munitions required for modern warfare.

With these inadequate means, we certainly did stem the invasion in the first year, but so long as the shortage in our effectives and material was not made good, we were not in a position to undertake the long-sustained offensive which alone could force a decision by arms. We were limited to local and spasmodic engagements, and the best that could be done was to endeavour to co-ordinate them as to space and time.

That is the explanation of the poor results obtained up to the year 1917. Happily for the Entente, the enemy was obliged during these years to cope first with the Russian and then with the Rumanian

Armies in the East. Consequently, he had employed on the Western front only a part of his forces, insufficient to gain a definite victory, or had put into operation, as at Verdun, only a narrow and limited conception of the offensive. The resulting weakness of the two opposing lines threatened to prolong for some time to come what has been called the war of attrition—that struggle of unmarked and unsustained advantages, which wears out both armies without bringing gain to either—a war without result. If a war is to end in victory, it must always be given a character different from this.

In the course of this struggle for a decision (a necessary phase be it said), Germany freed herself on the Eastern front in 1917 by means of the Russian Revolution and the Treaties of Brest-Litovsk and Bucharest. And when she turned the mass of her formidably equipped armies, more than 200 divisions strong, against the Western front to deliver the violent and, in the first instance, victorious attacks on the Somme in March, 1918, on the Lys in April, on the Chemin des Dames in May, on the Oise in June, and on the Marne in July, who could perceive the signs of that fatal attrition, or the dawn of victory for the Entente? Who will forget the danger of fresh enemy advances, along the Somme, to Amiens, to split the British Armies from the French, or towards Saint Omer and Dunkirk, to cut off the British Forces from Great Britain; or towards Paris itself, the heart of France and centre of communications vital to the Alliance? Where was the advantage claimed from the wastage of the German Armies during the preceding years? Was there no danger that the conflict of Armies, even Armies of the finest quality like the British, might end in disaster, unless they possessed a Higher Command capable of dominating the situation and controlling the turn of events, able to take the troops in hand again, to reorganize and so dispose them that they might first bring the enemy to a standstill, then attack him with such violence, dash and such repeated blows as were never surpassed?

At every stage, both Higher Command and Staffs proved more than equal to their tasks. Thanks to the activity they were to display after the German attacks in the spring of 1918, and in spite of the losses suffered, more than 60 British divisions, ten times the number in 1914, were to be kept in fighting order until the end of the year; and their moral was to be better than ever. Lines of resistance were multiplied before Amiens, Arras, Béthune, Hazebrouck, Saint Omer and Cassel. Preparations were also made to flood tracts of country, for the ground was to be contested bitterly, foot by foot. Above all, powerful supplies of Allied reserves were to be kept freely moving in constant play between all the Armies. Thus it was possible for French troops to relieve the Fifth British Army south of the Somme at the commencement of April, and for seven French divisions to support the Second British Army in Flanders in the same month; for five British divisions to reinforce the Sixth French Army on the Chemin des Dames; finally for two British divisions to assist the Fifth French Army in the Forest of Reims, and two other divisions the Tenth French Army at Villers-Cotterets, and join in the counter-offensive of July the 18th.

Thus it was that, thanks in particular to the activities of the British Higher Command and to their grasp of the needs of the situation, more than 200 German divisions were stopped short in their offensive by a smaller number of Allied divisions, and our defensive proved to be victorious. The same must be said for the support lent by the British troops to other armies during our actual offensive.

In order to estimate the ardour and endurance of these troops during this final stage, it will be enough to mention the dates and importance of the main events :—

> *Battle of Amiens.*—Aug. 8–13, in which the Fourth Army took 22,000 prisoners and more than 400 guns.
>
> *Battle of Bapaume.*—Aug. 21–Sept. 1, Third Army and Left Wing of the Fourth Army; 34,000 prisoners, 270 guns.
>
> *Battle of the Scarpe.*—Aug. 26–Sept. 3, First Army; 16,000 prisoners, 200 guns.
>
> *Battle of Havrincourt and Epéhy.*—Sept. 12–18, Fourth and Third Armies; 12,000 prisoners, 100 guns.
>
> *Battle of Cambrai and the Hindenburg Line.*—Sept. 27–Oct. 5, Fourth, Third and First Armies, which ended in the breaking of the Hindenburg Line and in the capture of 35,000 prisoners and 380 guns.
>
> *Battle of Flanders.*—Sept. 28–Oct. 14, Second Army.
>
> *Battle of Le Cateau.*—Oct. 6–12, Fourth, Third and First Armies.

INTRODUCTION

Battle of the Selle.—Oct. 17-25, Fourth and Third Armies; 20,000 prisoners, 475 guns.

Battle of the Sambre.—Nov. 1-11, Fourth, Third and First Armies; 19,000 prisoners, 450 guns.

The effect of these violent and repeated British attacks was greatly enhanced because they were linked up with the actions of other Allied armies, French, American, and also Belgian, who struck blows which told no less powerfully in the general plan of this converging assault, extending from the North Sea to the Moselle.

Never at any time in history has the British Army achieved greater results in attack than in this unbroken offensive lasting 116 days, from the 18th of July to the 11th of November. The victory gained was indeed complete, thanks to the excellence of the Commanders of Armies, Corps and Divisions, thanks above all to the unselfishness, to the wise, loyal and energetic policy of their Commander-in-Chief, who made easy a great combination, and sanctioned a prolonged and gigantic effort. Was it not the insight of an experienced and enlightened Commander which led him to intervene as he did, with his own Government on the 24th of March, 1918, and with the Allied Governments assembled at Doullens on the 26th, to the end that the French and British Armies might at once be placed under a single command, even though his personal position should thereby suffer? In the events that followed, did he not prove that he was above all anxious to anticipate and move in perfect harmony with the general Allied plan, framed by the new Supreme Command?

On this point the Despatches contain gaps which prevent the reader from grasping all the reasons for our victory; truth compelled me to complete their account.

CONTENTS

	PAGE
PREFACE BY FIELD-MARSHAL HAIG	v
INTRODUCTION BY FIELD-MARSHAL FOCH	ix
LOCAL OPERATIONS: ST. ELOI	1
THE OPENING OF THE WEARING-OUT BATTLE	17
THE RETREAT TO THE HINDENBURG LINE	61
THE CAMPAIGNS OF 1917	79
THE CAMBRAI OPERATIONS	149
THE GREAT GERMAN OFFENSIVE	175
THE ADVANCE TO VICTORY	243
THE FINAL DESPATCH	309
ORIGINAL TEXT OF MARSHAL FOCH'S INTRODUCTION	358
INDEX	363

PORTRAITS

FIELD-MARSHAL SIR DOUGLAS HAIG		*Frontispiece*
GENERAL SIR HENRY RAWLINSON		*facing page* 19
GENERAL SIR HUBERT GOUGH		,, 63
GENERAL SIR EDMUND ALLENBY		,, 81
GENERAL SIR HERBERT PLUMER		,, 103
GENERAL SIR JULIAN BYNG		,, 151
GENERAL SIR HENRY HORNE		,, 177
GENERAL SIR WILLIAM BIRDWOOD		,, 245

LIST OF SKETCH MAPS

THE ST. ELOI OPERATIONS	*facing page*	7
SOMME BATTLE: Attack of 1st July, 1916	,,	25
SOMME BATTLE: Attack of 14th July, 1916	,,	28
SOMME BATTLE: Attack of 15th September, 1916	,,	41
SOMME BATTLE: Attacks of 25th and 26th September, 1916	,,	43
ANCRE BATTLE: 13th November, 1916	,,	49
BATTLE OF ARRAS: 9th April, 1917	,,	89
BATTLE OF MESSINES: 7th June, 1917	,,	106
THIRD YPRES BATTLE: Attack of 31st July, 1917	,,	113
THIRD YPRES BATTLE: Attack of 20th September, 1917	,,	121
THIRD YPRES BATTLE: Attack of 26th September, 1917	,,	123
THIRD YPRES BATTLE: Attack of 4th October, 1917	,,	125
CAMBRAI BATTLE: British Attack, 20th November, 1917	,,	154

LIST OF SKETCH MAPS—continued

CAMBRAI BATTLE: German Attack, 30th November, 1917 . . . . *facing page* 163

SECOND SOMME BATTLE: German Attack, 21st March, 1918 . . . . " 186

SECOND SOMME BATTLE: Stages of Retreat . . " 196

THE LYS BATTLE: German Attacks of 9th and 10th April, 1918 . . . . " 220

VILLERS BRETONNEUX: 24th—25th April, 1918 . " 231

THE LYS BATTLE: German Attack, 25th April, 1918 . . . . " 232

OPENING OF FINAL BRITISH OFFENSIVE: 8th August—9th September, 1918 . . . . . " 262

BATTLE OF CAMBRAI AND HINDENBURG LINE: Cambrai Attack, 27th September, 1918 . . " 280

BATTLE OF CAMBRAI AND HINDENBURG LINE: Hindenburg Line Attack, 29th September, 1918 . " 282

SECOND BATTLE OF LE CATEAU: 8th October, 1918 . " 287

BATTLE OF THE SAMBRE: 4th November, 1918 . " 294

GENERAL BATTLE SITUATION ON WESTERN FRONT: 25th September, 1918 . . . . . " 378

LIST OF FOLDING MAPS
(IN PORTFOLIO)

1. THE SOMME BATTLE, 1916
2. THE GERMAN RETREAT, SPRING, 1917
3. THE ARRAS BATTLE, 1917
4. THE FLANDERS CAMPAIGN, 1917
5. THE CAMBRAI OPERATIONS, 1917
6. THE GERMAN ATTACK ON THE SOMME, 1918
7. THE GERMAN ATTACK ON THE LYS, 1918
8. THE GREAT BRITISH ADVANCE, 1918
9. STRATEGIC MAP OF ALLIED OFFENSIVE, 1918
10. THE ADVANCE INTO GERMANY, 1918

PREFACE TO THE 2001 EDITION

THIS edition of *Sir Douglas Haig's Despatches* is a reprint of J.M. Dent's edition, published in October1919, but with one major addition, contained in this preface – the text of phrases or sentences deleted by HMG, then led by Lloyd George, no admirer of Haig. The two relevant despatches are those dated 25 December 1917 and 20 July 1918, specifically pages 82, 177 and 178 where a series of asterisks denote the deleted passages. It is of interest that the references in the despatches that attracted HMG's attention were to the Third Ypres offensive (more commonly, if incorrectly, known as Passchendaele), and the BEF manpower shortage at the beginning of 1918. In a couple of instances the Government actually inserted its own words, altering the original.

These despatches were edited by Lt Col J.H. Boraston, private secretary to the Field Marshal, and the deleted phrases are preserved among his papers in the Imperial War Museum (71/13/2). These missing extracts were first published in G.A.B Dewar and J.H Boraston's *Sir Douglas Haig's Command* (Constable 1922, 2 volumes) and the authors commented critically on the Government's action. Referring to the July 1918 *Despatch*, published in the *London Gazette* on 21 October 1918 they have this to say (Vol 1 p28):

"By October 21, all risk of the Germans profiting by these [deleted] references was of course over. The enemy was retreating hastily...However, as the war was still in being...Let us, for the sake of peace, concede that censorship was reasonable. October 21, 1918, however, is one thing, the late autumn of 1919 is another; and yet at the latter period, when an opportunity was taken to issue...[the] Despatches in book form...permission was granted only on the explicit understanding that the text should be that of the *London Gazette*. That is - the offending passages must still be omitted!"

And referring to the deletions in the December 1917 *Despatch* they say:

"The public more than a year after the Armistice was not entitled to know what the Commander-in-Chief stated in his Despatch of December 25, 1917, concerning the great Flanders offensive of that year."

They conclude these comments thus:

"Truth in this world, said a cynic, must wait – she is used to it. The wait in this instance strikes one as being unconscionably long."

The authors were quite clearly angered by what they regarded as unjustified Government censorship.

SIR DOUGLAS HAIG'S DESPATCHES

In 1979 J.M Dent published a new edition of the *Despatches* with a Foreword by John Terraine, but it did not include the deleted passages.

In preparing this preface I would like to acknowledge the help given by my good friend John Hussey, military historian, whose knowledge of the Great War is formidable, who suggested incorporating the missing bits in this reprint. This led me to ferret through my copy of *Sir Douglas Haig's Command* (still, I am ashamed to say with many uncut pages, though now fewer) in search of the offending passages. I am indebted, too, for the summary of the changes as shown below which he prepared and sent me.

TERRY CAVE
WORTHING AUGUST 2001

THE ALTERATIONS MADE BY HMG TO HAIG'S DESPATCHES
DATED 25 DECEMBER 1917 AND 20 JULY 1918

DESPATCH OF 25 DECEMBER 1917, page 82, paragraph 4.

1. At the beginning of the paragraph restore the following phrase, deleted by the Government:

   4. The project of an offensive operation in Flanders, to which I was informed His Majesty's Government attached considerable importance, was one which I had held steadily in view since I had been first entrusted with the chief command of the British Armies in France, and even before that date.

2. After the sentence near the bottom of the page concerning the advantages of gaining the high ground at Broodseinde and Passchendaele, restore the next sentence, deleted by the Government:

   Moreover, once this high ground had been secured, further offensive possibilities would be opened up.

DESPATCH OF 20 JULY 1918.

1. Page 177, paragraph 2. In the first sentence restore the following phrase, deleted by the Government:

   to which the retention of British troops in Italy, the lack of the men required to fill up our divisions, and the urgent demands made upon us to extend the British front gave added force,

PREFACE TO THE 2001 EDITION

2. Page 178, paragraph 4. At the beginning of the paragraph restore the following sentence, deleted by the Government:

   4. The lack of adequate reinforcements and my consequent inability to keep the ranks of the fighting units within a measure of their establishment gave me cause for anxiety.

3. Page 179, paragraph 4 (cont).
   (a) Delete the Government's phrase: "At the same time a change took place in the organisation of the forces." and replace by:

   As regards our requirements of men, deficiencies were not being made good, and this necessitated a change in the organisation of the forces.

   (b) In the next sentence delete the asterisks after "to a 10 battalion basis was" and restore the original words:

   accordingly undertaken and...

   (c) In the next sentence delete the Government's words (italicised by Boraston): "to some extent affected" and replace by:

   lowered at a crucial moment.

   (d) In the next sub-paragraph, first sentence, delete the asterisks after "...we were faced" and restore the original wording:

   in connection with the reduction in numbers, the necessity for extensive training, and the construction of elaborate systems of rearward defences

LOCAL OPERATIONS: ST. ELOI

SIR DOUGLAS HAIG'S DESPATCHES

(DECEMBER 1915 — APRIL 1919)

LOCAL OPERATIONS: ST. ELOI

General Headquarters,
19th May, 1916.[1]

MY LORD,—

1. I have the honour to report the operations of the British Forces serving in France and Belgium since 19th December, 1915, on which date, in accordance with the orders of His Majesty's Government, I assumed the Chief Command.

During this period, the only offensive effort made by the enemy on a great scale was directed against our French Allies near Verdun. The fighting in that area has been prolonged and severe. The results have been worthy of the high traditions of the French Army and of great service to the cause of the Allies. The efforts made by the enemy have cost him heavy losses both in men and in prestige, and he has made these sacrifices without gaining any advantage to counterbalance them.

During this struggle my troops have been in readiness to cooperate as they might be needed, but the only assistance asked for by our Allies was of an indirect nature—viz., the relief of the French troops on a portion of their defensive front. This relief I was glad to be able to afford.

Its execution on a considerable front, everywhere in close touch with the enemy, was a somewhat delicate operation, but it was carried out with complete success, thanks to the cordial co-operation and goodwill of all ranks concerned and to the lack of enterprise shown by the enemy during the relief.

2. On the British front no action on a great scale, such as that at Verdun, has been fought during the past five months, nevertheless our troops have been far from idle or inactive. Although the struggle, in a general sense, has not been intense, it has been everywhere continuous, and there have been many sharp local actions.

[1] This Despatch was published as a Supplement, dated the 29th May, 1916, to the *London Gazette* of the 26th May, 1916.

The maintenance and repair of our defences alone, especially in winter, entails constant heavy work. Bad weather and the enemy combine to flood and destroy trenches, dug-outs and communications; all such damages must be repaired promptly, under fire, and almost entirely by night.

Artillery and snipers are practically never silent, patrols are out in front of the lines every night, and heavy bombardments by the artillery of one or both sides take place daily in various parts of the line. Below ground there is continual mining and counter-mining, which, by the ever-present threat of sudden explosion and the uncertainty as to when and where it will take place, causes perhaps a more constant strain than any other form of warfare. In the air there is seldom a day, however bad the weather, when aircraft are not busy reconnoitring, photographing, and observing fire. All this is taking place constantly at any hour of the day or night, and in any part of the line.

3. In short, although there has been no great incident of historic importance to record on the British front during the period under review, a steady and continuous fight has gone on, day and night, above ground and below it. The comparative monotony of this struggle has been relieved at short intervals by sharp local actions, some of which, although individually almost insignificant in a war on such an immense scale, would have been thought worthy of a separate despatch under different conditions, while their cumulative effect, though difficult to appraise at its true value now, will doubtless prove hereafter to have been considerable.

One form of minor activity deserves special mention, namely, the raids or " cutting-out parties " which are made at least twice or three times a week against the enemy's line. They consist of a brief attack, with some special object, on a section of the opposing trenches, usually carried out at night by a small body of men. The character of these operations—the preparation of a road through our own and the enemy's wire—the crossing of the open ground unseen—the penetration of the enemy's trenches—the hand-to-hand fighting in the darkness and the uncertainty as to the strength of the opposing force—gives peculiar scope to the gallantry, dash and quickness of decision of the troops engaged; and much skill and daring are frequently displayed in these operations.

The initiative in these minor operations was taken, and on the whole has been held, by us; but the Germans have recently attempted some bold and well-conceived raids against our lines, many of which have been driven back, although some have succeeded in penetrating, as has been reported by me from time to time.

4. Of the numerous local actions alluded to, the total number,

omitting the more minor raids, amounts to over 60 since December 19th, of which the most important have been :—

The operations at The Bluff, the Hohenzollern Redoubt, and at St. Eloi; the mining operations and crater fighting in the Loos salient and on the Vimy Ridge; and the hostile gas attacks north of Ypres in December, and opposite Hulluch and Messines in April.

The most recent local operations worthy of mention are the capture of some 500 yards of our trenches by the Germans at the Kink, on the 11th May, and the capture by us of 250 yards of their trenches near Cabaret Rouge, on the night of the 15th/16th May.

5. As an illustration of the nature of these local operations, it will suffice to describe two or three of the most important.

Ypres Salient and The Bluff, 8th February to 2nd March, 1916

During the period 8th to 19th February the enemy displayed increased activity in the Ypres salient, and carried out a series of infantry attacks, preceded, as a rule, by intense bombardment, and by the explosion of mines. These attacks may, no doubt, be regarded as a subsidiary operation, designed partly to secure local points of vantage, but probably also to distract attention from the impending operations near Verdun, which began on the 21st February.

After several days' heavy shelling over the whole of our line in this area, the first attack took place on 12th February at the extreme left of our line to the north of Ypres (14th and 20th Divisions, Major-Generals V. A. Couper and R. H. Davies commanding). A bombing attack was launched by the Germans in the early morning, and they succeeded in capturing our trenches. Our counter-attack, however, which was immediately organised, enabled us to clear our trenches of the enemy, and to pursue him to his own. After a period of further bombardment on both sides, the German fire again increased in intensity against our trenches and the French line beyond them; and in the evening a second attempt was made to rush our extreme left—this time entirely without success. Smaller attempts against other trenches in the neighbourhood were made at the same time, but were immediately repulsed by rifle and machine-gun fire. Throughout the operations our position in this part of the line remained intact, except that two isolated trenches of no tactical importance were captured by the enemy a day or two later; they were subsequently obliterated by our artillery fire. Throughout this fighting the French on our immediate left rendered us the prompt and valuable assistance which we have at all times received from them.

Another series of German attacks was launched about the same time in the neighbourhood of Hooge to the east of Ypres. The enemy had pushed out several saps in front of his trenches, and connected them up into a firing line some 150 yards from our lines. During the whole of the 13th February he heavily bombarded our front-line trenches in this neighbourhood and completely destroyed them. On the following afternoon an intense bombardment of our line began, and the enemy exploded a series of mines in front of our trenches, simultaneously launching infantry attacks against Hooge and the northern and southern ends of Sanctuary Wood (24th Division, Major-General J. E. Capper commanding). Each of these attacks was repulsed by artillery, machine-gun and rifle fire.

Further to the south, however, the enemy was more successful. On the northern bank of the Ypres-Comines Canal there is a narrow ridge, 30 to 40 feet high, covered with trees—probably the heap formed by excavation when the canal was dug—which forms a feature of the flat wooded country at the southern bend of the Ypres salient. It runs outward through our territory almost into the German area, so that our trenches pass over the eastern point of it, which is known as The Bluff. Here also our trenches were almost obliterated by the bombardment on the afternoon of the 14th, following which a sudden rush of hostile infantry was successful in capturing these and other front-line trenches immediately north of The Bluff— some 600 yards in all (17th Division, Major-General T. D. Pilcher commanding). Two of these trenches were at once regained, but the others were held by the enemy, in the face of several counter-attacks. On the night of the 15th/16th we made an unsuccessful counter-attack, with the object of regaining the lost trenches. An advance was begun across the open on the north side of the canal, combined with grenade attacks along the communication trenches immediately north of The Bluff. The night was very dark, and heavy rain had turned the ground into a quagmire, so that progress was difficult for the attacking force, which was unable to consolidate its position in the face of heavy machine-gun and rifle fire. After the failure of this attack it was decided to adopt slower and more methodical methods of recapturing the lost trenches, and nothing of special importance occurred in the Ypres salient during the rest of the month, although both sides displayed rather more than the usual activity.

The recapture of The Bluff took place after the enemy had held it for seventeen days. After several days' preliminary bombardment by our artillery, the assault was carried out at 4.29 a.m. on the 2nd March by troops of the 3rd Division, Major-General J. A. L. Haldane, and of the 17th Division. Measures taken to deceive the enemy were successful, and our infantry effected a complete surprise, finding the enemy with their bayonets unfixed, and many of them without rifles or equipment. About 50 Germans took refuge in a crater at the

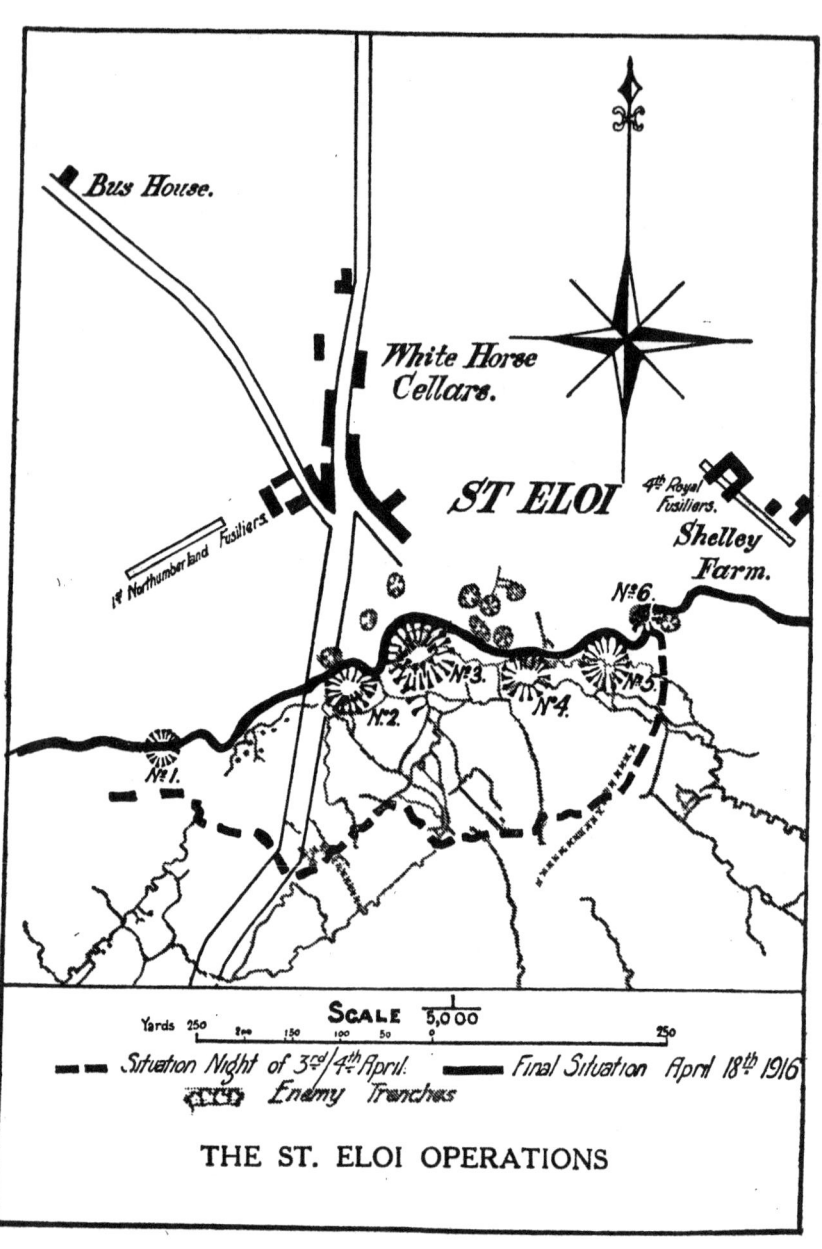

THE ST. ELOI OPERATIONS

eastern end of The Bluff, and these put up a brief resistance before taking refuge in the tunnels they had constructed, in which they were captured at leisure. Otherwise our right-hand attacking party, whose objective was The Bluff, met with little opposition.

The front line of the centre attack, reaching its assigned objective without much opposition, swept on past it and seized the German Third Line at the eastern side of the salient. This line was not suitable to hold permanently, but it proved useful as a temporary covering position while the captured trenches in rear were being consolidated, and at nightfall the covering party was withdrawn unmolested. The later waves of our centre attack met and captured, after some fighting, several Germans coming out of their dug-outs.

The left attacking party, at the first attempt, failed to reach the German trenches, but those who had penetrated to the German line on the right realised the situation and brought a Lewis gun to bear on the enemy's line of resistance, completely enfilading his trenches, and thus enabling the left company to reach its goal.

Thus our objective, which included a part of the German line, as well as the whole of the front lost by us on the 14th February, was captured, and is still held by us. Several counter-attacks were destroyed by our fire. The enemy's trenches were found full of dead as a result of our bombardment, and five officers and 251 other ranks were captured.

The support of the Heavy and Field Artillery, and a number of trench mortars, contributed largely to the success of the operation.

St. Eloi

6. On the 27th March our troops (9th Infantry Brigade, 3rd Division) made an attack with the object of straightening out the line at St. Eloi, and cutting away the small German salient which encroached on the semicircle of our line in the Ypres salient to a depth of about 100 yards over a front of some 600 yards. The operation was begun by the firing of six very large mines; the charge was so heavy that the explosion was felt in towns several miles behind the lines, and large numbers of the enemy were killed. Half a minute after the explosion our infantry attack was launched aiming at the German Second Line. The right attack (1st Battalion Northumberland Fusiliers) met with little opposition, and captured its assigned objective; but the left attack (4th Battalion Royal Fusiliers) was not so successful, and a gap was left in possession of the Germans, through which they entered one of the craters. The following days were spent by both sides in heavy bombardment and in unsuccessful attacks, intended on our part to capture the remaining trenches, and

on the part of the Germans to drive us from the positions we had occupied. In the very early morning of April 3rd troops of the 76th Infantry Brigade succeeded in recapturing the crater and the trenches still held by the enemy, thereby securing the whole of our original objective. We had, moreover, captured five officers and 195 men in the first attack on March 27th, and five officers and 80 men in the attack on April 3rd. The work of consolidating our new position, however, proved extremely difficult, owing to the wet soil, heavy shelling and mine explosions; though pumps were brought up and efforts at draining were instituted, the result achieved was comparatively small. By dint of much heavy work the brigade holding these trenches (6th Canadian Brigade, 2nd Canadian Division, Major-General R. E. W. Turner commanding the division) succeeded in reducing the water in the trenches by two feet by the morning of the 5th. This state of affairs could not, even so, be regarded as satisfactory; and during the 5th the enemy's bombardment increased in intensity, and the new trenches practically ceased to exist. On the morning of the 6th the enemy attacked with one battalion supported by another; he penetrated our new line, and gained the two westernmost craters. It is difficult to follow in detail the fighting of the next three weeks, which consisted in repeated attacks by both sides on more or less isolated mine craters, the trench lines having been destroyed by shell fire. Great efforts were made to maintain communication with the garrisons of these advanced posts, and with considerable success. But there were periods of uncertainty, and some misconception as to the state of affairs arose. On the 11th it was reported to me that we had recaptured all that remained of the position won by us on the 27th March and 3rd April. This report, probably due to old craters having been mistaken for new ones, was subsequently found to be incorrect. The new craters, being exposed to the enemy's view and to the full weight of his artillery fire, have proved untenable, and at the present time our troops are occupying trenches roughly in the general line which was held by them before the 27th.

German Gas Attacks, 27th/30th April

7. On the night of the 29th/30th April the enemy carried out a gas attack on a considerable scale near Wulverghem, on a front of 3,500 yards held by the 3rd and 24th Divisions. The operation was opened by heavy rifle and machine-gun fire under cover of which the gas was released. Immediately afterwards a heavy " barrage," or curtain of artillery fire, was placed on three parts of this area, and eight infantry attacks were launched. Of these attacks only two penetrated our trenches; one was immediately repelled, while the

LOCAL OPERATIONS: ST. ELOI

other was driven out by a counter-attack after about 40 minutes' occupation. The enemy's object would appear to have been the destruction of mine shafts, as a charge of gun-cotton was found unexploded in a disused shaft, to which the enemy had penetrated. But if this was his object he was completely unsuccessful.

Similar attacks were made by the Germans in front of Vermelles, to the south of La Bassée, on the 27th and 29th April, the discharge of a highly concentrated gas being accompanied by bombardment with lachrymatory and other shells and the explosion of a mine. On the first occasion two minor infantry attacks penetrated our trenches, but were driven out almost immediately; on the second occasion a small attack was repulsed, but the more serious advance which appears to have been intended was probably rendered impossible by the fact that a part of the enemy's gas broke back over his own lines, to the visible confusion of his troops, who were massing for the attack.

8. While many other units have done excellent work during the period under review, the following have been specially brought to my notice for good work in carrying out or repelling local attacks and raids:—

    3rd Divisional Artillery.
    17th Divisional Artillery.
    1st Canadian Divisional Artillery.
    62nd Brigade, Royal Field Artillery.
    B Battery, 153rd Brigade, Royal Field Artillery.
    83rd Battery, Royal Field Artillery (Lahore).
    22nd Canadian (Howitzer) Brigade.
    24th Heavy Battery, Royal Garrison Artillery.
    115th Heavy Battery, Royal Garrison Artillery.
    122nd Heavy Battery, Royal Garrison Artillery.
    3rd Siege Battery, Royal Garrison Artillery.
    12th Siege Battery, Royal Garrison Artillery.
    9th Field Company, Royal Engineers.
    56th Field Company, Royal Engineers.
    70th Field Company, Royal Engineers.
    77th Field Company, Royal Engineers.
    1st (Cheshire) Field Company, Royal Engineers.
    170th Tunnelling Company, Royal Engineers.
    172nd Tunnelling Company, Royal Engineers.
    173rd Tunnelling Company, Royal Engineers.
    253rd Tunnelling Company, Royal Engineers.
    12th Divisional Signal Company, Royal Engineers.
    24th Trench Mortar Battery.
    76/1st Trench Mortar Battery.
    No. 2 Squadron, Royal Flying Corps.

No. 6 Squadron, Royal Flying Corps.
2nd Battalion, Grenadier Guards.
1st Battalion, Coldstream Guards.
2nd Battalion, Irish Guards.
1st Battalion, Welsh Guards.
11th (Service) Battalion, The Royal Scots (Lothian Regiment).
1st Battalion, The Queen's (Royal West Surrey Regiment).
7th (Service) Battalion, The King's Own (Royal Lancaster Regiment).
8th (Service) Battalion, The King's Own (Royal Lancaster Regiment).
1st Battalion, Northumberland Fusiliers.
12th (Service) Battalion, Northumberland Fusiliers.
1st Battalion, Royal Warwickshire Regiment.
8th Battalion, Royal Warwickshire Regiment (Territorial).
8th (Service) Battalion, Royal Fusiliers (City of London Regiment).
9th (Service) Battalion, Royal Fusiliers (City of London Regiment).
4th (Extra Reserve) Battalion, The King's Liverpool Regiment.
1/8th (Irish) Battalion, The King's Liverpool Regiment (Territorial).
7th (Service) Battalion, Lincolnshire Regiment.
1/4th Battalion, Suffolk Regiment (Territorial).
7th (Service) Battalion, Suffolk Regiment.
8th (Service) Battalion, Somerset Light Infantry.
7th (Service) Battalion, Bedfordshire Regiment.
1/4th Battalion, The Prince of Wales's Own (West Yorkshire Regiment) (Territorial).
2nd Battalion, Lancashire Fusiliers.
11th (Service) Battalion, Lancashire Fusiliers.
15th (Service) Battalion, Lancashire Fusiliers.
17th (Service) Battalion, Lancashire Fusiliers.
2nd Battalion, Royal Welsh Fusiliers.
15th (Service) Battalion, Royal Welsh Fusiliers.
8th (Service) Battalion, King's Own Scottish Borderers.
7th (Service) Battalion, Royal Inniskilling Fusiliers.
9th (Service) Battalion, Royal Inniskilling Fusiliers.
10th (Service) Battalion, Royal Inniskilling Fusiliers.
1/6th Battalion, Gloucestershire Regiment (Territorial).
1st Battalion, East Lancashire Regiment.
7th (Service) Battalion, East Surrey Regiment.
8th (Service) Battalion, East Surrey Regiment.
9th (Service) Battalion, West Riding Regiment.
2nd Battalion, The Border Regiment.
7th (Service) Battalion, The Border Regiment.
11th (Service) Battalion, The Border Regiment.
7th (Service) Battalion, Royal Sussex Regiment.
8th (Service) Battalion, Royal Sussex Regiment.

LOCAL OPERATIONS: ST. ELOI

8th (Service) Battalion, South Staffordshire Regiment.
1st Battalion, Dorsetshire Regiment.
1/4th Battalion, Oxfordshire and Buckinghamshire Light Infantry (Territorial).
1st Battalion, Northamptonshire Regiment.
5th (Service) Battalion, Northamptonshire Regiment.
6th (Service) Battalion, Northamptonshire Regiment.
1st Battalion, The King's (Shropshire Light Infantry).
1st Battalion, Duke of Cambridge's Own (Middlesex Regiment).
2nd Battalion, Duke of Cambridge's Own (Middlesex Regiment).
2nd Battalion, King's Royal Rifle Corps.
6th (Service) Battalion, The Duke of Edinburgh's (Wiltshire Regiment).
18th (Service) Battalion, Manchester Regiment.
1st Battalion, The Prince of Wales's (North Staffordshire Regiment).
8th (Service) Battalion, The Prince of Wales's (North Staffordshire Regiment).
17th (Service) Battalion, Highland Light Infantry.
8th (Service) Battalion, Seaforth Highlanders (Ross-shire Buffs, The Duke of Albany's).
1st Battalion, The Gordon Highlanders.
2nd Battalion, The Royal Irish Rifles.
9th (Service) Battalion, The Royal Irish Rifles.
1st Battalion, Princess Victoria's (Royal Irish Fusiliers).
2nd Battalion, Princess Louise's (Argyll & Sutherland Highlanders).
9th (Service) Battalion, Royal Munster Fusiliers.
3rd Battalion, The Rifle Brigade (The Prince Consort's Own).
5th Canadian Infantry Battalion.
7th Canadian Infantry Battalion.
29th Canadian Infantry Battalion.
49th Canadian Infantry Battalion.

9. The activity described above has its counterpart in rear of our lines in the training which is carried out continuously. During the periods of relief all formations, and especially the newly created ones, are instructed and practised in all classes of the present and other phases of warfare. A large number of schools also exist for the instruction of individuals, especially in the use and theory of the less familiar weapons, such as bombs and grenades.

There are schools for young staff officers and regimental officers, for candidates for commissions, etc. In short, every effort is made to take advantage of the closer contact with actual warfare, and to put the finishing touches, often after actual experience in the trenches, to the training received at home.

10. During the period under review the forces under my command have been considerably augmented by the arrival of new formations from home, and the transfer of others released from service in the Near East. This increase has made possible the relief of a French Army, to which I have already referred, at the time of the Battle of Verdun. Among the newly arrived forces is the "Anzac" Corps. With them, the Canadians, and a portion of the South African Overseas Force which has also arrived, the Dominions now furnish a valuable part of the Imperial Forces in France.

Since the date of the last Despatch, but before I assumed command, the Indian Army Corps left this country for service in the East. They had given a year's valuable and gallant service under conditions of warfare which they had not dreamt of, and in a climate peculiarly difficult for them to endure. I regret their departure, but I do not doubt that they will continue to render gallant and effective service elsewhere, as they have already done in this country.

11. I take this opportunity to bring to notice the admirable work which the Royal Flying Corps has continued to perform, in spite of much unfavourable weather, in carrying out reconnaissance duties, in taking photographs—an important aid to reconnaissance which has been brought to a high pitch of perfection—and in assisting the work of our Artillery by registering targets and locating hostile batteries. In the performance of this work they have flown in weather when no hostile aeroplane ventured out, and they have not hesitated to fly low, under fire of the enemy's guns, when their duties made it necessary to do so. They have also carried out a series of bombing raids on hostile aerodromes and points of military importance. A feature of the period under review has been the increased activity of the enemy's aircraft, in suitable weather. But the enemy's activity has been mainly on his own side of the line, and has aimed chiefly at interrupting the work carried out by our machines. In order to carry on the work in spite of this opposition, which was for a time rendered more effective by the appearance in December of a new and more powerful type of enemy machine, it has been necessary to provide an escort to accompany our reconnaissance aeroplanes, and fighting in the air, which was formerly exceptional, has now become an everyday occurrence.

The observers, no less than the pilots, have done excellent service, and many fine feats have been performed by both. Developments on the technical side of the Air Service have been no less remarkable and satisfactory than the progress made on the purely military side. Much inventive genius has been displayed; and our equipment for photography, wireless telegraphy, bomb-dropping and offensive action generally has been immensely improved, while

LOCAL OPERATIONS: ST. ELOI

great skill has been shown in keeping the flying machines themselves in good flying condition.

12. The continuance of siege warfare has entailed for the Royal Engineers work of a particularly arduous and important kind, extending from the front trenches to the Base Ports.

In the performance of this work the officers, non-commissioned officers and men of the Field Companies and other units of the Corps have continued to exhibit a very high standard of skill, courage, and devotion to duty.

13. The work of the Tunnelling Companies calls for special mention. Increased mining activity on the part of the enemy has invariably been answered with enterprise combined with untiring energy on the part of our miners, who in carrying out duties always full of danger have shown that they possess in the highest degree the qualities of courage, perseverance, and self-sacrifice. Their importance in the present phase of warfare is very great.

14. The excellent work done by the Corps of Military Police is worthy of mention. This Corps is inspired by a high sense of duty, and in the performance of its share in the maintenance of discipline it has shown both zeal and discretion.

15. All branches of the Medical Services deserve the highest commendation for the successful work done by them, both at the Front and on the Lines of Communication. The sick rate has been consistently low; there has been no serious epidemic, and enteric fever, the bane of armies in the past, has almost completely disappeared owing to preventive measures energetically carried out.

The results of exposure incidental to trench warfare during the winter months were to a very great extent kept in check by careful application of the precautions recommended and taught by regimental Medical Officers.

The wounded have been promptly and efficiently dealt with, and their evacuation to the Base has been rapidly accomplished.

The close co-operation which has existed between the officers of the Regular Medical Service of the Army and those members of the civil medical profession who have patriotically given their valuable services to the Army, has largely contributed to the prevention of disease and to the successful treatment and comfort of the sick and wounded.

As part of the Medical Services, the Canadian Army Medical Corps has displayed marked efficiency and devotion to duty.

16. The Commission of Graves Registration and Enquiries has, since it first undertook this work eighteen months ago, registered and marked over 50,000 graves. Without its labours many would have remained unidentified. It has answered several thousand

enquiries from relatives and supplied them with photographs. Flowers and shrubs have been planted in most of the cemeteries which are sufficiently far removed from the firing line, and all cemeteries which it is possible to work in during the daytime are now being looked after by non-commissioned officers and men of this unit.

17. The valuable nature of the work performed by the officers of the Central Laboratory and the Chemical Advisers with the Armies in investigations into the nature of the gases and other new substances used in hostile attacks, and in devising and perfecting means of protecting our troops against them, is deserving of recognition. The efforts of these officers materially contributed to the failure of the Germans in their attack of 19th December, 1915, as well as in the various gas attacks since made.

18. The stream of additional personnel and material arriving from England, and the move of complete formations to and from the East during the period under review, have thrown a great deal of work on our Base Ports and on the Advanced Base. The staff and personnel at these stations have coped most ably with the work of forwarding and equipping the various units passing through their hands, and I desire to bring their good work to notice.

19. The large increases made to our forces have necessitated a great expansion in the resources of our Lines of Communication, and I have been greatly struck by the forethought shown by the Administrative Services in anticipating the requirements of the Armies in the Field and in the provision made to satisfy these requirements.

The Base Ports have been developed to the utmost possible extent, advanced Depôts have been provided, and communications have been improved to ensure punctual distribution to the troops.

Labour has been organised in order to develop local resources, especially in the matter of timber for defences and hutting, and stone for road maintenance, whereby considerable reductions have been made possible in the shipments from over sea.

Economy has attended the good methods adopted, and the greatest credit is due to all concerned for the results obtained.

20. I desire to acknowledge here the valuable assistance rendered by the naval transport officers on the Lines of Communication. They have worked with and for the Army most untiringly, efficiently, and with the utmost harmony.

I also desire to acknowledge the indebtedness of the Army to the Royal Navy for their unceasing and uniformly successful care in securing the safety of our transport service on the seas.

21. I wish to acknowledge the work done in the reproduction of maps by the Ordnance Survey Department. Over 90 per cent. of

LOCAL OPERATIONS: ST. ELOI

the maps used in this country are reproduced and printed in England by the Ordnance Survey, and the satisfactory supply is largely due to the foresight and initiative displayed by this Department. I can now count on obtaining an issue of as many as 10,000 copies of any map within one week of sending it home for reproduction.

22. I have forwarded under a separate letter the names of the officers, non-commissioned officers and men whom I wish to bring to notice for gallant and distinguished service.

23. I cannot close this Despatch without some reference to the work of my predecessor in Command, Field-Marshal Viscount French. The Field-Marshal, starting the war with our small Expeditionary Force, faced an enemy far superior in numbers and fully prepared for this great campaign. During the long and anxious time needed for the improvisation of the comparatively large force now serving in this country, he overcame all difficulties, and before laying down his responsibilities he had the satisfaction of seeing the balance of advantage swing steadily in our favour. Those who have served under him appreciate the greatness of his achievement.

 I have the honour to be
  Your Lordship's most obedient Servant,
   D. HAIG, General,
  Commander-in-Chief, The British Forces in France.

THE OPENING OF
THE WEARING-OUT BATTLE

THE OPENING OF
THE WEARING-OUT BATTLE

General Headquarters,
23rd December, 1916.[1]

MY LORD,—

I have the honour to submit the following report on the operations of the Forces under my Command since the 19th May, the date of my last Despatch.

The General Situation towards the end of May

1. The principle of an offensive campaign during the summer of 1916 had already been decided on by all the Allies. The various possible alternatives on the Western front had been studied and discussed by General Joffre and myself, and we were in complete agreement as to the front to be attacked by the combined French and British Armies.[2] Preparations for our offensive had made considerable progress; but as the date on which the attack should begin was dependent on many doubtful factors, a final decision on that point was deferred until the general situation should become clearer.

Subject to the necessity of commencing operations before the summer was too far advanced, and with due regard to the general situation, I desired to postpone my attack as long as possible. The British Armies were growing in numbers[3] and the supply of munitions was steadily increasing. Moreover a very large proportion of the officers and men under my command were still far from being fully trained, and the longer the attack could be deferred the more efficient they would become. On the other hand the Germans were continuing to press their attacks at Verdun, and both there and on the Italian front, where the Austrian offensive[4] was gaining ground, it was evident that the strain might become too great to be borne unless timely action were taken to relieve it. Accordingly, while

---

[1] This Despatch was published as a Supplement to the *London Gazette* of the 29th December, 1916.

[2] The choice of front for the Allied offensive was governed by the consideration that neither the French nor ourselves were at the moment deemed strong enough to undertake unaided an offensive on a really large scale. It was therefore necessary to deliver a combined attack.

[3] Between January, 1916, and July, 1916, the strength of the British Armies on the Western front in bayonets and sabres increased from 450,000 to 660,000.

[4] On the 14th May, 1916, the Austrians attacked in the Trentino and by the end of May had advanced to Arsiero and Asiago.

maintaining constant touch with General Joffre in regard to all these considerations, my preparations were pushed on, and I agreed, with the consent of H.M. Government, that my attack should be launched whenever the general situation required it with as great a force as I might then be able to make available.

2. By the end of May the pressure of the enemy on the Italian front had assumed such serious proportions that the Russian campaign was opened early in June, and the brilliant successes [1] gained by our Allies against the Austrians at once caused a movement of German troops from the Western to the Eastern front. This, however, did not lessen the pressure on Verdun. The heroic defence of our French Allies had already gained many weeks of inestimable value and had caused the enemy very heavy losses; but the strain continued to increase. In view, therefore, of the situation in the various theatres of war, it was eventually agreed between General Joffre and myself that the combined French and British offensive should not be postponed beyond the end of June.

The object of that offensive was threefold:

(i) To relieve the pressure on Verdun.
(ii) To assist our Allies in the other theatres of war by stopping any further transfer of German troops from the Western front.
(iii) To wear down the strength of the forces opposed to us.

3. While my final preparations were in progress the enemy made two unsuccessful attempts to interfere with my arrangements. The first, directed on the 21st May against our positions on the Vimy Ridge, south and south-east of Souchez, held by the 47th and 25th Divisions (Major-Generals Sir C. St. L. Barter and E. G. T. Bainbridge commanding), resulted in a small enemy gain of no strategic or tactical importance; and rather than weaken my offensive by involving additional troops in the task of recovering the lost ground, I decided to consolidate a position in rear of our original line.

The second enemy attack was delivered on the 2nd June on a front of over one and a half miles from Mount Sorrell to Hooge, held by the 3rd Division (Major-General L. J. Lipsett), and succeeded in penetrating to a maximum depth of 700 yards. As the southern part of the lost position commanded our trenches I judged it necessary to recover it, and by an attack launched on the 13th June, carefully prepared and well executed, this was successfully accomplished by the troops on the spot (1st Canadian Division, Major-General A. W. Currie).

[1] Brussilov's offensive on the Galician front in which Lutsk and Czernovitz were taken by the Russians.

OPENING OF THE WEARING-OUT BATTLE

Neither of these enemy attacks succeeded in delaying the preparations for the major operations which I had in view.

Preparations for the Somme Battle

4. These preparations were necessarily very elaborate and took considerable time.

Vast stocks of ammunition and stores of all kinds had to be accumulated beforehand within a convenient distance of our front. To deal with these many miles of new railways—both standard and narrow gauge—and trench tramways were laid. All available roads were improved, many others were made, and long causeways were built over marshy valleys. Many additional dug-outs had to be provided as shelter for the troops, for use as dressing stations for the wounded, and as magazines for storing ammunition, food, water, and engineering material. Scores of miles of deep communication trenches had to be dug, as well as trenches for telephone wires, assembly and assault trenches, and numerous gun emplacements and observation posts.

Important mining operations were undertaken, and charges were laid at various points beneath the enemy's lines.

Except in the river valleys, the existing supplies of water were hopelessly insufficient to meet the requirements of the numbers of men and horses to be concentrated in this area as the preparations for our offensive proceeded. To meet this difficulty many wells and borings were sunk, and over one hundred pumping plants were installed. More than one hundred and twenty miles of water mains were laid, and everything was got ready to ensure an adequate water supply as our troops advanced.

Much of this preparatory work had to be done under very trying conditions, and was liable to constant interruption from the enemy's fire. The weather, on the whole, was bad, and the local accommodation totally insufficient for housing the troops employed, who consequently had to content themselves with such rough shelter as could be provided in the circumstances. All this labour, too, had to be carried out in addition to fighting and to the everyday work of maintaining existing defences. It threw a very heavy strain on the troops, which was borne by them with a cheerfulness beyond all praise.

The Enemy's Position

5. The enemy's position to be attacked was of a very formidable character, situated on a high, undulating tract of ground, which rises to more than 500 feet above sea-level, and forms the watershed

between the Somme on the one side and the rivers of south-western Belgium on the other. On the southern face of this watershed, the general trend of which is from east-south-east to west-north-west, the ground falls in a series of long irregular spurs and deep depressions to the valley of the Somme. Well down the forward slopes of this face the enemy's first system of defence, starting from the Somme near Curlu (*vide* Map I.), ran at first northwards for 3,000 yards, then westwards for 7,000 yards to near Fricourt, where it turned nearly due north, forming a great salient angle in the enemy's line.

Some 10,000 yards north of Fricourt the trenches crossed the River Ancre, a tributary of the Somme, and still running northwards passed over the summit of the watershed, about Hébuterne and Gommecourt, and then down its northern spurs to Arras.

On the 20,000 yards front between the Somme and the Ancre the enemy had a strong second system of defence, sited generally on or near the southern crest of the highest part of the watershed, at an average distance of from 3,000 to 5,000 yards behind his first system of trenches.

During nearly two years' preparation he had spared no pains to render these defences impregnable. The first and second systems each consisted of several lines of deep trenches, well provided with bomb-proof shelters and with numerous communication trenches connecting them. The front of the trenches in each system was protected by wire entanglements, many of them in two belts forty yards broad, built of iron stakes interlaced with barbed wire, often almost as thick as a man's finger.

The numerous woods and villages in and between these systems of defence had been turned into veritable fortresses. The deep cellars usually to be found in the villages, and the numerous pits and quarries common to a chalk country, were used to provide cover for machine guns and trench mortars. The existing cellars were supplemented by elaborate dug-outs, sometimes in two storeys, and these were connected up by passages as much as thirty feet below the surface of the ground. The salients in the enemy's line, from which he could bring enfilade fire across his front, were made into self-contained forts, and often protected by mine fields; while strong redoubts and concrete machine gun emplacements had been constructed in positions from which he could sweep his own trenches should these be taken. The ground lent itself to good artillery observation on the enemy's part, and he had skilfully arranged for cross fire by his guns.

These various systems of defence, with the fortified localities and other supporting points between them, were cunningly sited to afford each other mutual assistance and to admit of the utmost possible development of enfilade and flanking fire by machine guns and artillery. They formed, in short, not merely a series of successive lines, but one composite system of enormous depth and strength.

Behind his second system of trenches, in addition to woods, villages and other strong points prepared for defence, the enemy had several other lines already completed ; and we had learnt from aeroplane reconnaissance that he was hard at work improving and strengthening these and digging fresh ones between them, and still further back.

In the area above described, between the Somme and the Ancre, our front line trenches ran parallel and close to those of the enemy, but below them. We had good direct observation on his front system of trenches and on the various defences sited on the slopes above us between his first and second systems ; but the second system itself, in many places, could not be observed from the ground in our possession, while, except from the air, nothing could be seen of his more distant defences.

North of the Ancre, where the opposing trenches ran transversely across the main ridge, the enemy's defences were equally elaborate and formidable. So far as command of ground was concerned, we were here practically on level terms ; but, partly as a result of this, our direct observation over the ground held by the enemy was not so good as it was further south. On portions of this front the opposing first line trenches were more widely separated from each other ; while in the valleys to the north were many hidden gun positions from which the enemy could develop flanking fire on our troops as they advanced across the open.

Arrangement

6. The period of active operations dealt with in this despatch divides itself roughly into three phases. The first phase opened with the attack of the 1st July, the success of which evidently came as a surprise to the enemy and caused considerable confusion and disorganisation in his ranks. The advantages gained on that date and developed during the first half of July may be regarded as having been rounded off by the operations of the 14th July and three following days, which gave us possession of the southern crest of the main plateau between Delville Wood and Bazentin-le-Petit.

We then entered upon a contest lasting for many weeks, during which the enemy, having found his strongest defences unavailing, and now fully alive to his danger, put forth his utmost efforts to keep his hold on the main ridge. This stage of the battle constituted a prolonged and severe struggle for mastery between the contending armies, in which, although progress was slow and difficult, the confidence of our troops in their ability to win was never shaken. Their tenacity and determination proved more than equal to their task, and by the first week in September they had established a fighting superiority that has left its mark on the enemy, of which possession of the ridge was merely the visible proof.

The way was then opened for the third phase, in which our advance was pushed down the forward slopes of the ridge and further extended on both flanks, until, from Morval to Thiepval, the whole plateau and a good deal of ground beyond were in our possession. Meanwhile our gallant Allies, in addition to great successes south of the Somme, had pushed their advance, against equally determined opposition and under most difficult tactical conditions, up the long slopes on our immediate right, and were now preparing to drive the enemy from the summit of the narrow and difficult portion of the main ridge which lies between the Combles Valley and the River Tortille, a stream flowing from the north into the Somme just below Peronne.

The Somme Battle—First Phase

The Over-running of the German Entrenched Positions

7. Defences of the nature described could only be attacked with any prospect of success after careful artillery preparation. It was accordingly decided that our bombardment should begin on the 24th June, and a large force of artillery was brought into action for the purpose.

Artillery bombardments were also carried out daily at different points on the rest of our front, and during the period from the 24th June to 1st July gas was discharged with good effect at more than forty places along our line, upon a frontage which in total amounted to over fifteen miles. Some 70 raids, too, were undertaken by our infantry between Gommecourt and our extreme left north of Ypres during the week preceding the attack, and these kept me well informed as to the enemy's dispositions, besides serving other useful purposes.

On the 25th June the Royal Flying Corps carried out a general attack on the enemy's observation balloons, destroying nine of them, and depriving the enemy for the time being of this form of observation.

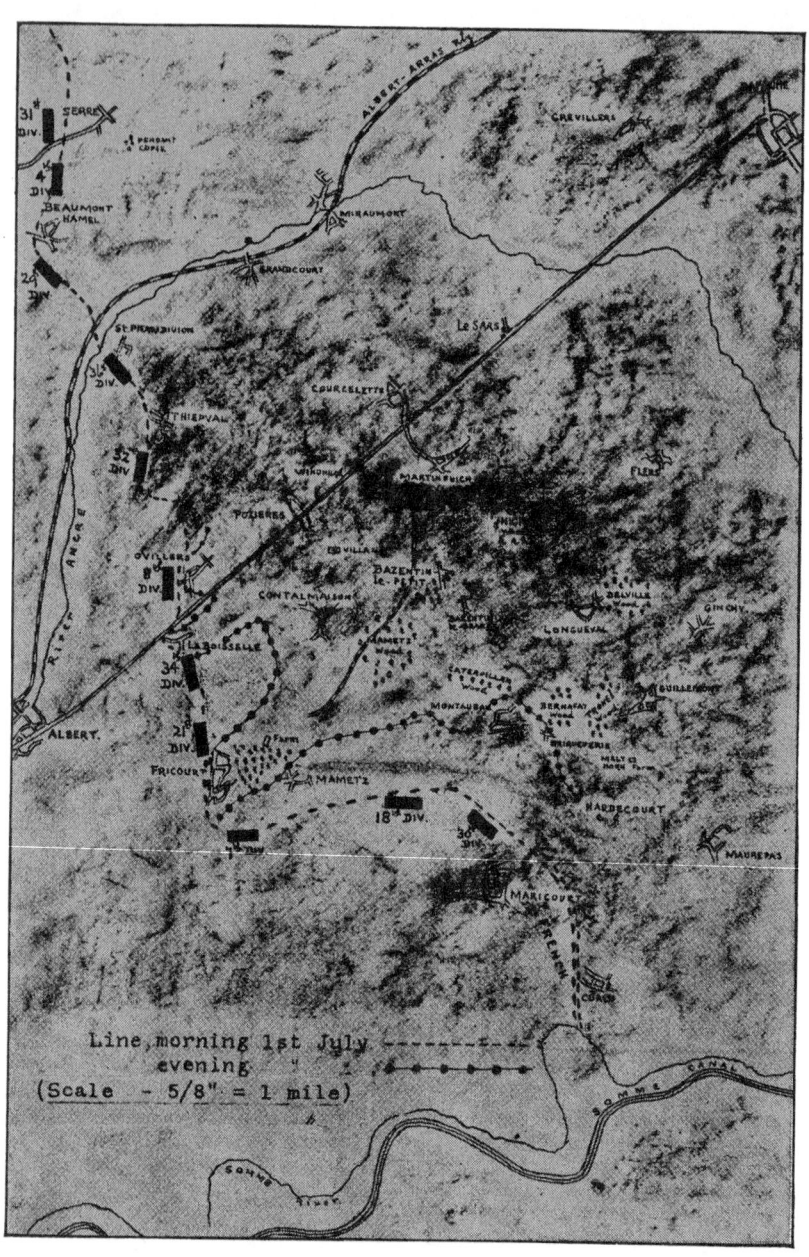

SOMME BATTLE;
Attack of July 1st, 1916.

OPENING OF THE WEARING-OUT BATTLE 25

The Opening Assault—1st July

8. On July 1st, at 7.30 a.m., after a final hour of exceptionally violent bombardment, our infantry assault was launched. Simultaneously the French attacked on both sides of the Somme, co-operating closely with us.

The British main front of attack extended from Maricourt on our right, round the salient at Fricourt, to the Ancre in front of St. Pierre Divion. To assist this main attack by holding the enemy's reserves and occupying his artillery, the enemy's trenches north of the Ancre, as far as Serre inclusive, were to be assaulted simultaneously; while further north a subsidiary attack was to be made on both sides of the salient at Gommecourt.

I had entrusted the attack on the front from Maricourt to Serre to the Fourth Army, under the command of General Sir Henry S. Rawlinson, with five Army Corps at his disposal. The subsidiary attack at Gommecourt was carried out by troops from the Third Army commanded by General Sir E. H. H. Allenby.[1]

Just prior to the attack the mines which had been prepared under the enemy's lines were exploded, and smoke was discharged at many places along our front. Through this smoke our infantry advanced to the attack with the utmost steadinesss, in spite of the very heavy barrage of the enemy's guns. On our right our troops met with immediate success, and rapid progress was made. Before midday Montauban had been carried by the 30th Division, and shortly

[1] The disposition of our forces from south to north at the moment of attack was as follows :—

Fourth Army
- *XIII. Corps* . . . . . Lt.-Gen. W. N. Congreve.
- 30th Div. . . . . . Maj.-Gen. J. S. M. Shea.
- 18th Div. . . . . . Maj.-Gen. F. I. Maxse.
- *XV. Corps* . . . . . Lt.-Gen. H. S. Horne.
- 7th Div. . . . . . Maj.-Gen. H. E. Watts.
- 21st Div. . . . . . Maj.-Gen. D. G. M. Campbell.
- *III. Corps* . . . . . Lt.-Gen. Sir W. P. Pulteney.
- 34th Div. . . . . . Maj.-Gen. E. C. Ingouville-Williams.
- 8th Div. . . . . . Maj.-Gen. H. Hudson.
- *X. Corps* . . . . . Lt.-Gen. Sir T. L. N. Morland.
- 32nd Div. . . . . . Maj.-Gen. W. H. Rycroft.
- 36th Div. . . . . . Maj.-Gen. O. S. W. Nugent.
- *VIII. Corps* . . . . . Lt.-Gen. Sir A. G. Hunter-Weston.
- 29th Div. . . . . . Maj.-Gen. H. de B. de Lisle.
- 4th Div. . . . . . Maj.-Gen. Hon. W. Lambton.
- 31st Div. . . . . . Maj.-Gen. R. Wanless O'Gowan.

Third Army
- *VII. Corps* . . . . . Lt.-Gen. Sir T. D'O. Snow.
- 56th Div. . . . . . Maj.-Gen. C. P. A. Hull.
- 46th Div. . . . . . Maj.-Gen. E. J. Montagu Stuart-Wortley.

afterwards the Briqueterie to the east, and the whole of the ridge to the west of the village were in our hands (18th Division). Opposite Mametz part of our assembly trenches had been practically levelled by the enemy artillery, making it necessary for our infantry (7th Division) to advance to the attack across 400 yards of open ground. None the less they forced their way into Mametz, and reached their objective in the valley beyond, first throwing out a defensive flank towards Fricourt on their left. At the same time the enemy's trenches were entered by the 21st Division north of Fricourt, so that the enemy's garrison in that village was pressed on three sides. Further north, though the villages of La Boisselle and Ovillers for the time being resisted our attack, our troops (34th and 8th Divisions) drove deeply into the German lines on the flanks of these strongholds, and so paved the way for their capture later. On the spur running south from Thiepval the work known as the Leipzig Salient was stormed by the 32nd Division, and severe fighting[1] took place for the possession of the village and its defences. Here and north of the valley of the Ancre as far as Serre on the left flank of our attack, our initial successes were not sustained. Striking progress was made at many points and parties of troops penetrated the enemy's positions to the outer defences of Grandcourt (36th Division), and also to Pendant Copse (4th Division) and Serre (31st Division); but the enemy's continued resistance at Thiepval and Beaumont Hamel (29th Division) made it impossible to forward reinforcements and ammunition, and, in spite of their gallant efforts, our troops were forced to withdraw during the night to their own lines.

The subsidiary attack at Gommecourt also forced its way into the enemy's positions; but there met with such vigorous opposition that as soon as it was considered that the attack had fulfilled its object our troops were withdrawn.

The Attack Continued

9. In view of the general situation at the end of the first day's operations, I decided that the best course was to press forward on a front extending from our junction with the French to a point halfway between La Boisselle and Contalmaison, and to limit the offensive on our left for the present to a slow and methodical advance. North of the Ancre such preparations were to be made as would hold the enemy to his positions, and enable the attack to be resumed there later if desirable. In order that General Sir Henry Rawlinson might be left free to concentrate his attention on the portion of the front where the attack was to be pushed home, I also decided

---

[1] In the course of this fighting, a brigade of the 49th Division, Major-General E. M. Percival, made a gallant attempt to force Thiepval from the north.

OPENING OF THE WEARING-OUT BATTLE 27

to place the operations against the front, La Boisselle to Serre, under the command of General Sir Hubert de la P. Gough, to whom I accordingly allotted the two northern corps of Sir Henry Rawlinson's Army. My instructions to Sir Hubert Gough were that his Army was to maintain a steady pressure on the front from La Boisselle to the Serre Road, and to act as a pivot on which our line could swing as our attacks on his right made progress towards the north.

10. During the succeeding days the attack was continued on these lines. In spite of strong counter-attacks on the Briqueterie and Montauban, by midday on the 2nd July our troops (17th Division, Major-General T. D. Pilcher) had captured Fricourt, and in the afternoon and evening stormed Fricourt Wood and the farm to the north. During the 3rd and 4th July Bernafay and Caterpillar Woods were also captured, and our troops pushed forward to the railway north of Mametz. On these days the reduction of La Boisselle was completed after hard fighting (19th Division, Major-General G. T. M. Bridges), while the outskirts of Contalmaison were reached on the 5th July (the 23rd Division, Major-General J. M. Babington, taking part in this fighting with the 17th and 7th Divisions). North of La Boisselle also the enemy's forces opposite us were kept constantly engaged, and our holding in the Leipzig Salient was gradually increased.

To sum up the results of the fighting of these five days, on a front of over six miles, from the Briqueterie to La Boisselle, our troops had swept over the whole of the enemy's first and strongest system of defence, which he had done his utmost to render impregnable. They had driven him back over a distance of more than a mile, and had carried four elaborately fortified villages.

The number of prisoners passed back to the Corps cages at the close of the 5th July had already reached the total of ninety-four officers and 5,724 other ranks.

11. After the five days' heavy and continuous fighting just described it was essential to carry out certain readjustments and reliefs of the forces engaged. In normal conditions of enemy resistance the amount of progress that can be made at any time without a pause in the general advance is necessarily limited. Apart from the physical exhaustion of the attacking troops and the considerable distances separating the enemy's successive main systems of defence, special artillery preparation was required before a successful assault could be delivered. Meanwhile, however, local operations were continued in spite of much unfavourable weather. The attack on Contalmaison and Mametz Wood was undertaken on the 7th July by the 38th Division (Major-General I. Philipps), and the 17th, 23rd and 19th

Divisions. After three days' obstinate fighting, in the course of which the enemy delivered several powerful counter-attacks, the village and the whole of the wood, except its northern border, were finally secured. On the 7th July also a footing was gained in the outer defences of Ovillers (25th and 12th Divisions, Major-General A. B. Scott commanding the 12th Division), while on the 9th July on our extreme right Maltz Horn Farm—an important point on the spur north of Hardecourt—was secured.

A thousand yards north of this farm our troops (30th Division) had succeeded at the second attempt in establishing themselves on the 8th July in the southern end of Trônes Wood. The enemy's positions in the northern and eastern parts of this wood were very strong, and no less than eight powerful German counter-attacks were made here during the next five days. In the course of this struggle portions of the wood changed hands several times; but we were left eventually, on the 13th July, in possession of the southern part of it.

12. Meanwhile Mametz Wood had been entirely cleared of the enemy (by the 21st Division), and with Trônes Wood also practically in our possession we were in a position to undertake an assault upon the enemy's second system of defences. Arrangements were accordingly made for an attack to be delivered at daybreak on the morning of the 14th July against a front extending from Longueval to Bazentin-le-Petit Wood, both inclusive. Contalmaison Villa, on a spur 1,000 yards west of Bazentin-le-Petit Wood, had already been captured to secure the left flank of the attack, and advantage had been taken of the progress made by our infantry to move our artillery forward into new positions. The preliminary bombardment had opened on the 11th July. The opportunities offered by the ground for enfilading the enemy's lines were fully utilised and did much to secure the success of our attack.

The Attack of the 14th July

13. In the early hours of the 14th July the attacking troops moved out over the open for a distance of from about 1,000 to 1,400 yards, and lined up in the darkness just below the crest and some 300 to 500 yards from the enemy's trenches. Their advance was covered by strong patrols, and their correct deployment had been ensured by careful previous preparations.[1] The whole movement was carried out unobserved and without touch being lost in any case. The decision to attempt a night operation of this magnitude with an Army,

---

[1] White tapes were laid out on the ground earlier in the night, to assist the attacking troops to form up in their proper positions.

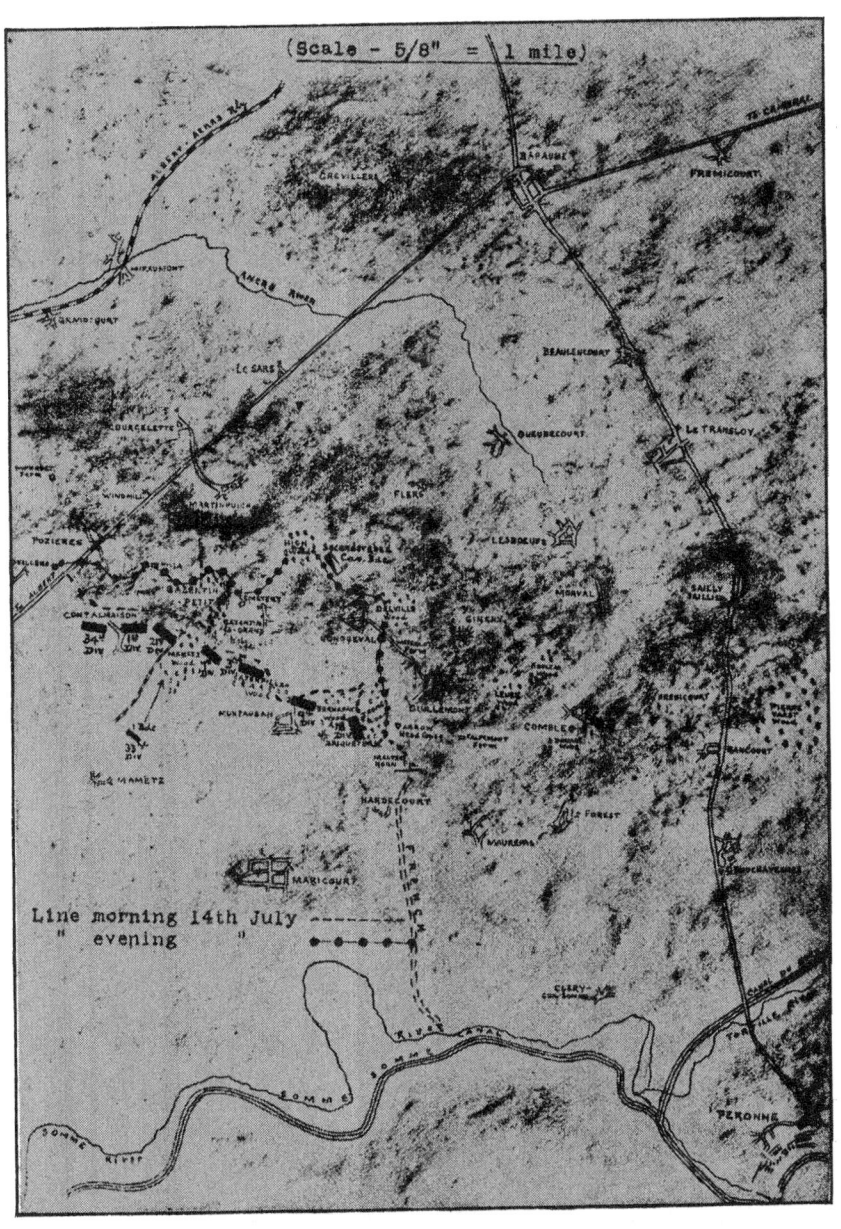

SOMME BATTLE;
Attack of 14th July, 1916.

the bulk of which has been raised since the beginning of the war, was perhaps the highest tribute that could be paid to the quality of our troops. It would not have been possible but for the most careful preparation and forethought, as well as thorough reconnaissance of the ground which was in many cases made personally by Divisional, Brigade and Battalion Commanders and their staffs before framing their detailed orders for the advance.

The actual assault was delivered at 3.25 a.m. on the 14th July, when there was just sufficient light to be able to distinguish friend from foe at short ranges, and along the whole front attacked our troops, preceded by a very effective artillery barrage, swept over the enemy's first trenches and on into the defences beyond.

On our right the enemy was driven by the 18th Division from his last foothold in Trônes Wood, and by 8.0 a.m. we had cleared the whole of it, relieving a body of 170 men (Royal West Kents and Queens) who had maintained themselves all night in the northern corner of the wood, although completely surrounded by the enemy. Our position in the wood was finally consolidated, and strong patrols were sent out from it in the direction of Guillemont and Longueval. The southern half of this latter village was already in the hands of the troops who had advanced west of Trônes Wood (9th Division, Major-General W. T. Furze). The northern half, with the exception of two strong points, was captured by 4.0 p.m. after a severe struggle.

In the centre of our attack Bazentin-le-Grand village and wood were also gained by the 3rd and 7th Divisions (Major-General J. A. L. Haldane commanding the 3rd Division), and our troops pushing northwards captured Bazentin-le-Petit village, and the cemetery to the east. Here the enemy counter-attacked twice about midday without success, and again in the afternoon, on the latter occasion momentarily reoccupying the northern half of the village as far as the church. Our troops immediately returned to the attack and drove him out again with heavy losses. To the left of the village Bazentin-le-Petit Wood was cleared by the 21st Division, in spite of the considerable resistance of the enemy along its western edge where we successfully repulsed a counter-attack. In the afternoon further ground was gained to the west of the wood (1st Division, Major-General E. P. Strickland), and posts were established immediately south of Pozières by the 34th Division.

The enemy's troops, who had been severely handled in these attacks and counter-attacks, began to show signs of disorganisation, and it was reported early in the afternoon that it was possible to advance to High Wood. General Rawlinson, who had held a force of cavalry in readiness for such an eventuality, decided to employ a part of it. As the fight progressed small bodies of this force had pushed forward gradually, keeping in close touch with the development of the action and prepared to seize quickly any opportunity that might occur. A squadron (7th Dragoon Guards, Secunderabad Brigade with the Deccan Horse operating with them) now came up on the flanks of our infantry (7th Division), who entered High Wood at about 8.0 p.m., and, after some hand-to-hand fighting, cleared the whole of the wood with the exception of the northern apex. Acting mounted in co-operation with the infantry, the cavalry came into action with good effect, killing several of the enemy and capturing some prisoners.

14. On the 15th July the battle still continued, though on a reduced scale. Arrow Head Copse, between the southern edge of Trônes Wood and Guillemont, and Waterlot Farm on the Longueval-Guillemont Road, were seized, and Delville Wood was captured and held against several hostile counter-attacks (18th and 9th Divisions). In Longueval fierce fighting continued until dusk for the possession of the two strong points and the orchards to the north of the village. The situation in this area made the position of our troops in High Wood somewhat precarious, and they now began to suffer numerous casualties from the enemy's heavy shelling. Accordingly orders were given for their withdrawal, and this was effected during the night of the 15/16th July without interference by the enemy. All the wounded were brought in.

In spite of repeated enemy counter-attacks, further progress was made by the 1st Division on the night of the 16th July along the enemy's main second line trenches north-west of Bazentin-le-Petit Wood to within 500 yards of the north-east corner of the village of Pozières, which our troops were already approaching from the south.

Meanwhile the operations further north had also made progress. Since the attack of the 7th July the enemy in and about Ovillers had been pressed relentlessly, and gradually driven back by incessant bombing attacks and local assaults (25th and 32nd Divisions), in accordance with the general instructions I had given to General Sir Hubert Gough. On the 16th July a large body of the garrison of Ovillers surrendered, and that night and during the following day, by a direct advance from the west across No Man's Land, our troops (48th Division, Major-General R. Fanshawe) carried the remainder of the village and pushed out along the spur to the north and eastwards towards Pozières.

Results, 17th July

15. The results of the operations of the 14th July and subsequent days were of considerable importance. The enemy's second main system of defence had been captured on a front of over three miles.

OPENING OF THE WEARING-OUT BATTLE

We had again forced him back more than a mile, and had gained possession of the southern crest of the main ridge on a front of 6,000 yards. Four more of his fortified villages and three woods had been wrested from him by determined fighting, and our advanced troops had penetrated as far as his third line of defence. In spite of a resolute resistance and many counter-attacks, in which the enemy had suffered severely, our line was definitely established from Maltz Horn Farm, where we met the French left, northwards along the eastern edge of Trônes Wood to Longueval, then westwards past Bazentin-le-Grand to the northern corner of Bazentin-le-Petit and Bazentin-le-Petit Wood, and then westwards again past the southern face of Pozières to the north of Ovillers. Posts were established at Arrow Head Copse and Waterlot Farm, while we had troops thrown forward in Delville Wood and towards High Wood, though their position was not yet secure.

I cannot speak too highly of the skill, daring, endurance and determination by which these results had been achieved. Great credit is due to Sir Henry Rawlinson for the thoroughness and care with which this difficult undertaking was planned; while the advance and deployment made by night without confusion, and the complete success of the subsequent attack, constitute a striking tribute to the discipline and spirit of the troops engaged, as well as to the powers of leadership and organisation of their commanders and staffs.

During these operations and their development on the 15th a number of enemy guns were taken, making our total captures since the 1st July 8 heavy howitzers, 4 heavy guns, 42 field and light guns and field howitzers, 30 trench mortars and 52 machine guns. Very considerable losses had been inflicted on the enemy, and the prisoners captured amounted to over 2,000, bringing the total since the 1st July to over 10,000.

THE SECOND PHASE—THE STRUGGLE FOR THE RIDGE

16. There was strong evidence that the enemy forces engaged on the battle front had been severely shaken by the repeated successes gained by ourselves and our Allies; but the great strength and depth of his defences had secured for him sufficient time to bring up fresh troops, and he had still many powerful fortifications, both trenches, villages and woods, to which he could cling in our front and on our flanks.

We had, indeed, secured a footing on the main ridge, but only on a front of 6,000 yards; and desirous though I was to follow up quickly the successes we had won, it was necessary first to widen this front.

West of Bazentin-le-Petit the villages of Pozières and Thiepval, together with the whole elaborate system of trenches round, between and on the main ridge behind them, had still to be carried. An advance further east would, however, eventually turn these defences, and all that was for the present required on the left flank of our attack was a steady, methodical, step by step advance as already ordered.

On our right flank the situation called for stronger measures. At Delville Wood and Longueval our lines formed a sharp salient, from which our front ran on the one side westwards to Pozières, and on the other southwards to Maltz Horn Farm. At Maltz Horn Farm our lines joined the French, and the Allied front continued still southwards to the village of Hem on the Somme.

This pronounced salient invited counter-attacks by the enemy. He possessed direct observation on it all round from Guillemont on the south-east to High Wood on the north-west. He could bring a concentric fire of artillery to bear not only on the wood and village, but also on the confined space behind, through which ran the French communications as well as ours, where great numbers of guns, besides ammunition and impedimenta of all sorts, had necessarily to be crowded together. Having been in occupation of this ground for nearly two years he knew every foot of it, and could not fail to appreciate the possibilities of causing us heavy loss there by indirect artillery fire; while it was evident that, if he could drive in the salient in our line and so gain direct observation on to the ground behind, our position in that area would become very uncomfortable.

If there had not been good grounds for confidence that the enemy was not capable of driving from this position troops who had shown themselves able to wrest it from him, the situation would have been an anxious one. In any case it was clear that the first requirement at the moment was that our right flank, and the French troops in extension of it, should swing up into line with our centre. To effect this, however, strong enemy positions had to be captured both by ourselves and by our Allies.

From Delville Wood (*vide* Map I.) the main plateau extends for 4,000 yards east-north-east to Les Bœufs and Morval, and for about the same distance south-eastwards to Leuze and Bouleaux Woods, which stand above and about 1,000 yards to the west of Combles. To bring my right up into line with the rest of my front it was necessary to capture Guillemont, Falfemont Farm and Leuze Wood, and then Ginchy and Bouleaux Wood. These localities were naturally very strong, and they had been elaborately fortified. The enemy's main

OPENING OF THE WEARING-OUT BATTLE 33

second line system of defence ran in front of them from Waterlot Farm, which was already in our hands, south-eastwards to Falfemont Farm, and thence southwards to the Somme. The importance of holding us back in this area could not escape the enemy's notice, and he had dug and wired many new trenches, both in front of and behind his original lines. He had also brought up fresh troops,[1] and there was no possibility of taking him by surprise.

The task before us was therefore a very difficult one and entailed a real trial of strength between the opposing forces. At this juncture its difficulties were increased by unfavourable weather. The nature of the ground limited the possibility of direct observation for our artillery fire, and we were consequently much dependent on observation from the air. As in that element we had attained almost complete superiority, all that we required was a clear atmosphere; but with this we were not favoured for several weeks. We had rather more rain than is usual in July and August, and even when no rain fell there was an almost constant haze and frequent low clouds.

In swinging up my own right it was very important that the French line north of the Somme should be advanced at the same time, in close combination with the movement of the British troops. The line of demarcation agreed on between the French commander and myself ran from Maltz Horn Farm due eastwards to the Combles Valley and then north-eastwards up that valley to a point midway between Sailly-Saillisel and Morval. These two villages had been fixed upon as the objectives, respectively, of the French left and of my right. In order to advance in co-operation with my right, and eventually to reach Sailly-Saillisel, our Allies had still to fight their way up that portion of the main ridge which lies between the Combles Valley on the west and the River Tortille on the east. To do so they had to capture, in the first place, the strongly fortified villages of Maurepas, Le Forest, Rancourt and Frégicourt, besides many woods and strong systems of trenches. As the high ground on each side of the Combles Valley commands the slopes of the ridge on the opposite side, it was essential that the advance of the two armies should be simultaneous and made in the closest co-operation. This was fully recognised by both armies, and our plans were made accordingly.

To carry out the necessary preparations to deal with the difficult situation outlined above, a short pause was necessary to enable tired

---

[1] On the 18th July the enemy had 138 battalions engaged in and behind the line north of the Somme, as compared with 62 at the commencement of the battle. By the end of August, 30 German divisions had been brought in to reinforce the 6 divisions located on the front of our attack on the 1st July.

troops to be relieved and guns to be moved forward; while at the same time old communications had to be improved and new ones made. Entrenchments against probable counter-attacks could not be neglected, and fresh dispositions of troops were required for the new attacks to be directed eastwards.

It was also necessary to continue such pressure on the rest of our front, not only on the Ancre but further south, as would make it impossible for the enemy to devote himself entirely to resisting the advance between Delville Wood and the Somme. In addition it was desirable further to secure our hold on the main ridge west of Delville Wood by gaining more ground to our front in that direction. Orders were therefore issued in accordance with the general considerations explained above, and, without relaxing pressure along the enemy's front from Delville Wood to the west, preparations for an attack on Guillemont were pushed on.

Attack and Counter-Attack

17. During the afternoon of the 18th July the enemy developed his expected counter-attack against Delville Wood, after heavy preliminary shelling. By sheer weight of numbers and at very heavy cost he forced his way through the northern and north-eastern portions of the wood and into the northern half of Longueval, which our troops (3rd Division) had cleared only that morning. In the south-east corner of the wood he was held up by a gallant defence (9th and 18th Divisions), and further south three attacks on our positions held by the 35th Division (Major-General R. J. Pinney) in Waterlot Farm failed.

This enemy attack on Delville Wood marked the commencement of the long, closely contested struggle which was not finally decided in our favour till the fall of Guillemont on the 3rd September, a decision which was confirmed by the capture of Ginchy six days later. Considerable gains were indeed made during this period; but progress was slow and bought only by hard fighting. A footing was established in High Wood by the 33rd Division (Major-General H. J. S. Landon) on the 20th July, and our line linked up thence with Longueval by the 7th and 5th Divisions (Major-General R. B. Stephens commanding the 5th Division). A subsequent advance by the Fourth Army on the 23rd July on a wide front from Guillemont to near Pozières found the enemy in great strength all along the line, with machine guns and forward troops in shell holes and newly constructed trenches, well in front of his main defences. Although ground was won, the strength of the resistance experienced showed that the hostile troops had recovered from their previous confusion

OPENING OF THE WEARING-OUT BATTLE

sufficiently to necessitate long and careful preparation before further successes on any great scale could be secured.

An assault delivered simultaneously on this date by General Gough's Army (1st Australian Division, Major-General H. B. Walker, and 48th Division) against Pozières gained considerable results, and by the morning of the 25th July the whole of that village was carried, including the cemetery, and important progress was made along the enemy's trenches to the north-east. That evening (24th July), after heavy artillery preparation, the enemy launched two more powerful counter-attacks, the one directed against our new position in and around High Wood (51st Division, Major-General G. M. Harper) and the other delivered from the north-west of Delville Wood. Both attacks were completely broken up with very heavy losses to the enemy.

On the 27th July the remainder of Delville Wood was recovered by the 2nd Division (Major-General W. G. Walker), and two days later the northern portion of Longueval and the orchards were cleared of the enemy by the 5th Division, after severe fighting, in which our own and the enemy's artillery were very active.

The Problem of Guillemont

18. On the 30th July the village of Guillemont and Falfemont Farm to the south-east were attacked, in conjunction with a French attack north of the Somme. A battalion (2nd Battalion Royal Scots Fusiliers, 30th Division) entered Guillemont, and part of it passed through to the far side; but as the battalions on either flank did not reach their objectives, it was obliged to fall back, after holding out for some hours on the western edge of the village. In a subsequent local attack on the 8th August our troops again entered Guillemont, but were again compelled to fall back owing to the failure of a simultaneous effort against the enemy's trenches on the flanks of the village.

The ground to the south of Guillemont was dominated by the enemy's positions in and about that village. It was therefore hoped that these positions might be captured first, before an advance to the south of them in the direction of Falfemont Farm was pushed further forward. It had now become evident, however, that Guillemont could not be captured as an isolated enterprise without very heavy loss, and, accordingly, arrangements were made with the French Army on our immediate right for a series of combined attacks, to be delivered in progressive stages, which should embrace Maurepas, Falfemont Farm, Guillemont, Leuze Wood and Ginchy.

An attempt on the 16th August to carry out the first stage of the prearranged scheme met with only partial success, and two days later, after a preliminary bombardment lasting thirty-six hours, a larger combined attack was undertaken. In spite of a number of enemy counter-attacks—the most violent of which, levelled at the point of junction of the British with the French, succeeded in forcing our Allies and ourselves back from a part of the ground won—very valuable progress was made, and our troops (3rd Division) established themselves in the outskirts of Guillemont Village and occupied Guillemont Station. A violent counter-attack on Guillemont Station was repulsed on the 23rd August by the 35th Division, and next day further important progress was made on a wide front north and east of Delville Wood (33rd and 14th Divisions).

Minor Operations

19. Apart from the operations already described, others of a minor character, yet involving much fierce and obstinate fighting,[1] continued during this period on the fronts of both the British Armies. Our lines were pushed forward wherever possible by means of local attacks and by bombing and sapping, and the enemy was driven out of various forward positions from which he might hamper our progress. By these means many gains were made which, though small in themselves, in the aggregate represented very considerable advances. In this way our line was brought to the crest of the ridge above Martinpuich, Pozières Windmill and the high ground north of the village were secured, and with them observation over Martinpuich and Courcelette and the enemy's gun positions in their neighbourhood and around Le Sars. At a later date our troops reached the defences of Mouquet Farm, north-west of Pozières, and made progress in the enemy's trenches south of Thiepval. The enemy's counter-attacks were incessant and frequently of great violence, but they were made in vain and at heavy cost to him. The fierceness of the fighting can be gathered from the fact that one regiment of the German Guard Reserve Corps, which had been in the Thiepval salient opposite Mouquet Farm, is known to have lost 1,400 men in fifteen days.

Guillemont Taken

20. The first two days of September on both Army fronts were spent in preparation for a more general attack, which the gradual

---

[1] The 1st, 12th, 15th Divisions (Major-General F. W. N. McCracken commanding the 15th Division); 19th, 23rd, 25th and 34th Divisions (Major-General C. L. Nicholson commanding the 34th Division); 48th, 51st, 1st Australian, 2nd Australian and 4th Australian Divisions (Major-General Sir H. V. Cox commanding the 4th Australian Division), were engaged in this fighting.

OPENING OF THE WEARING-OUT BATTLE 37

progress made during the preceding month had placed us in a position to undertake. Our assault was delivered at 12 noon on the 3rd September on a front extending from our extreme right to the enemy trenches on the right bank of the Ancre, north of Hamel. Our Allies attacked simultaneously on our right.

Guillemont was stormed [1] and at once consolidated, and our troops pushed on unchecked to Ginchy and the line of the road running south to Wedge Wood. Ginchy was also seized (7th Division), but here in the afternoon we were very strongly counter-attacked. For three days the tide of attack and counter-attack swayed backwards and forwards amongst the ruined houses of the village, till, in the end, for three days more the greater part of it remained in the enemy's possession. Three counter-attacks made on the evening of the 3rd September against our troops in Guillemont (47th Infantry Brigade, 16th Division) all failed with considerable loss to the enemy. We also gained ground north of Delville Wood and in High Wood, though here an enemy counter-attack recovered part of the ground won.

On the front of General Gough's Army, though the enemy suffered heavy losses in personnel, our gain in ground was slight.

21. In order to keep touch with the French who were attacking on our right, the assault on Falfemont Farm on the 3rd September was delivered, by the 5th Division, three hours before the opening of the main assault. In the impetus of their first rush our troops reached the farm, but could not hold it. Nevertheless, they pushed on to the north of it, and on the 4th September delivered a series of fresh assaults upon it from the west and north.

Ultimately this strongly fortified position was occupied piece by piece, and by the morning of the 5th September the whole of it was in our possession. Meanwhile further progress had been made to the north-east of the farm, where considerable initiative was shown by the local commanders. By the evening of the same day our troops were established strongly in Leuze Wood, which on the following day was finally cleared of the enemy.

The Barrier Broken.—Ginchy

22. In spite of the fact that most of Ginchy and of High Wood remained in the enemy's hands, very noteworthy progress had been made in the course of these four days' operations, exceeding anything that had been achieved since the 14th July. Our right was advanced on a front of nearly two miles to an average depth of nearly one mile, penetrating the enemy's original second line of

---

[1] 20th Division, Major-General W. D. Smith, and attached brigade of 16th Division, Major-General W. B. Hickie.

defence on this front, and capturing strongly fortified positions at Falfemont Farm, Leuze Wood, Guillemont, and south-east of Delville Wood, where we reached the western outskirts of Ginchy. More important than this gain in territory was the fact that the barrier which for seven weeks the enemy had maintained against our further advance had at last been broken. Over 1,000 prisoners were made and many machine guns taken or destroyed in the course of the fighting.

23. Preparations for a further attack upon Ginchy continued without intermission, and at 4.45 p.m. on the 9th September the attack was reopened on the whole of the Fourth Army front. At Ginchy and to the north of Leuze Wood it met with almost immediate success. On the right (56th Division) the enemy's line was seized over a front of more than 1,000 yards from the south-west corner of Bouleaux Wood in a north-westerly direction to a point just south of the Guillemont-Morval tramway. Our troops (49th Infantry Brigade, 16th Division) again forced their way into Ginchy, and passing beyond it, carried the line of enemy trenches to the east. Further progress was made east of Delville Wood and south and east of High Wood.

Over 500 prisoners were taken in the operations of the 9th September and following days, making the total since the 1st July over 17,000.

Results Achieved

24. Meanwhile the French had made great progress on our right, bringing their line forward to Louage Wood (just south of Combles)—Le Forest—Cléry-sur-Somme, all three inclusive. The weak salient in the Allied line had therefore disappeared, and we had gained the front required for further operations.

Still more importance, however, lay in the proof afforded by the results described of the ability of our new Armies not only to rush the enemy's strongest defences, as had been accomplished on the 1st and 14th July, but also to wear down and break his power of resistance by a steady, relentless pressure, as they had done during the weeks of this fierce and protracted struggle. As has already been recounted, the preparations made for our assault on the 1st July had been long and elaborate ; but though the enemy knew that an attack was coming, it would seem that he considered the troops already on the spot, secure in their apparently impregnable defences, would suffice to deal with it. The success of that assault, combined with the vigour and determination with which our troops pressed their advantage, and followed by the successful night attack of the 14th

July, all served to awaken him to a fuller realisation of his danger. The great depth of his system of fortification, to which reference has been made, gave him time to reorganise his defeated troops, and to hurry up numerous fresh divisions and more guns. Yet in spite of this, he was still pushed back, steadily and continuously. Trench after trench, and strong point after strong point were wrested from him. The great majority of his frequent counter-attacks failed completely, with heavy loss; while the few that achieved temporary local success purchased it dearly, and were soon thrown back from the ground they had for the moment regained.

The enemy had, it is true, delayed our advance considerably, but the effort had cost him dear; and the comparative collapse of his resistance during the last few days of the struggle justified the belief that in the long run decisive victory would lie with our troops, who had displayed such fine fighting qualities and such indomitable endurance and resolution.

The Third Phase—Exploitation of Success

25. Practically the whole of the forward crest of the main ridge, on a front of some 9,000 yards from Delville Wood to the road above Mouquet Farm, was now in our hands, and with it the advantage of observation over the slopes beyond. East of Delville Wood, for a further 3,000 yards to Leuze Wood, we were firmly established on the main ridge; while further east, across the Combles Valley, the French were advancing victoriously on our right. But though the centre of our line was well placed, on our flanks there was still difficult ground to be won.

From Ginchy the crest of the high ground runs northwards for 2,000 yards, and then eastwards, in a long spur, for nearly 4,000 yards. Near the eastern extremity of this spur stands the village of Morval, commanding a wide field of view and fire in every direction. At Leuze Wood my right was still 2,000 yards from its objective at this village, and between lay a broad and deep branch of the main Combles Valley, completely commanded by the Morval spur and flanked not only from its head north-east of Ginchy, but also from the high ground east of the Combles Valley, which looks directly into it.

Up this high ground beyond the Combles Valley the French were working their way towards their objective at Sailly-Saillisel, situated due east of Morval and standing at the same level. Between these two villages the ground falls away to the head of the Combles Valley, which runs thence in a south-westerly direction. In the bottom of this valley lies the small town of Combles, then well fortified and strongly held, though dominated by my right at Leuze Wood, and by the French left on the opposite heights. It had been agreed between the French and myself that an assault on Combles would not be necessary, as the place could be rendered untenable by pressing forward along the ridges above it on either side.

The capture of Morval from the south presented a very difficult problem, while the capture of Sailly-Saillisel, at that time some 3,000 yards to the north of the French left, was in some respects even more difficult. The line of the French advance was narrowed almost to a defile by the extensive and strongly fortified wood of St. Pierre Vaast on the one side, and on the other by the Combles Valley, which, with the branches running out from it and the slopes on each side, is completely commanded, as has been pointed out, by the heights bounding the valley on the east and west.

On my right flank, therefore, the progress of the French and British forces was still interdependent, and the closest co-operation continued to be necessary in order to gain the further ground required to enable my centre to advance on a sufficiently wide front. To cope with such a situation unity of command is usually essential, but in this case the cordial good feeling between the Allied Armies, and the earnest desire of each to assist the other, proved equally effective and removed all difficulties.

On my left flank the front of General Gough's Army bent back from the main ridge near Mouquet Farm down a spur descending south-westwards, and then crossed a broad valley to the Wonderwork, a strong point situated in the enemy's front-line system near the southern end of the spur on the higher slopes of which Thiepval stands. Opposite this part of our line we had still to carry the enemy's original defences on the main ridge above Thiepval and in the village itself, defences which may fairly be described as being as nearly impregnable as nature, art and the unstinted labour of nearly two years could make them.

Our advance on Thiepval and on the defences above it had been carried out up to this date in accordance with my instructions given on the 3rd July, by a slow and methodical progression, in which great skill and much patience and endurance had been displayed with entirely satisfactory results. General Gough's Army had, in fact, acted most successfully in the required manner as a pivot to the remainder of the attack. The Thiepval defences were known to be exceptionally strong, and as immediate possession of them was not necessary to the development of my plans after the 1st July, there had been no need to incur the heavy casualties to be expected in an attempt to rush them. The time was now approaching, although it had not yet arrived, when their capture would become necessary;

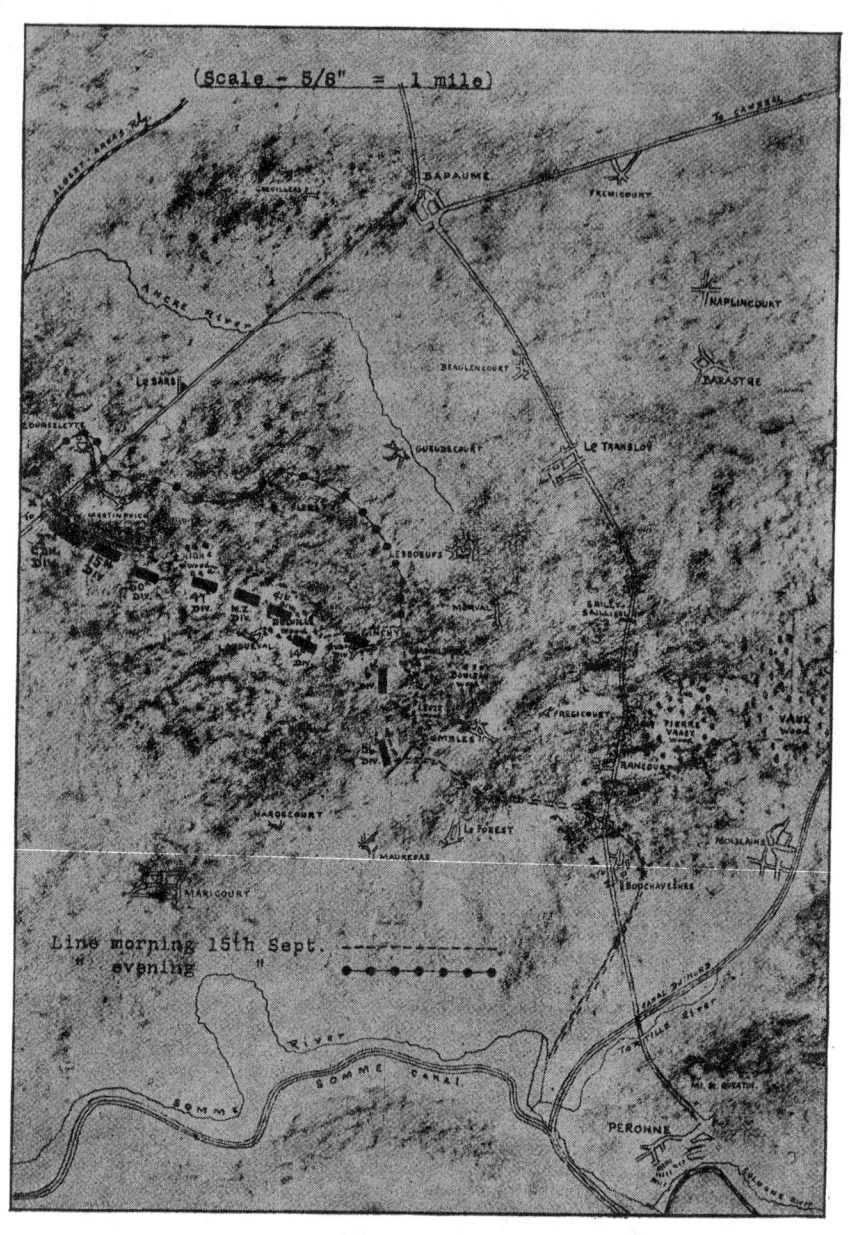

SOMME BATTLE;
Attack of 15th September, 1916.

OPENING OF THE WEARING-OUT BATTLE 41

but from the positions we had now reached and those which we expected shortly to obtain, I had no doubt that they could be rushed when required without undue loss. An important part of the remaining positions required for my assault on them was now won by a highly successful enterprise carried out by the 11th Division (Major-General Sir C. L. Woollcombe) on the evening of the 14th September, by which the Wonderwork was stormed.

26. The general plan of the combined Allied attack which was opened on the 15th September was to pivot on the high ground south of the Ancre and north of the Albert-Bapaume road, while the Fourth Army devoted its whole effort to the rearmost of the enemy's original systems of defence between Morval and Le Sars. Should our success in this direction warrant it, I made arrangements to enable me to extend the left of the attack to embrace the villages of Martinpuich and Courcelette. As soon as our advance on this front had reached the Morval line, the time would have arrived to bring forward my left across the Thiepval Ridge. Meanwhile on my right our Allies [1] arranged to continue the line of advance, in close co-operation with me, from the Somme to the slopes above Combles; but directing their main effort northwards against the villages of Rancourt and Frégicourt, so as to complete the isolation of Combles and open the way for their attack upon Sailly-Saillisel.

The Attack—15th September

27. A methodical bombardment was commenced at 6.0 a.m. on the 12th September and was continued steadily and uninterruptedly till the moment of attack.

At 6.20 a.m. on the 15th September the infantry assault commenced,[2] and at the same moment the bombardment

---

[1] At this time, the success of our attack had compelled the enemy to relax his pressure at Verdun. The forces at the disposal of the French were correspondingly increased. The British Armies south of the Ancre still constituted, however, the striking force of the offensive.

[2] The order of battle of the Fourth Army, from south to north, was as follows :—

XIV. Corps	Lt.-Gen. the Earl of Cavan.
56th Div.	Maj.-Gen. C. P. A. Hull.
6th Div.	Maj.-Gen. C. Ross.
Guards Div.	Maj.-Gen. G. P. T. Feilding.
XV. Corps	Lt.-Gen. H. S. Horne.
14th Div.	Maj.-Gen. V. A. Couper.
41st Div.	Maj.-Gen. S. T. B. Lawford.
N.Z. Div.	Maj.-Gen. A. H. Russell.
III. Corps	Lt.-Gen. Sir W. P. Pulteney.
47th Div.	Maj.-Gen. Sir C. St. L. Barter.
50th Div.	Maj.-Gen. P. S. Williams.
15th Div.	Maj.-Gen. F. W. N. McCracken.

became intense. Our new heavily armoured cars, known as "Tanks," now brought into action for the first time, successfully co-operated with the infantry, and coming as a surprise to the enemy rank and file, gave valuable help in breaking down their resistance.

The advance met with immediate success on almost the whole of the front attacked. At 8.40 a.m. tanks were seen to be entering Flers, followed by large numbers of troops. Fighting continued in Flers for some time, but by 10.0 a.m. our troops had reached the north side of the village, and by midday had occupied the enemy's trenches for some distance beyond. On our right our line was advanced to within assaulting distance of the strong line of defence running before Morval, Les Bœufs and Gueudecourt, and on our left High Wood was at last carried after many hours of very severe fighting, reflecting great credit on the attacking battalions of the 47th Division. Our success made it possible to carry out during the afternoon that part of the plan which provided for the capture of Martinpuich and Courcelette, and by the end of the day both these villages were in our hands (taken respectively by the 15th Division, and 2nd Canadian Division, Maj.-Gen. R. E. W. Turner). On the 18th September the work of this day was completed by the capture by the 6th Division of the Quadrilateral, an enemy stronghold which had hitherto blocked the progress of our right towards Morval. Further progress was also made between Flers and Martinpuich.

28. The result of the fighting of the 15th September and following days was a gain more considerable than any which had attended our arms in the course of a single operation since the commencement of the offensive. In the course of one day's fighting we had broken through two of the enemy's main defensive systems and had advanced on a front of over six miles to an average depth of a mile. In the course of this advance we had taken three large villages, each powerfully organised for prolonged resistance. Two of these villages had been carried by assault with short preparation in the course of a few hours' fighting. All this had been accomplished with a small number of casualties in comparison with the troops employed, and in spite of the fact that, as was afterwards discovered, the attack did not come as a complete surprise to the enemy.[1]

The total number of prisoners taken by us in these operations since their commencement on the evening of the 14th September amounted at this date to over 4,000, including 127 officers.

[1] In spite of the secrecy maintained, the enemy appears to have obtained some information regarding our intended use of tanks, and had issued warnings.

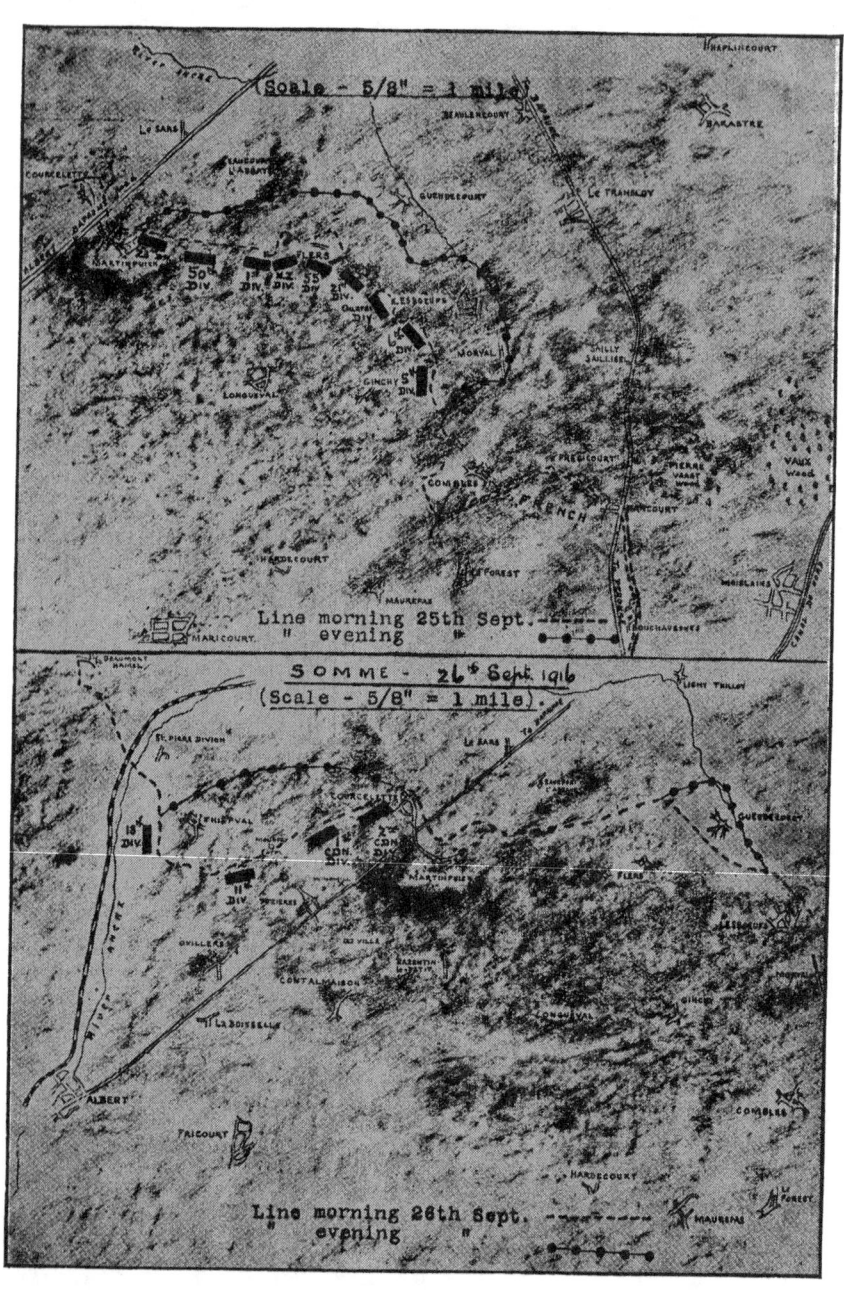

SOMME BATTLE;
Attacks of 25th & 26th September, 1916.

OPENING OF THE WEARING-OUT BATTLE 43

The Advance Renewed.—Combles

29. Preparations for our further advance were again hindered by bad weather, but at 12.35 p.m. on the 25th September, after a bombardment commenced early in the morning of the 24th, a general attack by the Allies was launched on the whole front between the Somme and Martinpuich. The objectives on the British front included the villages of Morval (5th Division), Les Bœufs (6th and Guards Divisions) and Gueudecourt (21st Division), and a belt of country about 1,000 yards deep, curving round the north of Flers to a point midway between that village and Martinpuich (55th Division, Major-General H. S. Jeudwine, and New Zealand and 1st Divisions). By nightfall the whole of these objectives were in our hands, with the exception of the village of Gueudecourt, before which our troops met with very serious resistance from a party of the enemy in a section of his fourth main system of defence.

On our right our Allies carried the village of Rancourt, and advanced their line to the outskirts of Frégicourt, capturing that village also during the night and early morning. Combles was therefore nearly surrounded by the Allied forces, and in the early morning of the 26th September the village was occupied simultaneously by the Allied forces, the British to the north and the French to the south of the railway. The capture of Combles in this inexpensive fashion represented a not inconsiderable tactical success. Though lying in a hollow, the village was very strongly fortified and possessed, in addition to the works which the enemy had constructed, exceptionally large cellars and galleries at a great depth underground, sufficient to give effectual shelter to troops and material under the heaviest bombardment. Great quantities of stores and ammunition of all sorts were found in these cellars when the village was taken.

On the same day Gueudecourt was carried by the 21st Division, after the protecting trench to the west had been captured in a somewhat interesting fashion. In the early morning a tank started from the north-west down the portion of the trench held by the enemy, firing its machine guns and followed by bombers. The enemy could not escape, as we held the trench at the southern end. At the same time an aeroplane flew down the length of the trench, also firing a machine gun at the enemy holding it. These then waved white handkerchiefs in token of surrender, and when this was reported by the aeroplane the infantry accepted the surrender of the garrison. By 8.30 a.m. the whole trench had been cleared, great numbers of the enemy had been killed, and 8 officers and 362 other ranks made prisoners. Our total casualties amounted to five.

Thiepval

30. The success of the Fourth Army had now brought our advance to the stage at which I judged it advisable that Thiepval should be taken, in order to bring our left flank into line and establish it on the main ridge above that village, the possession of which would be of considerable tactical value in future operations.

Accordingly at 12.25 p.m. on the 26th September, before the enemy had been given time to recover from the blow struck by the Fourth Army, a general attack was launched against Thiepval and the Thiepval Ridge. The objective consisted of the whole of the high ground still remaining in enemy hands, extending over a front of some 3,000 yards north and east of Thiepval, and including, in addition to that fortress, the Zollern Redoubt, the Stuff Redoubt, and the Schwaben Redoubt, with the connecting lines of trenches.

The attack was a brilliant success. On the right our troops (2nd and 1st Canadian Divisions of the Canadian Corps, Lieut.-General Sir J. H. G. Byng) reached the system of enemy trenches which formed their objectives without great difficulty. In Thiepval and the strong works to the north of it the enemy's resistance was more desperate. Three waves of our attacking troops (11th and 18th Divisions, II. Corps, Lieut.-General C. W. Jacob) carried the outer defences of Mouquet Farm, and, pushing on, entered Zollern Redoubt which they stormed and consolidated. In the strong point formed by the buildings of the farm itself, the enemy garrison, securely posted in deep cellars, held out until 6.0 p.m., when their last defences were forced by a working party of a Pioneer Battalion acting on its own initiative.

On the left of the attack fierce fighting, in which tanks again gave valuable assistance to our troops (18th Division), continued in Thiepval during that day and the following night, but by 8.30 a.m. on the 27th September the whole of the village of Thiepval was in our hands.

Some 2,300 prisoners were taken in the course of the fighting on the Thiepval Ridge on these and the subsequent days, bringing the total number of prisoners taken in the battle area in the operations of the 14th-30th September to nearly 10,000. In the same period we had captured 27 guns, over 200 machine guns, and some 40 trench mortars.

Further Successes

31. On the same date the south and west sides of Stuff Redoubt were carried by our troops (11th Division), together with the length of trench connecting that strong point with Schwaben Redoubt to the west, and also the greater part of the enemy's defensive line

OPENING OF THE WEARING-OUT BATTLE 45

eastwards along the northern slopes of the ridge. Schwaben Redoubt was assaulted during the afternoon of the 28th September (18th Division), and in spite of counter-attacks, delivered by strong enemy reinforcements, we captured the whole of the southern face of the redoubt and pushed out patrols to the northern face and towards St. Pierre Divion.

Our line was also advanced north of Courcelette, while on the Fourth Army front on the 27th September a further portion of the enemy's fourth system of defence north-west of Gueudecourt was carried on a front of a mile by the 55th and New Zealand Divisions. Between these two points the enemy fell back upon his defences running in front of Eaucourt l'Abbaye and Le Sars, and on the afternoon and evening of the 27th September our troops were able to make a very considerable advance in this area without encountering serious opposition until within a few hundred yards of this line. The ground thus occupied extended to a depth of from 500 to 600 yards on a front of nearly two miles between the Bazentin-le-Petit, Lingy Thilloy and Albert-Bapaume roads.

Destremont Farm, south-west of Le Sars, was carried by a single company (23rd Division) on the 29th September, and on the afternoon of the 1st October a successful attack was launched [1] against Eaucourt l'Abbaye and the enemy defences to the east and west of it, comprising a total front of about 3,000 yards. Our artillery barrage was extremely accurate, and contributed greatly to the success of the attack. Bomb fighting continued among the buildings during the next two days, but by the evening of the 3rd October the whole of Eaucourt l'Abbaye was in our hands.

32. At the end of September I had handed over Morval to the French, in order to facilitate their attacks on Sailly-Saillisel, and on the 7th October, after a postponement rendered necessary by three days' continuous rain, our Allies made a considerable advance in the direction of the latter village. On the same day the Fourth Army attacked along the whole front from Les Bœufs to Destremont Farm, in support of the operations of our Allies.

The village of Le Sars was captured by the 23rd Division, together with the quarry to the north-west, while considerable progress was made at other points along the front attacked. In particular, to the east of Gueudecourt, the enemy's trenches were carried by the 20th Division on a breadth of some 2,000 yards, and a footing gained on the crest of the long spur which screens the defences of Le Transloy from the south-west. Nearly 1,000 prisoners were secured by the Fourth Army in the course of these operations.

[1] By the New Zealand Division, the 47th Division, Major-General Sir G. F. Gorringe, and the 50th and 23rd Divisions.

The Situation

33. With the exception of his positions in the neighbourhood of Sailly-Saillisel, and his scanty foothold on the northern crest of the high ground above Thiepval, the enemy had now been driven from the whole of the ridge lying between the Tortille and the Ancre.

Possession of the north-western portion of the ridge north of the latter village carried with it observation over the valley of the Ancre between Miraumont and Hamel, and the spurs and valleys held by the enemy on the right bank of the river. The Germans, therefore, made desperate efforts to cling to their last remaining trenches in this area, and in the course of the three weeks following our advance made repeated counter-attacks at heavy cost in the vain hope of recovering the ground they had lost. During this period our gains in the neighbourhood of Stuff and Schwaben Redoubts were gradually increased and secured in readiness for future operations; and I was quite confident of the ability of our troops, not only to repulse the enemy's attacks, but to clear him entirely from his last positions on the ridge whenever it should suit my plans to do so. I was, therefore, well content with the situation on this flank.

Along the centre of our line from Gueudecourt to the west of Le Sars similar considerations applied. As we were already well down the forward slopes of the ridge on this front, it was for the time being inadvisable to make any serious advance. Pending developments elsewhere, all that was necessary or indeed desirable was to carry on local operations to improve our positions and to keep the enemy fully employed.

On our eastern flank, on the other hand, it was important to gain ground. Here the enemy still possessed a strong system of trenches covering the villages of Le Transloy and Beaulencourt and the town of Bapaume; but, although he was digging with feverish haste, he had not yet been able to create any very formidable defences behind this line. In this direction, in fact, we had at last reached a stage at which a successful attack might reasonably be expected to yield greater results than anything we had yet attained. The resistance of the troops opposed to us had seriously weakened in the course of our recent operations, and there was no reason to suppose that the effort required would not be within our powers.

This last completed system of defence, before Le Transloy, was flanked to the south by the enemy's positions at Sailly-Saillisel, and screened to the west by the spur lying between Le Transloy and Les Bœufs. A necessary preliminary, therefore, to an assault upon it was to secure the spur and the Sailly-Saillisel heights. Possession of the high ground at this latter village would at once give a far better

OPENING OF THE WEARING-OUT BATTLE 47

command over the ground to the north and north-west, secure the flank of our operations towards Le Transloy, and deprive the enemy of observation over the Allied communications in the Combles Valley. In view of the enemy's efforts to construct new systems of defence behind the Le Transloy line, it was desirable to lose no time in dealing with the situation.

Unfortunately, at this juncture, very unfavourable weather set in and continued with scarcely a break during the remainder of October and the early part of November. Poor visibility seriously interfered with the work of our artillery, and constant rain turned the mass of hastily dug trenches for which we were fighting into channels of deep mud. The country roads, broken by countless shell craters, that crossed the deep stretch of ground we had lately won, rapidly became almost impassable, making the supply of food, stores and ammunition a serious problem. These conditions multiplied the difficulties of attack to such an extent that it was found impossible to exploit the situation with the rapidity necessary to enable us to reap the full benefits of the advantages we had gained.[1]

None the less my right flank continued to assist the operations of our Allies against Saillisel, and attacks were made to this end whenever a slight improvement in the weather made the co-operation of artillery and infantry at all possible. The delay in our advance, however, though unavoidable, had given the enemy time to reorganise and rally his troops. His resistance again became stubborn and he seized every favourable opportunity for counter-attacks. Trenches changed hands with great frequency, the conditions of ground making it difficult to renew exhausted supplies of bombs and ammunition, or to consolidate the ground won, and so rendering it an easier matter to take a battered trench than to hold it.

Other Minor Operations

34. On the 12th and 18th September further gains were made to the east of the Les Bœufs-Gueudecourt line and east of Le Sars,

[1] The scheme of the Allied operations, if events went well, included an advance to the general line Le Transloy—South of Bapaume—Bois Loupart. The British forces would then have developed their successes in a northerly and north-easterly direction, turning the enemy's defences South of the Scarpe, and threatening his troops in that area with capture or destruction. The unfavourable weather, and consequent delay in the Allied advance against Sailly-Saillisel and Le Transloy, made it necessary to abandon this plan at the moment when our September successes seemed to have brought it almost within our grasp. As the season advanced and the bad weather continued the scope of our plan had constantly to be reduced, until finally it was only possible to undertake the much more limited operation of the 13th November against Beaumont Hamel. The brilliant success of this attack, carried out as it was under most difficult conditions of ground, affords some indication of what might have been accomplished had the weather permitted us to give fuller effect to our original plan.

D

and some hundreds of prisoners were taken. On these dates, despite all the difficulties of ground, the French first reached and then captured the village of Sailly-Saillisel, but the moment for decisive action was rapidly passing away, while the weather showed no signs of improvement. By this time, too, the ground had already become so bad that nothing less than a prolonged period of drying weather, which at that season of the year was most unlikely to occur, would suit our purpose.

In these circumstances, while continuing to do all that was possible to improve my position on my right flank, I determined to press on with preparations for the exploitation of the favourable local situation on my left flank. At midday on the 21st October, during a short spell of fine, cold weather, the line of Regina Trench and Stuff Trench, from the west Courcelette-Pys road westward to Schwaben Redoubt, was attacked with complete success by the 4th Canadian, 18th and 15th Divisions, and the 39th Division (Major-General R. Dawson). Assisted by an excellent artillery preparation and barrage, our infantry carried the whole of their objectives very quickly and with remarkably little loss, and our new line was firmly established in spite of the enemy's shell fire. Over 1,000 prisoners were taken in the course of the day's fighting, a figure only slightly exceeded by our casualties.

On the 23rd October, and again on the 5th November, while awaiting better weather for further operations on the Ancre, our attacks on the enemy's positions to the east of Les Bœufs and Gueudecourt were renewed, in conjunction with French operations against the Sailly-Saillisel heights and St. Pierre Vaast Wood. Considerable further progress was achieved by the 4th and 8th Divisions (Major-Generals the Hon. W. Lambton and H. Hudson). Our footing on the crest of the Le Transloy spur was extended and secured, and the much contested tangle of trenches at our junction with the French left at last passed definitely into our possession. Many smaller gains were made in this neighbourhood by local assaults during these days, in spite of the difficult conditions of the ground. In particular, on the 10th November, after a day of improved weather, the portion of Regina Trench lying to the east of the Courcelette-Pys road was carried by the 4th Canadian Division on a front of about 1,000 yards.

Throughout these operations the enemy's counter-attacks were very numerous and determined, succeeding indeed in the evening of the 23rd October in regaining a portion of the ground east of Le Sars taken from him by our attack on that day. On all other occasions his attacks were broken by our artillery or infantry, and the losses incurred by him in these attempts, made frequently with considerable effectives, were undoubtedly very severe.

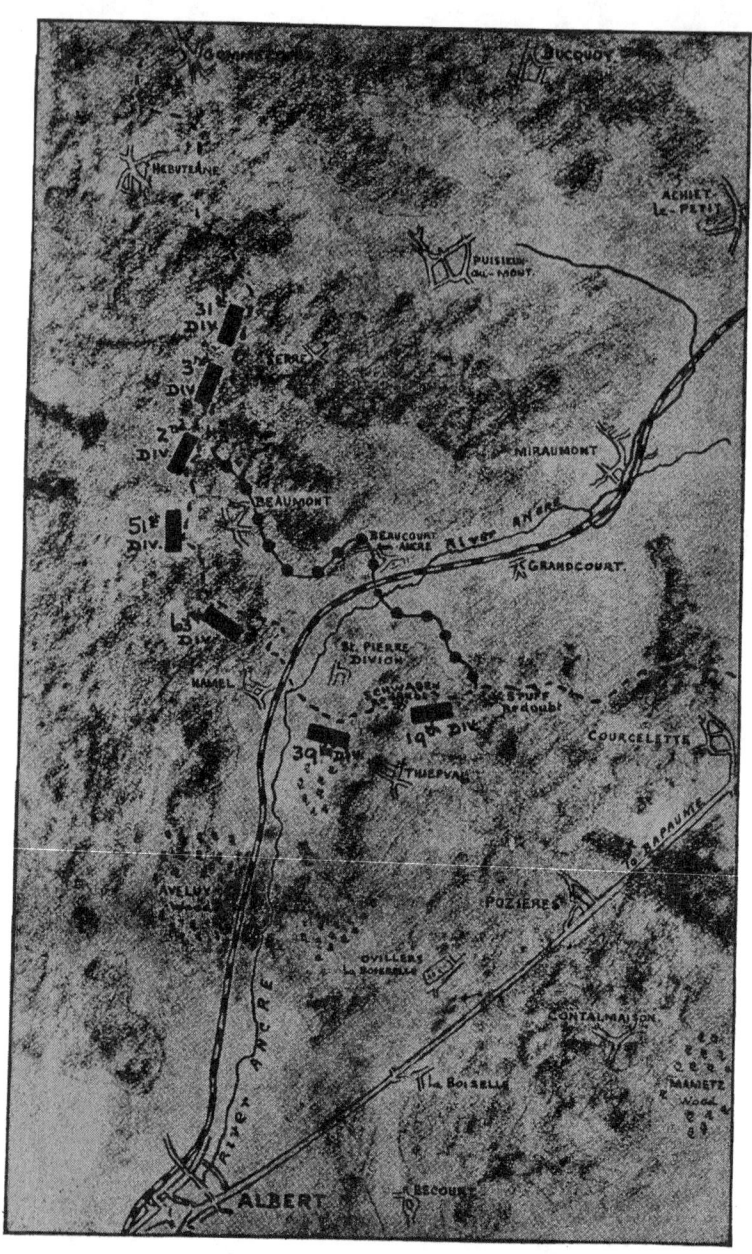

ANCRE BATTLE;
13th November, 1916.

OPENING OF THE WEARING-OUT BATTLE 49

Beaumont Hamel

35. On the 9th November the long-continued bad weather took a turn for the better, and thereafter remained dry and cold, with frosty nights and misty mornings, for some days. Final preparations were therefore pushed on for the attack on the Ancre, though, as the ground was still very bad in places, it was necessary to limit the operations to what it would be reasonably possible to consolidate and hold under the existing conditions.

The enemy's defences in this area were already extremely formidable when they resisted our assault on the 1st July, and the succeeding period of four months had been spent in improving and adding to them in the light of the experience he had gained in the course of our attacks further south. The hamlet of St. Pierre Divion and the villages of Beaucourt-sur-Ancre and Beaumont Hamel, like the rest of the villages forming part of the enemy's original front in this district, were evidently intended by him to form a permanent line of fortifications, while he developed his offensive elsewhere. Realising that his position in them had become a dangerous one, the enemy had multiplied the number of his guns covering this part of his line, and at the end of October introduced an additional division on his front between Grandcourt and Hébuterne.

The Assault

36. At 5 a.m. on the morning of the 11th November the special bombardment preliminary to the attack was commenced. It continued with bursts of great intensity until 5.45 a.m. on the morning of the 13th November, when it developed into a very effective barrage covering the assaulting infantry.

At that hour our troops advanced on the enemy's position through dense fog, and rapidly entered his first line trenches on almost the whole of the front attacked, from east of Schwaben Redoubt to the north of Serre. South of the Ancre, where our assault (19th and 39th Divisions) was directed northwards against the enemy's trenches on the northern slopes of the Thiepval Ridge, it met with a success altogether remarkable for rapidity of execution and lightness of cost. By 7.20 a.m. our objectives east of St. Pierre Divion had been captured, and the Germans in and about that hamlet were hemmed in between our troops and the river. Many of the enemy were driven into their dug-outs and surrendered, and at 9.0 a.m. the number of prisoners was actually greater than the attacking force. St. Pierre Divion soon fell, and in this area nearly 1,400 prisoners were taken by a single division (the 39th Division) at the expense of less than

600 casualties. The rest of our forces operating south of the Ancre attained their objectives with equal completeness and success.

North of the river the struggle was more severe, but very satisfactory results were achieved. Though parties of the enemy held out for some hours during the day in strong points at various places along his first line and in Beaumont Hamel, the main attack pushed on. The troops attacking close to the right bank of the Ancre (the 63rd Division, Major-General C. D. Shute) reached their second objectives to the west and north-west of Beaucourt during the morning, and held on there for the remainder of the day and night, though practically isolated from the rest of our attacking troops. Their tenacity was of the utmost value, and contributed very largely to the success of the operations.

At nightfall our troops were established on the western outskirts of Beaucourt, in touch with our forces south of the river, and held a line along the station road from the Ancre towards Beaumont Hamel (51st Division), where we occupied the village. Further north the enemy's first line system for a distance of about half a mile beyond Beaumont Hamel was also in our hands (2nd Division). Still further north—opposite Serre—the ground was so heavy that it became necessary to abandon the attack at an early stage; although, despite all difficulties, our troops (3rd Division, Major-General C. J. Deverell, and 31st Division) had in places reached the enemy's trenches in the course of their assault.

Next morning, at an early hour, the attack was renewed between Beaucourt and the top of the spur just north of Beaumont Hamel. The whole of Beaucourt was carried, and our line extended to the north-west along the Beaucourt road across the southern end of the Beaumont Hamel spur. The number of our prisoners steadily rose, and during this and the succeeding days our front was carried forward eastwards and northwards up the slopes of the Beaumont Hamel spur.

The results of this attack were very satisfactory, especially as before its completion bad weather had set in again. We had secured the command of the Ancre Valley on both banks of the river at the point where it entered the enemy's lines, and, without great cost to ourselves, losses had been inflicted on the enemy which he himself admitted to be considerable. Our final total of prisoners taken in these operations, and their development during the subsequent days, exceeded 7,200, including 149 officers.

Our other Armies

37. Throughout the period dealt with in this Despatch the rôle of the other armies holding our defensive line from the northern

OPENING OF THE WEARING-OUT BATTLE

limits of the battle front to beyond Ypres was necessarily a secondary one, but their task was neither light nor unimportant. While required to give precedence in all respects to the needs of the Somme battle, they were responsible for the security of the line held by them and for keeping the enemy on their front constantly on the alert. Their rôle was a very trying one, entailing heavy work on the troops and constant vigilance on the part of Commanders and Staffs. It was carried out to my entire satisfaction, and in an unfailing spirit of unselfish and broad-minded devotion to the general good, which is deserving of the highest commendation.

Some idea of the thoroughness with which their duties were performed can be gathered from the fact that in the period of four and a half months from the 1st July some 360 raids were carried out, in the course of which the enemy suffered many casualties and some hundreds of prisoners were taken by us. The largest of these operations was undertaken on the 19th July in the neighbourhood of Armentières. Our troops penetrated deeply into the enemy's defences, doing much damage to his works and inflicting severe losses upon him.

General Review

Our Main Objects Achieved

38. The three main objects with which we had commenced our offensive in July had already been achieved at the date when this account closes; in spite of the fact that the heavy autumn rains had prevented full advantage being taken of the favourable situation created by our advance, at a time when we had good grounds for hoping to achieve yet more important successes.

Verdun had been relieved; the main German forces had been held on the Western front; and the enemy's strength had been very considerably worn down.

Any one of these three results is in itself sufficient to justify the Somme battle. The attainment of all three of them affords ample compensation for the splendid efforts of our troops and for the sacrifices made by ourselves and our Allies. They have brought us a long step forward towards the final victory of the Allied cause.

The desperate struggle for the possession of Verdun had invested that place with a moral and political importance out of all proportion to its military value. Its fall would undoubtedly have been proclaimed as a great victory for our enemies, and would have shaken the faith of many in our ultimate success. The failure of the enemy to capture it, despite great efforts and very heavy losses, was a severe blow to his prestige, especially in view of the confidence he had openly expressed as to the results of the struggle.

Information obtained both during the progress of the Somme battle and since the suspension of active operations has fully established the effect of our offensive in keeping the enemy's main forces tied to the Western front. A movement of German troops eastward, which had commenced in June as a result of the Russian successes, continued for a short time only after the opening of the Allied attack. Thereafter the enemy forces that moved East consisted, with one exception, of divisions that had been exhausted in the Somme battle, and these troops were always replaced on the Western front by fresh divisions. In November the strength of the enemy in the Western theatre of war was greater than in July, notwithstanding the abandonment of his offensive at Verdun. It is possible that if Verdun had fallen large forces might still have been employed in an endeavour further to exploit that success. It is, however, far more probable, in view of developments in the Eastern theatre, that a considerable transfer of troops in that direction would have followed. It is therefore justifiable to conclude that the Somme offensive not only relieved Verdun, but held large forces which would otherwise have been employed against our Allies in the East.

The third great object of the Allied operations on the Somme was the wearing down of the enemy's powers of resistance. Any statement of the extent to which this has been attained must depend in some degree on estimates. There is, nevertheless, sufficient evidence to place it beyond doubt that the enemy's losses in men and material have been very considerably higher than those of the Allies, while morally the balance of advantage on our side is still greater.

During the period under review a steady deterioration took place in the moral of large numbers of the enemy's troops. Many of them, it is true, fought with the greatest determination, even in the latest encounters, but the resistance of still larger numbers became latterly decidedly feebler than it had been in the earlier stages of the battle. Aided by the great depth of his defences, and by the frequent reliefs which his resources in men enabled him to effect, discipline and training held the machine together sufficiently to enable the enemy to rally and reorganise his troops after each fresh defeat. As our advance progressed, four-fifths of the total number of divisions engaged on the Western front were thrown one after another into the Somme battle, some of them twice, and some three times; and towards the end of the operations, when the weather unfortunately broke, there can be no doubt that his power of resistance had been very seriously diminished.

The total number of prisoners taken by us in the Somme battle

OPENING OF THE WEARING-OUT BATTLE 53

between the 1st July and the 18th November is just over 38,000, including over 800 officers. During the same period we captured 29 heavy guns, 96 field guns and field howitzers, 136 trench mortars, and 514 machine guns.

Our Troops

So far as these results are due to the action of the British forces, they have been attained by troops the vast majority of whom had been raised and trained during the war. Many of them, especially amongst the drafts sent to replace wastage, counted their service by months, and gained in the Somme battle their first experience of war. The conditions under which we entered the war had made this unavoidable. We were compelled either to use hastily trained and inexperienced officers and men, or else to defer the offensive until we had trained them. In this latter case we should have failed our Allies. That these troops should have accomplished so much under such conditions, and against an Army and a nation whose chief concern for so many years has been preparation for war, constitutes a feat of which the history of our nation records no equal. The difficulties and hardships cheerfully overcome, and the endurance, determination and invincible courage shown in meeting them, can hardly be imagined by those who have not had personal experience of the battle, even though they have themselves seen something of war.

The events which I have described in this Despatch form but a bare outline of the more important occurrences. To deal in any detail even with these, without touching on the smaller fights and the ceaseless work in the trenches continuing day and night for five months, is not possible here.[1] Meanwhile, it must suffice to say that troops from every part of the British Isles, and from every Dominion and quarter of the Empire, whether Regulars, Territorials, or men of the New Armies, have borne a share in the Battle of the Somme. While some have been more fortunate than others in opportunities for distinction, all have done their duty nobly.

Among all the long roll of victories borne on the colours of our regiments, there has never been a higher test of the endurance and resolution of our infantry. They have shown themselves worthy of the highest traditions of our race, and of the proud records of former wars.

[1] In the original Despatch, which does not mention divisions or other units by name, the following passage occurs here :—" Nor have I deemed it permissible in this Despatch, much as I desired to do so, to particularise the units, brigades, or divisions especially connected with the different events described. It would not be possible to do so without giving useful information to the enemy. Recommendations for individual rewards have been forwarded separately, and in due course full details will be made known."

Against such defences as we had to assault—far more formidable in many respects than those of the most famous fortresses in history —infantry would have been powerless without efficient artillery preparation and support. The work of our artillery was wholly admirable, though the strain on the personnel was enormous. The excellence of the results attained was the more remarkable, in view of the shortness of the training of most of the junior officers and of the N.C.O.'s and men. Despite this, they rose to a very high level of technical and tactical skill, and the combination between artillery and infantry, on which above everything victory depends, was an outstanding feature of the battle. Good even in July, it improved with experience, until in the latter assaults it approached perfection.

In this combination between infantry and artillery the Royal Flying Corps played a highly important part. The admirable work of this Corps has been a very satisfactory feature of the battle. Under the conditions of modern war the duties of the Air Service are many and varied. They include the regulation and control of artillery fire by indicating targets and observing and reporting the results of rounds ; the taking of photographs of enemy trenches, strong points, battery positions, and of the effect of bombardments ; and the observation of the movements of the enemy behind his lines.

The greatest skill and daring has been shown in the performance of all these duties, as well as in bombing expeditions. Our Air Service has also co-operated with our infantry in their assaults, signalling the position of our attacking troops and turning machine guns on to the enemy infantry and even on to his batteries in action.

Not only has the work of the Royal Flying Corps to be carried out in all weathers and under constant fire from the ground, but fighting in the air has now become a normal procedure, in order to maintain the mastery over the enemy's Air Service. In these fights the greatest skill and determination have been shown, and great success has attended the efforts of the Royal Flying Corps. I desire to point out, however, that the maintenance of mastery in the air, which is essential, entails a constant and liberal supply of the most up-to-date machines, without which even the most skilful pilots cannot succeed.

The style of warfare in which we have been engaged offered no scope for cavalry action, with the exception of the one instance already mentioned in which a small body of cavalry gave useful assistance in the advance on High Wood.

Intimately associated with the artillery and infantry in attack and defence, the work of various special services contributed much towards the successes gained.

Trench mortars, both heavy and light, have become an important

OPENING OF THE WEARING-OUT BATTLE

adjunct to artillery in trench warfare, and valuable work has been done by the personnel in charge of these weapons. Considerable experience has been gained in their use, and they are likely to be employed even more frequently in the struggle in future.

Machine guns play a great part—almost a decisive part under some conditions—in modern war, and our Machine Gun Corps has attained to considerable proficiency in their use, handling them with great boldness and skill. The highest value of these weapons is displayed on the defensive rather than in the offensive, and we were attacking. Nevertheless, in attack also machine guns can exercise very great influence in the hands of men with a quick eye for opportunity and capable of a bold initiative. The Machine Gun Corps, though comparatively recently formed, has done very valuable work and will increase in importance.

The part played by the new armoured cars—known as "tanks"—in some of the later fights has been brought to notice by me already in my daily reports. These cars proved of great value on various occasions, and the personnel in charge of them performed many deeds of remarkable valour.

The employment by the enemy of gas and of liquid flame as weapons of offence compelled us, not only to discover ways to protect our troops from their effects, but also to devise means to make use of the same instruments of destruction. Great fertility of invention has been shown, and very great credit is due to the special personnel employed for the rapidity and success with which these new arms have been developed and perfected, and for the very great devotion to duty they have displayed in a difficult and dangerous service. The Army owes its thanks to the chemists, physiologists and physicists of the highest rank who devoted their energies to enabling us to surpass the enemy in the use of a means of warfare which took the civilised world by surprise. Our own experience of the numerous experiments and trials necessary before gas and flame could be used, of the great preparations which had to be made for their manufacture, and of the special training required for the personnel employed, shows that the employment of such methods by the Germans was not the result of a desperate decision, but had been prepared for deliberately.

Since we have been compelled, in self-defence, to use similar methods, it is satisfactory to be able to record, on the evidence of prisoners, of documents captured, and of our own observation, that the enemy has suffered heavy casualties from our gas attacks, while the means of protection adopted by us have proved thoroughly effective.

Throughout the operations Engineer troops, both from home and overseas, have played an important rôle, and in every engagement the Field Companies, assisted by Pioneers, have co-operated with the other arms with the greatest gallantry and devotion to duty.

In addition to the demands made on the services of the Royal Engineers in the firing line, the duties of the Corps during the preparation and development of the offensive embraced the execution of a vast variety of important works, to which attention has already been drawn in this Despatch. Whether in or behind the firing line, or on the lines of communication, these skilled troops have continued to show the power of resource and the devotion to duty by which they have ever been characterised.

The Tunnelling Companies still maintain their superiority over the enemy underground, thus safeguarding their comrades in the trenches. Their skill, enterprise and courage have been remarkable, and, thanks to their efforts, the enemy has nowhere been able to achieve a success of any importance by mining.

During the Battle of the Somme the work of the Tunnelling Companies contributed in no small degree to the successful issue of several operations.

The Field Survey Companies have worked throughout with ability and devotion, and have not only maintained a constant supply of the various maps required as the battle progressed, but have in various other ways been of great assistance to the artillery.

The Signal Service, created a short time before the war began on a very small scale, has expanded in proportion with the rest of the Army, and is now a very large organisation.

It provides the means of inter-communication between all the Armies and all parts of them, and in modern war requirements in this respect are on an immense and elaborate scale. The calls on this Service have been very heavy, entailing a most severe strain, often under most trying and dangerous conditions. Those calls have invariably been met with conspicuous success, and no service has shown a more whole-hearted and untiring energy in the fulfilment of its duty.

The great strain of the five months' battle was met with equal success by the Army Service Corps and the Ordnance Corps, as well as by all the other Administrative Services and Departments, both on the Lines of Communication and in front of them. The maintenance of large armies in a great battle under modern conditions is a colossal task. Though bad weather often added very considerably to the difficulties of transport, the troops never wanted for food, ammunition, or any of the other many and varied requirements for the supply of which these Services and Departments are responsible. This fact in itself is the highest testimony that can be given to the energy and efficiency with which the work was conducted.

OPENING OF THE WEARING-OUT BATTLE

In connection with the maintenance and supply of our troops, I desire to express the obligation of the Army to the Navy for the unfailing success with which, in the face of every difficulty, the large numbers of men and the vast quantities of material required by us have been transported across the seas.

I also desire to record the obligation of the Army in the Field to the various authorities at home, and to the workers under them—women as well as men—by whose efforts and self-sacrifice all our requirements were met. Without the vast quantities of munitions and stores of all sorts provided, and without the drafts of men sent to replace wastage, the efforts of our troops could not have been maintained.

The losses entailed by the constant fighting threw a specially heavy strain on the Medical Services. This has been met with the greatest zeal and efficiency. The gallantry and devotion with which officers and men of the Regimental Medical Service and Field Ambulances have discharged their duties is shown by the large number of the R.A.M.C. and Medical Corps of the Dominions who have fallen in the field. The work of the Medical Services behind the front has been no less arduous. The untiring professional zeal and marked ability of the surgical specialists and consulting surgeons, combined with the skill and devotion of the medical and nursing staffs, both at the Casualty Clearing Stations in the field and the Stationary and General Hospitals at the Base, have been beyond praise. In this respect also the Director-General has on many occasions expressed to me the immense help the British Red Cross Society have been to him in assisting the R.A.M.C. in their work.

The health of the troops has been most satisfactory, and, during the period to which this Despatch refers, there has been an almost complete absence of wastage due to disease of a preventable nature.

The Army Commanders and Staffs

With such large forces as we now have in the field, the control exercised by a Commander-in-Chief is necessarily restricted to a general guidance, and great responsibilities devolve on the Army Commanders.

In the Somme Battle these responsibilities were entrusted to Generals Sir Henry Rawlinson and Sir Hubert Gough, commanding respectively the Fourth and Fifth Armies, who for five months controlled the operations of very large forces in one of the greatest, if not absolutely the greatest struggle that has ever taken place.

It is impossible to speak too highly of the great qualities displayed by these commanders throughout the battle. Their thorough knowledge of their profession, and their cool and sound judgment, tact and determination proved fully equal to every call on them. They entirely justified their selection for such responsible commands.

The preparations for the battle, with the exception of those at Gommecourt, were carried out under Sir Henry Rawlinson's orders. It was not until after the assault of the 1st July that Sir Hubert Gough was placed in charge of a portion of the front of attack, in order to enable Sir Henry Rawlinson to devote his whole attention to the area in which I then decided to concentrate the main effort.

The Army Commanders have brought to my notice the excellent work done by their Staff Officers and Technical Advisers, as well as by the various commanders and staffs serving under them, and I have already submitted the names of the various officers and others recommended by them.

I desire also to record my obligation to my own Staff at General Head Quarters and on the Lines of Communication, and to the various Technical Advisers attached thereto for their loyal and untiring assistance.

Throughout the operations the whole Army has worked with a remarkable absence of friction and with a self-sacrifice and whole-hearted devotion to the common cause which is beyond praise. This has ensured and will continue to ensure the utmost concentration of effort. It is indeed a privilege to work with such officers and with such men.

Our Allies

I cannot close this Despatch without alluding to the happy relations which continue to exist between the Allied Armies and between our troops and the civil population in France and Belgium. The unfailing co-operation of our Allies, their splendid fighting qualities and the kindness and goodwill universally displayed towards us have won the gratitude, as well as the respect and admiration, of all ranks of the British Armies.

Future Prospects

In conclusion, I desire to add a few words as to future prospects.

The enemy's power has not yet been broken, nor is it yet possible to form an estimate of the time the war may last before the objects for which the Allies are fighting have been attained. But the Somme battle has placed beyond doubt the ability of the Allies to gain those objects. The German Army is the mainstay of the Central Powers, and a full half of that Army, despite all the advantages of the defensive, supported by the strongest fortifications, suffered defeat on the

Somme this year. Neither the victors nor the vanquished will forget this ; and, though bad weather has given the enemy a respite, there will undoubtedly be many thousands in his ranks who will begin the new campaign with little confidence in their ability to resist our assaults or to overcome our defence.

Our new Armies entered the battle with the determination to win and with confidence in their power to do so. They have proved to themselves, to the enemy, and to the world that this confidence was justified, and in the fierce struggle they have been through they have learned many valuable lessons which will help them in the future.

> I have the honour to be,
> Your Lordship's obedient Servant,
> D. HAIG, General,
> Commanding-in-Chief, British Armies in France.

THE RETREAT TO THE HINDENBURG LINE

THE RETREAT TO THE HINDENBURG LINE

General Headquarters,
British Armies in France,
31st May, 1917.[1]

MY LORD,—

I have the honour to submit the following Report on the operations of the British Armies in France from the 18th November, 1916, to the commencement of our present offensive.

Nature of Operations

1. My plans for the winter, already decided on at the opening of the period under review, were based on several considerations :—
The enemy's strength had been considerably reduced by the severe and protracted struggle on the Somme battlefields, and so far as circumstances and the weather would permit it was most desirable to allow him no respite during the winter.

With this object, although possibilities were limited by the state of the ground under winter conditions, I considered it feasible to turn to good account the very favourable situation then existing in the region of the River Ancre as a result of the Somme battle.

Our operations prior to the 18th November, 1916, had forced the enemy into a very pronounced salient in the area between the Ancre and the Scarpe Valleys, and had obtained for us greatly improved opportunities for observation over this salient. A comparatively short further advance would give us complete possession of the few points south of the Ancre to which the enemy still clung, and would enable us to gain entire command of the spur above Beaumont Hamel. Thereafter, the configuration of the ground in the neighbourhood of the Ancre Valley was such that every fresh advance would enfilade the enemy's positions and automatically open up to the observation of our troops some new part of his defences. Arrangements could therefore be made for systematic and deliberate attacks

---

[1] This Despatch was published as a Supplement to the *London Gazette* of the 19th June, 1917.

to be delivered on selected positions, to gain further observation for ourselves and deprive the enemy of that advantage. By these means the enemy's defences would be continually outflanked, and we should be enabled to direct our massed artillery fire with such accuracy against his trenches and communications as to make his positions in the Ancre Valley exceedingly costly to maintain.

With the same object in view a number of minor enterprises and raids were planned to be carried out along the whole front of the British Armies.

In addition to the operations outlined above, preparations for the resumption of a general offensive in the spring had to be proceeded with in due course. In this connection, steps had to be taken to overcome the difficulties which a temporary lack of railway facilities would place in the way of completing our task within the allotted time. Provision had also to be made to cope with the effect of winter conditions upon work and roads, a factor to which the prolonged frost at the commencement of the present year subsequently gave especial prominence.

Another very important consideration was the training of the forces under my command. It was highly desirable that during the winter the troops engaged in the recent prolonged fighting should be given an adequate period out of the line for training, rest and refitting.

Certain modifications of my programme in this respect eventually became necessary. To meet the wishes of our Allies in connection with the plan of operations for the spring of 1917, a gradual extension of the British front southwards as far as a point opposite the town of Roye was decided on in January, and was completed without incident of importance by the 26th February, 1917. This alteration entailed the maintenance by British forces of an exceptionally active front of 110 miles, including the whole of the Somme battle front, and, combined with the continued activity maintained throughout the winter, interfered to no small extent with my arrangements for reliefs. The training of the troops had consequently to be restricted to such limited opportunities as circumstances from time to time permitted.

The operations on the Ancre, however, as well as the minor enterprises and raids to which reference has been made, were carried out as intended. Besides gaining valuable positions and observation by local attacks in the neighbourhood of Bouchavesnes, Sailly-Saillisel and Grandcourt, these raids and minor enterprises were the means of inflicting heavy casualties on the enemy, and contributed very appreciably to the total of 5,284 prisoners taken from him in the period under review.

RETREAT TO THE HINDENBURG LINE 65

OPERATIONS ON THE ANCRE

The Enemy's Position

2. At the conclusion of the operations of the 13th November and following days the enemy still held the whole of the Ancre Valley from Le Transloy to Grandcourt, and his first line of defence lay along the lower northern slopes of the Thiepval Ridge. (See Map No. 2.)

North of the Ancre, he still held the greater part of the spur above Beaumont Hamel. Beyond that point the original German front line, in which the enemy had established himself two years previously, ran past Serre, Gommecourt and Monchy-au-Bois to the northern slopes of the main watershed, and then north-east down to the valley of the River Scarpe east of Arras.

Besides the positions held by him on our immediate front, and in addition to the fortified villages of the Ancre Valley with their connecting trenches, the enemy had prepared along the forward crest of the ridge north of the Ancre Valley a strong second system of defence. This consisted of a double line of trenches, heavily wired, and ran north-west from Saillisel past Le Transloy to the Albert-Bapaume Road, where it turned west past Grévillers and Loupart Wood and then north-west again past Achiet-le-Petit to Bucquoy. This system, which was known as the Le Transloy-Loupart line, both by reason of its situation and as a result of the skill and industry expended on its preparation, constituted an exceedingly strong natural defensive position; second only to that from which the enemy had recently been driven on the Morval-Thiepval Ridge. Parallel to this line, but on the far side of the crest, he had constructed towards the close of the past year a third defensive system on the line Rocquigny, Bapaume, Ablainzevelle.

Operations Commenced

3. The first object of our operations in the Ancre Valley was to advance our trenches to within assaulting distance of the Le Transloy-Loupart line.

Accordingly, on the 18th November, 1916, before the rapidly deteriorating condition of the ground had yet made an undertaking on so considerable a scale impossible, an attack was delivered against the next German line of defence, overlooking the villages of Pys and Grandcourt. Valuable positions were gained on a front of about 5,000 yards, while a simultaneous attack north of the Ancre considerably improved the situation of our troops in the Beaucourt Valley.[1]

[1] The 4th Canadian, 18th, 19th, 37th and 32nd Divisions, commanded respectively by Major-Generals D. Watson, F. I. Maxse, G. T. M. Bridges, H. B. Williams and W. H. Rycroft, carried out these attacks.

By this time winter conditions had set in, and along a great part of our new front movement across the open had become practically impossible. During the remainder of the month, therefore, and throughout December, our energies were principally directed to the improvement of our own trenches and of roads and communications behind them. At the same time the necessary rearrangement of our artillery was completed, so as to take full advantage of the opportunities afforded by our new positions for concentration of fire.

The Beaumont Hamel Spur

4. As soon as active operations again became possible, proceedings were commenced to drive the enemy from the remainder of the Beaumont Hamel Spur. In January a number of small operations were carried out with this object by the 3rd, 7th and 11th Divisions (Major-Generals C. J. Deverell, H. E. Watts and A. B. Ritchie), resulting in a progressive improvement of our position. Before the end of the month the whole of the high ground north and east of Beaumont Hamel was in our possession, we had pushed across the Beaucourt Valley 1,000 yards north of Beaucourt Village, and had gained a footing on the southern slopes of the spur to the east.

The most important of these attacks was undertaken at dawn on the morning of the 11th January by the 7th Division, against a system of hostile trenches extending for some 1,500 yards along the crest of the spur east and north-east of Beaumont Hamel. By 8.30 a.m. all our objectives had been captured, together with over 200 prisoners. That afternoon an enemy counter-attack was broken up by our artillery.

Throughout the whole of the month's fighting in this area, in which over 500 German prisoners were taken by us, our casualties were exceedingly light. This satisfactory circumstance can be attributed mainly to the close and skilful co-operation between our infantry and artillery, and to the excellence of our artillery preparation and barrages. These in turn were made possible by the opportunities for accurate observation afforded by the high ground north of Thiepval, and by the fine work done by our aircraft.

Grandcourt

5. Possession of the Beaumont Hamel Spur opened up a new and extensive field of action for our artillery. The whole of the Beaucourt Valley and the western slopes of the spur beyond from opposite Grandcourt to Serre now lay exposed to our fire. Operations were, therefore, at once commenced under the cover of our guns to clear

RETREAT TO THE HINDENBURG LINE 67

the remainder of the valley south of the Serre Hill, and to push our line forward to the crest of the spur.

On the night of the 3rd/4th February an important German line of defence on the southern slopes of this spur, forming part of the enemy's original second line system north of the Ancre, was captured by our troops (63rd Division, Major-General C. D. Shute) on a front of about three-quarters of a mile. The enemy's resistance was stubborn, and hard fighting took place, which lasted throughout the whole of the following day and night. During this period a number of determined counter-attacks were beaten off by our infantry or dispersed by our artillery, and by the 5th February we had gained the whole of our objectives. In this operation, in which the excellence of our artillery co-operation was very marked, we took 176 prisoners and four machine guns.

This success brought our front forward north of the Ancre to a point level with the centre of Grandcourt, and made the enemy's hold on his position in that village and in his more western defences south of the river very precarious. It was not unexpected, therefore, when on the morning of the 6th February our patrols reported that the last remaining portion of the old German second line system south of the river, lying between Grandcourt and Stuff Redoubt, had been evacuated. The abandoned trenches were occupied by our troops the same morning.

Constant reconnaissances were sent out by us to keep touch with the enemy and to ascertain his movements and intentions. Grandcourt itself was next found to be clear of the enemy, and by 10 a.m. on the morning of the 7th February was also in our possession (63rd Division). That night we carried Baillescourt Farm, about half-way between Beaucourt and Miraumont, capturing 87 prisoners.

The Advance against Serre

6. The task of driving the enemy from his position in the Beaucourt Valley was resumed on the night of the 10th/11th February. Our principal attack was directed against some 1,500 yards of a strong line of trenches, the western end of which was already in our possession, lying at the southern foot of the Serre Hill. Our infantry (32nd Division, Major-General R. W. R. Barnes) were formed up after dark, and at 8.30 p.m. advanced under our covering artillery barrage. After considerable fighting in the centre and towards the left of our attack, the whole of the trench line which formed our objective was gained, with the exception of two strong points which held out for a few days longer. At 5 a.m. a determined counter-attack from the direction of Puisieux-au-Mont was beaten off by our

artillery and machine gun fire. Two other counter-attacks on the 11th February and a third on the 12th February were equally unsuccessful.

The Advance towards Miraumont

7. The village of Serre now formed the point of a very pronounced salient, which our further progress along the Ancre Valley would render increasingly difficult, if not impossible, for the enemy to hold. Accordingly, an operation on a somewhat larger scale than anything hitherto attempted since the new year, was now undertaken. Its object was to carry our line forward along the spur which runs northwards from the main Morval-Thiepval Ridge about Courcelette, and so gain possession of the high ground at its northern extremity. The possession of this high ground, besides commanding the approaches to Pys and Miraumont from the south, would give observation over the upper valley of the Ancre, in which many hostile batteries were situated in positions enabling their fire to be directed for the defence of the Serre sector. At the same time arrangements were made for a smaller attack on the opposite bank of the river, designed to seize a portion of the sunken road lying along the eastern crest of the second spur north of the Ancre and so obtain control of the approaches to Miraumont from the west.

Our assault was delivered simultaneously on both banks of the Ancre at 5.45 a.m. on the 17th February by the 2nd, 18th and 63rd Divisions (Major-Generals C. E. Pereira and R. P. Lee commanding respectively the 2nd and 18th Divisions). The night was particularly dark, and thick mist and heavy conditions of ground, produced by the thaw that had just set in, added to the difficulties with which our troops had to contend. The enemy was, moreover, on the alert, and commenced a heavy barrage some time before the hour of our assault, while our attacking battalions were still forming up. None the less, our troops advanced to the assault with great gallantry. On the left of our attack (south of the river) our artillery preparation had been assisted by observation from the positions already won on the right bank of the Ancre. In consequence, our infantry were able to make a very considerable advance, and established themselves within a few hundred yards of Petit Miraumont. The right of our attack encountered more serious resistance, but here also valuable progress was made.

North of the Ancre our troops met with complete success. The whole of the position attacked, on a front of about half a mile, was secured without great difficulty, and an enemy counter-attack during the morning was easily driven off.

Next day, at 11.30 a.m., the enemy delivered a second counter-attack from the north with considerable forces, estimated at two battalions, upon our new positions north of the river. His advancing waves came under the concentrated fire of our artillery and machine guns while still some distance in front of our lines, and were driven back in disorder with exceedingly heavy losses.

Eleven officers and 588 other ranks were taken prisoners by us in these operations.

Miraumont and Serre Evacuated

8. The ground gained by these two attacks, and by minor operations carried out during the succeeding days, gave us the observation we desired, as well as complete command over the German artillery positions in the upper Ancre Valley and over his defences in and around Pys and Miraumont. The constant bombardment by our artillery, combined with the threat of an attack in which his troops would have been at great disadvantage, accordingly decided the enemy to abandon both villages. Our possession of Miraumont, however, gravely endangered the enemy's positions at Serre by opening up for us possibilities of a further advance northwards, while the loss of Serre would speedily render Puisieux-au-Mont and Gommecourt equally difficult of defence. There was, therefore, good ground to expect that the evacuation of Pys and Miraumont would shortly be followed by a withdrawal on a more considerable scale. This in fact occurred.

On the 24th February the enemy's positions before Pys, Miraumont and Serre were found by our patrols to have been evacuated, and were occupied by our troops. Our patrols were then at once pushed forward, supported by strong infantry detachments, and by the evening of the 25th February the enemy's first system of defence from north of Gueudecourt to west of Serre, and including Luisenhof Farm, Warlencourt-Eaucourt, Pys, Miraumont, Beauregard Dovecot and Serre, had fallen into our hands. The enemy offered some opposition with machine guns at selected strong points in his line, and his artillery actively shelled the areas from which he had withdrawn; but the measures taken to deal with such tactics proved adequate, and the casualties inflicted on our troops were light.

The enemy's retirement at this juncture was greatly favoured by the weather. The prolonged period of exceptional frost, following on a wet autumn, had frozen the ground to a great depth. When the thaw commenced in the third week of February the roads, disintegrated by the frost, broke up, the sides of trenches fell in, and the area across which our troops had fought their way forward returned to a condition of slough and quagmire even worse than that of the previous autumn. On the other hand, the condition of the roads and the surface of the ground behind the enemy steadily improved the further he withdrew from the scene of the fighting. He was also materially assisted by a succession of misty days, which greatly interfered with the work of our aeroplanes. Over such ground and in such conditions rapid pursuit was impossible. It is greatly to the credit of all ranks concerned that, in spite of all difficulties, constant touch was maintained with the enemy and that timely information was obtained of his movements.

Le Barque and Gommecourt

9. Resistance of a more serious character was encountered in a strong secondary line of defence which, from a point in the Le Transloy-Loupart line due west of the village of Beaulencourt, crossed in front of Ligny-Thilloy and Le Barque to the southern defences of Loupart Wood. Between the 25th February and the 2nd March a series of attacks were carried out by the 1st Anzac Corps (Lieut.-General Sir W. R. Birdwood) against this line, and the enemy was gradually driven out of his positions. By the evening of the latter day the whole line of trenches and the villages of Le Barque, Ligny-Thilloy and Thilloy had in turn been captured. One hundred and twenty-eight prisoners and a number of trench mortars and machine guns were taken in this fighting, in the course of which the enemy made several vigorous but unsuccessful counter-attacks.

Meanwhile rapid progress had been made on the remainder of the front of our advance. On the 27th February the enemy's rearguards in Puisieux-au-Mont were driven to their last positions of defence in the neighbourhood of the church, and to the north-west of the village our front was extended to within a few hundred yards of Gommecourt. That evening our patrols entered Gommecourt Village and Park, following closely upon the retreating enemy, and by 10.0 p.m. Gommecourt and its defences had been occupied. Next morning the capture of Puisieux-au-Mont was completed.

Irles

10. The enemy had, therefore, been driven back to the Le Transloy-Loupart line, except that he still held the village of Irles, which formed a salient to his position, and was linked up to it at Loupart Wood and Achiet-le-Petit by well-constructed and well-wired trenches.

Accordingly, our next step was to take Irles, as a preliminary to a larger undertaking against the Le Transloy-Loupart line itself; but before either operation could be attempted exceedingly heavy work had to be done in the improvement of roads and communications,

RETREAT TO THE HINDENBURG LINE 71

and in bringing forward guns and ammunition. The following week was devoted to these very necessary tasks. Meanwhile, operations were limited to small enterprises, designed to keep in touch with the enemy and to establish forward posts which might assist in the forthcoming attack.

The assault on Irles and its defences was delivered at 5.25 a.m. on the morning of the 10th March by the 2nd and 18th Divisions, and was completely successful. The whole of our objectives were captured, and in the village and the surrounding works 289 prisoners were taken, together with sixteen machine guns and four trench mortars. Our casualties were very light, being considerably less than the number of our prisoners.

The Loupart Line

11. The way was now open for the main operation against the centre of the Le Transloy-Loupart line, which throughout the 11th March was heavily shelled by all natures of our artillery. So effective was this bombardment that during the night of the 12th/13th March the enemy once more abandoned his positions, and fell back on the parallel system of defences already referred to on the reverse side of the ridge. Grévillers and Loupart Wood were thereupon occupied by our troops, and methodical preparations were at once begun for an attack on the enemy's next line of defence.

THE ENEMY'S RETREAT

The General Withdrawal

12. For some time prior to this date a number of indications had been observed which made it probable that the area of the German withdrawal would be yet further extended.

It had been ascertained that the enemy was preparing a new defensive system, known as the Hindenburg Line, which, branching off from his original defences near Arras, ran south-eastwards for twelve miles to Quéant, and thence passed west of Cambrai towards St. Quentin. Various " switches " branching off from this line were also under construction. The enemy's immediate concern appeared to be to escape from the salient between Arras and Le Transloy, which would become increasingly difficult and dangerous to hold as our advance on the Ancre drove ever more deeply into his defences. It was also evident, however, from the preparations he was making that he contemplated an eventual evacuation of the greater salient between Arras and the Aisne Valley, north-west of Rheims.

Constant watch had accordingly been kept along the whole front south of Arras, in order that instant information might be obtained of any such development. On the 14th March patrols found portions of the German front line empty in the neighbourhood of St. Pierre Vaast Wood. Acting on the reports of these patrols, during that night and the following day our troops occupied the whole of the enemy's trenches on the western edge of the wood. Little opposition was met, and by the 16th March we held the western half of Moislains Wood, the whole of St. Pierre Vaast Wood with the exception of its north-eastern corner, and the enemy's front trenches as far as the northern outskirts of Sailly-Saillisel.

Meanwhile, on the evening of the 15th March, further information had been obtained which led me to believe that the enemy's forces on our front south of the Somme had been reduced, and that his line was being held by rearguard detachments supported by machine guns, whose withdrawal might also be expected at any moment. The Corps Commanders concerned were immediately directed to confirm the situation by patrols. Orders were thereafter given for a general advance, to be commenced on the morning of the 17th March along our whole front from the Roye Road to south of Arras.

Bapaume and Peronne

13. Except at certain selected localities, where he had left detachments of infantry and machine guns to cover his retreat, such as Chaulnes, Vaux Wood, Bapaume and Achiet-le-Grand, the enemy offered little serious opposition to our advance on this front, and where he did so his resistance was rapidly overcome. Before nightfall on the 17th March Chaulnes and Bapaume had been captured (61st Division and 2nd Australian Division, Major-Generals C. J. Mackenzie and N. M. Smyth), and advanced bodies of our troops had pushed deeply into the enemy's positions at all points from Damery to Monchy-au-Bois. On our right our Allies made rapid progress also, and entered Roye.

On the 18th March and subsequent days our advance continued, in co-operation with the French. In the course of this advance the whole intricate system of German defences in this area, consisting of many miles of powerful, well-wired trenches which had been constructed with immense labour and worked on till the last moment, were abandoned by the enemy and passed into the possession of our troops.

At 7.0 a.m. on the 18th March our troops (48th Division, Major-General R. Fanshawe) entered Peronne and occupied Mont St. Quentin, north of the town. To the south our advanced troops

RETREAT TO THE HINDENBURG LINE

established themselves during the day along the western bank of the Somme from Peronne to just north of Epenancourt. By 10.0 p.m. on the same day Brie Bridge had been repaired by our engineers sufficiently for the passage of infantry in single file, and our troops crossed to the east bank of the river, in spite of some opposition. Further south French and British cavalry entered Nesle.

North of Peronne equal progress was made, and by the evening of the 18th March our troops had entered the German trench system known as the Beugny-Ytres Line, beyond which lay open country as far as the Hindenburg Line. On the same day the left of our advance was extended to Beaurains, which was captured after slight hostile resistance.

By the evening of the 19th March our infantry held the line of the Somme from Canizy to Peronne, and infantry outposts and cavalry patrols had crossed the river at a number of points. North of Peronne our infantry had reached the line Bussu, Barastre, Vélu, St. Leger, Beaurains, with cavalry in touch with the enemy at Nurlu, Bertincourt, Noreuil, and Hénin-sur-Cojeul. Next day considerable bodies of infantry and cavalry crossed to the east of the Somme, and a line of cavalry outposts with infantry in support was established from south of Germaine, where we were in touch with the French, through Hancourt and Nurlu to Bus. Further north we occupied Morchies.

Difficulty of Communications

14. By this time our advance had reached a stage at which the increasing difficulty of maintaining our communications made it imperative to slacken the pace of our pursuit. South of Peronne, the River Somme, the bridges over which had been destroyed by the retreating enemy, presented a formidable obstacle. North of Peronne, the wide belt of devastated ground over which the Somme Battle had been fought offered even greater difficulties to the passage of guns and transport.

We were advancing, therefore, over country in which all means of communication had been destroyed, against an enemy whose armies were still intact and capable of launching a vigorous offensive should a favourable opening present itself. Strong detachments of his infantry and cavalry occupied points of advantage along our line of advance, serving to keep the enemy informed of our progress and to screen his own movements. His guns, which had already been withdrawn to previously prepared positions, were available at any moment to cover and support a sudden counter-stroke, while the conditions of the country across which we were moving made the progress of our own artillery unavoidably slow. The bulk of the enemy's forces were known to be holding a very formidable defensive system, upon which he could fall back should his counter-stroke miss its aim. On the other hand, our troops as they moved forward left all prepared defences further and further behind them. In such circumstances the necessity for caution was obvious. At different stages of the advance successive lines of resistance were selected and put in a state of defence by the main bodies of our infantry, while cavalry and infantry outposts maintained touch with the enemy and covered the work of consolidation. Meanwhile, in spite of the enormous difficulties which the condition of ground and the ingenuity of the enemy had placed in our way, the work of repairing and constructing bridges, roads and railways was carried forward with most commendable rapidity.

Enemy Resistance Increasing

15. North of the Bapaume-Cambrai Road between Noreuil and Neuville-Vitasse our advance had already brought us to within two or three miles of the Hindenburg Line, which entered the old German front line system at Tilloy-lez-Mofflaines. The enemy's resistance now began to increase along our whole front, extending gradually southwards from the left flank of our advance, where our troops had approached most nearly to his new main defensive position.

A number of local counter-attacks were delivered by the enemy at different points along our line. In particular five separate attempts were made to recover Beaumetz-lez-Cambrai, which we had captured on the 21st March, and the farm to the north of the village. All failed with considerable loss to the enemy.

Meanwhile our progress continued steadily, and minor engagements multiplied from day to day all along our front. In these we were constantly successful, and at small cost to ourselves took many prisoners and numerous machine guns and trench mortars. In every fresh position captured, large numbers of German dead testified to the obstinacy of the enemy's defence and the severity of his losses.

Our cavalry took an active part in this fighting, and on the 27th March in particular carried out an exceedingly successful operation, in the course of which a squadron of the 5th Cavalry Division (Major-General H. J. M. Macandrew) drove the enemy from Villers Faucon and a group of neighbouring villages, capturing 23 prisoners and four machine guns. In another series of engagements on the 1st and 2nd April, in which Savy and Selency were taken by the 32nd Division (Major-General C. D. Shute) and our line advanced to within two miles of St. Quentin, we captured 91 prisoners and six German field guns. The enemy's casualties were particularly heavy.

On the 2nd April, also, an operation on a more important scale was undertaken against the enemy's positions north of the Bapaume-

Cambrai Road. The enemy here occupied in considerable strength a series of villages and well-wired trenches, forming an advanced line of resistance to the Hindenburg Line. A general attack on these positions was launched by the 4th Australian Division and the 7th Division (Major-Generals W. Holmes and T. H. Shoubridge) in the early morning of the 2nd April on a front of over ten miles, from Doignies to Hénin-sur-Cojeul, both inclusive. After fighting which lasted throughout the day the entire series of villages was captured by us, with 270 prisoners, four trench mortars and 25 machine guns.

The Hindenburg Line

16. By this date our troops were established on the general line Selency, Jeancourt, Epéhy, Ruyaulcourt, Doignies, Mercatel, Beaurains. East of Selency, and between Doignies and our old front line east of Arras, our troops were already close up to the main Hindenburg defences. Between Selency and Doignies the enemy still held positions some distance in advance of his new system. During the succeeding days our efforts were directed to driving him from these advanced positions, and to pushing our posts forward until contact had been established all along our front south of Arras with the main defences of the Hindenburg Line. Fighting of some importance again took place on the 4th and 5th April in the neighbourhood of Epéhy and Havrincourt Wood, in which Ronssoy, Lempire and Metz-en-Couture were captured by us, together with 100 prisoners, two trench mortars and eleven machine guns (48th, 8th and 20th Divisions, Major-Generals W. C. G. Heneker and T. G. Matheson commanding the two latter divisions).

GENERAL REVIEW

17. Certain outstanding features of the past five months' fighting call for brief comment before I close this Report.

In spite of a season of unusual severity, a winter campaign has been conducted to a successful issue under most trying and arduous conditions. Activity on our battle-front has been maintained almost without a break from the conclusion of last year's offensive to the commencement of the present operations. The successful accomplishment of this part of our general plan has already enabled us to realise no inconsiderable instalment of the fruits of the Somme Battle, and has gone far to open the road to their full achievement.[1] The courage and endurance of our troops have carried them triumphantly through a period of fighting of a particularly trying nature,

[1] In this connection it is interesting to note that according to his Memoirs Ludendorff expected in January, 1917 (*i.e.*, before the collapse of Russia), to be beaten before the end of the year, unless the submarine campaign forced an earlier and more favourable conclusion.

in which they have been subjected to the maximum of personal hardship and physical strain. I cannot speak too highly of the qualities displayed by all ranks of the Army.

I desire also to place on record here my appreciation of the great skill and energy displayed by the Army Commanders under whose immediate orders the operations described above were carried out. The ability with which the troops in the Ancre area were handled by General Sir Hubert Gough, and those further south on our front from Le Transloy to Roye by General Sir Henry Rawlinson, was in all respects admirable.

The retreat to which the enemy was driven by our continued success reintroduced on the Western front conditions of warfare which had been absent from that theatre since the opening months of the war. After more than two years of trench warfare considerable bodies of our troops have been engaged under conditions approximating to open fighting, and cavalry has been given an opportunity to perform its special duties. Our operations south of Arras during the latter half of March are, therefore, of peculiar interest, and the results achieved by all arms have been most satisfactory. Although the deliberate nature of the enemy's withdrawal enabled him to choose his own ground for resistance, and to employ every device to inflict losses on our troops, our casualties, which had been exceedingly moderate throughout the operations on the Ancre, during the period of the retreat became exceptionally light.[1] The prospect of a more general resumption of open fighting can be regarded with great confidence.

The systematic destruction of roads, railways and bridges in the evacuated area made unprecedented demands upon the Royal Engineers, already heavily burdened by the work entailed by the preparations for our spring offensive. Our steady progress, in the face of the great difficulties confronting us, is the best testimony to the energy and thoroughness with which those demands were met.

The bridging of the Somme at Brie, to which reference has already been made, is an example of the nature of the obstacles with which our troops were met and of the rapidity with which those obstacles were overcome. In this instance six gaps had to be bridged across the canal and river, some of them of considerable width and over a swift-flowing stream. The work was commenced on the morning of the 18th March, and was carried out night and day in three stages. By 10.0 p.m. on the same day foot-bridges for infantry had been completed, as already stated. Medium type bridges for horse transport and cavalry were completed by 5.0 a.m. on the 20th March,

---

[1] Our weekly casualties for all Armies, which had risen to 7,000 during the Ancre fighting, fell to 4,000 at the end of March.

RETREAT TO THE HINDENBURG LINE 77

and by 2.0 p.m. on the 28th March, or four and a half days after they had been begun, heavy bridges capable of taking all forms of traffic had taken the place of the lighter type. Medium type deviation bridges were constructed as the heavy bridges were begun, so that from the time the first bridges were thrown across the river traffic was practically continuous.

Throughout the past winter the question of transport, in all its forms, has presented problems of a most serious nature, both in the battle area and behind the lines. On the rapid solution of these problems the success or failure of our operations necessarily largely depended.

At the close of the campaign of 1916 the steady growth of our Armies and the rapid expansion of our material resources had already taxed to the utmost the capacity of the roads and railways then at our disposal. Existing broad and narrow gauge railways were insufficient to deal with the increasing volume of traffic, an undue proportion of which was thrown upon the roads. As winter conditions set in, these rapidly deteriorated, and the difficulties of maintenance and repair became almost overwhelming.[1] An increase of railway facilities of every type and on a large scale was therefore imperatively and urgently necessary to relieve the roads. For this purpose rails, material and rolling stock were required immediately in great quantities, while at a later date our wants in these respects were considerably augmented by a large programme of new construction in the area of the enemy's withdrawal.

The task of obtaining the amount of railway material required to meet the demands of our Armies, and of carrying out the work of construction at the rate rendered necessary by our plans, in addition to providing labour and material for the necessary repair of roads, was one of the very greatest difficulty. Its successful accomplishment reflects the highest credit on the Transportation Service, of whose efficiency and energy I cannot speak too highly. I desire to acknowledge in the fullest manner the debt that is owed to all who assisted in meeting a most difficult situation, and especially to Major-General Sir Eric Geddes, Director-General of Transportation, to whose great ability, organising power and energy the results achieved are primarily due. I am glad to take this opportunity also to acknowledge the valuable assistance given to us by the Chemin de Fer du Nord, by which the work of the Transportation Service was greatly facilitated.

[1] So great did these difficulties become, that it became necessary at this time to adopt a new system on our Lines of Communication, involving the creation of the new Department of Transportation, of which Sir Eric Geddes was the first Director-General. See also Sir Douglas Haig's final Despatch, page 337.

I wish also to place on record here the fact that the successful solution of the problem of railway transport would have been impossible had it not been for the patriotism of the railway companies at home and in Canada. They did not hesitate to give up the locomotives and rolling stock required to meet our needs, and even to tear up track in order to provide us with the necessary rails. The thanks of the Army are due also to those who have accepted so cheerfully the inconvenience caused by the consequent diminution of the railway facilities available for civil traffic.

The various other special services, to the excellence of whose work I was glad to call attention in my last Despatch, have continued to discharge their duties with the same energy and efficiency displayed by them during the Somme Battle, and have rendered most valuable assistance to our artillery and infantry.

I desire also to repeat the well-merited tribute paid in my last Despatch to the different Administrative Services and Departments. The work entailed by the double task of meeting the requirements of our winter operations and preparing for our next offensive was very heavy, demanding unremitting labour and the closest attention to detail.

The fighting on the Ancre and subsequent advance made large demands upon the devotion of our Medical Services. The health of the troops during the period covered by this Despatch has been satisfactory, notwithstanding the discomfort and exposure to which they were subjected during the extreme cold of the winter, especially in the areas taken over from the enemy.

The loyal co-operation and complete mutual understanding that prevailed between our Allies and ourselves throughout the Somme Battle have been continued and strengthened by the events of the past winter, and in particular by the circumstances attending the enemy's withdrawal. During the latter part of the period under review, a very considerable tract of country has been won back to France by the combined efforts of the Allied troops. This result is regarded with lively satisfaction by all ranks of the British Armies in France. At the same time I wish to give expression to the feelings of deep sympathy and profound regret provoked among us by the sight of the destruction that war has wrought in a once fair and prosperous countryside.

I have the honour to be,
My Lord,
Your Lordship's obedient Servant,
D. HAIG, Field-Marshal,
Commanding-in-Chief, British Armies in France.

THE CAMPAIGNS OF 1917

THE CAMPAIGNS OF 1917

General Headquarters,
British Armies in the Field,
25th December, 1917.[1]

MY LORD,—
I have the honour to submit the following Report on the operations of the Forces under my Command from the opening of the British offensive on the 9th April, 1917, to the conclusion of the Flanders offensive in November. The subsequent events of this year will form the subject of a separate Despatch, to be rendered a little later.

INTRODUCTORY

The General Allied Plan

1. The general plan of campaign to be pursued by the Allied Armies during 1917 was unanimously agreed on by a conference of military representatives of all the Allied Powers held at French General Headquarters in November, 1916.[2]

This plan comprised a series of offensives on all fronts, so timed as to assist each other by depriving the enemy of the power of weakening any one of his fronts in order to reinforce another.

A general understanding had also been arrived at between the then French Commander-in-Chief and myself as to the rôles of our respective Armies in this general plan, and with the approval of His Majesty's Government preparations based upon these arrangements had at once been taken in hand.

2. Briefly stated, my plan of action for the Armies under my command in the proposed general offensive was as follows :—

In the spring, as soon as all the Allied Armies were ready to commence operations, my first efforts were to be directed against the enemy's troops occupying the salient between the Scarpe and the Ancre, into which they had been pressed as a result of the Somme Battle.

It was my intention to attack both shoulders of this salient

[1] This Despatch was published as a Supplement dated the 8th January, 1918, to the *London Gazette* of the 4th January, 1918.
[2] At Chantilly; General Joffre was the French Commander-in-Chief at this time.

simultaneously, the Fifth Army operating on the Ancre front while the Third Army attacked from the north-west about Arras. These converging attacks, if successful, would pinch off the whole salient, and would be likely to make the withdrawal of the enemy's troops from it a very costly manœuvre for him if it were not commenced in good time.

The front of attack on the Arras side was to include the Vimy Ridge, possession of which I considered necessary to secure the left flank of the operations on the south bank of the Scarpe. The capture of this ridge, which was to be carried out by the First Army, also offered other important advantages. It would deprive the enemy of valuable observation and give us a wide view over the plains stretching from the eastern foot of the ridge to Douai and beyond. Moreover, although it was evident that the enemy might, by a timely withdrawal, avoid a battle in the awkward salient still held by him between the Scarpe and the Ancre, no such withdrawal from his important Vimy Ridge positions was likely. He would be almost certain to fight for this ridge, and, as my object was to deal him a blow which would force him to use up reserves, it was important that he should not evade my attack.

3. With the forces at my disposal, even combined with what the French proposed to undertake in co-operation, I did not consider that any great strategical results were likely to be gained by following up a success on the front about Arras and to the south of it, beyond the capture of the objectives aimed at as described above. It was therefore my intention to transfer my main offensive to another part of my front after these objectives had been secured.

The front selected for these further operations was in Flanders. They were to be commenced as soon as possible after the Arras offensive, and continued throughout the summer, so far as the forces at my disposal would permit.

4. * * * * The positions held by us in the Ypres salient since May, 1915, were far from satisfactory.[1] They were completely overlooked by the enemy. Their defence involved a considerable strain on the troops occupying them, and they were certain to be costly to maintain against a serious attack, in which the enemy would enjoy all the advantages in observation and in the placing of his artillery. Our positions would be much improved by the capture of the Messines-Wytschaete Ridge, and of the high ground which extends thence north-eastwards for some seven miles and then trends north through Broodseinde and Passchendaele. * * * *

The operation in its first stages was a very difficult one, and in 1916 I had judged that the general situation was not yet ripe to

[1] *Vide* Map No. 4.

attempt it. In the summer of 1917, however, as larger forces would be at my disposal, and as, in the Somme Battle, our new Armies had proved their ability to overcome the enemy's strongest defences, and had lowered his power of resistance, I considered myself justified in undertaking it. Various preliminary steps had already been taken, including the necessary development of railways in the area, which had been proceeding quietly from early in 1916. I therefore hoped, after completing my spring offensive further south, to be able to develop this Flanders attack without great delay, and to strike hard in the north before the enemy realised that the attack in the south would not be pressed further.

5. Subsequently, unexpected developments in the early weeks of the year necessitated certain modifications in my plans above described.

New proposals for action were made by our French Allies [1] which entailed a considerable extension of my defensive front, a modification of the rôle previously allotted to the British Armies, and an acceleration of the date of my opening attack.

As a result of these proposals, I received instructions from His Majesty's Government to readjust my previous plans to meet the wishes of our Allies. Accordingly, it was arranged that I should commence the offensive early in April on as great a scale as the extension of my front would permit, with due regard to defensive requirements on the rest of my line. The British attack, under the revised scheme, was, in the first instance, to be preparatory to a more decisive operation to be undertaken a little later by the French Armies, in the subsequent stages of which the British Forces were to co-operate to the fullest extent possible.

It was further agreed that if this combined offensive did not produce the full results hoped for within a reasonable time, the main efforts of the British Armies should then be transferred to Flanders as I had originally intended. In this case our Allies were to assist me by taking over as much as possible of the front held by my troops, and by carrying out, in combination with my Flanders attacks, such offensives on the French front as they might be able to undertake.

6. My original plan for the preliminary operations on the Arras front fortunately fitted in well with what was required of me under the revised scheme, and the necessary preparations were already in progress. In order to give full effect, however, to the new rôle allotted to me in this revised scheme, preparations for the attack in Flanders had to be restricted for the time being to what could be done by such troops and other labour as could not in any case be made available on the Arras front. Moreover, the carrying out of any

---

[1] In December, 1916, General Nivelle succeeded Marshal Joffre as Commander-in-Chief, and a new plan of campaign was adopted by the French.

offensive this year on the Flanders front became contingent on the degree of success attained by the new plan.

7. The chief events to note during the period of preparations for the spring offensive were the retirement of the enemy on the Arras-Soissons front and the revolution in Russia.

As regards the former, the redistribution of my forces necessitated by the enemy's withdrawal was easily made. The front decided on for my main attack on the Arras front lay almost altogether outside the area from which the enemy retired, and my plans and preparations on that side were not deranged thereby. His retirement, however, did enable the enemy to avoid the danger of some of his troops being cut off by the converging attacks arranged for, and to that extent reduced the results which might have been attained by my operation as originally planned. The rôle of the Fifth Army, too, had to be modified. Instead of attacking from the line of the Ancre simultaneously with the advance of the Third Army from the northwest, it had now to follow up the retiring enemy and establish itself afresh in front of the Hindenburg Line to which the enemy withdrew. This line had been very strongly fortified, and sited with great care and skill to deny all advantages of position to any force attempting to attack it.

The adjustments necessary, however, to enable me to carry out the more subsidiary rôle which had been allotted to my Armies since the formation of my original plans, were comparatively simple, and caused no delay in my preparation for the spring offensive.

My task was, in the first instance, to attract as large hostile forces as possible to my front before the French offensive was launched, and my forces were still well placed for this purpose. The capture of such important tactical features as the Vimy Ridge and Monchy-le-Preux by the First and Third Armies, combined with pressure by the Fifth Army from the south against the front of the Hindenburg Line, could be relied on to use up many of the enemy's divisions and to compel him to reinforce largely on the threatened front.

The Russian revolution was of far more consequence in the approaching struggle. Even though the Russian Armies might still prove capable of co-operating in the later phases of the 1917 campaign, the revolution at once destroyed any prospect that may previously have existed of these Armies being able to combine with the spring offensive in the West by the earlier date which had been fixed for it in the new plans made since the conference of November, 1916. Moreover, as the Italian offensive also could not be ready until some time after the date fixed by the new arrangement with the French for our combined operation, the situation became very different from that contemplated at the Conference.

THE CAMPAIGNS OF 1917

It was decided, however, to proceed with the spring offensive in the West, notwithstanding these serious drawbacks. Even though the prospects of any far-reaching success were reduced, it would at least tend to relieve Russia of pressure on her front while she was trying to reorganise her Government; and if she should fail to reorganise it, the Allies in the West had little, if anything, to gain by delaying their blow.

Preparations were pushed on accordingly, the most urgent initial step being the development of adequate transport facilities.

THE SPRING CAMPAIGN

Preparations for the Arras Offensive

8. When transport requirements on the front in question were first brought under consideration, the neighbourhood was served by two single lines of railway, the combined capacity of which was less than half our estimated requirements. Considerable constructional work, therefore, both of standard and narrow gauge railway, had to be undertaken to meet our programme. Roads also had to be improved and adapted to the circumstances for which they were required, and preparations made to carry them forward rapidly as our troops advanced.

For this latter purpose considerable use was made, both in this and in the later offensives, of plank roads. These were built chiefly of heavy beech slabs laid side by side, and were found of great utility, being capable of rapid construction over almost any nature of ground.

By these means the accumulation of the vast stocks of munitions and stores of all kinds required for our offensive, and their distribution to the troops, were made possible. The numberless other preparatory measures taken for the Somme offensive were again repeated, with such improvements and additions as previous experience dictated. Hutting and other accommodation for the troops concentrated in the area had to be provided in great quantity. An adequate water supply had to be guaranteed, necessitating the erection of numerous pumping installations, the laying of many miles of pipe lines, and the construction of reservoirs.

Very extensive mining and tunnelling operations were carried out. In particular, advantage was taken of the existence of a large system of underground quarries and cellars in Arras and its suburbs to provide safe quarters for a great number of troops. Electric light was installed in these caves and cellars, which were linked together by tunnels, and the whole connected by long subways with our trench system east of the town.

A problem peculiar to the launching of a great offensive from a town arose from the difficulty of ensuring the punctual debouching of troops and the avoidance of confusion and congestion in the streets both before the assault and during the progress of the battle. This problem was met by the most careful and complete organisation of routes, reflecting the highest credit on the staffs concerned.

The Enemy's Defences

9. Prior to our offensive, the new German lines of defence on the British front ran in a general north-westerly direction from St. Quentin to the village of Thilloy-lez-Mofflaines, immediately south-east of Arras (*vide* Map No. 3). Thence the German original trench systems continued northwards across the valley of the Scarpe River to the dominating Vimy Ridge, which, rising to a height of some 475 feet, commands a wide view to the south-east, east and north. Thereafter the opposing lines left the high ground, and, skirting the western suburbs of Lens, stretched northwards to the Channel across a flat country of rivers, dykes and canals, the dead level of which is broken by the line of hills stretching from Wytschaete north-eastwards to Passchendaele and Staden.

The front attacked by the Third and First Armies on the morning of the 9th April extended from just north of the village of Croisilles, south-east of Arras, to just south of Givenchy-en-Gohelle at the northern foot of Vimy Ridge, a distance of nearly 15 miles. It included between four and five miles of the northern end of the Hindenburg Line, which had been built to meet the experience of the Somme Battle.

Further north, the original German defences in this sector were arranged on the same principle as those which we had already captured further south. They comprised three separate trench systems, connected by a powerful switch line running from the Scarpe at Fampoux to Liévin, and formed a highly organised defensive belt some two to five miles in depth.

In addition, from three to six miles further east a new line of resistance was just approaching completion. This system, known as the Drocourt-Quéant Line, formed a northern extension of the Hindenburg Line, with which it linked up at Quéant.

Final Preparations.—Fight for Aerial Supremacy

10. The great strength of these defences demanded very thorough artillery preparation, and this in turn could only be carried out effectively with the aid of our air services.

THE CAMPAIGNS OF 1917

Our activity in the air, therefore, increased with the growing severity of our bombardment. A period of very heavy air fighting ensued, culminating in the days immediately preceding the attack in a struggle of the utmost intensity for local supremacy in the air. Losses on both sides were severe, but the offensive tactics most gallantly persisted in by our fighting aeroplanes secured our artillery machines from serious interference and enabled our guns to carry out their work effectively. At the same time bombing machines caused great damage and loss to the enemy by a constant succession of successful raids against his dumps, railways, aerodromes, and billets.

The Bombardment

11. Three weeks prior to the attack the systematic cutting of the enemy's wire was commenced, while our heavy artillery searched the enemy's back areas and communications. Night firing, wire cutting, and bombardment of hostile trenches, strong points, and billets continued steadily and with increasing intensity on the whole battle front, till the days immediately preceding the attack when the general bombardment was opened.

During this latter period extensive gas discharges were carried out, and many successful raids were undertaken by day and night along the whole front to be attacked.

Organised bombardments took place also on other parts of our front, particularly in the Ypres sector.

The Troops Employed

12. The main attack was entrusted to the Third and First Armies, under the command of General Sir E. H. H. Allenby, and General Sir H. S. Horne, respectively.

Four Army Corps (the VII., VI., XVII. and XVIII. Corps, under command respectively of Lieut.-Generals Sir T. D'O. Snow, J. A. L. Haldane, Sir C. Fergusson and Sir F. I. Maxse) were placed at the disposal of General Allenby, with an additional Army Corps Headquarters (the XIX. Corps, Lieut.-General H. E. Watts) to be used as occasion might demand. Cavalry also (the Cavalry Corps, Lieut.-General Sir C. T. McM. Kavanagh) was brought up into the Third Army area, in case the development of the battle should give rise to an opportunity for the employment of mounted troops on a considerable scale.

The attack of the First Army on the Vimy Ridge was carried out by the Canadian Corps (Lieut.-General Sir J. H. G. Byng). It was further arranged that, as soon as the Vimy Ridge had been secured, the troops in line on the left of the Canadian Corps (I. Corps, Lieut.-General A. E. A. Holland) should extend the area of attack northwards as far as the left bank of the Souchez River. An additional Army Corps (the XIII. Corps, Lieut.-General Sir W. N. Congreve) was also at the disposal of the First Army in reserve.

The greater part of the divisions employed in the attack were composed of troops drawn from the English counties. These, with Scottish, Canadian, and South African troops, accomplished a most striking success.[1]

My plans provided for the co-operation of the Fourth and Fifth Armies, under the command respectively of General Sir Henry S. Rawlinson, and General Sir H. de la P. Gough, as soon as the development of my main assault should permit of their effective action.

The Method of Attack

13. The attack on the front of the Third and First Armies was planned to be carried out by a succession of comparatively short advances, the separate stages of which were arranged to correspond approximately with the enemy's successive systems of defence. As each stage was reached a short pause was to take place, to enable the troops detailed for the attack on the next objective to form up for the assault.

Tanks, which on many occasions since their first use in September of last year had done excellent service, were attached to each Corps for the assault, and again did admirable work in co-operation with our infantry. Their assistance was particularly valuable in the capture of hostile strong points, such as Telegraph Hill and the Harp, two powerful redoubts situated to the south of Tilloy-lez-Mofflaines, and Railway Triangle, a stronghold formed by the junction of the Lens and Douai Lines east of Arras.

---

[1] The disposition of our troops for the attack was as follows, from South to North :—

Third Army
  VII. Corps
    21st Div. . . . . Maj.-Gen. D. G. M. Campbell.
    30th Div. . . . . Maj.-Gen. J. S. M. Shea.
    56th Div. . . . . Maj.-Gen. C. P. A. Hull.
    14th Div. . . . . Maj.-Gen. V. A. Couper.
  VI. Corps
    3rd Div. . . . . Maj.-Gen. C. J. Deverell.
    12th Div. . . . . Maj.-Gen. A. B. Scott.
    15th Div. . . . . Maj.-Gen. F. W. N. McCracken,
        with the
    37th Div. . . . . Maj.-Gen. H. B. Williams
        going through.

BATTLE OF ARRAS;
9th April, 1917.

THE CAMPAIGNS OF 1917

The Arras Battle

14. The general attack on the 9th April was launched at 5.30 a.m. under cover of a most effective artillery barrage. Closely following the tornado of our shell fire, our gallant infantry poured like a flood across the German lines, overwhelming the enemy's garrisons.

Within forty minutes of the opening of the battle, practically the whole of the German front line system on the front attacked had been stormed and taken. Only on the extreme left fierce fighting was still taking place for the possession of the enemy's trenches on the slopes of Hill 145 at the northern end of the Vimy Ridge.

At 7.30 a.m. the advance was resumed against the second objectives. Somewhat greater opposition was now encountered, and at the hour at which these objectives were timed to have been captured strong parties of the enemy were still holding out on the high ground north of Tilloy-lez-Mofflaines, known as Observation Ridge, and in Railway Triangle.

North of the Scarpe, North-country and Scottish Territorial troops (34th and 51st Divisions), attacking east of Roclincourt, were met by heavy machine gun fire. Their advance was delayed, but not checked. On the left, the Canadians rapidly over-ran the German positions, and by 9.30 a.m., in spite of difficult going over wet and sticky ground, had carried the village of Les Tilleuls and La Folie Farm.

By 12 noon men from the Eastern counties of England (12th Division) had captured Observation Ridge and, with the exception of Railway Triangle, the whole of our second objectives were in our possession, from south of Neuville Vitasse, stormed by London Territorials (56th Division), to north of La Folie Farm. A large number of prisoners had already been taken, including practically a whole battalion of the 162nd German Regiment at the Harp.

XVII. Corps
9th Div. . . . . Maj.-Gen. T. Lukin,
                 with the
4th Div. . . . . Maj.-Gen. Hon. W. Lambton
                 going through.
34th Div. . . . . Maj.-Gen. C. L. Nicholson.
51st Div. . . . . Maj.-Gen. G. M. Harper.
First Army
  Canadian Corps
    1st Cdn. Div. . . . Maj.-Gen. A. W. Currie.
    2nd Cdn. Div. . . . Maj.-Gen. H. E. Burstall.
    13th Bde., 5th Div. . . Maj.-Gen. R. B. Stephens.
    3rd Cdn. Div. . . . Maj.-Gen. L. J. Lipsett.
    4th Cdn. Div. . . . Maj.-Gen. D. Watson.

Meanwhile our artillery had begun to move forward to positions from which they could support our attack upon our third objectives. The enemy's determined resistance at Observation Ridge, however, had delayed the advance of our batteries in this area. The bombardment of the German third line on this front had consequently to be carried out at long range, with the result that the enemy's wire was not well cut.

None the less, when the advance was resumed, shortly after midday, great progress was made all along the line. In the course of this attack many of the enemy's battery positions were captured, together with a large number of guns.

South of the Scarpe, Manchester and Liverpool troops (30th Division) took St. Martin-sur-Cojeul, and our line was carried forward between that point and Feuchy Chapel on the Arras-Cambrai road. Here a counter-attack was repulsed at 2.0 p.m. by the 12th Division, and at about the same hour Scottish troops (15th Division) carried Railway Triangle, after a long struggle. Thereafter this division continued their advance rapidly and stormed Feuchy Village, making a breach in the German third line. An attempt by the 37th Division to widen this breach, and to advance beyond it in the direction of Monchy-le-Preux, was held up for the time by the condition of the enemy's wire.

North of the Scarpe our success was even more complete. Troops from Scotland and South Africa (9th Division), who had already stormed St. Laurent Blangy, captured Athies. They then gave place, in accordance with programme, to an English division (the 4th), who completed their task by the capture of Fampoux Village and Hyderabad Redoubt, breaking another wide gap in the German third line system. The North-country troops (34th Division) on their left seized the strong work known as the Point du Jour, in the face of strong hostile resistance from the German switch line to the north.

Further north, the Canadian divisions, with an English brigade (13th Infantry Brigade, 5th Division) in the centre of their attack, completed the capture of the Vimy Ridge from Commandant's House to Hill 145, in spite of considerable opposition, especially in the neighbourhood of Thélus and the high ground north of this village. These positions were taken by 1.0 p.m., and early in the afternoon our final objectives in this area had been gained. Our troops then dug themselves in on the eastern side of Farbus Wood and along the steep eastern slopes of the ridge west and north-west of Farbus, sending out cavalry and infantry patrols in the direction of Willerval and along the front of their position.

The left Canadian division (the 4th), meanwhile, had gradu-

THE CAMPAIGNS OF 1917

ally fought their way forward on Hill 145, in the face of a very desperate resistance. The enemy defended this dominating position with great obstinacy, and his garrison, reinforced from dug-outs and underground tunnels, launched frequent counter-attacks. In view of the severity of the fighting, it was decided to postpone the attack upon the crest line until the following day.

At the end of the day, therefore, our troops were established deeply in the enemy's positions on the whole front of attack. We had gained a firm footing in the enemy's third line on both banks of the Scarpe, and had made an important breach in the enemy's last fully completed line of defence.

During the afternoon cavalry had been brought up to positions east of Arras, in readiness to be sent forward should our infantry succeed in widening this breach sufficiently for the operations of mounted troops. South of Feuchy, however, the unbroken wire of the German third line constituted a complete barrier to a cavalry attack, while the commanding positions held by the enemy on Monchy-le-Preux Hill blocked the way of advance along the Scarpe. The main body of our mounted troops was accordingly withdrawn in the evening to positions just west of the town. Smaller bodies of cavalry were employed effectively during the afternoon on the right bank of the Scarpe to maintain touch with our troops north of the river, and captured a number of prisoners and guns.

The Advance Continued

15. For some days prior to the 9th April the weather had been fine, but on the morning of that day heavy showers had fallen, and in the evening the weather definitely broke. Thereafter for many days it continued stormy, with heavy falls of snow and squalls of wind and rain. These conditions imposed great hardships on our troops and greatly hampered operations. The heavy snow, in particular, interfered with reliefs, and rendered all movements of troops and guns slow and difficult. It would be hard to overestimate the importance of the resultant delay in bringing up our guns, at a time when the enemy had not yet been able to assemble his reserves, or to calculate the influence which a further period of fine weather might have had upon the course of the battle.[1]

North of the Scarpe little remained to be done to complete the

---

[1] The following passage in Ludendorff's Memoirs is of interest here :—" The battle near Arras on April 9th formed a bad beginning to the capital fighting during this year. April 10th and the succeeding days were critical days. A breach 12,000 to 15,000 yards wide, and as much as 6,000 yards or more in depth is not a thing to be mended without more ado. It takes a good deal to repair the inordinate wastage of men and guns, as well as munitions, that results from such a breach."

capture of our objectives. South of the river we still required to gain the remainder of the German third line and Monchy-le-Preux. Despite the severity of the weather, our troops set themselves with the utmost gallantry to the accomplishment of these tasks.

During the night English troops (37th Division) made considerable progress through the gap in the German defences east of Feuchy and occupied the northern slopes of Orange Hill, south-east of the village.

Throughout the morning of the 10th April every effort was made to gain further ground through this gap, and our troops succeeded in reaching the enclosures north-west of Monchy-le-Preux.

At noon the advance became general, and the capture of the whole of the enemy's third-line system south of the Scarpe was completed. The progress of our right beyond this line was checked by machine gun fire from the villages of Héninel, Wancourt and Guémappe, with which our artillery were unable to deal effectively. Between the Arras-Cambrai Road and the Scarpe, English and Scottish troops (12th and 15th Divisions) pushed on as far as the western edge of Monchy-le-Preux. Here our advance was held up as a result of the unavoidable weakness of our artillery support, and for the same reason an attempt to pass cavalry south and north of Monchy-le-Preux (3rd and 2nd Cavalry Divisions, Major-Generals J. Vaughan and W. H. Greenly) and along the left bank of the Scarpe (1st Cavalry Division, Major-General R. L. Mullens) proved impossible in the face of the enemy's machine gun fire.

Meanwhile, on the left flank of our battle front the Canadians had renewed their attack at 4.0 p.m. on the portion of Hill 145 still remaining in the enemy's possession, and captured it after sharp fighting, together with over 200 prisoners and a number of trench mortars and machine guns.

Monchy-le-Preux

16. Heavy fighting, in which cavalry again took part, continued south of the Scarpe on the 11th April. Two English infantry brigades (37th Division), acting in co-operation with cavalry (3rd Cavalry Division), attacked Monchy-le-Preux at 5.0 a.m., and, after hard fighting in which tanks arrived at an opportune moment, carried the position. As our men pushed through the village, the enemy was seen retreating eastwards over the open, and many casualties were inflicted on him by our machine guns. By 9.0 a.m. the whole of Monchy-le-Preux was in our hands, with a number of prisoners. During the afternoon and evening several determined counter-attacks were beaten off by our infantry and cavalry, assisted by the fire of our artillery.

THE CAMPAIGNS OF 1917

On other parts of the front our attacks had to be made across open forward slopes, which were swept from end to end by the enemy's machine guns. The absence of adequate artillery support again made itself felt, and little ground was gained.

In combination with this attack on the Third Army front, the Fifth Army launched an attack at 4.30 a.m. on the 11th April against the Hindenburg Line in the neighbourhood of Bullecourt (4th Australian Division and 62nd Division, Major-Generals W. Holmes and W. P. Braithwaite). The Australian and West Riding battalions engaged showed great gallantry in executing a very difficult attack across a wide extent of open country. Considerable progress was made, and parties of Australian troops, preceded by tanks, penetrated the German positions as far as Riencourt-lez-Cagnicourt. The obstinacy of the enemy's resistance, however, in Héninel and Wancourt, which held up the advance of the Third Army at these points, prevented the troops of the two Armies from joining hands, and the attacking troops of the Fifth Army were obliged to withdraw to their original line.

Héninel, Wancourt and the Souchez River

17. On the 12th April the relief of a number of divisions most heavily engaged was commenced, and on the same day the cavalry were withdrawn to areas west of Arras. Great efforts were made to bring forward guns, and, in spite of the difficulties presented by weather and ground, several batteries of howitzers and heavy guns reached positions in rear of the old German third line.

On this day our attacks upon Héninel and Wancourt were renewed, and our troops (21st and 56th Divisions) succeeded in carrying both villages, as well as in completing the capture of the Hindenburg Line for some 2,000 yards south of the Cojeul River. North of the Scarpe attacks were made against Roeux Village and the chemical works near Roeux Station, and proved the commencement of many days of fierce and stubbornly-contested fighting.

On our left flank operations of the First Army astride the Souchez River met with complete success. Attacks were delivered simultaneously at 5.0 a.m. on the 12th April by English and Canadian troops (4th Canadian Division and 24th Division, Major-General J. E. Capper) against the two small hills known as the Pimple and the Bois-en-Hache, situated on either side of the Souchez River. Both of these positions were captured, with a number of prisoners and machine guns. Steps were at once taken to consolidate our gains, and patrols were pushed forward to maintain touch with the enemy.

Withdrawal of the Enemy

18. The results of this last success at once declared themselves. Prior to its accomplishment there had been many signs that the enemy was preparing to make strong counter-attacks from the direction of Givenchy and Hirondelle Woods to recover the Vimy Ridge. The positions captured on the 12th April commanded both these localities, and he was therefore compelled to abandon the undertaking. His attitude in this neighbourhood forthwith ceased to be aggressive, and indications of an immediate withdrawal from the areas commanded by the Vimy Ridge multiplied rapidly.

The withdrawal commenced on the morning of the 13th April. Before noon on that day Canadian patrols had succeeded in occupying the southern portion of Givenchy-en-Gohelle, had pushed through Petit Vimy, and had reached the cross-roads 500 yards north-east of the village. That afternoon English patrols north of the Souchez River crossed No Man's Land and entered Angres, while Canadian troops completed the occupation of Givenchy-en-Gohelle and the German trench system east of it. Further south our troops seized Petit Vimy and Vimy, and Willerval and Bailleul were occupied in turn.

Our patrols, backed by supports, continued to push forward on the 14th April, keeping contact with the retreating enemy, but avoiding heavy fighting. By midday the general line of our advanced troops ran from a point about 1,000 yards east of Bailleul, through Mont Forêt Quarries on the Farbus-Méricourt road, to the eastern end of Hirondelle Wood. North of the river we had reached Riaumont Wood and the southern outskirts of Liévin. By the evening the whole of the town of Liévin was in our hands, and our line ran thence to our old front line north of the Double Crassier. Great quantities of ammunition of all calibres, as well as several guns, and stores and materials of every kind were abandoned by the enemy in his retreat.

Meanwhile, on the 13th and 14th April, fighting south of the Scarpe continued, and some progress was made in the face of strong hostile resistance. On the right of our attack our troops (21st Division) fought their way eastwards down the Hindenburg Line till they had reached a point opposite Fontaine-lez-Croisilles, about seven miles south-east of Arras. In the centre a Northumberland brigade of the 50th Division (Major-General P. S. Wilkinson), advancing in open order, carried the high ground east of Héninel and captured Wancourt Tower. Three counter-attacks against this position were successfully driven off, and further ground was gained on the ridge south-east of Héninel.

THE CAMPAIGNS OF 1917

On other parts of our line heavy counter-attacks developed on the 14th April, the most violent of which were directed against Monchy-le-Preux. The struggle for this important position (held by the 29th Division, Major-General Sir H. de B. de Lisle) was exceedingly fierce. The enemy's attacks were supported by the full weight of his available artillery, and at one time parties of his infantry reached the eastern defences of the village. To the south and the north, however, our posts held their ground, and in the end the enemy was completely repulsed, with great loss.

Results of First Attacks

19. Our advance had now reached a point at which the difficulty of maintaining communications and of providing adequate artillery support for our infantry began seriously to limit our progress. Moreover, the enemy had had time to bring up reserves and to recover from the temporary disorganisation caused by our first attacks. Both the increasing strength of his resistance and the weight and promptness of his counter-attacks made it evident that, except at excessive cost, our success could not be developed further without a return to more deliberate methods.

Already a very remarkable success had been gained, whether measured by our captures in territory, prisoners and guns, or judged by the number of German divisions attracted to the front of our attack.

At the end of six days' fighting our front had been rolled four miles farther east, and all the dominating features, forming the immediate objects of my attack, which I considered it desirable to hold before transferring the bulk of my resources to the north, had passed into our possession. So far, therefore, as my own plans were concerned, it would have been possible to have stopped the Arras offensive at this point, and, while maintaining a show of activity sufficient to mislead the enemy as to my intentions, to have diverted forthwith to the northern theatre of operations the troops, labour and material required to complete my preparations there.

At this time, however, the French offensive was on the point of being launched.[1] It was important that the full pressure of the British offensive should be maintained in order to assist our Allies, and that we might be ready to seize any opportunity which might follow their success. Accordingly, active preparations were undertaken to renew my attack, but, in view both of the weather and of the strength already developed by the enemy, it was necessary to

---

[1] The French attack was planned originally to follow within two or three days of the first British attack, but it was postponed owing to weather conditions.

postpone operations until my communications had been re-established and my artillery dispositions completed. The following week, therefore, saw little change in our front, though the labours of our troops continued incessantly under conditions demanding the highest qualities of courage and endurance.

So far as my object was to draw the enemy's reserves from the front of the French attack, much had already been accomplished. In addition to the capture of more than 13,000 prisoners and over 200 guns, a wide gap had been driven through the German prepared defences. The enemy had been compelled to pour in men and guns to stop this gap, while he worked feverishly to complete the Drocourt-Quéant Line. Ten days after the opening of our offensive the number of German infantry engaged on the front of our attack had been nearly doubled, in spite of the casualties the enemy's troops had sustained. The massing of such large forces within the range of our guns, and the frequent and costly counter-attacks rendered necessary by our successes, daily added to the enemy's losses.

Subsidiary Operations

20. In addition to the main attack east of Arras, successful minor operations were carried out on the 9th April by the Fourth and Fifth Armies, by which a number of fortified villages covering the Hindenburg Line were taken, with some hundreds of prisoners, and considerable progress was made in the direction of St. Quentin and Cambrai.

Throughout the remainder of the month the two Southern Armies maintained constant activity. By a succession of minor enterprises our line was advanced closer and closer to the Hindenburg Line, and the enemy was kept under the constant threat of more serious operations on this front.

The only offensive action taken by the enemy during this period in this area occurred on the 15th April. At 4.30 a.m. on that morning the enemy attacked our positions[1] from Hermies to Noreuil with considerable forces, estimated at not less than sixteen battalions. Heavy fighting took place, in the course of which parties of German infantry succeeded in penetrating our lines at Lagnicourt for some distance, and at one time reached our advanced battery positions. By 1.0 p.m., however, the whole of our original line had been re-established, and the enemy left some seventeen hundred dead on the field as well as 360 prisoners in our hands. During the attack our heavy batteries remained in action at very close range and materially assisted in the enemy's repulse.

[1] This front was then held by the 1st Anzac Corps, Lieut.-General Sir W. R. Birdwood.

THE CAMPAIGNS OF 1917

The Attack Resumed.—Guémappe and Gavrelle

21. On the 16th April our Allies launched their main offensive on the Aisne, and shortly after that date the weather on the Arras front began to improve. Our preparations made more rapid progress, and plans were made to deliver our next attack on the 21st April. High winds and indifferent visibility persisted, however, and so interfered with the work of our artillery and aeroplanes that it was found necessary to postpone operations for a further two days. Meanwhile local fighting took place frequently, and our line was improved slightly at a number of points.

At 4.45 a.m. on the 23rd April British troops attacked on a front of about nine miles from Croisilles to Gavrelle. At the same hour a minor operation was undertaken by us south-west of Lens.

On the main front of attack good progress was made at first at almost all points. By 10.0 a.m. the remainder of the high ground west of Chérisy had been captured by the attacking English brigades (30th and 50th Divisions), and Scottish troops (15th Division) had pushed through Guémappe. East of Monchy-le-Preux British battalions (29th Division) gained the western slopes of the rising ground known as Infantry Hill. North of the Scarpe Highland Territorials (51st Division) were engaged in heavy fighting on the western outskirts of Rœux Wood and the chemical works. On their left English county troops (37th Division) had reached the buildings west of Rœux Station and gained the line of their objectives on the western slopes of Greenland Hill, north of the railway. On the left of our main attack the Royal Naval Division (63rd Division, Major-General C. E. Laurie) had made rapid progress against Gavrelle, and the whole of the village was already in their hands.

At midday and during the afternoon counter-attacks in great force developed all along the line, and were repeated by the enemy with the utmost determination, regardless of the heavy losses inflicted by our fire. Many of these counter-attacks were repulsed after severe fighting, but on our right our troops were ultimately compelled by weight of numbers to withdraw from the ridge west of Chérisy and from Guémappe. North of the Scarpe fierce fighting continued for the possession of Rœux, the chemical works and the station to the north, but without producing any lasting change in the situation. Not less than five separate counter-attacks were made by the enemy on this day against Gavrelle, and on the 24th April he thrice repeated his attempts. All these attacks were completely crushed by our artillery barrage and machine gun fire.

As soon as it was clear that the whole of our objectives for the 23rd April had not been gained, orders were issued to renew the advance at 6.0 p.m. In this attack Guémappe was retaken, but further south our troops were at once met by a counter-attack in force, and made no progress. Fighting of a more or less intermittent character continued in this area all night.

In the early morning of the 24th April the enemy's resistance weakened all along the front of our attack south of the Arras-Cambrai Road. Our troops reaped the reward of their persistence, and gained their objectives of the previous day without serious opposition.

After twenty-four hours of very fierce fighting, therefore, in which the severity of the enemy's casualties was in proportion to the strength and determination of his numerous counter-attacks, we remained in possession of the villages of Guémappe and Gavrelle, as well as of the whole of the high ground overlooking Fontaine-lez-Croisilles and Chérisy. Very appreciable progress had also been made east of Monchy-le-Preux, on the left bank of the Scarpe, and on Greenland Hill.

In the minor operation south-west of Lens Cornish troops (1st D.C.L.I., 5th Division) established themselves on the railway loop east of Cité des Petits Bois, and succeeded in maintaining their position in spite of numerous hostile counter-attacks.

In the course of these operations of the 23rd and 24th April we captured a further 3,000 prisoners and a few guns. On the battlefield, which remained in our possession, great numbers of German dead testified to the costliness of the enemy's obstinate defence.

Policy of Subsequent Operations at Arras

22. The strength of the opposition encountered in the course of this attack was in itself evidence that my offensive was fulfilling the part designed for it in the Allied plans. As the result of the fighting which had already taken place, twelve German divisions had been withdrawn exhausted from the battle or were in process of relief. A month after the commencement of our offensive the number of German divisions so withdrawn had increased to twenty-three. On the other hand, the strengthening of the enemy's forces opposite my front necessarily brought about for the time being the characteristics of a wearing-out battle.

On the Aisne and in Champagne, also, the French offensive had met with very obstinate resistance. It was becoming clear that many months of heavy fighting would be necessary before the enemy's troops could be reduced to a condition which would permit of a more rapid advance. None the less, very considerable results had already been achieved, and our Allies continued their efforts against the long plateau north of the Aisne traversed by the Chemin des Dames.

THE CAMPAIGNS OF 1917

In order to assist our Allies, I arranged that until their object had been attained I would continue my operations at Arras. The necessary readjustment of troops, guns and material required to complete my preparations for my northern operations was accordingly postponed, and preparations were undertaken for a repetition of my attacks on the Arras front until such time as the results of the French offensive should have declared themselves.

The Final Arras Attacks.—Arleux

23. The first of these attacks was delivered on the 28th April on a front of about eight miles north of Monchy-le-Preux. With a view to economising my troops, my objectives were shallow, and for a like reason, and also in order to give the appearance of an attack on a more imposing scale, demonstrations were continued southwards to the Arras-Cambrai Road and northwards to the Souchez River.

The assault was launched at 4.25 a.m. by British and Canadian troops, and resulted in heavy fighting, which continued throughout the greater part of the 28th and 29th April. The enemy delivered counter-attack after counter-attack with the greatest determination and most lavish expenditure of men. Our positions at Gavrelle alone were again attacked seven times with strong forces, and on each occasion the enemy was repulsed by the 63rd Division with great loss.

In spite of the enemy's desperate resistance, the village of Arleux-en-Gohelle was captured by Canadian troops (1st Canadian Division), after bitter hand-to-hand fighting, and English troops (2nd Division, Major-General C. E. Pereira) made further progress in the neighbourhood of Oppy, on Greenland Hill (37th Division), and between Monchy-le-Preux and the Scarpe (12th Division). In addition to these advances, another 1,000 German prisoners were taken by us in the course of the two days' fighting.

Fresnoy

24. Five days later, at 3.45 a.m. on the 3rd May, another attack was undertaken by us of a similar nature to that of the 28th April, which in the character of the subsequent fighting it closely resembled.

In view of important operations which the French were to carry out on the 5th May, I arranged for a considerable extension of my active front. While the Third and First Armies attacked from Fontaine-lez-Croisilles to Fresnoy, the Fifth Army launched a second attack upon the Hindenburg Line in the neighbourhood of Bullecourt. This gave a total front of over sixteen miles.

Along practically the whole of this front our troops broke into the enemy's position. Australian troops (2nd Australian Division, Major-General N. M. Smyth) carried the Hindenburg Line east of Bullecourt. Eastern county battalions took Chérisy (18th Division, Major-General R. P. Lee). Other English troops entered Rœux (4th Division) and captured the German trenches south of Fresnoy (2nd Division). Canadian battalions (1st Canadian Division) found Fresnoy full of German troops assembled for a hostile attack which was to have been delivered at a later hour. After hard fighting, in which the enemy lost heavily, the Canadians carried the village, thereby completing an unbroken series of successes.

Later in the day, strong hostile counter-attacks once more developed, accompanied by an intense bombardment with heavy guns. Fierce fighting lasted throughout the afternoon and far into the night, and our troops were obliged to withdraw from Rœux and Chérisy. They maintained their hold, however, on Fresnoy and the Hindenburg Line east of Bullecourt, as well as upon certain trench elements west of Fontaine-lez-Croisilles and south of the Scarpe (12th Division).

Nine hundred and sixty-eight prisoners, including twenty-nine officers, were captured by us in these operations.

Situation Reviewed

25. On the 5th May the French delivered their attack against the Chemin des Dames and successfully achieved the objects they had in view. This brought to an end the first half of our general plan, and marked the close of the spring campaign on the Western front. The decisive action which it had been hoped might follow from the French offensive had not yet proved capable of realisation; but the magnitude of the results actually achieved strengthened our belief in its ultimate possibility.[1]

On the British front alone, in less than one month's fighting, we had captured over 19,500 prisoners, including over 400 officers, and had also taken 257 guns, including 98 heavy guns, with 464 machine guns, 227 trench mortars, and immense quantities of other war material. Our line had been advanced to a greatest depth exceeding five miles on a total front of over twenty miles, representing a gain of some sixty square miles of territory. A great improvement had been effected in the general situation of our troops on the front attacked,

---

[1] The agreement to give immediate effect to the British plan of a Northern offensive was reached at a Conference held at Paris on the 4th and 5th May. This marked the abandonment of General Nivelle's plan, and ten days later that General was replaced by General Petain.

THE CAMPAIGNS OF 1917

and the capture of the Vimy Ridge had removed a constant menace to the security of our line.

I was at length able to turn my full attention and to divert the bulk of my resources to the development of my northern plan of operations. Immediate instructions were given by me to General Sir Herbert Plumer, commanding the Second Army, to be prepared to deliver an attack on the 7th June against the Messines-Wytschaete Ridge, the capture of which, owing to the observation from it over our positions farther north in the Ypres salient, was an essential preliminary to the completion of the preparations for my principal offensive east and north of Ypres.

In order to assist me to concentrate troops on the new scene of operations, it was agreed that the French should take over once more a portion of the front taken over by me from them at the commencement of the year. This relief was completed without incident on the 20th May, the French extending their front to the Omignon River.

Arras Activity Maintained

26. A necessary part of the preparations for the Messines attack was the maintenance of activity on the Arras front, sufficient to keep the enemy in doubt as to whether our offensive there would be proceeded with. I therefore directed the Armies concerned to continue active operations with such forces as were left to them. The required effect was to be attained by a careful selection of important objectives of a limited nature, deliberate preparation of attack, concentration of artillery and economy of infantry.

Importance was to be given to these operations by combining them with feint attacks, and by the adoption of various measures and devices to extend the apparent front of attack. These measures would seem to have had considerable success, if any weight may be attached to the enemy's reports concerning them. They involved, however, the disadvantage that I frequently found myself unable to deny German accounts of the bloody repulse of extensive British attacks which in fact never took place.[1]

---

[1] The most noteworthy of these feint attacks was that of the 28th June on the Lens front, referred to on page 110 below. On this occasion large numbers of dummy men and some dummy tanks were employed, being raised up at zero hour by pulling ropes. These dummies drew a very heavy fire and were shot to pieces. The Germans duly reported that an attack had been annihilated, and that rows of British dead could be seen lying before our lines ! The impression of a great British attack was further heightened by the fact that about this date the First Army held their Horse Show. This involved much road traffic which might be taken by the enemy to indicate the concentration of troops in preparation for an attack.

Bullecourt and Rœux

27. To secure the footing gained by the Australians in the Hindenburg Line on the 3rd May it was advisable that Bullecourt should be captured without loss of time. During the fortnight following our attack, fighting for the possession of this village went on unceasingly; while the Australian troops [1] in the sector of the Hindenburg Line to the east beat off counter-attack after counter-attack. The defence of this 1,000 yards of double trench line, exposed to counter-attack on every side, through two weeks of almost constant fighting, deserves to be remembered as a most gallant feat of arms.

On the morning of the 7th May, English troops (7th Division, Major-General T. H. Shoubridge) gained a footing in the southeast corner of Bullecourt. Thereafter gradual progress was made, in the face of the most obstinate resistance, and on the 17th May London and West Riding Territorials [2] completed the capture of the village.

On other parts of the Arras front also heavy fighting took place, in which we both lost and gained ground.

On the 8th May the enemy regained Fresnoy Village. Three days later London troops (56th Division) captured Cavalry Farm, while other English battalions (4th Division) carried Rœux Cemetery and the chemical works. Further ground was gained in this neighbourhood on the 12th May, and on the night of the 13th/14th our troops (51st Division) captured Rœux.

On the 20th May fighting was commenced by the 33rd Division (Major-General R. J. Pinney) for the sector of the Hindenburg Line lying between Bullecourt and our front line west of Fontaine-lez-Croisilles. Steady progress was made, until by the 16th June touch had been established by us between these two points. Ten days prior to this event, on the 5th and 6th June, Scottish and North-country regiments (9th and 34th Divisions) captured the German positions on the western face of Greenland Hill and beat off two counter-attacks.

In these different minor operations over 1,500 prisoners were captured by us.

[1] 1st, 2nd and 5th Australian Divisions, Major-Generals H. B. Walker and J. J. T. Hobbs commanding respectively the 1st and 5th Australian Divisions.

[2] 58th and 62nd Divisions, Major-General H. D. Fanshawe commanding the 58th Division.

The Summer Campaign
Preparations for the Messines Attack

28. The preparations for the attack on the Messines-Wytschaete Ridge were necessarily as elaborate as those undertaken before either the Somme or the Arras Battles, and demanded an equal amount of time, forethought and labour. They were carried out, moreover, under circumstances of exceptional difficulty, for the enemy's positions completely overlooked our lines, and much of the area behind them.

Neither labour nor material were available in sufficient quantity for the Messines offensive until the prior demands of the Arras operations had been satisfied. Nevertheless, our preparations in the northern area had been proceeded with steadily, so far as the means at our disposal would allow, ever since the formation of definite plans in the late autumn of 1916.

A large railway programme had been commenced, and as soon as it was possible to divert larger supplies northwards, work was pushed on with remarkable speed. Great progress was made with road construction, and certain roads were selected for extension as soon as our objectives should be gained. Forward dumps of material were made for this purpose, and in the days following the 7th June roads were carried forward with great rapidity to Messines, Wytschaete, and Oosttaverne, across country so completely destroyed by shell fire that it was difficult to trace where the original road had run.

A special problem arose in connection with the water supply. Pipe lines were taken well forward from existing lakes, from catch pits constructed on the Kemmel Hills, and from sterilising barges on the Lys. Provision was made for the rapid extension of these lines. By the 15th June they had reached Messines, Wytschaete and the Dam Strasse, and were supplying water at the rate of between 450,000 and 600,000 gallons daily.

In addition, arrangements were made for the transport of water, rations and stores by pack animals and carrying parties. So efficiently did these arrangements work that during the attack water reached the troops within twenty to forty minutes of the taking of new positions, while in one case carrying parties arrived with packs, and dumps were formed within four minutes of the capture of the objective.

Underground Warfare

29. A special feature of the attack on the Messines-Wytschaete Ridge, and one unique in warfare, was furnished by the explosion of nineteen deep mines at the moment of assault.

The inception of a deep mining offensive on the Second Army front dated from July, 1915; but the proposal to conduct offensive mining on a grand scale was not definitely adopted till January, 1916. From that date onwards, as the necessary labour became available, deep mining for offensive purposes gradually developed, in spite of great difficulties from water-bearing strata and active counter-mining by the enemy.

In all, twenty-four mines were constructed, four of which were outside the front ultimately selected for our offensive, while one other was lost as the result of a mine blown by the enemy. Many of these mines had been completed for twelve months prior to our offensive, and constant and anxious work was needed to ensure their safety. The enemy also had a deep mining system, and was aware of his danger.

At Hill 60 continuous underground fighting took place for over ten months prior to our attack, and only by the greatest skill, persistence and disregard of danger on the part of our tunnellers were the two mines laid by us at this point saved from destruction. At the time of our offensive the enemy was known to be driving a gallery which ultimately would have cut into the gallery leading to the Hill 60 mines. By careful listening it was judged that, if our offensive took place on the date arranged, the enemy's gallery would just fail to reach us. So he was allowed to proceed.

At the Bluff, also, underground fighting went on incessantly. Between the 16th January, 1916, and the 7th June, 1917, twenty-seven camouflets were blown in this locality alone, of which seventeen were blown by us and ten by the enemy. After the 1st February, 1917, the enemy showed signs of great uneasiness, and blew several heavy mines and camouflets in the endeavour to interfere with our working. One of these blows destroyed our gallery to the Spanbroekmolen mine. For three months this mine was cut off, and was only recovered by strenuous efforts on the day preceding the Messines attack. The Spanbroekmolen mine formed the largest crater of any of those blown, the area of complete obliteration having a diameter of over 140 yards.

A total of 8,000 yards of gallery were driven in the construction of these mines, and over one million pounds of explosives were used in them. The simultaneous discharge of such an enormous aggregate of explosive is without parallel in land mining, and no actual experience existed of the effects which would be produced. In these circumstances, the fact that no hitch of any kind occurred in the operation, and that the effects of the discharges were precisely such as had been foretold, reflects the very highest credit upon those responsible for the planning and construction of the mines.

THE CAMPAIGNS OF 1917

The Messines Battle.—Description of Front [1]

30. The group of hills known as the Messines-Wytschaete Ridge lies about midway between the towns of Armentières and Ypres. Situated at the eastern end of the range of abrupt, isolated hills which divides the valleys of the River Lys and the River Yser, it links up that range with the line of rising ground which from Wytschaete stretches north-eastwards to the Ypres-Menin road, and then northwards past Passchendaele to Staden.

The village of Messines, situated on the southern spur of the ridge, commands a wide view of the valley of the Lys, and enfiladed the British lines to the south. North-west of Messines the village of Wytschaete, situated at the point of the salient and on the highest part of the ridge, from its height of about 260 feet commands even more completely the town of Ypres and the whole of the old British positions in the Ypres salient.

The German Defences

31. The German front line skirted the western foot of the ridge in a deep curve from the River Lys opposite Frelinghien to a point just short of the Menin road. The line of trenches then turned north-west past Hooge and Wieltje, following the slight rise known as the Pilckem Ridge to the Yser Canal at Boesinghe. The enemy's second line system followed the crest of the Messines-Wytschaete Ridge, forming an inner curve.

In addition to these defences of the ridge itself, two chord positions had been constructed across the base of the salient from south to north. The first lay slightly to the east of the hamlet of Oosttaverne, and was known as the Oosttaverne Line. The second chord position, known as the Warneton Line, crossed the Lys at Warneton, and ran roughly parallel to the Oosttaverne Line a little more than a mile to the east of it.

The natural advantages of the position were exceptional, and during more than two years of occupation the enemy had devoted the greatest skill and industry to developing them to the utmost. Besides the villages of Messines and Wytschaete, which were organised as main centres of resistance, numerous woods, farms and hamlets lent themselves to the construction of defensive points.

Captured documents and the statements of prisoners proved the importance attached by the enemy to the position. His troops in the line were told that the coming battle might well prove decisive, and

[1] *Vide* **Map No. 4.**

that they were to resist to the last. They were assured that strong reserves were available to come to their assistance and to restore the battle should the British attack succeed in penetrating their lines.

Preparations Completed

32. The final preparations for the assault on the Messines-Wytschaete Ridge were completed punctually, and with a thoroughness of organisation and attention to detail which is beyond praise. The excellence of the arrangements reflects the highest credit on the Second Army Commander, General Sir Herbert Plumer, and his Staff, as well as on the Commanders and Staffs of the various formations engaged.

The actual front selected for attack extended from a point opposite St. Yves to Mount Sorrel inclusive, a distance following the curve of the salient of between nine and ten miles. Our final objective was the Oosttaverne Line, which lay between these two points. The greatest depth of our attack was therefore about two and a half miles.

As the date for the attack drew near fine weather favoured the work of our airmen and artillery, and wire cutting, the bombardment of the enemy's defences and strong points, and the shelling of his communications, billets and back areas continued steadily. Counter-battery work was undertaken with great energy and with striking success.

The Assault

33. At 3.10 a.m. on the 7th June the nineteen mines were exploded simultaneously beneath the enemy's defences. At the same moment our guns opened and our infantry assault was launched. Covered by a concentrated bombardment, which overwhelmed the enemy's trenches and to a great extent neutralised his batteries, our troops swept over the German foremost defences all along the line.

The attack proceeded from the commencement in almost exact accordance with the time-table. The enemy's first trench system offered little resistance to our advance, and the attacking brigades—English, Irish, Australian and New Zealand [1]—pressed on up the slopes of the ridge to the assault of the crest line.

---

[1] The arrangement of our troops from south to north was as follows :—

II. Anzac Corps	Lt.-Gen. Sir A. J. Godley.
3rd Aust. Div.	Maj.-Gen. J. Monash.
N.Z. Div.	Maj.-Gen. Sir A. H. Russell.
25th Div.	Maj.-Gen. E. G. T. Bainbridge.
In support—	
4th Aust. Div.	Maj.-Gen. W. Holmes.

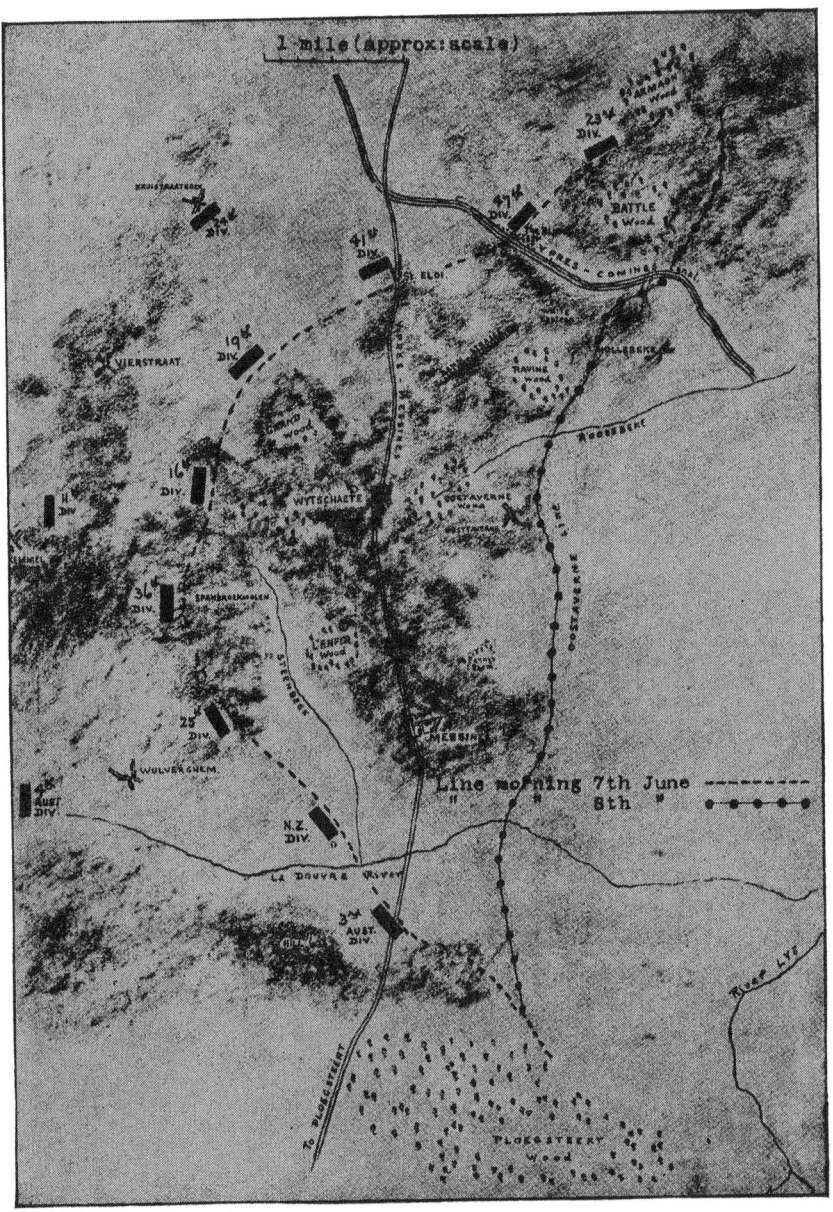

BATTLE OF MESSINES;
7th June, 1917.

At 5.30 a.m. Ulster regiments (36th Division) had already reached their second objectives, including l'Enfer Hill and the southern defences of Wytschaete, while on their left a South of Ireland division (16th Division) fought their way through Wytschaete Wood. At 7.0 a.m. New Zealand troops had captured Messines. Men from the western counties of England (19th Division) had cleared the Grand Bois. Other English county regiments (41st Division) had reached the Dam Strasse, and all along the battle front our second objectives had been gained.

Only at a few isolated points did the resistance of the enemy's infantry cause any serious delay. North-east of Messines our infantry (New Zealand Division) were held up for a time by machine gun fire from a strong point known as Fanny's Farm, but the arrival of a tank enabled our progress to be resumed. So rapid was the advance of our infantry, however, that only a few tanks could get forward in time to come into action. Heavy fighting took place in Wytschaete, and further north London troops (47th Division) encountered a serious obstacle in another strong point known as the White Château. This redoubt was captured while the morning was yet young, and before midday the two Irish divisions had fought their way side by side through the defences of Wytschaete.

Our troops then began to move down the eastern slopes of the ridge, and the divisions in the centre of our attack who had farthest to go, gradually drew level with those on either flank. About 2,000 prisoners had already been brought in, and Australian and English troops had reached the first of the enemy's guns. Our own guns had begun to move forward.

Further fighting took place in Ravine Wood, where English county regiments and London troops (41st and 47th Divisions) killed many Germans, and short-lived resistance was encountered at other points among the many woods and farm houses. Bodies of the enemy continued to hold out in the eastern end of Battle Wood and in strong points constructed in the spoil-banks of the Ypres-Comines

---

IX. Corps	Lt.-Gen. A. Hamilton-Gordon.
36th Div.	Maj.-Gen. O. S. W. Nugent.
16th Div.	Maj.-Gen. W. B. Hickie.
19th Div.	Maj.-Gen. G. T. M. Bridges.
In support—	
11th Div.	Maj.-Gen. H. R. Davies.
X. Corps	Lt.-Gen. Sir T. L. N. Morland.
41st Div.	Maj.-Gen. S. T. B. Lawford.
47th Div.	Maj.-Gen. Sir G. F. Gorringe.
23rd Div.	Maj.-Gen. Sir J. M. Babington.
In support—	
24th Div.	Maj.-Gen. L. J. Bols.

Canal. Except at these points, our troops gained their final objectives on both flanks early in the afternoon. In the centre we had reached a position running approximately parallel to the Oosttaverne Line and from 400 to 800 yards to the west of it. The guns required for the attack upon this line had been brought forward, and the troops and tanks detailed to take part were moving up steadily. Meanwhile the bridges and roads leading out of the triangle formed by the River Lys and the canal were kept under the fire of our artillery.

The final attack began soon afterwards, and by 3.45 p.m. the village of Oosttaverne had been captured. At 4.0 p.m. troops from the northern and western counties of England (11th and 19th Divisions) entered the Oosttaverne Line east of the village and captured two batteries of German field guns. Half an hour later other English battalions (24th Division) broke through the enemy's position further north. Parties of the enemy were surrendering freely, and his casualties were reported to be very heavy. By the evening the Oosttaverne Line had been taken, and our objectives had been gained.

The rapidity with which the attack had been carried through, and the destruction caused by our artillery, made it impossible at first to form more than a rough estimate of our captures. When the final reckoning had been completed, it was found that they included 7,200 prisoners, 67 guns, 94 trench mortars and 294 machine guns.

Subsequent Operations

34. During the night our infantry consolidated the captured positions; while tanks patrolled the ground east of the Oosttaverne Line, and in the early morning of the 8th June assisted in the repulse of an enemy counter-attack up the Wambeke valley. At 4.0 a.m. on the same morning our troops captured a small portion of German trench near Septième Barn, where the enemy had resisted our first attack. That evening, at 7.0 p.m., after an intense bombardment, the enemy counter-attacked along practically the whole of our new line, but was repulsed at all points.

Consolidation and the establishment of advanced posts continued during the following four days, in the course of which Australian troops captured La Potterie Farm, south-east of Messines, and the hamlet of Gapaard was occupied.

Our progress on the right of the battle front made the enemy's positions between the Lys River and St. Yves very dangerous, and he now gradually began to evacuate them. Our patrols kept close touch with the enemy, and by the evening of the 14th June the whole of the old German front and support lines north of the Lys had passed into our possession.

THE CAMPAIGNS OF 1917

That evening we again attacked south and east of Messines and on both sides of the Ypres-Comines Canal, and met with complete success. The strong points in which the enemy had held out north of the canal were captured, and our line was advanced on practically the whole front from the River Warnave to Klein Zillebeke.

By this operation the Second Army front was pushed forward as far as was then desirable. Henceforward our efforts in this area were directed to putting the line gained in a state of defence and establishing forward posts.

The Northern Operations.—Preparations Renewed

35. As soon as this preliminary operation had been successfully accomplished, it became possible to take in hand our final dispositions for our main offensive east and north of Ypres. Owing to the great extent of front to be dealt with, the Fifth Army took over command of the front from Observatory Ridge to Boesinghe on the 10th June, and the whole of our available resources were directed to completing the preparations for the attack.

It had been agreed that French troops should take part in these operations, and should extend my left flank northwards beyond Boesinghe. The relief by British troops of the French troops holding the coast sector from St. Georges to the sea was accordingly arranged for, and was successfully completed ten days later. In the first week of July the Belgian troops holding the front from Boesinghe to Noordschoote were relieved by the First French Army, under the command of General Anthoine.

The various problems inseparable from the mounting of a great offensive, the improvement and construction of roads and railways, the provision of an adequate water supply and of accommodation for troops, the formation of dumps, the digging of dug-outs, subways and trenches, and the assembling and registering of guns, had all to be met and overcome in the new theatre of battle, under conditions of more than ordinary disadvantage.

On no previous occasion, not excepting the attack on the Messines-Wytschaete Ridge, had the whole of the ground from which we had to attack been so completely exposed to the enemy's observation. Even after the enemy had been driven from the Messines-Wytschaete Ridge, he still possessed excellent direct observation over the salient from the east and south-east, as well as from the Pilckem Ridge to the north. Nothing existed at Ypres to correspond with the vast caves and cellars which proved of such value in the days prior to the Arras battle, and the provision of shelter for the troops presented a very serious problem.

The work of the Tunnelling Companies of the Royal Engineers

deserves special mention in this connection. It was carried on under great difficulties, both from the unreliable nature of the ground and also from hostile artillery, which paid particular attention to all indications of mining activity on our part.

Minor Operations Continued

36. Meanwhile the policy of maintaining activity on other parts of my front was continued.

Further ground was gained on Greenland Hill, and on the 14th June British troops (3rd Division) captured by a surprise attack the German trench lines on the crest of Infantry Hill, east of Monchy-le-Preux, with 175 prisoners. This important position had already been the scene of a great deal of fierce fighting, and during the following six weeks was frequently counter-attacked. Our advanced posts changed hands frequently; but the principal line, giving the observation which lent importance to the position, remained consistently in our possession.

Early in May local attacks had been undertaken by Canadian troops in the neighbourhood of the Souchez River, which formed the prelude to a long-sustained series of minor operations directed against the defence of Lens. Substantial progress was made in this area on the 5th and 19th June, and five days later North Midland troops (46th Division, Major-General W. Thwaites) captured an important position on the slopes of a small hill south-west of Lens, forcing the enemy to make a considerable withdrawal on both sides of the river. Canadian troops (3rd and 4th Canadian Divisions) took La Coulotte on the 26th June, and by the morning of the 28th June had reached the outskirts of Avion.

On the evening of the 28th June a deliberate and carefully-thought-out scheme was put into operation by the First Army, to give the enemy the impression that he was being attacked on a twelve-mile front from Gavrelle to Hulluch.[1]

Elaborate demonstrations were made on the whole of this front, accompanied by discharges of gas, smoke and thermit, and a mock raid was successfully carried out south-east of Loos. At the same time real attacks were made, with complete success, by English troops (31st Division, Major-General R. Wanless O'Gowan, and the 5th Division) on a front of 2,000 yards opposite Oppy, and by Canadian and North Midland troops (3rd and 4th Canadian Divisions, and the 46th Division) on a front of two and a half miles astride the Souchez River. All our objectives were gained, including Eleu dit Leauvette and the southern half of Avion, with some 300 prisoners and a number of machine guns.

[1] See previous footnote on page 101 above.

THE CAMPAIGNS OF 1917

The Lombartzyde Attack

37. The appearance of British troops on the coast seems to have alarmed the enemy and caused him to launch a small counter-offensive.[1]

The positions which we had taken over from the French in this area included a narrow strip of polder and dune, some two miles in length and from 600 to 1,200 yards in depth, lying on the right bank of the canalised Yser between the Plasschendaele Canal, south of Lombartzyde, and the coast. Midway between the Plasschendaele Canal and the sea these positions were divided into two parts by the dyke known as the Geleide Creek, which flows into the Yser south-west of Lombartzyde. If the enemy could succeed in driving us back across the canal and river on the whole of this front, he would render the defence of the sector much easier for him.

Early on the morning of the 10th July an intense bombardment was opened against these positions, held by the 1st Division (Major-General E. P. Strickland) and the 32nd Division (Major-General C. D. Shute). Our defences, which consisted chiefly of breastworks built in the sand, were flattened, and all the bridges across the Yser below the Geleide Creek, as well as the bridges across the creek itself, were destroyed.

At 6.30 p.m. the enemy's infantry attacked, and the isolated garrison of our positions north of the Geleide Creek, consisting of troops from a Northamptonshire battalion and a Rifle battalion,[2] were overwhelmed after an obstinate and most gallant resistance. Of these two battalions some seventy men and four officers succeeded during the nights of the 10th/11th and 11th/12th July in swimming across the Yser to our lines.

On the southern half of the point attacked, opposite Lombartzyde, the enemy also broke into our lines; but here, where our positions had greater depth and communication across the Yser was still possible, his troops were ejected by our counter-attack.

THE THIRD BATTLE OF YPRES

Preliminary Stages

38. By this date the preparations for the combined Allied offensive were far advanced, and the initial stages of the battle had already begun.

A definite aerial offensive had been launched, and the effective

[1] The Germans were not altogether wrong in their appreciation of the situation. Had the weather permitted the Ypres offensive to proceed more rapidly, it had been intended to develop offensive operations also along the coast. Subsequent events made it necessary to abandon this plan, though the enemy's attack at Lombartzyde had failed to deprive us of a sufficient bridgehead.

[2] 1st Battalion Northampton Regiment and 2nd Battalion K.R.R.C., 1st Division.

H

work of our airmen once more enabled our batteries to carry out successfully a methodical and comprehensive artillery programme.

So effective was our counter-battery work, that the enemy commenced to withdraw his guns to places of greater security. On this account, and also for other reasons, the date of our attack, which had been fixed for the 25th July, was postponed for three days. This postponement enabled a portion of our own guns to be moved farther forward, and gave our airmen the opportunity to locate accurately the enemy's new battery positions. Subsequently a succession of days of bad visibility, combined with the difficulties experienced by our Allies in getting their guns into position in their new area, decided me to sanction a further postponement until the 31st July.

In addition to our artillery bombardment, gas was used extensively during the fortnight preceding the attack, and a number of highly successful raids were carried out along the whole front north of the Lys.

The Yser Canal Crossed

39. As the date of the attack drew near, careful watch was maintained lest the enemy should endeavour to disarrange our plans by withdrawing to one of his rear lines of defence. On the 27th July the German forward defence system was found to be unoccupied on the northern portion of the Fifth Army front. British Guards and French troops seized the opportunity to cross the Yser Canal, and established themselves firmly in the enemy's first and support trenches on a front of about 3,000 yards east and north of Boesinghe. All hostile attempts to eject them failed, and during the night seventeen bridges were thrown across the canal by our troops.

This operation greatly facilitated the task of the Allied troops on this part of the battle front, to whose attack the Yser Canal had previously presented a formidable obstacle. Whether the withdrawal which made it possible was due to the desire of the German infantry to escape our bombardment, or to their fear that our attack would be inaugurated by the explosion of a new series of mines, is uncertain.

Plan of First Attack

40. The front of the Allied attack extended from the Lys River opposite Deulemont northwards to beyond Steenstraat, a distance of over fifteen miles, but the main blow was to be delivered by the Fifth Army on a front of about seven and a half miles, from the Zillebeke-Zandvoorde Road to Boesinghe, inclusive.

Covering the right of the Fifth Army, the task of the Second Army was to advance a short distance only. Its principal object at this stage was to increase the area threatened by the attack and so

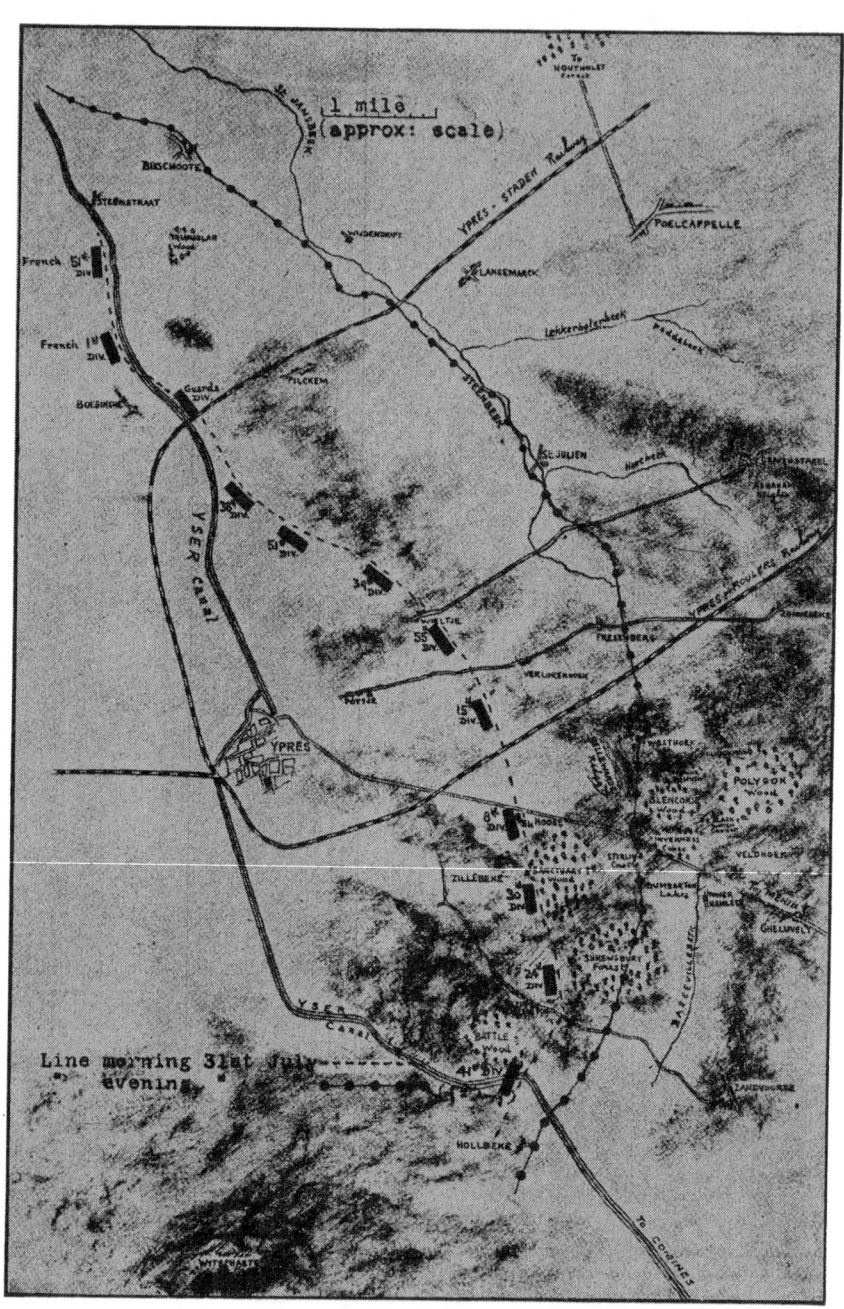

THIRD YPRES BATTLE;
Attack of 31st July, 1917.

THE CAMPAIGNS OF 1917

force the enemy to distribute the fire of his artillery. I had other tasks in view for it at a later period.[1]

On the left of the Fifth Army the First French Army was to advance its right in close touch with the British forces and secure them from counter-attack from the north. This entailed an advance of considerable depth over difficult country, and ultimately involved the capture of the whole peninsula lying between the Yser Canal and the floods of the St. Jansbeek and the Martjevaart.

The plan of attack on the Fifth Army front was to advance in a series of bounds, with which the right of the First French Army was to keep step. These bounds were arranged so as to suit as far as possible both the position of the principal lines of the enemy's defences and the configuration of the ground.

It was hoped that in this first attack our troops would succeed in establishing themselves on the crest of the high ground east of Ypres, on which a strong flank could be formed for subsequent operations, and would also secure the crossings of the Steenbeek. For this purpose four Army Corps were placed at the disposal of General Sir Hubert Gough: namely, the II. Corps, Lieut.-General Sir C. W. Jacob; the XIV. Corps, Lieut.-General F. R., Earl of Cavan; the XVIII. and XIX. Corps.

The Battle Opened

41. At 3.50 a.m. on the morning of the 31st July the combined attack was launched. English, Irish, Scottish and Welsh troops delivered the main assault on the British front.[2]

---

[1] Had our attack made more rapid progress, the Second Army would have taken an immediate part in our operations, on much the same lines as the attacks actually carried out by the Second Army in the autumn of 1918.

[2] The disposition of the attacking troops of the Fifth Army was as follows, from south to north :—

II. Corps
- 24th Div. . . . . Maj.-Gen. L. J. Bols.
- 30th Div. . . . . Maj.-Gen. W. de L. Williams, with a Brigade of the
- 18th Div. . . . Maj.-Gen. R. P. Lee going through.
- 8th Div. . . . . Maj.-Gen. W. C. G. Heneker.

XIX Corps
- 15th Div. . . . . Maj.-Gen. H. F. Thuillier.
- 55th Div. . . . . Maj.-Gen. H. S. Jeudwine.

XVIII. Corps
- 39th Div. . . . . Maj.-Gen. G. J. Cuthbert.
- 51st Div. . . . . Maj.-Gen. G. M. Harper.

XIV. Corps
- 38th Div. . . . . Maj.-Gen. C. G. Blackader.
- Guards Div. . . . . Maj.-Gen. G. P. T. Feilding.

Preceded at zero hour by discharges of thermit and oil drums, and covered by an accurate artillery barrage from a great number of guns, the Allied infantry entered the German lines at all points. The enemy's barrage was late and weak, and our casualties were light.

On the greater part of the front of the main attack the resistance of the German infantry was quickly overcome and rapid progress was made. The difficult country east of Ypres, where the Menin Road crosses the crest of the Wytschaete-Passchendaele Ridge, formed, however, the key to the enemy's position, and here the most determined opposition was encountered. None the less, the attacking brigades, including a number of Lancashire battalions, regiments from all parts of England and a few Scottish and Irish battalions (24th, 30th and 8th Divisions), fought their way steadily forward through Shrewsbury Forest and Sanctuary Wood and captured Stirling Castle, Hooge and the Bellewaarde Ridge.

Farther north, British and French troops carried the whole of the first German trench system with scarcely a check, and proceeded in accordance with the time-table to the assault of the enemy's second line of defence. Scottish troops (15th Division) took Verlorenhoek, and, continuing their advance, by 6.0 a.m. had reached Frezenberg, where for a short time stiff fighting took place before the village and the strong defences round it were captured. South of Pilckem a Prussian Guard battalion was broken up by Welsh troops (38th Division) after a brief resistance, and Pilckem was taken. Sharp fighting occurred also at a number of other points, but in every instance the enemy's opposition was overcome.

At 9.0 a.m. the whole of our second objectives north of the Ypres-Roulers Railway were in our possession, with the exception of a strong point north of Frezenberg, known as Pommern Redoubt, where fighting was still going on. Within an hour this redoubt also had been captured by West Lancashire Territorials (55th Division). On our left French troops made equal progress, capturing their objective in precise accordance with programme and with little loss.

By this time our field artillery had begun to move up, and by 9.30 a.m. a number of batteries were already in action in their forward positions. The Allied advance on this portion of our front was resumed at the hour planned. English county troops (39th Division) captured St. Julien, and from that point northwards our final objectives were reached and passed. Highland Territorials (51st Division), Welsh and Guards battalions secured the crossings of the Steenbeek, and French troops, having also taken their final objectives, advanced beyond them and seized Bixschoote. A hostile counter-attack launched against the point of junction of the French and British Armies was completely repulsed.

THE CAMPAIGNS OF 1917   115

Meanwhile, south of the Ypres-Roulers Railway, very heavy and continuous fighting was taking place on both sides of the Menin Road. After the capture of the German first line system our troops on this part of our front had advanced in time with the divisions on their left against their second objectives. Great opposition was at once encountered in front of two small woods known as Inverness Copse and Glencorse Wood, while further south a strong point in Shrewsbury Forest held out against our attacks till the morning of the 1st August. North of Glencorse Wood English troops (8th Division) continued their advance in spite of the enemy's resistance, and reached the village of Westhoek.

Later in the day heavy counter-attacks began to develop from south of the Menin Road northwards to St. Julien. Our artillery caused great loss to the enemy in these attacks, although the weather was unfavourable for aeroplane work and observation for our batteries was difficult. At Inverness Copse and Glencorse Wood a few tanks succeeded in reaching the fighting line, in spite of exceedingly bad ground, and came into action with our infantry. Fierce fighting took place all day, but the enemy was unable to shake our hold upon the ridge.

Results of First Day

42. At the end of the day, therefore, our troops on the Fifth Army front had carried the German first system of defence south of Westhoek. Except at Westhoek itself, where they were established on the outskirts of the village, they had already gained the whole of the crest of the ridge and had denied the enemy observation over the Ypres plain. Farther north they had captured the enemy's second line also as far as St. Julien. North of that village they had passed beyond the German second line, and held the line of the Steenbeek to our junction with the French.

On our left flank our Allies had admirably completed the important task allotted to them. Close touch had been kept with the British troops on their right throughout the day. All and more than all their objectives had been gained rapidly and at exceptionally light cost, and the flank of the Allied advance had been effectively secured.

Meanwhile, the attack on the Second Army front had also met with complete success. On the extreme right New Zealand troops had carried La Basse Ville after a sharp fight lasting some fifty minutes. On the left English troops (41st Division) had captured Hollebeke and the difficult ground north of the bend of the Ypres-Comines Canal and east of Battle Wood. Between these two points our line had been advanced on the whole front for distances varying from 200 to 800 yards.

Over 6,100 prisoners, including 133 officers, were captured by us in this battle. In addition to our gains in prisoners and ground we also captured some 25 guns, while a further number of prisoners and guns were taken by our Allies.

Effect of the Weather

43. The weather had been threatening throughout the day, and had rendered the work of the aeroplanes very difficult from the commencement of the battle. During the afternoon, while fighting was still in progress, rain began, and fell steadily all night. Thereafter, for four days, the rain continued without cessation, and for several days afterwards the weather remained stormy and unsettled. The low-lying, clayey soil, torn by shells and sodden with rain, turned to a succession of vast muddy pools. The valleys of the choked and overflowing streams were speedily transformed into long stretches of bog, impassable except by a few well-defined tracks, which became marks for the enemy's artillery. To leave these tracks was to risk death by drowning, and in the course of the subsequent fighting on several occasions both men and pack animals were lost in this way. In these conditions operations of any magnitude became impossible, and the resumption of our offensive was necessarily postponed until a period of fine weather should allow the ground to recover.

As had been the case in the Arras battle, this unavoidable delay in the development of our offensive was of the greatest service to the enemy. Valuable time was lost, the troops opposed to us were able to recover from the disorganisation produced by our first attack, and the enemy was given the opportunity to bring up reinforcements.

Hostile Counter-Attacks.—St. Julien and Westhoek

44. During the night of the 31st July and on the two following days, the enemy delivered further counter-attacks against our new line, and in particular made determined efforts to dislodge us from the high ground between the Menin Road and the Ypres-Roulers Railway, and to recover his second line system between Frezenberg and St. Julien. In this he completely failed. The violence of his artillery fire compelled us, however, to withdraw temporarily from St. Julien, though we retained a bridgehead across the Steenbeek, just north of the village.

In spite of these counter-attacks and the great but unavoidable hardships from which our troops were suffering, steady progress was made with the consolidation of the captured ground, and every opportunity was taken to improve the line already gained.

THE CAMPAIGNS OF 1917

On the 3rd August St. Julien was reoccupied without serious opposition, and our line linked up with the position we had retained on the right bank of the Steenbeek further north. A week later a successful minor operation carried out by English troops (18th and 25th Divisions) gave us complete possession of Westhoek. Seven hostile counter-attacks within the following four days broke down before our defence.

During this period certain centres of resistance in the neighbourhood of Kortekeer Cabaret were cleared up by our Allies, and a number of fortified farm houses, lying across the front of the French position, were reduced in turn.

Lens Operations Resumed.—Hill 70

45. Towards the middle of August a slight improvement took place in the weather, and advantage was taken of this to launch our second attack east of Ypres. Thereafter unsettled weather again set in, and the month closed as the wettest August that has been known for many years.

On the day preceding this attack at Ypres a highly successful operation was carried out in the neighbourhood of Lens, whereby the situation of our forces in that sector was greatly improved. At the same time the threat to Lens itself was rendered more immediate and more insistent, and the enemy was prevented from concentrating the whole of his attention and resources upon the front of our main offensive.

At 4.25 a.m. on the 15th August the Canadian Corps (Lieut.-General A. W. Currie) attacked with the 2nd and 1st Canadian Divisions (Major-General A. C. Macdonell commanding the 1st Canadian Division) on a front of 4,000 yards south-east and east of Loos. The objectives consisted of the strongly fortified hill known as Hill 70, which had been reached, but not held, in the battle of Loos on the 25th September, 1915, and also the mining suburbs of Cité Ste. Élizabeth, Cité St. Émile, and Cité St. Laurent, together with the whole of Bois Rasé and the western half of Bois Hugo. The observation from Hill 70 had been very useful to the enemy, and in our possession materially increased our command over the defences of Lens.

Practically the whole of these objectives were gained rapidly at light cost, and in exact accordance with plan. Only at the farthest apex of our advance a short length of German trench west of Cité St. Auguste resisted our first assault. This position was again attacked on the afternoon of the following day and captured after a fierce struggle lasting far into the night.

A number of local counter-attacks on the morning of the 15th August were repulsed, and in the evening a powerful attack delivered across the open by a German reserve division was broken up with heavy loss. In addition to the enemy's other casualties, 1,120 prisoners from three German divisions were captured by us.

The Ypres Battle.—Langemarck

46. Close upon the heels of this success, at 4.45 a.m. on the 16th August our second attack was launched east and north of Ypres; on a front extending from the north-west corner of Inverness Copse to our junction with the French south of St. Janshoek. On our left the French undertook the task of clearing up the remainder of the Bixshoote peninsula.

On the left of the British attack the English brigades detailed for the assault (29th and 20th Divisions, Major-General W. D. Smith commanding the 20th Division) captured the hamlet of Wijdendrift and reached the southern outskirts of Langemarck. Here some resistance was encountered, but by 8.0 a.m. the village had been taken, after sharp fighting. Our troops then proceeded to attack the portion of the Langemarck-Gheluvelt Line which formed their final objective, and an hour later had gained this also, with the exception of a short length of trench north-east of Langemarck. Two small counter-attacks were repulsed without difficulty.

The attack of the First French Army delivered at the same hour was equally successful. On the right a few fortified farms in the neighbourhood of the Steenbeek again gave trouble, and held out for a time. Elsewhere our Allies gained their objectives rapidly, and once more at exceptionally light cost. The bridge-head of Drie Grachten was secured, and the whole of the peninsula cleared of the enemy.

In the centre of the British attack the enemy's resistance was more obstinate. The difficulty of making deep mined dug-outs in soil where water lay within a few feet of the surface of the ground had compelled the enemy to construct in the ruins of farms and in other suitable localities a number of strong points or " pill-boxes " built of reinforced concrete often many feet thick.

These field forts, distributed in depth all along the front of our advance, offered a serious obstacle to progress. They were heavily armed with machine guns and manned by men determined to hold on at all costs. Many were reduced as our troops advanced, but others held out throughout the day, and delayed the arrival of our supports. In addition, weather conditions made aeroplane observation practically impossible, with the result that no warning was received of the enemy's counter-attacks and our infantry obtained little artillery help against them. When, therefore, later in the morning a heavy counter-attack developed in the neighbourhood of the Wieltje-Passchendaele Road, our troops, who had reached their final objectives at many points in this area also, were gradually compelled to fall back.

On the left centre West Lancashire Territorials and troops from other English counties (48th and 11th Divisions, Major-General R. Fanshawe commanding the 48th Division) established themselves on a line running north from St. Julien to the old German third line due east of Langemarck. This line they maintained against the enemy's attacks, and thereby secured the flank of our gains further north.

On the right of the British attack the enemy again developed the main strength of his resistance. At the end of a day of very heavy fighting, except for small gains of ground on the western edge of Glencorse Wood and north of Westhoek by the 56th Division (Major-General F. A. Dudgeon) and the 8th Division, the situation south of St. Julien remained unchanged.

In spite of this partial check on the southern portion of our attack, the day closed as a decided success for the Allies. A wide gap had been made in the old German third line system, and over 2,100 prisoners and some thirty guns had been captured.

Effect of Hostile Resistance.—Methods Revised

47. The strength of the resistance developed by the enemy at this stage in the neighbourhood of the Menin Road decided me to extend the flank of the next attack southwards. It was undesirable, however, either to increase the already wide front of attack for which the Fifth Army was responsible, or to divide between two Armies the control of the attack against the main ridge itself. I therefore determined to extend the left of the Second Army northwards, entrusting the attack upon the whole of the high ground crossed by the Menin Road to General Sir Herbert Plumer as a single self-contained operation, to be carried out in conjunction with the attacks of the Fifth Army farther north.

During the wet weather which prevailed throughout the remainder of the month, our efforts were confined to a number of small operations east and north-east of Ypres, designed to reduce certain of the more important of the enemy's strong points. In the meantime the necessary re-arrangements of the British forces were pushed on as rapidly as possible, so that our new attack might be ready directly the weather should improve sufficiently to enable it to be undertaken.

These arrangements included a modification of our artillery tactics, to meet the situation created by the change in the enemy's methods of defence.

Our recent successes had conclusively proved that the enemy's infantry were unable to hold the strongest defences against a properly mounted attack, and that increasing the number of his troops in his forward defence systems merely added to his losses. Accordingly, the enemy had adopted a system of elastic defence, in which his forward trench lines were held only in sufficient strength to disorganise the attack, while the bulk of his forces were kept in close reserve, ready to deliver a powerful and immediate blow which might recover the positions over-run by our troops before we had had time to consolidate them.

In the heavy fighting east of Ypres, these tactics had undoubtedly met with a certain measure of success. While unable to drive us back from the ridge, they had succeeded, in combination with the state of the ground and weather, in checking our progress. This new policy, for our early knowledge of which, as well as for other valuable information concerning the enemy's dispositions and intentions throughout the battle, much credit is due to the zeal and efficiency of my Intelligence Service, necessarily entailed corresponding changes in our method of attack.[1]

Minor Operations

48. In the interval, on the 19th, 22nd and 27th August, positions of considerable local importance in the neighbourhood of St. Julien were captured with some hundreds of prisoners, as the result of minor attacks conducted under the most unfavourable conditions of ground and weather. The ground gained represented an advance of about 800 yards on a front of over two miles. In combination with the attack of the 22nd August, English troops (14th Division) also attacked astride the Menin Road, and after six days of continuous local fighting established themselves in the western edge of Inverness Copse.

Meanwhile, in pursuance of my policy of compelling the enemy to guard himself on other fronts, successful minor operations had been undertaken elsewhere. On the Lens front, Canadian troops (4th and 2nd Canadian Divisions) attacked on the 21st August, and carried the line of German trenches skirting the town to the southwest and west, taking 200 prisoners. Farther south, north-country troops (34th Division) attacked on the 26th August east of Hargi-

---

[1] These changes consisted, speaking generally, in limiting the depth of our objectives and in making very careful artillery arrangements to deal with hostile concentrations and counter-attacks.

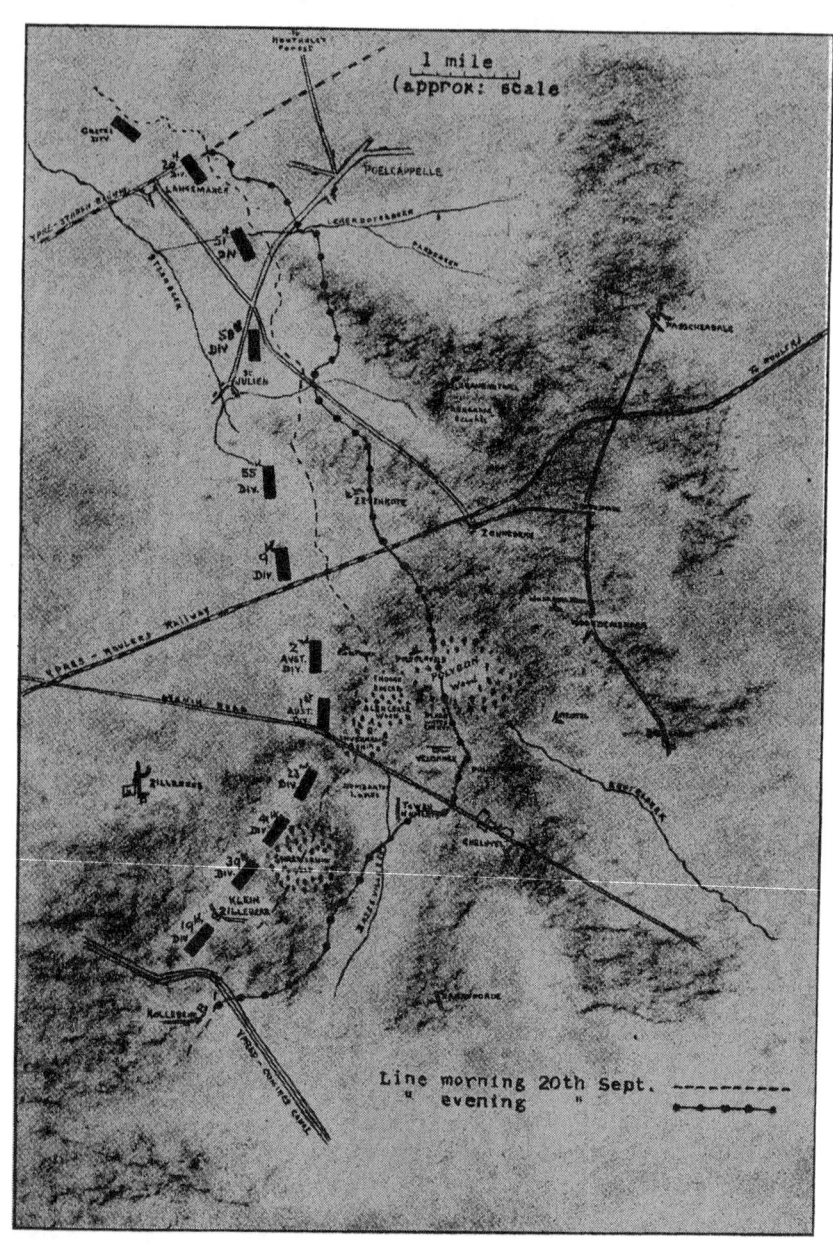

THIRD YPRES BATTLE;
Attack of 20th September, 1917.

THE CAMPAIGNS OF 1917

court, and captured the enemy's advanced positions on a front of a mile. In this operation 136 prisoners were taken, and on the 9th and 11th September our gains were extended and further prisoners secured.

The Ypres Battle.—Preparations for the Third Attack Completed

49. At the beginning of September the weather gradually improved, and artillery and other preparations for my next attack proceeded steadily. Both the extent of the preparations required, however, and the need to give the ground time to recover from the heavy rains of August rendered a considerable interval unavoidable before a new advance could be undertaken. The 20th September was therefore chosen for the date of our attack, and before that day our preparations had been completed.

The front selected extended from the Ypres-Comines Canal north of Hollebeke to the Ypres-Staden Railway north of Langemarck, a distance of just over eight miles along the line held by us. The average depth of our objectives was 1,000 yards, which increased to a depth of a mile in the neighbourhood of the Menin Road. Australian, English, Scottish and South African troops were employed in the attack, and gained a success conspicuous for precision and thoroughness of execution.

The Menin Road Ridge

50. During the night of the 19th/20th September rain again fell steadily, and when dawn broke thick mist made observation impossible. Despite this disadvantage, the assembling of our troops was carried out in good order, and at 5.40 a.m. on the 20th September the assault was launched.

Good progress was made from the start, and as the morning wore on the mist cleared. Our aeroplanes were able to establish contact with our infantry, to assist them by engaging parties of the enemy with machine gun fire, and to report hostile concentrations and counter-attacks to our artillery.

On our right Welsh and west-country troops (19th Division) advanced down the spur east of Klein Zillebeke, and, after sharp fighting in the small woods north of the Ypres-Comines Canal, gained the whole of their objectives. English battalions (39th Division, Major-General E. Feetham) pushed through the eastern portions of Shrewsbury Forest and reached their objectives in the valley of the Bassevillebeek. Regiments from the south-east counties of England (41st Division) had some trouble from snipers and machine guns early in their advance, but ultimately fought their way forward across the upper valley of the Bassevillebeek and up the slopes of Tower Hamlets. Here strong opposition was encountered, with heavy machine gun fire from Tower Hamlets and the Veldhoek Ridge.

In the meantime, however, north-country troops (23rd Division) had already carried Inverness Copse, and, after beating off a counter-attack in the neighbourhood of Dumbarton Lakes, captured Veldhoek and the line of their final objectives some 500 yards farther east. Their progress assisted the south-east county battalions on their right to establish themselves across the Tower Hamlets spur.

On the left of the north-country division Australian troops (1st and 2nd Australian Divisions) carried the remainder of Glencorse Wood and Nonne Boschen. Before 10.0 a.m. they had taken the hamlet of Polygonveld and the old German third line to the north of it. This advance constituted a fine performance, in which the capture of a difficult piece of ground that had much delayed us was successfully completed. Sharp fighting took place at a strong point known as Black Watch Corner at the south-western end of Polygon Wood. By midday this had been captured, the western portion of Polygon Wood had been cleared of the enemy, and the whole of our objectives on this part of our front had been gained.

On the Fifth Army front our attack met with equal success. Scottish and South African troops (9th Division) advancing on both sides of the Ypres-Roulers Railway, stormed the line of fortified farms immediately in front of their position, and, pressing on, captured Zonnebeke and Bremen Redoubts and the hamlet of Zevenkote. By 8.45 a.m. our final objectives on this front had been gained.

West Lancashire Territorial battalions (55th Division) found the ground south-east of St. Julien very wet and heavy after the night's rain. None the less, they made steady progress, reaching the line of their final objectives early in the afternoon. North of the Zonnebeke-Langemarck Road London and Highland Territorials (58th and 51st Divisions) gained the whole of their objectives by midday, though stiff fighting took place for a number of farms and strong places.[1]

As the result of this most successful operation the whole of the high ground crossed by the Menin Road, for which such desperate fighting had taken place during our previous attacks, passed into our possession. Important positions were won also on the remainder of our front, by which the right of our attack was rendered more secure, and the way opened for the advance of our left. In the attack, as well as in the repeated counter-attacks which followed, exceedingly heavy casualties were inflicted on the enemy, and 3,243 prisoners, together with a number of guns, were captured by us.

[1] Progress was also made by the 20th Division on the extreme left of the attack.

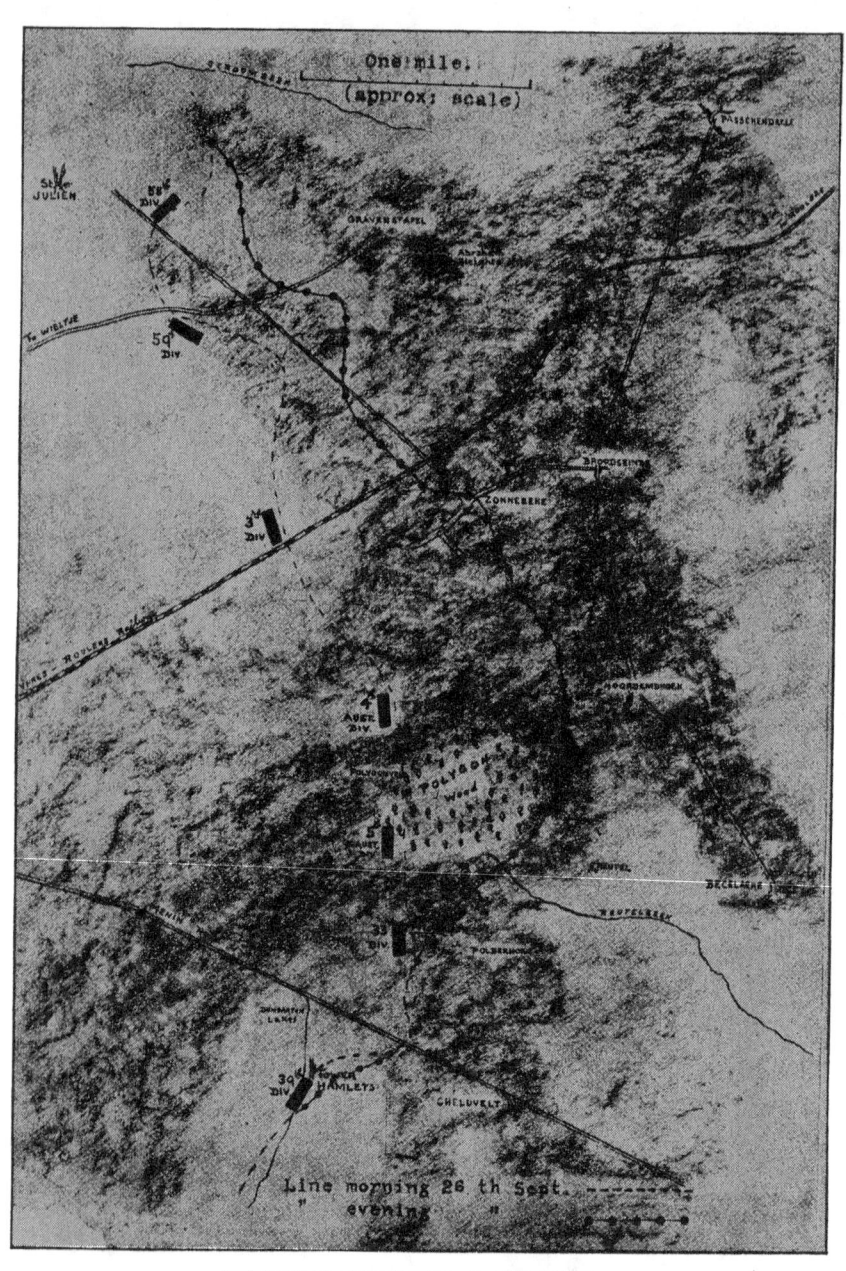

THIRD YPRES BATTLE;
Attack of 26th September, 1917.

THE CAMPAIGNS OF 1917

Counter-Attacks

51. The enemy did not abandon these important positions without further severe struggles. During the afternoon and evening of the 20th September no less than eleven counter-attacks were made without success against different parts of our new front, in addition to several concentrations of hostile infantry, which were broken up by our artillery before any attack could be launched.

East of St. Julien the enemy at his third attempt succeeded in forcing back our troops to the west of Schuler Farm, but on the following day the farm was retaken by us and our line re-established. North-east of Langemarck stubborn fighting took place for the possession of the short length of trench which, as already recounted, had resisted our attacks on the 16th August. It was not till the morning of the 23rd September that the position was finally captured by us (20th Division).

Fierce fighting took place also on the 21st September in the neighbourhood of Tower Hamlets (41st Division). In the course of this and the following four days three powerful attacks were launched by the enemy on wide fronts between Tower Hamlets and Polygon Wood, and a fourth north-east of St. Julien. All these attacks were repulsed, except that on the 25th September parties of German infantry succeeded in entering our lines north of the Menin Road. Heavy and confused fighting took place in this area throughout the day, in which English, Scottish and Australian troops (33rd Division and 5th Australian Division) gradually drove the enemy from the limited foothold he had gained.

The enemy's casualties in these many counter-attacks, as well as in all those subsequently delivered by him on the Ypres front, were consistently very heavy. Our constant successful resistance reflects the greatest credit on the high fighting qualities of our infantry, on the courage and devotion of our airmen, and upon the excellence of our artillery arrangements.

Polygon Wood and Zonnebeke

52. All this heavy fighting was not allowed to interfere with the arrangements made for a renewal of the advance by the Second and Fifth Armies on the 26th September.

The front of our attack on that date extended from south of Tower Hamlets to north-east of St. Julien, a total distance of rather less than six miles; but on the portion of this front south of the Menin Road (39th Division) only a short advance was intended. North of the Menin Road, our object was to reach a position from which a direct attack could be made upon the portion of the main ridge between Noordemdhoek and Broodseinde, traversed by the Becelaere-Passchendaele Road.

The assault was delivered at 5.50 a.m., and, after hard and prolonged fighting, in which over 1,600 prisoners were taken by us, achieved a success as striking as that of the 20th September.

Australian troops (5th and 4th Australian Divisions, Major-General E. G. Sinclair-MacLagan commanding the latter division) carried the remainder of Polygon Wood, together with the German trench line to the east of it, and established themselves on their objectives beyond the Becelaere-Zonnebeke Road. On the left of the Australians, English troops (3rd Division) took Zonnebeke Village and Church, and North Midland and London Territorial battalions (59th Division, Major-General C. F. Romer, and 58th Division) captured a long line of hostile strong points on both sides of the Wieltje-Gravenstafel Road.

South of Polygon Wood an obstinate struggle took place for a group of fortified farms and strong points. English, Scottish and Welsh battalions of the same divisions [1] that had borne the brunt of the enemy's attacks in this area on the previous day, gallantly fought their way forward. In their advance they effected the relief of two companies of Argyll and Sutherland Highlanders, who, with great courage and resolution, had held out in our forward line all night, although isolated from the rest of our troops. It was not until the evening of the 27th September, however, that the line of our objectives in this locality was completely gained.

Further Counter-Attacks

53. As had been the case on the 20th September, our advance was at once followed by a series of powerful counter-attacks.

There is evidence that our operations had anticipated a counter-stroke which the enemy was preparing for the evening of the 26th September, and the German troops brought up for this purpose were now hurled in to recover the positions he had lost. In the course of the day at least seven attacks were delivered at points covering practically the whole front from Tower Hamlets to St. Julien. The fiercest fighting prevailed in the sector between the Reutelbeek and Polygon Wood, but here, as elsewhere, all the enemy's assaults were beaten off.

On the 30th September, when the enemy had recovered from the disorganisation caused by his defeat, he recommenced his attacks. Two attempts to advance with flammenwerfer north of the Menin

---

[1] 33rd Division, Major-General P. R. Wood, and 39th Division.

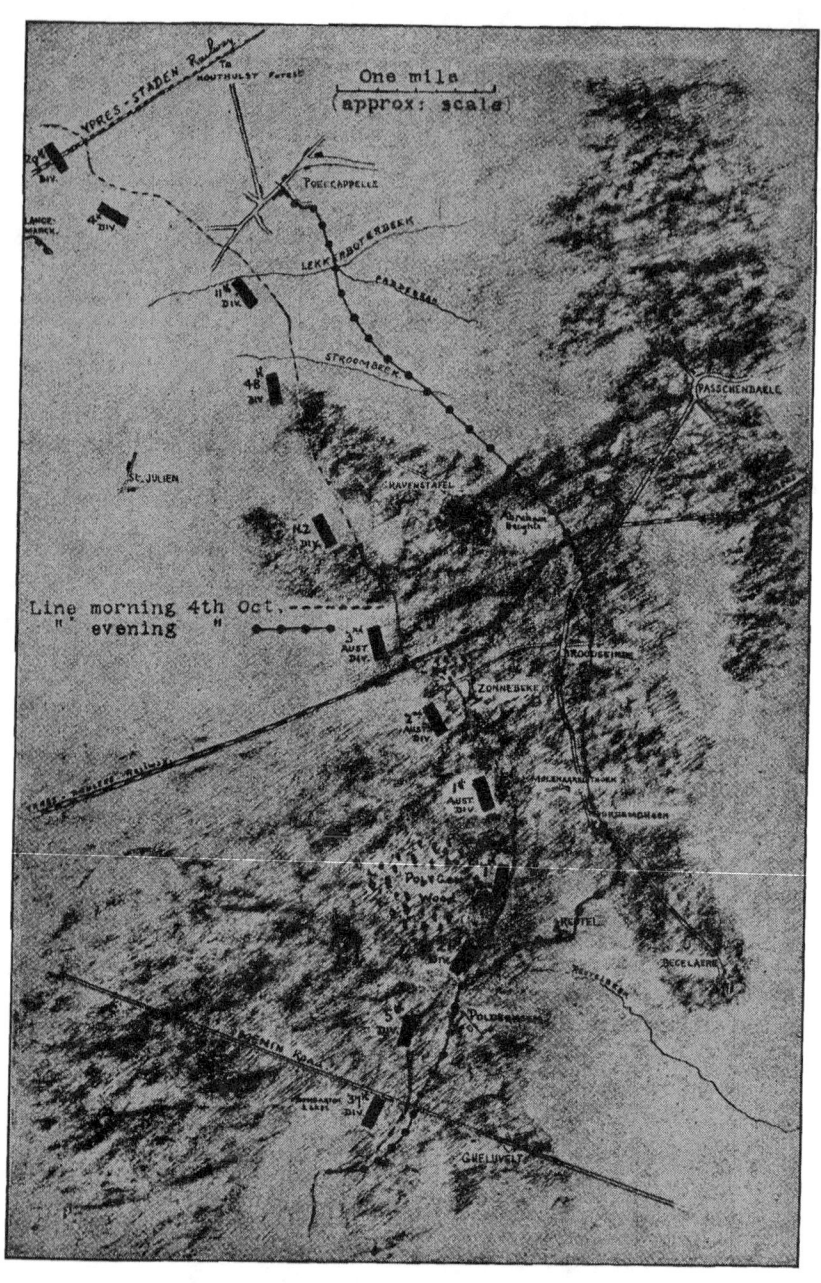

THIRD YPRES BATTLE;
Attack of 4th October, 1917.

THE CAMPAIGNS OF 1917

Road were followed on the 1st October by five other attacks in this area, and on the same day a sixth attack was made south of the Ypres-Roulers Railway. Except for the temporary loss of two advanced posts south-east of Polygon Wood, all these attacks were repulsed with great loss by the 37th, 23rd Divisions, 5th and 4th Australian Divisions, and 3rd Division. At dawn on the 3rd October another attempt in the neighbourhood of the Menin Road broke down before our positions.

A Further Advance on the Main Ridge.—Broodseinde

54. The spell of fine weather was broken on the evening of the 3rd October by a heavy gale and rain from the south-west. These conditions serve to emphasise the credit due to the troops for the completeness of the success gained by them on the following day.

At 6.0 a.m. on the 4th October our advance was renewed, in accordance with plan, against the main line of the ridge east of Zonnebeke. The front of our principal attack extended from the Menin Road to the Ypres-Staden Railway, a distance of about seven miles. South of the Menin Road a short advance was undertaken on a front of about a mile, with the object of capturing certain strong points required to strengthen our position in this sector.

The attack was carried out by Australian, New Zealand and English divisions, including among the latter a few Scottish, Irish and Welsh battalions, and was successful at all points.

On the right of the main attack troops from Kent, Devon and Cornwall, and a battalion of the King's Own Scottish Borderers (5th Division) carried their objectives after heavy fighting in the neighbourhood of Polderhoek Château. Battalions from Yorkshire, Northumberland, Surrey and Lincolnshire (21st Division) cleared the small enclosures east of Polygon Wood and seized the village of Reutel, meeting with strong opposition. On their left Surrey, Staffordshire, Devon, Border and Highland troops (7th Division), advancing across the crest of the ridge, captured the hamlet of Noordemdhoek.

Farther north, Australian troops (1st, 2nd and 3rd Australian Divisions) advanced beyond the Becelaere-Passchendaele Road, storming Molenaarelsthoek and Broodseinde, and established themselves well to the east of the crest line. New Zealand troops carried Gravenstafel, and drove the enemy from a network of trenches and strong points on the Gravenstafel spur.

On the whole of this front the enemy was met in great strength. In addition to the two German divisions already in line, the enemy had brought up three fresh divisions, with a view to launching an attack in force upon the positions captured by us on the 26th September. Our advance anticipated this attack by ten minutes, and the German infantry were forming up for the assault when our artillery barrage opened. Very serious casualties were inflicted on the enemy by our artillery, and our infantry, advancing with the bayonet, quickly overcame the resistance of those of his troops who had escaped our shell fire. Great numbers of prisoners were taken.

On the left of our attack South Midland troops (48th Division) forced their way across the valley of the Stroombeek, in spite of difficulties due to the rain of the previous night, and gained their objectives according to programme, with the exception of a single strong point at the limit of their advance. Other English divisions (11th and 4th Divisions, Major-General T. G. Matheson commanding the latter division), advancing on both sides of the Poelcappelle Road, stormed the western half of that village, including the church, and captured the whole of their objectives for the day. Tanks took part in the attack on Poelcappelle and contributed to the success of our troops.

On the extreme left (29th Division) considerable opposition was met with, and determined fighting took place for the possession of the rising ground known as 19 Metre Hill. Early in the afternoon a hostile counter-attack forced us back from a portion of this position, but later in the day our troops returned to the attack and recovered the lost ground.

Meanwhile, south of the Menin Road English troops (37th Division) had gained the whole of their limited objectives with the exception of two strong points. Soon after midday our final objectives had been gained, and large numbers of prisoners had already been brought in. The final total of German prisoners captured in these operations exceeded 5,000, including 138 officers.[1] A few guns and many machine guns and trench mortars were also taken by us.

The destruction of the divisions which the enemy had assembled for his intended attack made immediate serious counter-attacks impossible for him on a great part of our front. Between the Menin Road and the neighbourhood of Reutel, however, no less than seven counter-attacks were beaten off in turn. Exceedingly heavy fighting took place in this area, and later in the day an eighth attack succeeded in dislodging us from Polderhoek Château and from the eastern portions of Reutel. Another determined counter-attack, delivered in three waves early in the afternoon north of the Ypres-Roulers Railway, was broken up by our artillery, rifle and machine gun fire. Hostile concentrations east of Zonnebeke and west of Passchendaele were dispersed by our artillery.

[1] Ludendorff speaking of this attack refers to the German losses as " enormous."

THE CAMPAIGNS OF 1917

Results of this Attack

55. The success of this operation marked a definite step in the development of our advance. Our line had now been established along the main ridge for 9,000 yards from our starting point near Mount Sorrel. From the farthest point reached the well-marked Gravenstafel Spur offered a defensible feature along which our line could be bent back from the ridge.

The year was far spent. The weather had been consistently unpropitious, and the state of the ground, in consequence of rain and shelling combined, made movement inconceivably difficult. The resultant delays had given the enemy time to bring up reinforcements and to organise his defence after each defeat. Even so, it was still the difficulty of movement far more than hostile resistance which continued to limit our progress, and now made it doubtful whether the capture of the remainder of the ridge before winter finally set in was possible.

On the other hand, there was no reason to anticipate an abnormally wet October. The enemy had suffered severely, as was evidenced by the number of prisoners in our hands, by the number of his dead on the battlefield, by the costly failure of his repeated counter-attacks, and by the symptoms of confusion and discouragement in his ranks.

In this connection, documents captured in the course of the battle of the 4th October throw an interesting light upon the success of the measures taken by us to meet the enemy's new system of defence by counter-attack. These documents show that the German Higher Command had already recognised the failure of their methods, and were endeavouring to revert to something approximating to their old practice of holding their forward positions in strength.

After weighing these considerations, as well as the general situation and various other factors affecting the problem,[1] among them

---

[1] In a speech in the House of Commons on the 6th August, 1919 (Vol. 119 of the Official Reports), Major-General Sir John Davidson, M.P., gave a more complete account of the reasons which led to the continuing of the Ypres offensive. Briefly summarised, they are as follows :—
  1. Since the breakdown of their July offensive the Russian Armies had ceased to be a fighting force.
  2. The fighting capacity of the French Armies was at this time very seriously diminished by grave internal troubles.
  3. The solidarity of the Allied front in the west was jeopardised by the great reverse suffered in the October of 1917 by the Italian Armies.
  4. America was not yet in a position to give any assistance on land.
  5. The Russian collapse had set free large hostile forces which were rapidly being transferred to the Western front.
  6. The only Allied Army capable of conducting serious offensive operations at this time was the British.
  7. If the British offensive ceased, the enemy would regain the initiative, and be free

the desirability of assisting our Allies in the operations to be carried out by them on the 23rd October in the neighbourhood of Malmaison, I decided to continue the offensive further and to renew the advance at the earliest possible moment consistent with adequate preparation.

Accordingly, I determined to deliver the next combined French and British attack on the 9th October.

Houthulst Forest Reached

56. Unfortunately, bad weather still persisted in the early part of October, and on the 7th October heavy rain fell all day. The unfavourable conditions interfered with our artillery preparations; but every effort was made to engage the enemy's batteries in their new positions, and on the date last mentioned our artillery co-operated effectively in the repulse of two hostile attacks.

On the 8th October rain continued, and the slippery state of the ground, combined with an exceptionally dark night, made the assembling of our troops a matter of considerable difficulty. No interference, however, was encountered from the enemy's artillery, and at 5.20 a.m. on the 9th October our attack was renewed on a front of over six miles, from a point east of Zonnebeke to our junction with the French north-west of Langemarck. On our left our Allies prolonged the front of attack to a point opposite Draaibank. At the same time, minor operations were undertaken on the right of our main attack, east and south-east of Polygon Wood.

The greatest depth of our advance was on the left, where the Allied troops penetrated the German positions to a distance of nearly one and a half miles. French troops and British Guards crossed the flooded valley of the Broenbeek, and, making steady progress towards their objectives, captured the hamlet of Koekuit, Veldhoek, Mangelare and St. Janshoek, besides woods and a great number of farm houses and strong points. Early in the afternoon both French and British troops had established themselves on their final objectives on the outskirts of Houthulst Forest.

On the right of the Guards, other English divisions (29th and 4th Divisions) made equal progress along the Ypres-Staden Railway

> to attack wherever he thought the Allied line weakest. The condition of our Allies at this period was such that it was impossible to accept this risk while any alternative remained.
> 8. It followed, that the British must continue to attack, until the coming of winter put an end for the time being to the danger of a German counter-stroke.
> 9. The German submarine campaign was at its height. Our own Admiralty were anxious about our communications across the Channel so long as Ostend and Zeebrugge remained in the enemy's hands.

and secured a line well to the east of the Poelcappelle-Houthulst Road. Stiff fighting took place around certain strong points, in the course of which a hostile counter-attack was repulsed.

Farther south, English battalions (11th Division) fought their way forward in the face of great opposition to the eastern outskirts of Poelcappelle Village. Australian troops and East Lancashire, Yorkshire and South Midland Territorials [1] carried our line forward in the direction of Passchendaele and up the western slopes of the main ridge, capturing Nieuwemolen and Keerselaarhoek and a number of strong points and fortified farms.

In the subsidiary attack east of Polygon Wood Warwickshire and H.A.C. battalions (7th Division) successfully regained the remainder of Reutel.

Over 2,100 prisoners were taken by the Allies in the course of these operations, together with a few guns.

Progress Continued

57. Though the condition of the ground continued to deteriorate, the weather after this was unsettled rather than persistently wet, and progress had not yet become impossible. I accordingly decided to press on while circumstances still permitted, and arrangements were made for a renewal of the attack on the 12th October. On the night of the 11th/12th October, however, heavy rain commenced again, and, after a brief interval during the morning, continued steadily throughout the whole of the following day.

Our attack, launched at 5.25 a.m. on the 12th October between the Ypres-Roulers Railway and Houthulst Forest, made progress along the spurs and higher ground; but the valleys of the streams which run westward from the main ridge were found to be impassable. It was therefore determined not to persist in the attack, and the advance towards our more distant objectives was cancelled.

Certain strong points and fortified farms on the western slopes of the ridge were captured by the I. and II. Anzac Corps on this day, and were incorporated in our line. Farther north, on both sides of the Ypres-Staden Railway, English County divisions (4th and 17th Divisions, Major-General P. R. Robertson commanding the latter Division) and the Guards gained their objectives in spite of all difficulties. Though for many hours the position of our advanced troops on this part of our front was uncertain, communication was at length established and the captured ground maintained.

[1] These troops were the 2nd Australian Division, the 66th Division (Major-General Hon. Sir H. A. Lawrence), 49th Division (Major-General E. M. Perceval), and the 48th Division.

Over 1,000 prisoners were taken by us in this attack, in which the troops employed displayed remarkable gallantry, steadfastness and endurance in circumstances of extreme hardship.

Plan of Subsequent Operations

58. By this time the persistent continuation of wet weather had left no further room for hope that the condition of the ground would improve sufficiently to enable us to capture the remainder of the ridge this year. By limited attacks made during intervals of better weather, however, it would still be possible to progress as far as Passchendaele, and in view of other projects which I had in view it was desirable to maintain the pressure on the Flanders front for a few weeks longer.

To maintain his defence on this front the enemy had been obliged to reduce the garrison of certain other parts of his line to a degree which justified the expectation that a sudden attack at a point where he did not expect it might attain a considerable local success. The front for such an attempt had been selected, and plans had already been quietly made. But certain preparations and movements of troops required time to complete, and the 20th November had been fixed as the earliest date for the attack.

No large force could be made available for the enterprise. The prospects of success, therefore, depended on complete secrecy and on maintaining sufficient activity in Flanders to induce the enemy to continue his concentration of troops in that theatre.

As has been indicated above, our Allies also had certain limited operations in view which would be likely to benefit by the maintenance of pressure on my front, and, reciprocally, would add to the prospects of success of my intended surprise attack. Accordingly, while preparing for the latter, operations of limited scope were continued in Flanders.

The Merckem Peninsula

59. After the middle of October the weather improved, and on the 22nd October two successful operations, in which we captured over 200 prisoners and gained positions of considerable local importance east of Poelcappelle and within the southern edge of Houthulst Forest, were undertaken by us, in the one case by east-county and Northumberland troops (18th and 34th Divisions), and in the other by west-county and Scots battalions (35th Division, Major - General G. McK. Franks) in co-operation with the French.

THE CAMPAIGNS OF 1917

The following two days were unsettled, but òn the 25th October a strong west wind somewhat dried the surface of the ground. It was therefore decided to proceed with the Allied operations which had been planned for the 26th October.

At an early hour on that morning rain unfortunately began again and fell heavily all day. The assembling of our troops was completed successfully none the less, and at 5.45 a.m. English and Canadian troops attacked on a front extending from the Ypres-Roulers Railway to beyond Poelcappelle.

The Canadians (4th and 3rd Canadian Divisions) attacked on the right on both sides of the small stream known as the Ravebeek, which flows south-westwards from Passchendaele. On the left bank of the stream they advanced astride the main ridge and established themselves securely on the small hill south of Passchendaele. North of the Ravebeek strong resistance was met on the Bellevue Spur, a very strong point which had resisted our efforts in previous attacks. With splendid determination the Canadians renewed their attack on this point in the afternoon, and captured it. Two strong counter-attacks south and west of Passchendaele were beaten off, and by nightfall the Canadians had gained practically the whole of their objectives.

On the left of the Canadians the Royal Naval Division and battalions of London Territorials (58th Division, Major-General A. B. E. Cator) also advanced, and, in spite of immense difficulties from marsh and floods in the more low-lying ground, made progress.

In a subsidiary attack undertaken by us at the same hour English troops (7th and 5th Divisions) entered Gheluvelt and recaptured Polderhoek Château, with a number of prisoners. Our men's rifles, however, had become choked with mud in their advance, and when later in the morning strong German counter-attacks developed, they were obliged to withdraw.

The operations of our Allies on this day were limited to establishing bridgeheads across the floods of the St. Jansbeek. This was successfully accomplished, in spite of considerable opposition. Next day the French continued their advance in concert with Belgian troops, who crossed the Yser opposite Knockehoek, and captured Aschhoop, Kippe, and Merckem. The southern end of Blankaart Lake was reached on the same day, and early on the 28th October French and Belgian troops completed the capture of the whole Merckem peninsula.

Over 400 prisoners were taken by our Allies in these operations, bringing the total Allied captures since the commencement of our attacks on the 26th October to over 1,200.

Passchendaele

60. At this date the need for the policy of activity outlined above had been still further emphasised by recent developments in Italy. Additional importance was given to it by the increasing probability that a time was approaching when the enemy's power of drawing reinforcements from Russia would increase considerably. In pursuance of this policy, therefore, two short advances were made on the 30th October and the 6th November, by which we gained possession of Passchendaele.

In the first operation Canadian and English troops attacked at 5.50 a.m. on a front extending from the Ypres-Roulers Railway to the Poelcappelle-Westroosebeke Road.

On the right the Canadians (4th and 3rd Canadian Divisions) continued their advance along the high ground and reached the outskirts of Passchendaele, capturing an important position at Crest Farm on a small hill south-west of the village. Fighting was severe at all points, but particularly on the spur west of Passchendaele. Here no less than five strong counter-attacks were beaten off in the course of the day, our troops being greatly assisted by the fire of captured German machine guns in Crest Farm.

Farther north, battalions of the same London and Naval divisions (58th and 63rd Divisions) that had taken part in the attack on the 26th October again made progress wherever it was possible to find a way across the swamps. The almost impassable nature of the ground in this area, however, made movement practically impossible, and it was only on the main ridge that much could be effected.

During the succeeding days small advances were made by night south-west of Passchendaele, and a hostile attack on both sides of the Ypres-Roulers Railway was successfully repulsed.

At 6.0 a.m. on the 6th November Canadian troops (2nd and 1st Canadian Divisions) renewed their attack and captured the village of Passchendaele, together with the high ground immediately to the north and north-west. Sharp fighting took place for the possession of "pill-boxes" in the northern end of the village, around Mosselmarkt, and on the Goudberg Spur. All objectives were gained at an early hour, and at 8.50 a.m. a hostile counter-attack north of Passchendaele was beaten off.

Over 400 prisoners were captured in this most successful attack, by which for the second time within the year Canadian troops achieved a record of uninterrupted success. Four days later, in extremely unfavourable weather, British and Canadian troops (2nd and 1st Canadian Divisions and 1st Division) attacked northwards from Passchendaele and Goudberg, and captured further ground on the main ridge, after heavy fighting.

THE CAMPAIGNS OF 1917

General Review

61. These operations concluded our Flanders offensive for the time being, although considerable activity was still continued for another fortnight for purposes already explained.

This offensive, maintained for three and a half months under the most adverse conditions of weather, had entailed almost superhuman exertions on the part of the troops of all arms and services. The enemy had done his utmost to hold his ground, and in his endeavours to do so had used up no less than seventy-eight divisions, of which eighteen had been engaged a second or third time in the battle, after being withdrawn to rest and refit. Despite the magnitude of his efforts, it was the immense natural difficulties, accentuated manifold by the abnormally wet weather, rather than the enemy's resistance, which limited our progress and prevented the complete capture of the ridge.

What was actually accomplished under such adverse conditions is the most conclusive proof that, given a normally fine August, the capture of the whole ridge, within the space of a few weeks, was well within the power of the men who achieved so much. They advanced every time with absolute confidence in their power to overcome the enemy, even though they had sometimes to struggle through mud up to their waists to reach him. So long as they could reach him they did overcome him, but physical exhaustion placed narrow limits on the depth to which each advance could be pushed, and compelled long pauses between the advances. The full fruits of each success were consequently not always obtained. Time after time the practically beaten enemy was enabled to reorganise and relieve his men and to bring up reinforcements behind the sea of mud which constituted his main protection.

Notwithstanding the many difficulties, much has been achieved. Our captures in Flanders since the commencement of operations at the end of July amount to 24,065 prisoners, 74 guns, 941 machine guns and 138 trench mortars. It is certain that the enemy's losses considerably exceeded ours. Most important of all, our new and hastily trained Armies have shown once again that they are capable of meeting and beating the enemy's best troops, even under conditions which favoured his defence to a degree which it required the greatest endurance, determination and heroism to overcome.[1]

In this respect I desire once more to lay emphasis upon the supreme importance of adequate training prior to placing troops in

---

[1] Ludendorff in his Memoirs pays a striking tribute to the disastrous effect which the fighting in Flanders had upon the moral of the German Army.

the line of battle, whether for offence or defence. It is essential, if preventable sacrifice is to be avoided and success assured, that troops that are going into battle should first be given an opportunity for special training, under the officers who are to command them in the fight, for the task which they are to be called upon to perform.

Owing to the necessity, already referred to, of taking over line from the French, our offensive at the beginning of the year was commenced under a very definite handicap in this respect. This initial disadvantage was subsequently increased by the difficulty of obtaining adequate drafts a sufficient length of time before divisions were called upon to take their place in the battle, to enable the drafts to be assimilated into divisions and divisions to be trained.

The general conditions of the struggle this year have been very different from those contemplated at the conference of the Allied Commanders held in November, 1916. The great general and simultaneous offensive then agreed on did not materialise. Russia, though some of her leaders made a fine effort at one period, not only failed to give the help expected of her, but even failed to prevent the enemy from transferring some forty fresh divisions from her front in exchange for tired ones used up in the Western theatre, or from replacing losses in his divisions on this side by drafts of fresh and well-trained men drawn from divisions in the East.

The combined French and British offensive in the spring was launched before Italy could be ready; and the splendid effort made by Italy at a later period was, unfortunately, followed by developments which resulted in a weakening of the Allied forces in this theatre before the conclusion of our offensive.

In these circumstances the task of the British and French Armies has been a far heavier one throughout the year than was originally anticipated, and the enemy's means of meeting our attack have been far greater than either he or we could have expected.

That under such conditions the victories of Arras, Vimy, Messines and Flanders were won by us, and those at Moronvilliers, Verdun and Malmaison by the French, constitutes a record of which the Allied Armies, working in close touch throughout, have a right to be proud.

The British Armies have taken their full share in the fighting on the Western front. Save for such short intervals as were enforced by the weather or rendered necessary for the completion of the preparations for our principal attacks, they have maintained a vigorous and continuous offensive throughout practically the whole of the period covered by this Despatch. No other example of offensive action on so large a scale, so long and so successfully sustained, has yet been furnished by the war.

THE CAMPAIGNS OF 1917

In the operations of Arras, Messines, Lens and Ypres as many as 131 German divisions have been engaged and defeated by less than half that number of British divisions.

The number of prisoners and guns captured by us is an indication of the progress we have made. The total number of prisoners taken between the opening of our spring offensive on the 9th April, 1917, and the conclusion of the Flanders offensive, exclusive of prisoners captured in the Cambrai Battle, is 57,696, including 1,290 officers. During the same period and in the same offensives we have also captured 393 guns, including 109 heavy guns, 561 trench mortars and 1,976 machine guns.

Without reckoning, therefore, the possibilities which have been opened up by our territorial gains in Flanders, and without considering the effect which a less vigorous prosecution of the war by us might have had in other theatres, we have every reason to be satisfied with the results which have been achieved by the past year's fighting. The addition of strength which the enemy has obtained, or may yet obtain, from events in Russia and Italy has already largely been discounted, and the ultimate destruction of the enemy's field forces has been brought appreciably nearer.

The Defensive Fronts

62. Before passing from the subject of the operations of the past eight months, tribute must be paid to the work accomplished on the defensive portions of our line.

In order to meet the urgent demands of battle, the number of divisions in line on other fronts has necessarily been reduced to the minimum consistent with safety. In consequence, constant vigilance and heavy and unremitting labour have been required at all times of the troops holding these fronts.

The numerous feint attacks which have been organised from time to time have called for great care, forethought and ingenuity on the part of Commanders and Staffs concerned, and have demanded much courageous, skilful and arduous work from the troops entrusted with the task of carrying them out. In addition, raids and local operations have continued to form a prominent feature of our general policy on our defensive front, and have been effectively combined with our feint attacks and with gas discharges. In the course of the 270 successful raids carried out by us during the period covered by this Despatch, the greatest enterprise and skill have been displayed by our troops, and many hundreds of prisoners, together with much invaluable information, have been obtained at comparatively light cost.

Our Troops

63. In my Despatch dealing with the Somme Battle I endeavoured to express something of the profound admiration inspired in me by the indomitable courage, tireless energy and cheerful endurance of the men by whose efforts the British Armies in France were brought triumphantly through that mighty ordeal. To-day the Armies of the Empire can look back with yet greater pride upon still severer tests successfully withstood and an even higher record of accomplishment.

No one acquainted with the facts can review the general course of the campaigns of 1916 and 1917 without acquiring the sense of a steady progression, in which the fighting superiority of the British soldier has been asserted with ever-increasing insistence. This feeling permeates the troops themselves, and is the greatest guarantee of victory.

Infantry

Throughout the northern operations our troops have been fighting over ground every foot of which is sacred to the memory of those who, in the first and second battles of Ypres, fought and died to make possible the victories of the armies which to-day are rolling back the tide stayed by their sacrifice. It is no disparagement of the gallant deeds performed on other fronts to say that, in the stubborn struggle for the line of hills which stretches from Wytschaete to Passchendaele, the great armies that to-day are shouldering the burden of our Empire have shown themselves worthy of the regiments which, in October and November of 1914, made Ypres take rank for ever amongst the most glorious of British battles.

Throughout the months of strenuous fighting which have wiped the old Ypres salient from the battle map of Flanders, the finest qualities of our infantry have been displayed. The great material disadvantages of the position from which they had to attack, the strength of the enemy's fortifications, and the extraordinary hardships imposed by the conditions of ground and weather during August and throughout the later stages of the attack, called for the exercise of courage, determination and endurance to a degree which has never been surpassed in war.

Artillery

The courage of our infantry would have been in vain but for the skill, steadfastness and devotion of the artillery. Their task in the Ypres Battle was again a peculiarly hard one. The long preparatory bombardments had to be conducted from a narrow and confined

THE CAMPAIGNS OF 1917

space, for the most part destitute alike of cover and protection, and directly overlooked by the enemy.

As our infantry advanced, our guns had to follow, at the cost of almost incredible exertion, over ground torn by shell fire and sodden with rain. When at length the new positions had been reached, our batteries had to remain in action, practically without protection of any kind, day after day, week after week, and even month after month, under a continuous bombardment of gas and high explosive shell.

It would be easy to multiply instances of individual heroism, to quote cases where, when the signal from our infantry for urgent artillery support and the warning of German gas have been given at the same moment, our gunners have thrown aside their half-adjusted gas masks and, with full knowledge of the consequences, have fought their guns in response to the call of the infantry till the enemy's attack has been beaten off.

A single incident which occurred during the preparation for the attack of the 31st July may be taken as a general example. A howitzer battery had received orders to cut a section of German wire in the neighbourhood of Hooge, and 400 rounds had been allocated for the purpose. The battery, situated in an unavoidably exposed position in the neighbourhood of Zillebeke Lake, had already been subjected to constant shelling. On the occasion referred to, not more than 50 rounds had been fired at the German wire, when a hostile 15 cm. battery opened a steady and accurate fire in enfilade. Each time the British battery opened, salvos of 15 cm. shells raked its position. Four of its six guns were put out of action, and two ammunition dumps were blown up, but the remaining two guns continued in action until the last of the 400 rounds had been fired. A few days later, when our infantry advanced over the sector this battery had shelled, the enemy's wire was found to have been completely cut.

The debt owed to the artillery throughout the whole of this year's fighting, and particularly in the Ypres Battle, is very great. Despite the extraordinary strain to which the gunners have been subjected, yet, wherever conditions of weather and light have made accurate shooting possible, they have never failed to dominate the German batteries. As the result of their close and loyal co-operation through long periods of continuous fighting, hostile artillery has never succeeded in stopping our attacks. Our infantry would be the first to acknowledge their admirable devotion and self-sacrifice.

Royal Flying Corps

During the past year the part played by the Royal Flying Corps in modern battles has grown more and more important. Each successive attack has served to demonstrate with increasing clearness the paramount necessity for the closest co-operation between air and land arms. All must work together on a general plan towards our end—the defeat of the enemy forces.

In accordance with this governing consideration, co-operation with artillery, photography and reconnaissance have been greatly developed and actively continued. Air fighting has taken place on an ever-increasing scale in order to enable the machines engaged upon these tasks to carry out their work. In addition, a definite aerial offensive, in which long-distance raiding has taken a prominent place, has become a recognised part of the preparations for infantry attack.

Throughout the progress of the battle itself low-flying aeroplanes not only maintain contact with our advancing infantry, reporting their position and signalling the earliest indications of hostile counter-attack, but themselves join directly in the attack by engaging the enemy's infantry in line and in support with machine gun fire and bombs, by assisting our artillery to disperse hostile concentrations, and by spreading confusion among the enemy's transport, reinforcements and batteries.

In answer to the concentrations of hostile machines on our front and the strenuous efforts made by the enemy to reassert himself in the air, the bombing of German aerodromes has been intensified, and has been carried out at great distances behind the enemy's lines. In more than one instance the enemy has been compelled to abandon particular aerodromes altogether as the result of our constant raids.

Besides his aerodromes, the enemy's railway stations and communications, his dumps and billets, have also been attacked with increasing frequency and with most successful results.

The persistent raiding by hostile aeroplanes and airships of English cities and towns, and the enemy's open disregard of the losses thereby caused to civilian life and property, have recently decided our own Government to adopt counter-measures. In consequence of this decision a series of bombing raids into Germany were commenced in October, 1917, and have since been continued whenever weather conditions have permitted.

In the discharge of duties constantly increasing in number and importance, the Royal Flying Corps throughout the whole of the past year has shown the same magnificent offensive spirit which characterised its work during the Somme Battle, combined with unsurpassed technical knowledge and practical skill.

The enemy, however, shows no sign of relaxing his endeavours in this department of war. While acknowledging, therefore, most fully the great effort that has been made to meet the ever-increasing

THE CAMPAIGNS OF 1917

demands of this most important service, I feel it my duty to point out once more that the position which has been won by the skill, courage and devotion of our pilots can only be maintained by a liberal supply of the most efficient machines.

Before passing from the artillery and air services I wish to refer to the increasingly efficient work of the Anti-Aircraft and Searchlight Sections in France. The growing activity of the enemy's bombing squadrons has thrown a corresponding strain on these units. They have responded to the call with considerable success, and the frequency with which hostile aircraft are brought down by our ground defences shows a satisfactory tendency to increase.

Cavalry

During the first days of the Battle of Arras the depth of our advance enabled a limited use to be made of bodies of mounted troops. The cavalry showed much promptness and resource in utilising such opportunities as were offered them, and at Monchy-le-Preux, in particular, performed most valuable service in support of and in co-operation with the infantry.

Special Services

The gradual development of modern warfare during the past year has shown a very definite tendency to emphasise the importance of the various Special Services, while at the same time bringing their employment into closer co-ordination with the work of the principal arms.

Tanks

Although throughout the major part of the Ypres Battle, and especially in its latter stages, the condition of the ground made the use of tanks difficult or impossible, yet whenever circumstances were in any way favourable, and even when they were not, very gallant and valuable work has been accomplished by tank commanders and crews on a great number of occasions. Long before the conclusion of the Flanders offensive these new instruments had proved their worth and amply justified the labour, material and personnel diverted to their construction and development.

In the course of the various operations in which tanks have taken part, at Arras, Messines and Ypres, officers and men have given frequent examples of high and self-sacrificing courage as well as strong esprit-de-corps.

Trench Mortars

Trench mortars have continued to play an important part in supplementing the work of our artillery in trench warfare, and have also been used most effectively in the preliminary stages of our offensives. The personnel concerned have shown great skill and enterprise in obtaining the best results from the various types of mortars.

Machine Gun Corps

During the past year the use of the machine gun in offensive warfare has been considerably extended. The machine gun barrage has taken a definite place with the artillery barrage in covering the advance of our infantry, while the lighter forms of machine guns have proved of great assistance in the capture of hostile strong points. In these directions, as well as in the repulse of hostile counter-attacks, great boldness and skill have been shown, and very valuable work has been done by all ranks of the Machine Gun Corps.

Royal Engineers

The prolonged period of active fighting and the vast amount of work involved by our different offensives have thrown a peculiarly heavy burden on the Royal Engineers, both preparatory to and during operations.

The Field, Signal, Army Troops and Tramway Companies, together with Pioneer and Labour Battalions, from home and overseas, have played an increasingly important part, not only in the preparation for our offensives, but also during the latter stages of the battles. The courage and enduring self-sacrifice displayed by all ranks, whether in the organisation of captured positions or in the maintenance of forward communications under heavy shell fire, are deserving of the highest praise.

The Tunnelling Companies have maintained their superiority over the enemy underground, and the important tactical success achieved by the Messines mines is a sufficient testimony of their untiring efforts. They have taken a large share in the construction of dug-outs and road-making during operations, and have worked with great courage and cheerfulness under conditions of much hardship and danger.

The successful manner in which the difficult problem of water supply during operations was overcome reflects great credit upon the Royal Engineers. My thanks are also due to the War Office Staff concerned, and the manufacturers and their employees, for the special efforts made by them to meet the demands of the Army in respect of the necessary machinery and plant.

The other Engineer units, both in forward areas and on the lines of communication, have discharged their various special duties with an equal skill and perseverance. The increased demand for accom-

THE CAMPAIGNS OF 1917   141

modation, hospitals and workshops [1] on the lines of communication has been met with commendable promptitude, and the supply of Engineer stores and materials, now required in vast quantities, has throughout been most efficiently maintained. A notable feature also is the progress which has been made in the devices for the concealment of troops and material.

Signal Services

The Signal Service, which at the end of the battle of the Somme had already grown into a great and intricate organisation, has had even larger demands made upon it during the past year.

Apart from the perfecting and maintenance of rear communications, special provision has had to be made for carrying our communications forward as our troops have advanced. The measures adopted to this end have been skilfully devised and admirably carried out. In many cases within a few hours of a successful operation large numbers of buried telephone circuits have been extended into the captured zone under very trying conditions; the provision of communications for artillery Forward Observation Officers, etc., proceeding simultaneously with the organisation of the new line. Thanks to the rapidity with which communications in the forward areas have been established, information of hostile concentrations has frequently been transmitted by their means from the front in time to enable the artillery to break up impending counter-attacks.

The success which has attended the establishment of these forward communications has been largely due to the untiring energy and devotion to duty of the officers and men of the numerous small Signal Sections and Detachments. On them has devolved, in circumstances of great difficulty and danger, the execution of the complicated schemes of communication necessitated by the present form of warfare.

The Carrier Pigeon Service has also been greatly developed during the present year, and has proved extremely valuable for conveying information from attacking units to the headquarters of their formations.

Gas Services

Reference has been made earlier in this Despatch to the valuable services rendered by the Special Brigade, both on the defensive fronts and in the battle areas where large quantities of gas were

[1] The development of the German submarine campaign in this year led to a vigorous and successful attempt to make the British Armies in France self-supporting in all possible respects. The great increase in hospitals, workshops, etc., was due to this cause, as was largely the expansion of Forestry and Quarry services in France (see below).

successfully discharged in preparation for our different offensives. These special troops have taken an active part also in our feint attacks and in the various measures taken to harass German divisions sent by the enemy to recuperate on the quieter portions of his front. Gas discharges have become matters of almost nightly occurrence, and have been carried out with success on all portions of the front from the right of our line to the sea. In the period covered by this Despatch a total weight of nearly 2,000 tons of gas has been liberated in the course of 335 separate discharges.

Numerous new methods and devices have been put into practice with excellent results. Many of these have entailed very heavy work and great courage and devotion on the part of the personnel employed; but all demands have been met with unfailing cheerfulness and carried out with the greatest efficiency. Evidence of the serious casualties inflicted on the enemy by gas and kindred methods of offence continues to accumulate.

Field Survey Companies

Special mention again deserves to be made of the Field Survey Companies, who throughout the year's operations have carried out their important functions with the utmost zeal and efficiency. With the assistance of the Ordnance Survey they have enabled an adequate supply of maps to be maintained in spite of the constant changes of the battle front. Their assistance has also been invaluable to our artillery in locating the enemy's new battery positions during the actual progress of battle.

Meteorological Section

The Meteorological Section has kept me furnished with valuable information concerning the probable course of the weather, in spite of the limited area from which the necessary data are now procurable.

Transportation Services

In describing the preparations for our offensive, constant reference has been made in the body of this Despatch to the work of the Transportation Services. The year has been one of rapid expansion in all branches of the various Transportation Services, and the manner in which the calls made upon them have been met is deserving of the highest praise.

During the present year the dock capacity allotted to the British Armies in France has been thoroughly organised, and its equipment, efficiency of working and capacity greatly improved. In the first nine months of this year the number of working cranes was more

THE CAMPAIGNS OF 1917

than doubled, and during the year the discharging capacity of the docks has proved equal to the maximum import requirements. The rate of discharge of vessels has been accelerated by 100 per cent., and the weekly average of ship-days lost has been reduced to nearly one-fifth of its January figures.

As regards railway expansion, the number of imported broad gauge locomotives in traffic in France in October, 1917, was nearly ten times as great as at the end of 1916. The number of imported broad gauge waggons in traffic shows a corresponding growth, and the necessary erecting and repairing shops for this increased rolling stock have been provided and equipped. Many hundred miles of broad gauge track have been laid, also, both in immediate connection with our offensives and for the general service of our Armies.

The result of these different measures has naturally had a most marked effect upon the traffic-carrying capacity of the broad gauge railway system as a whole. The average number of trains run daily during October, 1917, showed an increase of nearly 50 per cent. on the daily average for March.

Light railways have grown with a like rapidity, and the track operated at the end of October was already eight times as great as that working at the commencement of the year. During the same period the plant used in the making and upkeep of roads has been multiplied nearly seven times, rendering possible a very considerable improvement in the conditions of road transport. At the same time, the possibilities of Inland Water Transport have been further developed, resulting in October, 1917, in an increase of 50 per cent. in the weekly traffic handled, as compared with the figures for January, 1917.

Forestry and Quarry Units

In the spring of 1917 the activities of the Army were extended by the formation of a Forestry Directorate, controlling Royal Engineer and Canadian Forestry Companies, to work certain forest areas in France and provide material for the use of our own and the French Armies. Quarry companies have also been formed in immediate connection with the Transportation Services.

Some idea of the magnitude of the work involved can be gained from the fact that from quarries worked in a single locality [1] over 600,000 tons of material were produced in the nine months ending 31st August, 1917. Between March and October of this year the total weekly output of road metal received in the Army areas has nearly doubled. The average area of new and re-made roads completed weekly during October was seven and a half times greater than the weekly average for March.

[1] The Marquise Quarries.

By September, 1917, the Army had become practically self-supporting as far as regards timber, and during the active period of working, from May to October, over three-quarters of a million tons of timber were supplied for the use of the British Army. Included in this timber was material sufficient to construct over 350 miles of plank roads and to provide sleepers for 1,500 miles of railway, besides great quantities of sawn timber for hutting and defences and many thousand tons of round timber for fascines and fuel. The bulk of the fuel wood is being obtained from woods already devastated by artillery fire.

These Forestry and Quarry units have proved of great value, and have been the source of very considerable economy. My special thanks are due to the French Forestry authorities, as well as to the Comité inter-Allié des Bois de Guerre, for their assistance in our negotiations regarding the acquisition of woods and forest areas.

Army Service Corps

The long period of active fighting, combined with the magnitude of our operations, has once more placed a heavy strain upon the personnel of the Army Service Corps and of the Administrative Services and Departments generally. The difficulties of supply have been increased by the unavoidable congestion of the areas in which operations were taking place, as well as by the inevitable deterioration of roads and by long-distance shelling and bombing by the enemy.

In spite of all difficulties the Army Service Corps has never failed to meet the needs of our troops in food, ammunition, material and stores of all kinds. Particularly good work has been done by the Motor Transport drivers, who have shown the greatest gallantry and devotion to duty in getting forward the requisites of the Army under heavy shell fire and during long hours of exposure.

Ordnance Corps

The energy and zeal of the Ordnance Corps have also been admirable. The intensity of our artillery preparations and bombardments has placed the heaviest demands upon the Ordnance workshops in the repair and the overhauling of guns of all calibres. Work has been continued by day and night in order to keep our guns in action, and the unsparing efforts of officers and men have contributed in no small degree to the success of our operations.

Medical Services

The work of the Medical Service in all its branches has continued to afford me most valuable assistance. The high standard of efficiency displayed by all ranks of the Medical Service has resulted in an almost entire freedom from epidemic disease, and has been the cause of much saving of life and limb amongst the wounded.

The devotion and gallantry of the Royal Army Medical Corps and of the Medical Corps of the Overseas Dominions during the recent operations have earned universal admiration and praise. Their work of collecting the wounded from the front has been of an exceptionally arduous nature, owing to the condition of the ground and weather. I regret that so many gallant officers and men have lost their lives in carrying out their duties.

The Medical Service of the United States of America has shared in the work of the British Medical Service, and has given very valuable help.

I am much indebted to the devotion and work of the consulting surgeons and physicians and to the Auxiliary Services of the British Red Cross Society and Order of St. John of Jerusalem.

The Nursing services, several of whose members have unfortunately lost their lives from hostile air raids, have, as always, devoted themselves with untiring care and zeal to their work of mercy.

The excellent organisation and administrative work of the Medical Services as a whole have given me entire satisfaction.

Veterinary Corps

The work of the Army Veterinary Corps and of the Mobile Veterinary Sections has been ably carried out, and has contributed largely to the general efficiency of the Army.

The Chaplains' Department

I take this opportunity to express, on behalf of all ranks of the British Armies in France, our great appreciation of the devotion and self-sacrifice of the Army Chaplains serving in France. No considerations of personal convenience or safety have at any time interfered with their work among the troops, the value of which is incalculable.

Army Commanders

My thanks are again due to the Army Commanders for the complete loyalty and conspicuous ability with which they have carried out my plans during the past year. The task of launching three great offensives on different sectors of the British front, in addition to the almost constant fighting that has taken place in the neighbourhood of Lens, has demanded professional knowledge, determination and soundness of judgment of a very high order on the part of the

Commanders of the Armies concerned. It required, moreover, the most willing and unselfish co-operation between Armies, and an absolute subservience of all personal interests to the common good.

In all these respects the different Army Commanders have most completely fulfilled the high standard of character and ability required of them.

Staff

In the heavy and responsible work which they have so admirably performed, the Army Commanders have been most loyally supported and assisted by their Staff Officers and Technical Advisers, as well as by the Commanders and Staffs of the units serving under them.

My Chief of the General Staff, Lieut.-General Sir L. E. Kiggell, my Adjutant-General, Lieut.-General Sir G. H. Fowke, and my Quartermaster-General, Lieut.-General Sir R. C. Maxwell, as well as the other officers of my Staff and my Technical Advisers at General Headquarters and on the Lines of Communication, have given me the greatest and most valuable assistance. I am glad once more to place on record the debt that I owe to them.

The entire absence of friction or discord which characterised the work of all Services and Departments during the Somme Battle has constituted a most pleasing feature of the operations of the past year. There could be no better evidence of the singleness of purpose and determination of the Armies as a whole, and no stronger guarantee of victory.

The Army's Acknowledgments

To the Navy.

64. The debt which the Army owes to the Navy grows ever greater as the years pass, and is deeply realised by all ranks of the British Armies in France. As the result of the unceasing vigilance of the Navy, the enemy's hope that his policy of unrestricted submarine warfare would hamper our operations in France and Flanders has been most signally disappointed. The immense quantities of ammunition and material required by the Army, and the large numbers of men sent to us as drafts, continue to reach us with unfailing regularity.

To Home Authorities.

In this connection, I desire once more to record the obligation of the Army in the Field to the different authorities at home, both civil and military, and to the great mass of men and women in Great

THE CAMPAIGNS OF 1917

Britain and throughout the Empire who are working with such loyalty to enable our manifold requirements to be met.

The confidence which is felt throughout the Army that the enemy can and will be beaten is founded on the firm conviction that their own efforts in the field will be supported to the limits of their power and resources by all classes at home.

To our Allies.

At the close of another year of fighting in France and Belgium, it is a source of great gratification to me to be able to record that nothing has occurred to mar the happy relations existing between the Allied Armies, or between our troops and the civil population in France and Belgium.

The feelings of good will and comradeship which existed between the French and British Armies on the Somme have been continued in Flanders, where the same excellent relations have characterised the combined operations of the Belgian, French and British troops.

During the present year the Portuguese Expeditionary Force has taken its place in the line, and for many months has held a sector of the British front. Though they have not been engaged in major offensive operations, yet in a number of raids and minor engagements the officers and men of the Portuguese Expeditionary Force have shown themselves gallant and efficient soldiers.

During the present year, also, the United States of America have entered the war, and have taken up their part in it with all the well-known energy and ability of that great nation. Already many thousands of American soldiers are in France. Warm as is the welcome they have received from the French people, nowhere will they find a more genuine or a more friendly greeting than among all ranks of the other great English-speaking Armies.

> I have the honour to be,
> My Lord,
> Your Lordship's obedient Servant,
> D. HAIG, Field-Marshal,
> Commanding-in-Chief, British Armies in France.

THE CAMBRAI OPERATIONS

THE CAMBRAI OPERATIONS

General Headquarters,
British Armies in the Field,
20th February, 1918.[1]

MY LORD,—

I have the honour to submit the following Report on the operations on the Cambrai front during November and December, 1917.

General Plan

1. As pointed out in my last Despatch, the object of these operations was to gain a local success by a sudden attack at a point where the enemy did not expect it. Our repeated attacks in Flanders and those of our Allies elsewhere had brought about large concentrations of the enemy's forces on the threatened fronts, with a consequent reduction in the garrisons of certain other sectors of his line.

Of these weakened sectors the Cambrai front had been selected as the most suitable for the surprise operation in contemplation. The ground there was, on the whole, favourable for the employment of tanks which were to play an important part in the enterprise, and facilities existed for the concealment of the necessary preparations for the attack.

If, after breaking through the German defence systems on this front, we could secure Bourlon to the north and establish a good flank position to the east, in the direction of Cambrai, we should be well placed to exploit the situation locally between Bourlon and the Sensée River and to the north-west. The capture of Cambrai itself was subsidiary to this operation, the object of our advance towards that town being primarily to cover our flank and puzzle the enemy regarding our intentions.

The enemy was laying out fresh lines of defence behind those which he had already completed on the Cambrai front; and it was to be expected that his troops would be redistributed as soon as our pressure in Flanders was relaxed. He had already brought large forces from Russia in exchange for divisions exhausted in the struggle in the Western theatre, and it was practically certain that heavy reinforcements would be brought from East to West during

[1] This Despatch was published as a Supplement dated the 4th March to the *London Gazette* of the 1st March, 1918.

the winter. Moreover his tired divisions, after a winter's rest, would recover their efficiency.

For all these reasons, if the existing opportunity for a surprise attack were allowed to lapse, it would probably be many months before an equally favourable one would again offer itself. Furthermore, having regard to the future, it was desirable to show the enemy that he could not with impunity reduce his garrisons beyond a certain point without incurring grave risks.

Against these arguments in favour of immediate action I had to weigh the fact that my own troops had been engaged for many months in heavy fighting, and that, though their efforts had been uniformly successful, the conditions of the struggle had greatly taxed their strength. Only part of the losses in my divisions had been replaced, and many recently arrived drafts, still far from being fully trained, were included in the ranks of the Armies. Under these conditions it was a serious matter to make a further heavy call on my troops at the end of such a strenuous year.

On the other hand, from the nature of the operation, the size of the force which could be employed was bound, in any case, to be comparatively small, since success depended so much on secrecy, and it is impossible to keep secret the concentration of very large forces. The demand made upon my resources, therefore, should not be a great one.

While considering these different factors, preparations were quietly carried on, so that all might be ready for the attack if I found it possible to carry it out. The success of the enemy's offensive in Italy[1] subsequently added great force to the arguments in favour of undertaking the operation, although the means at my disposal for the purpose were further reduced as a consequence of the Italian situation.

Eventually I decided that, despite the various limiting factors, I could muster enough force to make a first success sufficiently sure to justify undertaking the attack, but that the degree to which this success could be followed up must depend on circumstances.

It was calculated that, provided secrecy could be maintained to the last moment, no large hostile reinforcements were likely to reach the scene of action for forty-eight hours after the commencement of the attack. I informed General Sir Julian Byng, to whom the execution of the plans in connection with the Cambrai operations was entrusted, that the advance would be stopped by me after that time, or sooner if necessary, unless the results then gained and the general situation justified its continuance.

The general plan of attack was to dispense with previous

---

[1] The Austro-German attack on the Isonzo front was launched on the 24th October. By the 10th November the Italians had fallen back to the line of the Piave.

THE CAMBRAI OPERATIONS

artillery preparation, and to depend instead on tanks to smash through the enemy's wire, of which there was a great quantity protecting his trenches.

As soon as the advance of the tanks and infantry, working in close co-operation, began, the artillery was to assist with counter-battery and barrage work; but no previous registration of guns for this purpose could be permitted, as it would rouse the enemy's suspicions. The artillery of our new Armies was therefore necessarily subjected to a severe test in this operation, and proved itself entirely worthy of the confidence placed in it.

The infantry, tanks and artillery thus working in combination were to endeavour to break through all the enemy's lines of defence on the first day. If this were successfully accomplished and the situation developed favourably, cavalry were then to be passed through to raid the enemy's communications, disorganise his system of command, damage his railways and interfere as much as possible with the arrival of his reinforcements. It was explained to all Commanders that everything depended on secrecy up to the moment of starting, and after that on bold, determined and rapid action. Unless opposition could be beaten down quickly, no great results could be looked for.

The Commander-in-Chief of the French Armies, to whom I secretly communicated my plans, most readily agreed to afford me every assistance. In addition to the steps taken by him to engage the enemy's attention elsewhere, he arranged for a strong force of French infantry and cavalry to be in a position whence they could be moved forward rapidly to take part in the exploitation of our success, if the situation should render it possible to bring them into action. On the 20th November certain of these French units were actually put in motion. The course of events, however, did not open out the required opportunity for their employment, but the French forces were held in readiness and within easy reach so long as there appeared to be any hope of it. Had the situation on the 20th November developed somewhat more favourably in certain directions, the nature of which will become apparent in the course of this report, the presence and co-operation of these French troops would have been of the greatest value.

The Enemy's Defences

2. The German defences on this front had been greatly improved and extended since the opening of our offensive in April, and comprised three main systems of resistance. (*Vide* Map No. 5.)

The first of these three trench systems, constituting part of the Hindenburg Line proper, ran in a general north-westerly direction for a distance of six miles from the Canal de l'Escaut[1] at Banteux to Havrincourt. There it turned abruptly north along the line of the Canal du Nord for a distance of four miles to Mœuvres, thus forming a pronounced salient in the German front.

In advance of the Hindenburg Line the enemy had constructed a series of strong forward positions, including La Vacquerie and the north-eastern corner of Havrincourt Wood. Behind it, and at distances respectively varying from a little less to rather more than a mile, and from three-and-a-half to four-and-a-half miles, lay the second and third main German systems, known as the Hindenburg Reserve Line, and the Beaurevoir, Masnières, Marquion Lines.

The Attack

3. All necessary preparations were completed in time, and with a secrecy reflecting the greatest credit on all concerned. At 6.20 a.m. on the 20th November, without any previous artillery bombardment, tanks and infantry attacked on a front of about six miles from east of Gonnelieu to the Canal du Nord opposite Hermies.

At the same hour, demonstrations with gas, smoke and artillery took place on practically the whole of the British front south of the Scarpe, and subsidiary attacks were launched east of Epéhy and between Bullecourt and Fontaine-lez-Croisilles.

On the principal front of attack, the tanks moved forward in advance of the infantry, crushing down the enemy's wire and forming great lanes through which our infantry could pass. Protected by smoke barrages from the view of the enemy's artillery, they rolled on across the German trenches, smashing up the enemy's machine guns and driving his infantry to ground. Close behind our tanks our own infantry followed and, while the tanks patrolled the line of hostile trenches, cleared the German infantry from their dug-outs and shelters.

In this way, both the main system of the Hindenburg Line and its outer defences were rapidly over-run, and tanks and infantry proceeded in accordance with programme to the attack upon the Hindenburg Reserve Line.

In this advance, the 12th (Eastern) Division[2] (Major-General A. B.

[1] The Scheldt Canal.
[2] This was the first occasion on which the full descriptions of divisions taking part in operations were mentioned in the Despatches sent from France. The change of practice, however, did not indicate a change of policy. During the winter of 1917-1918 divisions were reduced from a 13 battalion to a 10 battalion basis and our Order of Battle was altered in the process. The mentioning of units by name in this Despatch did not, therefore, give the enemy information of any value. In the following Despatch, describing the great German attacks of March and April, the identifications obtained by the enemy in his advance made secrecy impossible. In the Victory Despatch secrecy was unnecessary.

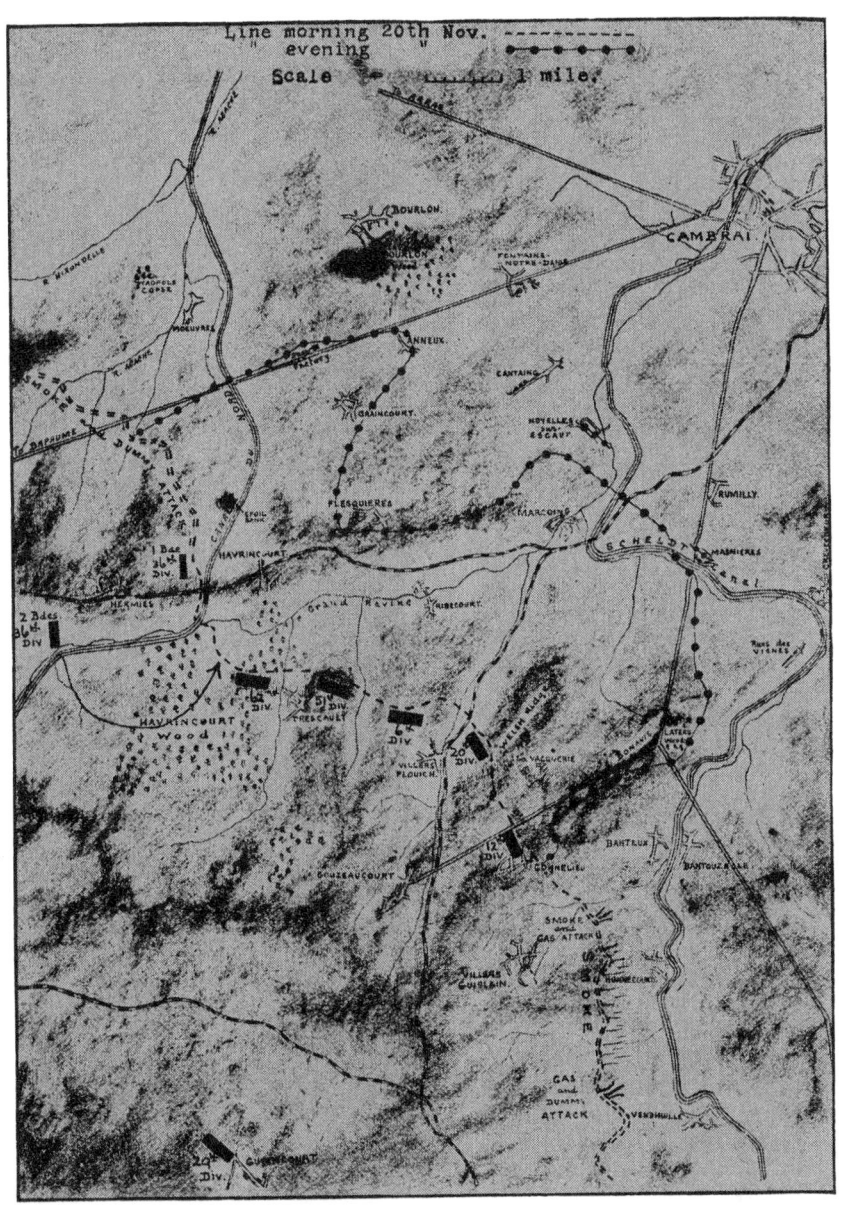

CAMBRAI BATTLE;
British Attack, 20th November, 1917.

Scott), moving along the Bonavis Ridge on the right of our attack, encountered obstinate resistance at Lateau Wood, which sheltered a number of German batteries. Fierce fighting, in which infantry and tank crews displayed the greatest gallantry, continued throughout the morning at this point, and ended in the capture of the position, together with the enemy's guns.

Meanwhile, the 20th (Light) Division (Major-General W. D. Smith), which had captured La Vacquerie at the opening of its attack, stormed the powerful defences of Welsh Ridge. The 6th Division (Major-General T. O. Marden) carried the village of Ribécourt, after sharp fighting among the streets and houses, while the 62nd (West Riding) Division (T.) (Major-General W. P. Braithwaite) stormed Havrincourt, where also parties of the enemy held out for a time.

The capture of these two villages secured the flanks of the 51st (Highland) Division (T.) (Major-General G. M. Harper), advancing on the left centre of our attack up the slopes of Flesquières Hill against the German trench lines on the southern side of Flesquières Village. Here very heavy fighting took place. The stout brick wall skirting the Château grounds opposed a formidable obstacle to our advance, while German machine guns swept the approaches. A number of tanks were knocked out by direct hits from German field batteries in position beyond the crest of the hill. None the less, with the exception of the village itself, our second objectives in this area were gained before midday.

Many of the hits upon our tanks at Flesquières were obtained by a German artillery officer who, remaining alone at his battery, served a field gun single-handed until killed at his gun. The great bravery of this officer aroused the admiration of all ranks.[1]

On the left of our attack west of the Canal du Nord, the 36th (Ulster) Division (Major-General O. S. W. Nugent), captured a German strong point on the spoil bank of the canal and pushed northwards in touch with the West Riding troops, who, as the first stage in a most gallant and remarkably successful advance, had taken Havrincourt. By 10.30 a.m. the general advance beyond the Hindenburg Reserve Line to our final objectives had begun, and cavalry were moving up behind our infantry.

In this period of the attack tanks and British infantry battalions of the 29th Division (Major-General Sir H. de B. De Lisle) entered Masnières and captured Marcoing and Neuf Wood, securing the passages of the Canal de l'Escaut at both villages.

At Marcoing the tanks arrived at the moment when a party of the enemy were in the act of running out an electrical connection to blow up one of the bridges. This party was fired on by a tank and

[1] He was not identified.

the bridges secured intact. At Masnières, however, the retreating enemy succeeded in destroying partially the bridge carrying the main road. In consequence the first tank which endeavoured to cross at this point fell through the bridge, completing its destruction.

The advance of a number of our guns had been unavoidably delayed in the sunken roads which served this part of the battle-field, and though our infantry continued their progress beyond Masnières, without the assistance of tanks and artillery they were not able at first to clear the enemy entirely from the northern portion of the village. Here parties of Germans held out during the afternoon, and gave the enemy time to occupy Rumilly and the section of the Beaurevoir-Masnières line south of it; while the destruction of the bridge also prevented the cavalry from crossing the canal in sufficient strength to overcome his resistance.

In spite of this difficulty, a squadron of the Fort Garry Horse, Canadian Cavalry Brigade (5th Cavalry Division, Major-General H. J. M. Macandrew), succeeded during the afternoon in crossing the canal by a temporary bridge constructed during the day. This squadron passed through the Beaurevoir-Masnières line and charged and captured a German battery in position to the east of it. Continuing its advance, it dispersed a body of about 300 German infantry, and did not cease its progress until the greater part of its horses had been killed or wounded. The squadron thereupon took up a position in a sunken road, where it maintained itself until night fell. It then withdrew to our lines, bringing with it several prisoners taken in the course of a most gallant exploit.

Meanwhile, west of the Canal de l'Escaut patrols of the 6th Division during the afternoon entered Noyelles-sur-l'Escaut, where they were reinforced by cavalry, and other cavalry units pushed out towards Cantaing. West of Flesquières, the 62nd Division, operating northwards from Havrincourt, made important progress. Having carried the Hindenburg Reserve Line north of that village, it rapidly continued its attack and captured Graincourt, where two anti-tank guns were destroyed by the tanks accompanying our infantry. Before nightfall infantry and cavalry had entered Anneux, though the enemy's resistance in this village does not appear to have been entirely overcome until the following morning.

This attack of the 62nd (West Riding) Division constitutes a brilliant achievement, in which the troops concerned completed an advance of four and a half miles from their original front, overrunning two German systems of defence and gaining possession of three villages.

On the left flank of our attack Ulster battalions pushed northwards along the Hindenburg Line and its forward defences, maintaining touch with the West Riding troops, and carried the whole of the German trench systems west of the Canal du Nord as far north as the Bapaume-Cambrai Road.

At the end of the first day of the attack, therefore, three German systems of defence had been broken through to a depth of some four and a half miles on a wide front, and over 5,000 prisoners had already been brought in. But for the wrecking of the bridge at Masnières and the check at Flesquières, still greater results might have been attained.

Throughout these operations the value of the services rendered by the tanks was very great, and the utmost gallantry, enterprise and resolution were displayed by both officers and crews. In combination with the other arms they helped to make possible a remarkable success. Without their aid in opening a way through the German wire, success could only have been attained by methods which would have given the enemy ample warning of our attack, and have allowed him time to mass troops to oppose it. As has been pointed out above, to enable me to undertake such an operation with the troops at my disposal, secrecy to the last moment was essential. The tanks alone made it possible to dispense with artillery preparation, and so to conceal our intentions from the enemy up to the actual moment of attack.

Great credit is due also to the Royal Flying Corps for very gallant and most valuable work carried out under conditions of the greatest difficulty from low clouds and driving mist.

In the subsidiary attack at Bullecourt battalions of the 3rd Division (Major-General C. J. Deverell) and the 16th (Irish) Division (Major-General W. B. Hickie) successfully completed the work begun by our operations in this area in May and June, 1917, capturing the remainder of the Hindenburg support trench on their front, with some 700 prisoners. A number of counter-attacks against our new positions at Bullecourt on this and the following day were repulsed, with great loss to the enemy.

The Advance Continued

4. On the morning of the 21st November the attack on Flesquières was resumed, and by 8.0 a.m. the village had been turned from the north-west and captured. The obstacle which more than anything else had limited the results of the 20th November was thereby removed, and later in the morning the advance once more became general.

Masnières had been cleared of the enemy during the previous evening, and at 11.0 a.m. our troops attacked the Beaurevoir-Masnières line and established themselves in the portion to the east and north of Masnières. Heavy fighting took place, and a counter-attack from the direction of Rumilly was beaten off. At the same hour we attacked and captured Les Rues des Vignes, but later in the morning the enemy counter-attacked and compelled our troops to fall back from this position. Progress was also made towards Crèvecœur; but though the canal was crossed during the afternoon, it was found impossible to force the passage of the river in face of the enemy's machine gun fire.

That evening orders were issued by the Third Army to secure the ground already gained in this area of the battle, and to capture Rumilly on the morrow; but in consequence of the exhaustion of the troops engaged it was found necessary later in the night to cancel the orders for this attack.

West of the Canal de l'Escaut infantry of the 29th Division and dismounted regiments of the 1st and 5th Cavalry Divisions,[1] including the Ambala Brigade, were heavily engaged throughout the day in Noyelles, and beat off all attacks in continuous fighting.

Following upon the capture of Flesquières, the 51st and 62nd Divisions, in co-operation with a number of tanks and squadrons of the 1st Cavalry Division, attacked at 10.30 a.m. in the direction of Fontaine-notre-Dame and Bourlon.

In this attack the capture of Anneux was completed, and early in the afternoon Cantaing was seized, with some hundreds of prisoners. Progress was made on the outskirts of Bourlon Wood, and late in the afternoon Fontaine-notre-Dame was taken by troops of the 51st Division and tanks. The attack on Bourlon Wood itself was checked by machine gun fire, though tanks advanced some distance into the wood.

Farther west, the 36th Division advanced north of the Bapaume-Cambrai Road, and reached the southern outskirts of Mœuvres, where strong opposition was encountered.

The Position on the 21st November

5. On the evening of the second day of the attack, therefore, our troops held a line which ran approximately as follows :—

From our old front line east of Gonnelieu the right flank of our new positions lay along the eastern slopes of the Bonavis Ridge, passing east of Lateau Wood and striking the Masnières-Beaurevoir line north of the Canal de l'Escaut at a point about half way between Crèvecœur and Masnières. From this point our line ran roughly north-west, past and including Masnières, Noyelles and Cantaing, to Fontaine, also inclusive. Thence it bent back to the south for a short distance, making a sharp salient round the latter village, and ran in a general westerly direction along the southern edge of Bourlon Wood and across the southern face of the spur to the west of the

---

[1] Major-General R. L. Mullens commanding the 1st Cavalry Division.

THE CAMBRAI OPERATIONS

wood, to the Canal du Nord, south-east of the village of Mœuvres. From Mœuvres the line linked up once more with our old front at a point about midway between Boursies and Pronville.

The forty-eight hours after which it had been calculated that the enemy's reserves would begin to arrive had in effect expired, and the high ground at Bourlon Village and Wood, as well as certain important tactical features to the east and west of the wood, still remained in the enemy's possession. It now became necessary to decide whether to continue the operation offensively or to take up a defensive attitude and rest content with what had been attained.

The Decision to Go On

6. It was not possible, however, to let matters stand as they were. The positions captured by us north of Flesquières were completely commanded by the Bourlon Ridge, and unless this ridge were gained it would be impossible to hold them, except at excessive cost. If I decided not to go on, a withdrawal to the Flesquières Ridge would be necessary and would have to be carried out at once.

On the other hand, the enemy showed certain signs of an intention to withdraw. Craters had been formed at road junctions, and troops could be seen ready to move east. The possession of Bourlon Ridge would enable our troops to obtain observation over the ground to the north, which sloped gently down to the Sensée River. The enemy's defensive lines south of the Scarpe and Sensée Rivers would thereby be turned, his communications exposed to the observed fire of our artillery, and his positions in this sector jeopardised. In short, so great was the importance of the ridge to the enemy that its loss would probably cause the abandonment by the Germans of their carefully prepared defence systems for a considerable distance to the north of it.

The successive days of constant marching and fighting had placed a very severe strain upon the endurance of the troops, and, before a further advance could be undertaken, some time would have to be spent in resting and relieving them. This need for delay was regrettable, as the enemy's forces were increasing, and fresh German divisions were known to be arriving, but, with the limited number of troops at my command, it was unavoidable.

It was to be remembered, however, that the hostile reinforcements coming up at this stage could at first be no more than enough to replace the enemy's losses; and although the right of our advance had definitely been stayed, the enemy had not yet developed such strength about Bourlon as it seemed might not be overcome by the numbers at my disposal. As has already been pointed out, on the

Cambrai side of the battlefield I had only aimed at securing a defensive flank to enable the advance to be pushed northwards and north-westwards, and this part of my task had been to a large extent achieved.

An additional and very important argument in favour of proceeding with my attack was supplied by the situation in Italy, upon which a continuance of pressure on the Cambrai front might reasonably be expected to exercise an important effect, no matter what measure of success attended my efforts. Moreover, two divisions previously under orders for Italy had on this day been placed at my disposal, and with this accession of strength the prospect of securing Bourlon seemed good.

After weighing these various considerations, therefore, I decided to continue the operations to gain the Bourlon position.

The 22nd November was spent in organising the captured ground, in carrying out certain reliefs, and in giving other troops the rest they greatly needed. Soon after midday the enemy regained Fontaine-notre-Dame; but, with our troops already on the outskirts of Bourlon Wood and Cantaing held by us, it was thought that the recapture of Fontaine should not prove very difficult. The necessary arrangements for renewing the attack were therefore pushed on, and our plans were extended to include the recapture of Fontaine-notre-Dame.

Meanwhile, early in the night of the 22nd November, a battalion of the Queen's Westminsters (56th Division, Major-General F. A. Dudgeon) stormed a commanding tactical point in the Hindenburg Line west of Mœuvres known as Tadpole Copse, the possession of which would be of value in connection with the left flank of the Bourlon position when the latter had been secured.

The Struggle for Bourlon Wood

7. On the morning of the 23rd November the 51st Division, supported by tanks, attacked Fontaine-notre-Dame, but was unable to force an entrance. Early in the afternoon this division repeated its attack from the west, and a number of tanks entered Fontaine, where they remained till dusk, inflicting considerable loss on the enemy. We did not succeed, however, in clearing the village, and at the end of the day no progress had been made on this part of our front.

At 10.30 a.m. the 40th Division (Major-General J. Ponsonby) attacked Bourlon Wood, and after four and a half hours of hard fighting, in which tanks again rendered valuable assistance to our infantry, captured the whole of the wood and entered Bourlon

Village. Here hostile counter-attacks prevented our further progress, and though the village was at one time reported to have been taken by us, this proved later to be erroneous. A heavy hostile attack upon our positions in the wood, in which all three battalions of the 9th Grenadier Regiment appear to have been employed, was completely repulsed.

Throughout this day, also, the 36th Division and troops of the 56th (London) Division (T.) were engaged in stubborn fighting in the neighbourhood of Mœuvres and Tadpole Copse, and made some progress.

This struggle for Bourlon resulted in several days of fiercely contested fighting, in which English, Scottish, Welsh and Irish battalions, together with dismounted cavalry, performed most gallant service and inflicted heavy loss on the enemy.

During the morning of the 24th November the enemy twice attacked, and at his second attempt pressed back our troops in the north-eastern corner of the wood. An immediate counter-attack delivered by the 14th Battalion, Argyll and Sutherland Highlanders, the 15th Hussars, dismounted, and the remnants of the 119th Infantry Brigade (40th Division and 1st Cavalry Division), drove back the enemy in turn, and by noon our line had been re-established. Meanwhile, dismounted cavalry had repulsed an attack on the high ground west of Bourlon Wood, and in the afternoon a third hostile attack upon the wood was stopped by our artillery and rifle fire.

On this afternoon our infantry again attacked Bourlon Village, and captured the whole of it. Later in the evening a fourth attack upon our positions in the wood was beaten off after fierce fighting. Further progress was made on this day in the Hindenburg Line west of Mœuvres, but the enemy's resistance in the whole of this area was very strong.

On the evening of the 25th November a fresh attack by the enemy regained Bourlon Village, though our troops offered vigorous resistance, and parties of the 13th Battalion, East Surrey Regiment (40th Division), held out in the south-east corner of the village until touch was re-established with them two days later. The continual fighting and the strength of the enemy's attacks, however, had told heavily on the 40th Division, which had borne the brunt of the struggle. This division was accordingly withdrawn, and on the following day our troops were again pressed back slightly in the northern outskirts of Bourlon Wood.

With the enemy in possession of the shoulder of the ridge above Fontaine-notre-Dame, as well as of part of the high ground west of Bourlon Wood, our position in the wood itself was a difficult one, and much of the ground to the south of it was still exposed to the enemy's observation. It was decided, therefore, to make another effort on the 27th November to capture Fontaine-notre-Dame and Bourlon Village, and to gain possession of the whole of the Bourlon Ridge.

In this attack, in which tanks co-operated, British Guards (Major-General G. P. T. Feilding) temporarily regained possession of Fontaine-notre-Dame, taking some hundreds of prisoners, and troops of the 62nd Division once more entered Bourlon Village. Later in the morning, however, heavy counter-attacks developed in both localities, and our troops were unable to maintain the ground they had gained. During the afternoon the enemy also attacked our positions at Tadpole Copse, but was repulsed.

As the result of five days of constant fighting, therefore, we held a strong position on the Bourlon Hill and in the wood, but had not yet succeeded in gaining all the ground required for the security of this important feature. The two following days passed comparatively quietly, while the troops engaged were relieved and steps were undertaken to prepare for a deliberate attack which might give us the tactical points we sought.

Meanwhile, on other parts of the front the organisation of our new positions was proceeding as rapidly as conditions would allow. In particular, troops of the 12th Division had effected some improvement on the right flank of our advance opposite Banteux, and the 16th Division had made further progress in the Hindenburg Line north-west of Bullecourt.

At the end of November the number of prisoners taken in our operations south-west of Cambrai exceeded 10,500. We had also captured 142 guns, some 350 machine guns, and 70 trench mortars, with great quantities of ammunition, material and stores of all kinds.

THE GERMAN ATTACK

Early Warnings

8. During the last days of November increased registration of hostile artillery, the movements of troops and transport observed behind the German lines, together with other indications of a like nature, pointed to further efforts by the enemy to regain the positions we had wrested from him.

The front affected by this increased activity included that of our advance, as well as the ground to Vendhuille and beyond. The massing of the enemy's infantry, however, his obvious anxiety concerning

CAMBRAI BATTLE ;
German Attack, 30th November, 1917.

the security of his defences south of the Sensée River, the tactical importance of the high ground about Bourlon, and the fact that we were still only in partial possession of it, all pointed to the principal attack being delivered in the Bourlon sector.

Our Dispositions for Defence

9. Measures were accordingly taken, both by the Third Army and by the lower formations concerned, to prepare for eventualities. Arrangements had been made after our last attack to relieve the troops holding the Bourlon positions by such fresh divisions as were available, and when these reliefs had been satisfactorily completed, I felt confident that the defence of this sector could be considered secure.

Covering our right flank from Cantaing to the Banteux Ravine, a distance of about 16,000 yards, five British divisions were disposed, and, though these had been fighting for several days and were consequently tired, I felt confident that they would prove equal to stopping any attack the enemy could make on them.

From the Banteux Ravine southwards the divisions in line were weak and held very extended fronts. On the other hand, the line held by us in this southern sector had been in our possession for some months. Its defences were for this reason more complete and better organised than those of the ground gained by us in our attack. Moreover, the capture of the Bonavis Ridge had added to the security of our position farther south.

The reserve divisions immediately available in the area consisted of the Guards and 2nd Cavalry Divisions (Major-General W. H. Greenly commanding 2nd Cavalry Division), both of which had been engaged in the recent fighting at Fontaine and Bourlon Wood. These were located behind the La Vacquerie-Villers Guislain front, while another division, the 62nd, which had also been recently engaged, was placed farther to the north-west in the direction of the Bapaume-Cambrai Road. A fresh South Midland division (61st Division, Major-General C. J. Mackenzie) was assembling farther back, two other cavalry divisions were within two or three hours' march of the battle area, and another cavalry division but a little farther distant.

In view of the symptoms of activity observed on the enemy's front, special precautions were taken by local commanders, especially from Villers Guislain to the south. Troops were warned to expect attack, additional machine guns were placed to secure supporting points, and divisional reserves were closed up. Special patrols were also sent out to watch for signs of any hostile advance.

The Battle Reopened

10. Between the hours of 7.0 and 8.0 a.m. on the last days of November the enemy attacked, after a short but intense artillery preparation, on the greater part of a front of some ten miles from Vendhuille to Masnières inclusive. From Masnières to Banteux, both inclusive, four German divisions would seem to have been employed against the three British divisions holding this area (29th, 20th and 12th Divisions). Between Banteux exclusive and Vendhuille one German division and portions of two others were employed against the northern half of the British division holding that front (the 55th Division, Major-General H. S. Jeudwine).

On the Masnières front the 29th Division, composed of English, Scottish, Welsh, Irish, Guernsey and Newfoundland battalions, although seriously threatened as the day wore on by the progress made by the enemy farther south, where their battery positions had been taken in reverse, most gallantly beat off a succession of powerful assaults and maintained their line intact.

At the northern end of the Bonavis Ridge and in the Gonnelieu sector the swiftness with which the advance of the enemy's infantry followed the opening of his bombardment appears to have overwhelmed our troops, both in line and in immediate support, almost before they had realised that the attack had begun.

The nature of the bombardment, which seems to have been heavy enough to keep our men under cover without at first seriously alarming them, contributed to the success of the enemy's plans. No steadily advancing barrage gave warning of the approach of the German assault columns, whose secret assembly was assisted by the many deep folds and hollows typical of a chalk formation, and shielded from observation from the air by an early morning mist. Only when the attack was upon them great numbers of low-flying German aeroplanes rained machine gun fire upon our infantry, while an extensive use of smoke shell and bombs made it extremely difficult for our troops to see what was happening on other parts of the battlefield, or to follow the movements of the enemy. In short, there is little doubt that, although an attack was expected generally, yet in these areas of the battle at the moment of delivery the assault effected a local surprise.

None the less, stubborn resistance was offered during the morning by isolated parties of our troops and by machine gun detachments in the neighbourhood of Lateau Wood and south-east of La Vacquerie, as well as at other points. In more than one instance heavy losses are known to have been inflicted on the enemy by machine gun fire at short range. North-east of La Vacquerie the 92nd Field

Artillery Brigade (20th Division) repulsed four attacks, in some of which the enemy's infantry approached to within 200 yards of our guns, before the surviving gunners were finally compelled to withdraw, after removing the breech-blocks from their pieces. East of Villers Guislain the troops holding our forward positions on the high ground were still offering a strenuous resistance to the enemy's attack on their front, at a time when large forces of German infantry had already advanced up the valley between them and Villers Guislain. South of this village a single strong point known as Limerick Post, garrisoned by troops of the 1/5th Battalion (King's Own), Royal Lancaster Regiment, and the 1/10th Battalion, Liverpool Regiment (both of the 55th Division), held out with great gallantry throughout the day, though heavily attacked.

The progress made by the enemy, however, across the northern end of the Bonavis Ridge and up the deep gully between Villers Guislain and Gonnelieu, known as 22 Ravine, turned our positions on the ridge as well as in both villages. Taken in flank and rear, the defences of Villers Guislain, Gonnelieu and Bonavis were rapidly over-run. Gouzeaucourt was captured about 9.0 a.m., the outer defences of La Vacquerie were reached, and a number of guns which had been brought up close to the line, in order to enable them to cover the battle-front about Masnières and Marcoing, fell into the hands of the enemy.

At this point the enemy's advance was checked by the action of our local reserves, and meanwhile measures had been taken with all possible speed to bring up additional troops. About midday the Guards came into action west of Gouzeaucourt, while cavalry (4th and 5th Cavalry Divisions, Major-General A. A. Kennedy commanding 4th Cavalry Division) moved up to close the gap on their right and made progress towards Villers Guislain from the south and south-west.

The attack of the Guards, which was delivered with the greatest gallantry and resolution, drove the enemy out of Gouzeaucourt and made progress on the high ground known as the St. Quentin Ridge, east of the village. In this operation the Guards were materially assisted by the gallant action of a party of the 29th Division, who, with a company of North Midland Royal Engineers, held on throughout the day to a position in an old trench near Gouzeaucourt. Valuable work was also done by a brigade of field artillery of the 47th Division, which moved direct into action from the line of march.

During the afternoon three battalions of tanks, which when they received news of the attack were preparing to move away from the battlefield to refit, arrived at Gouzeaucourt and aided the infantry to hold the recaptured ground. Great credit is due to the officers and men of the Tank Brigade concerned for the speed with which they brought their tanks into action.

Meanwhile, the defence of La Vacquerie had been successfully maintained, and our line had been established to the north of that village, in touch with our troops in Masnières.

The Northern Attack

11. In the northern area, from Fontaine-notre-Dame to Tadpole Copse, the German attack was not launched until some two hours later. This was the enemy's main attack, and was carried out with large forces and great resolution.

After a heavy preliminary bombardment, and covered by an artillery barrage, the enemy's infantry advanced shortly after 9.0 a.m. in dense waves, in the manner of his attacks in the first battle of Ypres. In the course of the morning and afternoon no less than five principal attacks were made in this area, and on one portion of the attack as many as eleven waves of German infantry advanced successively to the assault. On the whole of this front a resolute endeavour was made to break down by sheer weight of numbers the defence of the London Territorials and other English battalions holding the sector.

In this fighting the 47th (London) Division (T.) (Major-General Sir G. F. Gorringe), the 2nd Division (Major-General C. E. Pereira) and the 56th (London) Division (T.) greatly distinguished themselves, and there were accomplished many deeds of great heroism.

Under the fury of the enemy's bombardment a company of the 17th Battalion, Royal Fusiliers, were in the course of being withdrawn from an exposed position in a sap-head in advance of our line between Bourlon Wood and Mœuvres when the German attack burst upon them. The officer in command sent three of his platoons back, and with a rearguard composed of the remainder of his company held off the enemy's infantry until the main position had been organised. Having faithfully accomplished their task, this rearguard died fighting to the end with their faces to the enemy.

Somewhat later in the morning an attack in force between the Canal du Nord and Mœuvres broke into our foremost positions and isolated a company of the 13th Battalion, Essex Regiment, in a trench just west of the canal. After maintaining a splendid and successful resistance throughout the day, whereby the pressure upon our main line was greatly relieved, at 4.0 p.m. this company held a council of war, at which the two remaining company officers, the company sergeant-major, and the platoon sergeants were present, and unanimously determined to fight to the last and have " no surrender."

THE CAMBRAI OPERATIONS

Two runners who were sent to notify this decision to Battalion Headquarters succeeded in getting through to our lines and delivered their message. During the remainder of the afternoon and far into the following night this gallant company were heard fighting, and there is little room for doubt that they carried out to a man their heroic resolution.

Early in the afternoon large masses of the enemy again attacked west of Bourlon Wood, and, though beaten off with great loss at most points, succeeded in overwhelming three out of a line of posts held by a company of the 1st Battalion, Royal Berks Regiment, on the right of the 2nd Division. Though repeatedly attacked by vastly superior numbers the remainder of these posts stood firm, and when, two days later, the three posts which had been overpowered were regained, such a heap of German dead lay in and around them that the bodies of our own men were hidden.

All accounts go to show that the enemy's losses in the whole of his constantly repeated attacks on this sector of the battle front were enormous. One battery of eight machine guns fired 70,000 rounds of ammunition into ten successive waves of Germans. Long lines of attacking infantry were caught by our machine gun fire in enfilade, and were shot down in line as they advanced. Great execution also was done by our field artillery, and in the course of the battle guns were brought up to the crest line and fired direct upon the enemy at short range.

At one point west of Bourlon the momentum of his first advance carried the enemy through our front line and a short way down the southern slopes of the ridge. There, however, the German masses came under direct fire from our field artillery at short range and were broken up. Our local reserves at once counter-attacked, and succeeded in closing the gap that had been made in our line. Early in the afternoon the enemy again forced his way into our foremost positions in this locality, opening a gap between the 1/6th Battalion and the 1/15th Battalion, London Regiments. Counter-attacks, led by the two battalion commanders, with all available men, including the personnel of their headquarters, once more restored the situation. All other attacks were beaten off with the heaviest losses to the enemy.

The greatest credit is due to the troops at Masnières, Bourlon and Mœuvres for the very gallant service performed by them on this day. But for their steady courage and staunchness in defence, the success gained by the enemy on the right of our battle front might have had serious consequences.

I cannot close the account of this day's fighting without recording my obligation to the Commander-in-Chief of the French Armies for the prompt way in which he placed French troops within reach for employment in case of need at the unfettered discretion of the Third Army Commander. Part of the artillery of this force actually came into action, rendering valuable service, and though the remainder of the troops were not called upon, the knowledge that they were available should occasion arise was a great assistance.

The Fighting at Gonnelieu and Masnières

12. On the 1st December fighting continued fiercely on the whole front.

The Guards completed the capture of the St. Quentin Ridge and entered Gonnelieu, where they captured over 350 prisoners and a large number of machine guns. Tanks took an effective part in the fighting for the ridge. At one point, where our infantry were held up by fire from a hostile trench, a single tank attacked and operated up and down the trench, inflicting heavy losses on the enemy's garrison. Our infantry were then able to advance and secure the trench, which was found full of dead Germans. In it were also found fifteen machine guns that had been silenced by the tank. In the whole of this fighting splendid targets were obtained by all tank crews, and the German casualties were seen to be very great.

Farther south, a number of tanks co-operated with dismounted Indian cavalry of the 5th Cavalry Division and with the Guards in the attacks upon Villers Guislain and Gauche Wood, and were in great measure responsible for the capture of the wood. Heavy fighting took place for this position, which it is clear the enemy had decided to hold at all costs. When the infantry and cavalry finally took possession of the wood, great numbers of German dead and smashed machine guns were found. In one spot four German machine guns, with dead crews lying round, were discovered within a radius of twenty yards. Three German field guns, complete with teams, were also captured in this wood.

Other tanks proceeded to Villers Guislain, and, in spite of heavy direct artillery fire, three reached the outskirts of the village, but the fire of the enemy's machine guns prevented our troops advancing from the south from supporting them, and the tanks ultimately withdrew.

Severe fighting took place, also, at Masnières. During the afternoon and evening at least nine separate attacks were beaten off by the 29th Division on this front, and other hostile attacks were repulsed in the neighbourhood of Marcoing, Fontaine-notre-Dame and Bourlon. With the Bonavis Ridge in the enemy's hands, however, Masnières was exposed to attack on three sides, and on the night of the 1st/2nd December our troops were withdrawn under orders to a line west of the village.

On the afternoon of the 2nd December a series of heavy attacks developed against Welsh Ridge in the neighbourhood of La Vacquerie, and further assaults were made on our positions in the neighbourhood of Masnières and Bourlon. These attacks were broken in succession by our machine gun fire, but the enemy persisted in his attempts against Welsh Ridge and gradually gained ground. By nightfall our line had been pushed back to a position west and north of Gonnelieu.

Next day the enemy renewed his attacks in great force on the whole front from Gonnelieu to Marcoing, and ultimately gained possession of La Vacquerie. North of La Vacquerie repeated attacks made about Masnières and Marcoing were repulsed in severe fighting, but the positions still retained by us beyond the Canal de l'Escaut were extremely exposed, and during the night our troops were withdrawn under orders to the west bank of the canal.

The Withdrawal from Bourlon

13. By this time the enemy had evidently become exhausted by the efforts he had made and the severity of his losses, and the 4th December passed comparatively quietly. For some days, however, local fighting continued in the neighbourhood of La Vacquerie, and his attitude remained aggressive. Local attacks in this sector were repulsed on the 5th December, and on this and the following two days further fierce fighting took place, in which the enemy again endeavoured without success to drive us from our positions on Welsh Ridge.

The strength which the enemy had shown himself able to develop in his attacks made it evident that only by prolonged and severe fighting could I hope to re-establish my right flank on the Bonavis Ridge. Unless this was done, the situation of my troops in the salient north of Flesquières would be difficult and dangerous, even if our hold on Bourlon Hill were extended.

I had therefore to decide either to embark on another offensive battle on a large scale, or to withdraw to a more compact line on the Flesquières Ridge.

Although this decision involved giving up important positions most gallantly won, I had no doubt as to the correct course under the conditions. Accordingly, on the night of the 4th/5th December the evacuation of the positions held by us north of the Flesquières Ridge was commenced. On the morning of the 7th December this withdrawal was completed successfully without interference from the enemy.

Before withdrawing, the more important of the enemy's field defences were destroyed, and those of his guns which we had been unable to remove were rendered useless. The enemy did not discover our withdrawal for some time, and when, on the afternoon of the 5th December, he began to feel his way forward, he did so with great caution. In spite of his care, on more than one occasion bodies of his infantry were caught in the open by our artillery.

Much skill and courage were shown by our covering troops in this withdrawal, and an incident which occurred on the afternoon of the 6th December in the neighbourhood of Graincourt deserves special notice. A covering party, consisting of two companies of the 1/15th Battalion, London Regiment, 47th Division, much reduced in strength by the fighting at Bourlon Wood, found their flank exposed by a hostile attack farther east, and were enveloped and practically cut off. These companies successfully cut their way through to our advanced line of resistance, where they arrived in good order, after having inflicted serious casualties on the enemy.

The new line taken up by us corresponded roughly to the old Hindenburg Reserve Line, and ran from a point about one and a half miles north by east of La Vacquerie, north of Ribécourt and Flesquières to the Canal du Nord, about one and a half miles north of Havrincourt—*i.e.*, between two and two and a half miles in front of the line held by us prior to the attack of the 20th November. We therefore retained in our possession an important section of the Hindenburg trench system, with its excellent dug-outs and other advantages.

The Results of the Battle

14. The material results of the three weeks' fighting described above can be stated in general terms very shortly.

We had captured and retained in our possession over 12,000 yards of the former German front line from La Vacquerie to a point opposite Boursies, together with between 10,000 and 11,000 yards of the Hindenburg Line and Hindenburg Reserve Line and the villages of Ribécourt, Flesquières and Havrincourt. A total of 145 German guns were taken or destroyed by us in the course of the operations, and 11,100 German prisoners were captured.

On the other hand, the enemy had occupied an unimportant section of our front line between Vendhuille and Gonnelieu.

There is little doubt that our operations were of considerable indirect assistance to the Allied forces in Italy. Large demands were made upon the available German reserves at a time when a great concentration of German divisions was still being maintained in Flanders. There is evidence that German divisions intended for the Italian theatre were diverted to the Cambrai front, and it is probable that the further concentration of German forces against Italy was suspended for at least two weeks at a most critical period, when our Allies were making their first stand on the Piave Line.

GENERAL REVIEW

15. I have already summarised in the opening paragraphs of this Despatch both the reasons which decided me to undertake the Cambrai operations and the limitations to which those operations were subject.

In view of the strength of the German forces on the front of my attack, and the success with which secrecy was maintained during our preparations, I had calculated that the enemy's prepared defences would be captured in the first rush. I had good hope that his resisting power behind those defences would then be so enfeebled for a period that we should be able on the same day to establish ourselves quickly and completely on the dominating Bourlon Ridge from Fontaine-notre-Dame to Mœuvres, and to secure our right flank along a line including the Bonavis Ridge, Crèvecœur and Rumilly to Fontaine-notre-Dame. Even if this did not prove possible within the first twenty-four hours, a second day would be at our disposal before the enemy's reserves could begin to arrive in any formidable numbers.

Meanwhile, with no wire and no prepared defences to hamper them, it was reasonable to hope that masses of cavalry would find it possible to pass through, whose task would be thoroughly to disorganise the enemy's systems of command and inter-communication in the whole area between the Canal de l'Escaut, the River Sensée and the Canal du Nord, as well as to the east and north-east of Cambrai.

My intentions as regards subsequent exploitation were to push westward and north-westward, taking the Hindenburg Line in reverse from Mœuvres to the River Scarpe, and capturing all the enemy's defences and probably most of his garrisons lying west of a line from Cambrai northwards to the Sensée, and south of that river and the Scarpe.

Time would have been required to enable us to develop and complete the operation; but the prospects of gaining the necessary time, by the use of cavalry in the manner outlined above, were in my opinion good enough to justify the attempt to execute the plan. I am of opinion that on the 20th and 21st November we went very near to a success sufficiently complete to bring the realisation of our full programme within our power.

The reasons for my decision to continue the fight after the 21st November have already been explained. Though in the event no advantage was gained thereby, I still consider that, as the problem presented itself at the time, the more cautious course would have been difficult to justify. It must be remembered that it was not a question of remaining where we stood, but of abandoning tactical positions of value, gained with great gallantry, the retention of which seemed not only to be within our power, but likely even yet to lead to further success.

Whatever may be the final decision on this point, as well as on the original decision to undertake the enterprise at all with the forces available, the continuation of our efforts against Fontaine-notre-Dame gave rise to severe fighting, in which our troops more than held their own.

On the 30th November risks were accepted by us at some points in order to increase our strength at others. Our fresh reserves had been thrown in on the Bourlon front, where the enemy brought against us a total force of seven divisions to three and failed. I do not consider that it would have been justifiable on the indications to have allotted a smaller garrison to this front.

Between Masnières and Vendhuille the enemy's superiority in infantry over our divisions in line was in the proportion of about four to three,[1] and we were sufficiently provided with artillery. That his attack was partially successful may tend to show that the garrison allotted to this front was insufficient, either owing to want of numbers, lack of training, or exhaustion from previous fighting.

Captured maps and orders have made it clear that the enemy aimed at far more considerable results than were actually achieved by him. Three convergent attacks were to be made on the salient formed by our advance; two of them delivered approximately simultaneously about Gonnelieu and Masnières, followed later by a still more powerful attack on the Bourlon front. The objectives of these attacks extended to the high ground at Beaucamp and Trescault, and the enemy's hope was to capture and destroy the whole of the British forces in the Cambrai salient.

This bold and ambitious plan was foiled on the greater part of our front by the splendid defence of the British divisions engaged; and, though the defence broke down for a time in one area, the recovery made by the weak forces still left and those within immediate reach is worthy of the highest praise. Numberless instances

---

[1] The strengths of the 55th, 12th, 20th and 29th Divisions just prior to the German attack totalled some 43,000 rifles. The estimated strength of a German division at this time was some 8,500 rifles. Only a part of the front of the 55th Division was involved in the attack.

of great gallantry, promptitude and skill were shown, some few of which have been recounted.

I desire to acknowledge the skill and resource displayed by General Byng throughout the Cambrai operations, and to express my appreciation of the manner in which they were conducted by him, as well as by his Staff and the subordinate commanders.

In conclusion, I would point out that the sudden breaking through by our troops of an immense system of defence has had a most inspiring moral effect on the Armies I command, and must have a correspondingly depressing influence upon the enemy. The great value of the tanks in the offensive has been conclusively proved. In view of this experience, the enemy may well hesitate to deplete any portion of his front, as he did last summer, in order to set free troops to concentrate for decisive action at some other point.

    I have the honour to be,
        My Lord,
           Your obedient Servant,
                D. HAIG, Field-Marshal,
        Commanding-in-Chief, British Armies in France.

THE
GREAT GERMAN OFFENSIVE

THE GREAT GERMAN OFFENSIVE

General Headquarters,
20th July, 1918.[1]

My Lord,—

I have the honour to submit the following report upon the operations of the Forces under my Command during the period following the actions in the vicinity of Cambrai in the first week of December, 1917.

General Situation

1. The broad facts of the change which took place in the general war situation at the close of 1917, and the causes which led to it, have long been well known, and need be referred to but shortly.

The disappearance of Russia as a belligerent country on the side of the Entente Powers had set free the great bulk of the German and Austrian divisions on the Eastern Front. Already at the beginning of November, 1917, the transfer of German divisions from the Russian to the Western front had begun.[2] It became certain that the movement would be continued steadily until numerical superiority lay with the enemy.

It was to be expected, moreover, that large numbers of guns and munitions formerly in the possession of the Russian Armies would fall into the hands of our enemies, and at some future date would be turned against the Allies.

Although the growing Army of the United States of America might be expected eventually to restore the balance in our favour, a considerable period of time would be required to enable that Army to develop its full strength. While it would be possible for Germany to complete her new dispositions early in the new year, the forces which America could send to France before the season would permit active operations to be recommenced would not be large.

Transition from an Offensive to a Defensive Policy

2. In view of the situation described above, * * * * it became necessary to change the policy governing the conduct of the operations

[1] This Despatch was published as a Supplement to the *London Gazette* of the 21st October, 1918.
[2] Prior to this date, many thousands of fresh troops had been brought from the Eastern front as drafts.

of the British Armies in France. Orders accordingly were issued early in December having for their object immediate preparation to meet a strong and sustained hostile offensive. In other words, a defensive policy was adopted, and all necessary arrangements consequent thereon were put in hand with the least possible delay.

Extension of the British Front

3. Since the month of September, 1917, pursuant to a decision taken by the British Government towards the end of that month, negotiations had been proceeding with the French authorities regarding the extension of the front held by the British Armies. After considerable discussion on the subject, it was finally decided that the British should relieve the French troops on my right as far as the vicinity of the village of Barisis, immediately south of the River Oise. The additional front to be taken over by me amounted to over twenty-eight miles.

This relief, which was to have taken place in December, was delayed until January in consequence of the further development of the Cambrai battle. In the meantime, the French forces which had co-operated so successfully on the left of the British in Flanders had been withdrawn, and French troops again assumed responsibility for the coastal sector at Nieuport.

By the end of January, 1918, the relief of the French as far as Barisis had been completed without incident. At that date the British Armies were holding some 125 miles of active front.

Man-power and Training

4. * * * * * * * *

The strenuous efforts made by the British forces during 1917 had left the Army at a low ebb in regard both to training and numbers. It was therefore of the first importance, in view of the expected German offensive, to fill up the ranks as rapidly as possible and provide ample facilities for training.

So far as the second of these requirements was concerned, two factors materially affected the situation. Firstly, training had hitherto been primarily devoted to preparation for offensive operations. Secondly, the necessity for maintaining the front line systems of defence and the construction of new lines on ground recently captured from the enemy had precluded the development of rear line systems to any great degree.

Under the new conditions the early construction of these latter systems, involving the employment of every available man on the work, became a matter of vital importance. In consequence it was difficult to carry out any elaborate course of training in defensive tactics. On the other hand, in the course of the strenuous fighting in 1916 and 1917, great developments had taken place in the methods of conducting a defensive battle. It was essential that the lessons learned therein should be assimilated rapidly and thoroughly by all ranks.

* * * * *At the same time* a change *took place* in the organisation of the forces. Under instructions from the Army Council, the reorganisation of divisions from a 13 battalion to a 10 battalion basis was * * * * completed during the month of February. Apart from the reduction in fighting strength involved by this reorganisation, the fighting efficiency of units was *to some extent affected.* An unfamiliar grouping of units was introduced thereby, necessitating new methods of tactical handling of the troops and the discarding of old methods to which subordinate commanders had been accustomed.

The difficulties with which we were faced * * * * were accentuated by the increase in the British front described in the preceding paragraph. Meanwhile, in marked contrast to our own position, the large reserves in the Western theatre, which the enemy was able to create for himself by the transfer of numerous divisions from the East, enabled him to carry out extensive training with units completed to establishment.

Preparations for Defence

5. Orders issued early in December, as stated above, had defined the defensive policy to be adopted and the methods of defence. A vast amount of work was required to be done in the construction of defences, old systems had to be remodelled and new systems created. The construction of new communications and the extension of old, more especially in the area south-east of Arras which the enemy had devastated in his retirement last year, involved the building of a number of additional roads and the laying out of railways, both narrow and normal gauge. Work of this nature was particularly necessary on the Somme battlefield and in the area recently taken over from the French.

All available men of the fighting units, with the exception of a very small proportion undergoing training, and all labour units were employed on these tasks. Though the time and labour available were in no way adequate if, as was suspected, the enemy intended to commence his offensive operations in the early spring, a large portion of the work was in fact completed before the enemy launched his great attack. That so much was accomplished is due to the untiring energy of all ranks of the fighting units, the Transportation Service and the Labour Corps.

Arrangements for Co-operation with the French

6. In addition to our own defensive schemes, completion of arrangements for the closest possible co-operation with the French was recognised to be a matter of great importance and urgency. A comprehensive investigation was undertaken into the various problems connected with the co-operation of the two Allied forces. Plans were drawn up in combination with the French military authorities, and were worked out in great detail to meet the different situations which might arise on different parts of the Allied front. Measures were taken to ensure the smooth and rapid execution of these plans.

Among the many problems studied by the Allied Staffs, those involved by a hostile offensive on the line of the Somme River and the passage of that river by the enemy had been worked out. The plans applicable to such a situation had been drawn up and were ready to be put into execution when required.

Operations during the Winter

7. In order to ensure the greatest possible concentration of effort upon training, reorganisation and defences, and also in order to allow my divisions the maximum amount of rest after the continuous fighting of 1917, only such minor enterprises were undertaken by the British forces during the winter months as were essential to keep us informed regarding the dispositions and intentions of the German forces opposed to us. Special attention was directed to disposing our forces in line in such manner as would best promote economy in men and reduce casualties.

On the enemy side, some little activity continued until the end of the year, and local attacks were made by him both on the Cambrai front and in the Ypres sector; resulting in certain small modifications in the line held by us. In these engagements, the policy followed by me was to avoid involving troops in struggles for non-essential positions, and subordinate commanders were instructed accordingly.

The first of the enemy's minor attacks took place on the 12th December in the neighbourhood of Bullecourt, and after sharp fighting led to the loss of the point of the salient held by us east of that village, with a consequent shortening of our line. Other local attacks on the 14th and 22nd December at Polderhoek Château and astride the Ypres-Staden Railway also resulted in small and unimportant withdrawals of portions of our outpost line in these localities.

THE GREAT GERMAN OFFENSIVE 181

On the 30th December a somewhat more serious attempt was made by the enemy against our positions on Welsh Ridge, on the Cambrai front. The attack, made in the early morning on a front of over two miles from La Vacquerie northwards towards Marcoing, was delivered in considerable strength, and elaborate precautions were taken by the enemy to effect surprise.[1] South of Marcoing, the enemy gained possession of a somewhat isolated trench sited on the northern slopes of Welsh Ridge, compelling our troops to fall back to a sunken road lying across the base of the salient, where they organised a successful resistance. At the southern end of the ridge near La Vacquerie the enemy's attack succeeded in over-running not only our forward posts but also the trench line on the crest of the ridge, with all its advantages of observation. During the afternoon, however, an admirably executed counter-attack by two companies of the 63rd Division drove the enemy from the crest of the ridge and regained all the essential parts of our former positions.

On the 5th, and again on the 8th January, the enemy made two other local attacks east of Bullecourt, both of which were unsuccessful.

Early in March there was a recrudescence of hostile activity in the northern sector. Following upon an unsuccessful attack on the Belgian advanced positions north of Dixmude on the 6th March, two local attacks were made by the enemy two days later on the British front, the one south and north of the Menin Road, and the other on a front of over a mile south of Houthulst Forest. Both these attacks were repulsed after sharp fighting and our line maintained or re-established by counter-attacks.

During the whole of this period hostile raiding parties displayed greatly increased activity, but the vigilance of our troops prevented them from achieving any success in more than a small proportion of instances. On our side, during the earlier part of the winter, raiding activity was deliberately cut down to the lowest limits consonant with the maintenance of an adequate knowledge of the enemy's dispositions. In the three and a half months extending from the morning of the 8th December, 1917, to the opening of the German offensive, some 225 raids were attempted by the enemy. Not more than 62 of these were successful in obtaining any identification from our lines, while in 67 cases his raiding parties left prisoners or dead in our hands. During the same period some 125 raids were carried out by us, 77 of which were successful in obtaining prisoners or identifications ; while in 31 other cases the enemy's trenches were found to have been evacuated.

Besides raids, considerable patrolling activity took place on both sides. In this form of warfare our troops maintained a marked

[1] The leading parties of the enemy were clad in white in order that they might be the less readily seen against the background of snow.

superiority over the enemy on almost all occasions and secured many prisoners, in addition to inflicting frequent casualties on hostile patrols and working parties.

THE STORM GATHERS

Indications of the Coming Attack

8. Towards the middle of February, 1918, it became evident that the enemy was preparing for a big offensive on the Western front. It was known from various sources that he had been steadily increasing his forces in the Western theatre since the beginning of November, 1917. In three and a half months 28 infantry divisions had been transferred from the Eastern theatre and 6 infantry divisions from the Italian theatre. There were reports that further reinforcements were on their way to the West, and it was also known that the enemy had greatly increased his heavy artillery in the Western theatre during the same period. These reinforcements were more than were necessary for defence, and, as they were moved at a time when the distribution of food and fuel to the civil population in Germany was rendered extremely difficult through lack of rolling stock, I concluded that the enemy intended to attack at an early date.

Constant air reconnaissances over the enemy's lines showed that rail and road communications were being improved and ammunition and supply dumps increased along the whole front from Flanders to the Oise. By the end of February, 1918, these preparations had become very marked opposite the front held by the Third and Fifth British Armies, and I considered it probable that the enemy would make his initial effort from the Sensée River southwards.[1] As the 21st March approached it became certain that an attack on this sector was imminent, and counter-preparation was carried out nightly by our artillery on the threatened front. By the 21st March the number of German infantry divisions in the Western theatre had risen to 192, an increase of 46 since the 1st November, 1917.

British Dispositions to Meet the Enemy's Offensive

9. In making the necessary distribution of the forces under my command to meet the threatened German attack, the enemy's possible objectives and the relative importance of ground in the various sectors had to be taken into consideration. These objectives

[1] No small interest was aroused about this time by the appearance in the fields near St. Quentin of great numbers of small objects that, from the tracks leading to them, were at one time thought to be German tanks. It is probable that they were dumps of ammunition brought up on tractors.

and their bearing on the distribution of the troops are set forth below :—

(i) In the northern portion of the British area lie the northern Channel ports of Dunkirk, Calais and Boulogne, the security of which necessitated the maintenance of sufficient troops in the neighbourhood. Little or no ground could be given up on this front, and therefore the necessary reserves must be kept in close proximity.

Although, as a rule, the state of the ground would preclude a general offensive in this sector early in the year, the weather had been exceptionally dry, and preparations for an attack by the enemy astride the Menin Road were known to be in an advanced state.

(ii) In the central portion lie the northern collieries of France and certain important tactical features which cover our lateral communications.

Here, also, little or no ground could be given up, except in the Lys Valley itself.

(iii) In the southern portion of the British area south-east of Arras, in contrast to the central and northern portions, ground could be given up under great pressure without serious consequences, the forward area of this sector consisting chiefly of a wide expanse of territory devastated by the enemy last spring in his withdrawal.

As shown in paragraph 8, it was evident that the enemy was about to make a great effort south of Arras. An attack on this front would undoubtedly have as its object the separation of the French and British Armies and the capture of the important centre of communications of Amiens. To meet this eventuality more than half my available troops were allocated to the defence of this sector, together with the whole of the cavalry. In addition, as previously stated, arrangements had been made for the movement of a French force to the southern portion of the British area north of the River Oise in case of need.

(iv) Arrangements were made in detail for the rapid transport by rail or bus of a force of such British divisions as could be held back in reserve to meet any emergency on any sector of the British front.

The Situation on the Eve of the Attack

10. On the 19th March my Intelligence Department reported that the final stages of the enemy's preparations on the Arras-St. Quentin front were approaching completion, and that from

information obtained it was probable that the actual attack would be launched on the 20th or 21st March. On our side our dispositions to meet the expected offensive were as complete as the time and troops available could make them.

The front of the Fifth Army,[1] at that date commanded by General Sir H. de la P. Gough, extended from our junction with the French just south of Barisis to north of Gouzeaucourt, a distance of about forty-two miles, and was held by the III., XVIII., XIX. and VII. Corps, commanded respectively by Lieut.-General Sir R. H. K. Butler, Lieut.-General Sir F. I. Maxse, Lieut.-General Sir H. E. Watts, and Lieut.-General Sir W. N. Congreave. Over ten miles of this front between Amigny Rouy and Alaincourt were protected by the marshes of the Oise River and Canal, and were therefore held more lightly than the remainder of the line; but on the whole front of this Army the number of divisions in line only allowed of an average of one division to some 6,750 yards of front.

The Third Army, under the command of General the Hon. Sir J. H. G. Byng, held a front of about 27 miles from north of Gouzeaucourt to south of Gavrelle with the V., IV., VI. and XVII. Corps, under the respective commands of Lieut.-General Sir E. A. Fanshawe, Lieut.-General Sir G. M. Harper, Lieut.-General Sir J. A. L. Haldane, and Lieut.-General Sir C. Fergusson, Bt. The average length of front held by each division in line on the Third Army front was about 4,700 yards.

The general principle of our defensive arrangements on the fronts of these Armies was the distribution of our troops in depth. With this object three defensive belts, sited at considerable distances from each other, had been constructed or were approaching completion in the forward area, the most advanced of which was in the nature of a lightly-held outpost screen covering our main positions. On the morning of the attack the troops detailed to man these various defences were all in position.

Behind the forward defences of the Fifth Army, and in view of the smaller resources which could be placed at the disposal of that Army, arrangements had been made for the construction of a strong and carefully-sited bridgehead position covering Peronne and the crossings of the River Somme south of that town. Considerable progress had been made in the laying out of this position, though at the outbreak of the enemy's offensive its defences were incomplete.

The Enemy's Dispositions

11. From the information at my disposal, it was expected that the enemy's heaviest attack would fall between the Sensée River and

[1] *Vide* Map No. 6.

THE GREAT GERMAN OFFENSIVE 185

the neighbourhood of the Bapaume-Cambrai Road, and on this front of some 16,000 yards eighteen German divisions are known to have been employed in line and in immediate reserve on the 21st March. It was correctly anticipated that the Flesquières salient itself would not be directly attacked in strength, but that the attack would be continued in great force from the southern flank of the salient to St. Quentin. On this front of some 48,000 yards, from Gouzeaucourt to the Oise River at Moy, forty German divisions were set in motion on the first day.

An event which, having regard to the nature of the ground, was not considered probable, was that the enemy would be able to extend the flank of his attack in any considerable strength beyond Moy. The rapid drying of the marshes, due to an exceptionally dry spring, in fact enabled the enemy to attack this lightly-held front with three fresh divisions, in addition to the three divisions already in line.

Comparison of Forces Engaged

12. In all, at least sixty-four German divisions took part in the operations of the first day of the battle, a number considerably exceeding the total forces composing the entire British Army in France. The majority of these divisions had spent many weeks and even months in concentrated training for offensive operations, and had reached a high pitch of technical excellence in the attack.

To meet this assault the Third Army disposed of eight divisions in line on the front of the enemy's initial attack, with seven divisions available in reserve. The Fifth Army disposed of fourteen divisions and three cavalry divisions, of which three infantry divisions and three cavalry divisions were in reserve. The total British force on the original battle front, therefore, on the morning of the 21st March was twenty-nine infantry divisions and three cavalry divisions, of which nineteen infantry divisions were in line.

Launched on a front of about fifty-four miles on the 21st March, the area of the German offensive spread northwards on the 28th March, until from La Fère to beyond Gavrelle some sixty-three miles of our former line were involved. On this front a total of seventy-three German divisions were engaged during March against the Third and Fifth Armies and the right of the First Army, and were opposed in the first place by twenty-two British infantry divisions in line, with twelve infantry divisions and three cavalry divisions in close reserve.

As soon as it became evident that the enemy had thrown practically the whole of his striking force against this one battle front, it became both possible and necessary to collect additional reserves from the remainder of my front, and hurry them to the battlefield. Plans previously drawn up to meet such an eventuality were put into execution at once, and before the end of March, by which date the principal German effort had been broken, a further force of eight British divisions was brought south and sent into the fight. Prior to the 9th April four other British divisions were engaged, making a total of forty-six British infantry divisions and three cavalry divisions employed on the Somme battle front.

THE SECOND SOMME BATTLE

The Attack Opened

13. Shortly before 5.0 a.m. on the 21st March a bombardment of great intensity, with gas and high explosive shell from all natures of artillery and trench mortars, was opened against practically the whole fronts of the Fifth and Third Armies from the Oise to the Scarpe River, while road centres and railways as far back as St. Pol were engaged by high velocity guns. Violent bombardments were opened also on the French front in wide sectors east and north-east of Reims, and on portions of the British front between the Scarpe River and Lens. Our positions from south of the La Bassée Canal to the River Lys were heavily shelled with gas, and battery areas between the Scarpe and the Ypres-Comines Canal were actively engaged. Dunkirk was bombarded from the sea.

The hour of the enemy's assault varied in different sectors, but by about 9.45 a.m. a general attack had been launched on a battle front of fifty-four miles between the Oise and the Sensée Rivers. Later in the day, as visibility improved, large numbers of low-flying aeroplanes attacked our troops and batteries.

Favoured by a thick white fog, which hid from our artillery and machine gunners the S.O.S. signals sent up by our outpost line, and in numbers which made loss of direction impossible, the attacking German infantry forced their way into our foremost defensive zone. Until 1.0 p.m. the fog made it impossible to see more than fifty yards in any direction, and the machine guns and forward field guns which had been disposed so as to cover this zone with their fire were robbed almost entirely of their effect. The detachments holding the outpost positions were consequently overwhelmed or surrounded, in many cases before they were able to pass back information concerning the enemy's attack.

The attack being expected, reserves had been brought forward and battle stations manned. On all parts of the battle front garrisons

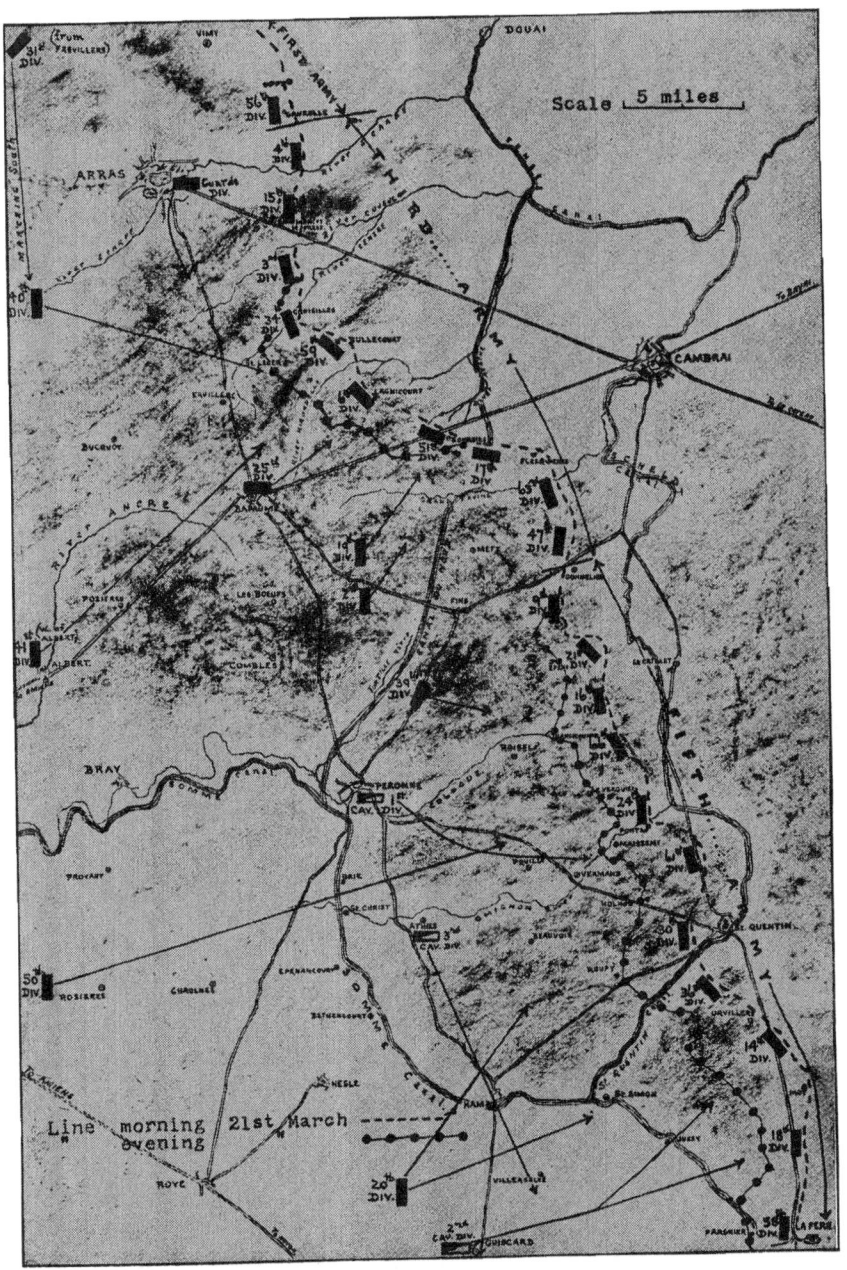

SECOND SOMME BATTLE;
German Attack, 21st March, 1918.

THE GREAT GERMAN OFFENSIVE 187

of redoubts and strong points in the forward zone held out with the utmost gallantry for many hours. From some of them wireless messages were received up to a late hour in the day, giving information of much value. The losses which they were able to inflict upon the enemy were undoubtedly very great, and materially delayed his advance. The prolonged defence of these different localities, under conditions which left little hope of any relief, deserves to rank among the most heroic actions in the history of the British Army.

So intense was the enemy's bombardment that at an early hour our communications were severed, and so swift was his advance under the covering blanket of the mist that certain of our more advanced batteries found the German infantry close upon them before they had received warning from their own infantry that the expected attack had been launched. Many gallant deeds were performed by the personnel of such batteries, and on numerous occasions heavy losses were inflicted on bodies of hostile troops by guns firing over open sights at point-blank range.

Ronssoy Captured

14. During the morning reports were received that the enemy had penetrated our front line opposite La Fère, and had also broken into our forward positions north of the Bapaume-Cambrai Road, and opposite Lagnicourt and Bullecourt. The first indication that the progress made by him was developing a serious aspect was the news that at noon German infantry were entering Ronssoy. This meant that in this sector the attack had already reached and penetrated a considerable distance into the second defensive belt which constituted our battle positions.

The enemy's success at this point was followed up vigorously. Templeux-le-Guérard fell into his hands shortly afterwards, while the villages of Hargicourt and Villeret, attacked simultaneously in flank and rear, were practically surrounded, and were entered about midday.

Thereafter the enemy was held up by the resistance of our troops in the rear defences of the battle zone, greatly assisted by the very gallant action of the 24th Division in Le Verguier and the 21st Division at Epéhy, on the two flanks of his advance. Both these divisions, under command respectively of Major-General A. C. Daly, and Major-General D. G. M. Campbell, held out throughout the day against repeated attacks delivered in great strength, and killed large numbers of the enemy. In this fighting parties of German troops who had entered Peizière on the northern outskirts of Epéhy were driven out by our infantry, with the assistance of tanks, which on this and many subsequent occasions did valuable and gallant work.

The Situation at Midday

15. At midday the enemy's infantry had reached the first line of our battle positions in strength on practically the whole front of his attack, except at the Flesquières salient, where his assaults were not pressed with the same weight as elsewhere. Save in the neighbourhood of Ronssoy, however, and at certain other points in a less serious degree, our battle positions themselves had not been entered, while at numerous localities in front of them fierce fighting was taking place around strong points still occupied by our troops.

Assisted by the long spell of dry weather, hostile infantry had crossed the river and canal north of La Fère, and south of St. Quentin had penetrated into the battle zone between Essigny and Benay. At Maissemy also our battle positions were entered at about noon, but the vigorous resistance of the 61st and 24th Divisions, assisted by troops of the 1st Cavalry Division, prevented the enemy from developing his success.

On the Third Army front also the attack had succeeded by midday in breaking into the battle zone at certain points, and heavy fighting was taking place all along the line from the Canal du Nord north-westwards to the Sensée River. Astride the canal the enemy was held up by the 17th Division, under command of Major-General P. R. Robertson, and made no progress. Farther west he had entered Doignies and had taken Louverval. In Lagnicourt and to the south of it the 6th Division, under command of Major-General T. O. Marden, were still maintaining a gallant fight for the possession of the first line of their battle positions; but beyond that village the battle zone had been entered at Noreuil, Longatte and Ecoust St. Mein, all of which places had fallen into the enemy's hands.

The Struggle for the Battle Zone

16. Fighting in and in front of our battle positions continued with the greatest intensity throughout the afternoon and evening. Except for certain small gains, the enemy were held by our defence, and even driven back in places by our counter-attacks. Reports received from all parts of the front testified to the unusual severity of his losses.

The most serious progress made by the enemy during this part of the struggle was on the right, south of St. Quentin. At Fargnier, having reached the eastern portion of the village by 4.0 p.m., during the remainder of the day his troops pressed on to the Crozat Canal and captured Quessy. North of this point the 18th Division, under command of Major-General R. P. Lee, reinforced by troops of the 2nd Cavalry Division, still held their battle positions intact, though threatened on both flanks by the enemy's progress at Quessy and at Benay, and successfully restored the situation in the neighbourhood of Ly-Fontaine by a counter-attack. Many of the strong points in the forward zone on the front of this division were also holding out, though surrounded. Wireless messages from their gallant defenders were received as late as 8.30 p.m., and rifle fire was heard in their vicinity until midnight.

Between the neighbourhood of Benay and the Somme Canal, the enemy by the evening had forced back our troops, after heavy fighting, to the rear line of their battle positions. Parties of our infantry, however, were still holding out east and north-east of Essigny, and certain of our keeps in front of this line were still intact.

About Roupy and Savy all hostile attempts, in which tanks were used, to break into the battle positions of the 30th Division, under command of Major-General W. de L. Williams, were repulsed with the heaviest losses, our troops carrying out a number of successful counter-attacks. In this sector, the advancing German infantry frequently bunched together and offered good targets to our artillery and machine guns.

On the remainder of the Fifth Army front our battle positions still held, the 9th Division, under command of Major-General H. H. Tudor, retaining also nearly the whole of their forward positions, having twice retaken by counter-attack the important local feature on their right flank known as Chapel Hill.

On the Third Army front, our line in the Flesquières salient had not been heavily attacked, and was substantially intact. Beyond this sector, fierce fighting took place around Demicourt and Doignies, and north of the village of Beaumetz-lez-Cambrai. In this area the 51st Division, under command of Major-General G. T. C. Carter-Campbell, was heavily engaged, but from noon onwards practically no progress was made by the enemy. A counter-attack carried out by two battalions of the 19th Division, Major-General G. D. Jeffreys commanding the division, with a company of tanks recovered a portion of this ground in the face of strong resistance, and secured a few prisoners, though it proved unable to clear the village of Doignies.

Lagnicourt fell into the enemy's hands during the afternoon, and heavy attacks were made also between Noreuil and Croisilles. At one time, hostile infantry were reported to have broken through the rear line of our battle positions in this sector in the direction of Mory. By nightfall the situation had been restored; but meanwhile the enemy had reached the outskirts of St. Leger and was attacking the 34th Division, under command of Major-General C. L. Nicholson, about Croisilles heavily from the south-west. A strong attack launched at 5.0 p.m. against the 3rd Division, under command of Major-General C. J. Deverell, north of Fontaine-les-Croisilles on the left bank of the Sensée River, was broken up by machine gun fire.

At the end of the first day, therefore, the enemy had made very considerable progress, but he was still firmly held in the battle zone, in which it had been anticipated that the real struggle would take place. Nowhere had he effected that immediate break-through for which his troops had been training for many weeks, and such progress as he had made had been bought at a cost which had already greatly reduced his chances of carrying out his ultimate purpose.

The First Withdrawals

17. In view of the progress made by the enemy south of St. Quentin, the thinness of our line on that front, and the lack of reserves with which to restore the situation in our battle positions, the Fifth Army Commander decided on the evening of the 21st March, after consultation with the G.O.C. III. Corps, to withdraw the divisions of that Corps behind the Crozat Canal. The movement involved the withdrawal of the 36th Division, on the right of the XVIII. Corps, to the line of the Somme Canal.

The enemy's advance south and north of the Flesquières salient rendered a withdrawal by the V. Corps and by the 9th Division on its right necessary also. Orders were accordingly issued to the divisions concerned for a line to be taken up, as a first stage, along the high ground known as Highland Ridge, and thence westwards along the Hindenburg Line to Havrincourt and Hermies.

These different withdrawals were carried out successfully during the night. The bridges across the Crozat and Somme Canals were destroyed, though in some cases not with entire success, it being probable that certain of them were still practicable for infantry. Instances of great bravery occurred in the destruction of these bridges. In one case, when the electrical connection for firing the demolition charge had failed, the officer responsible for the destruction of the bridge personally lit the instantaneous fuse and blew up the bridge.[1] Many of the bridges were destroyed in the close presence of the enemy.

---

[1] By extraordinary good fortune, he was not killed.

THE GREAT GERMAN OFFENSIVE 191

As by this time it had become clear that practically the whole of the enemy's striking force had been committed to this one battle, my plans already referred to for collecting reserves from other parts of the British front were put into immediate execution. By drawing away local reserves and thinning out the front not attacked, it was possible, as pointed out above, to reinforce the battle by eight divisions before the end of the month. Steps were taken also to set in operation at once the schemes previously agreed upon with the French for taking over a portion of the battle front.

The Second Day of the Battle

18. On the morning of the 22nd March the ground was again enveloped in thick mist, under cover of which the enemy renewed his attacks in great strength all along the line. Fighting was again very heavy, and short-range fire from guns, rifles and machine guns caused enormous losses to the enemy's troops. The weight of his attack, however, combined with the impossibility of observing beforehand and engaging with artillery the massing of his troops, enabled him to press forward.

The Fight for the Crozat Canal

19. In the south the enemy advanced during the morning as far as the line of the canal at Jussy, and a fierce struggle commenced for the passage of the canal, his troops bringing up trench mortars and machine guns, and endeavouring to cross on rafts under cover of their fire. At 1.0 p.m. he succeeded in effecting a crossing at Quessy, and made progress during the afternoon in the direction of Vouel. His further advance in this sector, however, was delayed by the gallant resistance of troops of the 58th Division, under command of Major-General A. B. E. Cator, at Tergnier, and it was not until evening, after many costly attempts and much sanguinary fighting, that the enemy gained possession of this village. During the afternoon hostile infantry crossed the canal also at La Montagne and at Jussy, but in both cases were counter-attacked and driven back by troops of the 18th Division and 2nd Cavalry Division, Major-General T. T. Pitman commanding the 2nd Cavalry Division.

Le Verguier and Epéhy Lost

20. In the centre of the battle front the enemy made a strong and determined effort to develop the success gained at Templeux-le-Guérard on the previous day, and in the early morning captured Ste. Émilie and Hervilly. Hervilly was retaken by troops of the 1st

Cavalry Division (under command of Major-General R. L. Mullens), assisted by tanks, at 9.0 a.m.[1] At midday, after heavy fighting in the neighbourhood of Roisel, the 66th Division, under command of Major-General N. Malcolm, still held their positions in this sector, having for the time being definitely stopped the enemy's advance.

To the south and north, however, the progress of the German infantry continued. Constantly attacked from almost every direction, Le Verguier fell into the enemy's hands at about 10.0 a.m., after a most gallant defence. On the left bank of the Cologne River the capture of Ste. Émilie was followed by the fall of Villers Faucon, and both Roisel and Epéhy were threatened with envelopment from the rear.

Accordingly, our troops about Roisel were withdrawn during the afternoon under orders, the enemy making no attempt to interfere, and were directed to reorganise behind the line of our third defensive belt between Bernes and Boucly, which was already manned by the 50th Division, temporarily commanded by Brig.-General A. F. U. Stockley. Later in the afternoon the troops of the 21st Division in Epéhy also fell back under orders, though with more difficulty, as parties of hostile infantry were west of the village. To the north the 9th Division held their battle positions practically intact until the late afternoon, when they were withdrawn under orders to the rear line of defence between Nurlu and Equancourt. This retirement also was made with great difficulty.

The Battle on the Third Army Front

21. The divisions holding the Flesquières salient were not seriously involved during the morning of the 22nd March, but in the evening strong attacks were made both at Villers Plouich and at Havrincourt. All these attacks were repulsed with great slaughter.

Farther north fighting was severe and continuous throughout the day. Shortly before noon the enemy attacked Hermies strongly from the north-west, and repeated his attacks at intervals during the remainder of the day. These attacks were completely repulsed by the 17th Division. Heavy losses were inflicted on the German infantry in the fighting in this area, the leading wave of a strong attack launched between Hermies and Beaumetz-lez-Cambrai being destroyed by our fire.

In the neighbourhood of Beaumetz the enemy continued his assaults with great determination, but was held by the 51st Division and a brigade of the 25th Division until the evening (Major-General Sir E. G. T. Bainbridge commanding the 25th Division).

---

[1] The capture by the enemy of Hervilly itself at this hour is disputed. It is certain that we had troops east of Herbécourt until after midday.

Our troops were then withdrawn under orders to positions south of the village. Very severe fighting took place at Vaulx Wood and Vaulx Vraucourt, as well as about St. Leger and north of Croisilles, which latter village our troops had evacuated during the night.

At Vraucourt the enemy broke through the rear line of the battle zone and penetrated into the village. There he was counter-attacked by infantry and tanks, and driven out. Farther west, after heavy fighting, his troops forced their way into our positions along the line of the Croisilles—Hénin-sur-Cojeul Road. On the left of this attack troops of the 34th Division maintained themselves in St. Leger until the afternoon, when they fell back to a line of trenches just west of the village. To the north the 3rd Division brought back their right flank to a line facing south-east, and in this position successfully beat off a heavy attack.

The Break Through at St. Quentin

22. With Maissemy already in the enemy's hands, the fall of Le Verguier greatly weakened the defence of the centre of the Fifth Army. The rear line of our battle positions was held during the morning, in spite of unceasing pressure from large hostile forces, but as the day wore on the great concentration of German divisions attacking west of St. Quentin had its effect. During the early afternoon our troops east of Holnon Wood were forced to withdraw from their battle zone trenches; while after repulsing heavy attacks throughout the morning, the 30th Division were again attacked during the afternoon and evening and compelled to give ground. Our troops, fighting fiercely and continuously, were gradually forced out of the battle zone on the whole of this front, and fell back through the 20th Division, under command of Major-General W. D. Smith, and the 50th Division holding the third defensive zone between Happencourt, Villéveque and Boucly, in the hope of reorganising behind them.

In this fighting the action of the 1st Battalion Royal Inniskilling Fusiliers, 36th Division, deserves special mention. This battalion held a redoubt in the forward zone near Fontaine-les-Clercs throughout the whole of the first day of the battle, and on the following day, after the troops on their right had withdrawn in accordance with orders, still maintained their position, although surrounded by the enemy. After a magnificent fight, in which all the enemy's attacks were repulsed with great loss, at 3.0 p.m. the officer commanding the battalion sent back a small party of troops, who succeeded in getting through to our lines. The remainder of the battalion continued the fight to the end.

By 5.30 p.m. the enemy had reached the third zone at different points, and was attacking the 50th Division heavily between Villéveque and Boucly. Though holding an extended front of some 10,500 yards, the division succeeded in checking the enemy's advance, and by a successful counter-attack drove him temporarily from the village of Coulaincourt. At the close of the engagement, however, the troops of the 50th Division about Pœuilly had been forced back, and by continued pressure along the south bank of the Omignon River the enemy had opened a gap between their right flank and the troops of the 61st Division, under command of Major-General C. J. Mackenzie, and of the 20th Division farther south. At this gap, during the late afternoon and evening, strong bodies of German troops broke through the third defensive zone about Vaux and Beauvois.

All available reserves at the disposal of the Fifth Army had already been thrown into the fight, and except for one French division and some French cavalry in the III. Corps area, no further support was within reach of the fighting line. There remained, therefore, no course open but to fall back on the bridgehead positions east of the Somme.

The Withdrawal to the Somme

23. Accordingly, at 11.0 p.m., on the 22nd March, orders were issued by the Fifth Army Commander that the troops of the XVIII. Corps should fall back during the night behind the line of the Somme south of Voyennes, in touch with the III. Corps on their right; while the XIX. and VII. Corps endeavoured to secure the main Peronne bridgehead on the line Croix Molignaux—Monchy Lagache —Vraignes, and thence northwards along the third zone of defence to the junction with the Third Army about Equancourt.

These withdrawals were carried out under constant pressure from the enemy, covered by rearguards of the 20th, 50th and 39th Divisions (Major-General E. Feetham commanding the last-mentioned division), which were continually in action with the German troops.

On the Third Army front also, certain necessary readjustments of our line were carried out during the night. On the right, the evacuation of the Flesquières salient was continued, our troops withdrawing to a line covering Equancourt and Metz-en-Couture in touch with the Fifth Army about Equancourt. In the centre, the troops still in advance of the third defensive zone were brought back to that system. On the left, our troops withdrew from the remainder of their forward positions south of the Scarpe, taking up the rear line of their battle positions between Hénin-sur-Cojeul and Fampoux.

As on the southern portion of the battle front, the enemy followed up our troops closely, except on the left, where for a time he was unaware of what we had done. Elsewhere, more or less continuous fighting took place throughout the night, and in the early morning parties of the enemy succeeded in finding a gap in our new line about Mory.

The Decision to Abandon the Peronne Bridgehead

24. Reports that the enemy had forced the line of the Crozat Canal, combined with the loss of the Vaux-Pœuilly positions, and information obtained by the Air Service that the German front as far back as Mont D'Origny was packed with advancing troops, led the Fifth Army Commander to reconsider his decision to offer battle afresh east of the Somme. Considering that if involved in a general engagement his tired troops might be exposed to a decisive defeat before help could arrive, and that the situation might then be exploited by the enemy to a disastrous extent, he decided to continue the withdrawal at once to the west bank of the Somme.

On the morning of the 23rd March, therefore, confirming instructions previously given by telephone, orders were issued by the Fifth Army to the XIX. Corps to carry out a gradual withdrawal to the line of the Somme. The VII. Corps was directed to conform to this movement, and to take up a position on the general line Doingt-Nurlu.

This order involved the abandonment of the main Peronne bridgehead position. It greatly shortened the time available for clearing our troops and removable material from the east bank of the river, for completing the necessary final preparations for the destruction of the river and canal bridges, for re-forming west of the river the divisions which had suffered most in the previous fighting, and generally for securing the adequate defence of the river line.

The Crozat Canal Crossed

25. Meanwhile, the enemy had recommenced his attacks. The footing obtained by him on the west bank of the Crozat Canal was gradually increased, in spite of counter-attacks by British and French troops at Tergnier and at other points. During the morning, he forced the passage of the canal at Jussy, where he was reported to have employed tanks east of the canal. Shortly afterwards hostile infantry crossed at Mennessis, though suffering great loss from the

fire of a machine gun detachment of the Canadian Cavalry Brigade. By midday our troops had been pressed back from the line of the canal to the wooded ground to the west, where fierce confused fighting continued throughout the afternoon about Noureuil, Faillouel and Cugny, infantry and cavalry offering a most resolute resistance to the enemy's advance and performing many gallant actions.

The Crossing at Ham

26. In the course of the withdrawal to the Somme on the previous night, a gap occurred in our line in the neighbourhood of Ham, and the enemy, following closely upon our troops, entered the town during the early morning. Before midday bodies of German infantry, though at first only in small numbers, succeeded in crossing the river about Ham and Pithon, where the bridges had not been completely destroyed. In the afternoon these forces increased in strength, gradually pressing back our troops, until a spirited counter-attack by troops of the 20th and 61st Divisions about Verlaines restored the situation in this locality. To the east of this point, heavy fighting took place around Ollezy, which the 36th Division, under command of Major-General O. S. W. Nugent, regained and held until a late hour, and around Aubigny and Brouchy, both of which villages, however, fell into the enemy's hands before night.

Farther north, the withdrawal to the west bank of the Somme was carried out successfully during the morning and early afternoon, effectively covered by troops of the 50th Division. By 3.15 p.m. all troops were across the river, and the bridges for the most part destroyed.

All bridges over the canals and rivers in the Fifth Army area had been carefully listed early in February and reconnoitred for demolition. The necessary explosives were stored in the neighbourhood of each bridge, and a definite party of Royal Engineers detailed for its destruction. As has been seen, however, owing to the effects of the enemy's artillery fire, which blew up some of the charges and cut the leads of others, the destruction of the bridges was in certain cases incomplete.

None the less, the situation on the Somme front north of Ham was for the time being not unsatisfactory. In the course of the afternoon, strong attacks at Offoy and Bethencourt were repulsed with heavy loss by rifle and machine gun fire. In the evening, the enemy's attempts to come down the open slopes on the east bank of the river were heavily punished by artillery fire, as they were on several subsequent occasions. It is believed that north of Ham none of the enemy succeeded in crossing the river before nightfall.

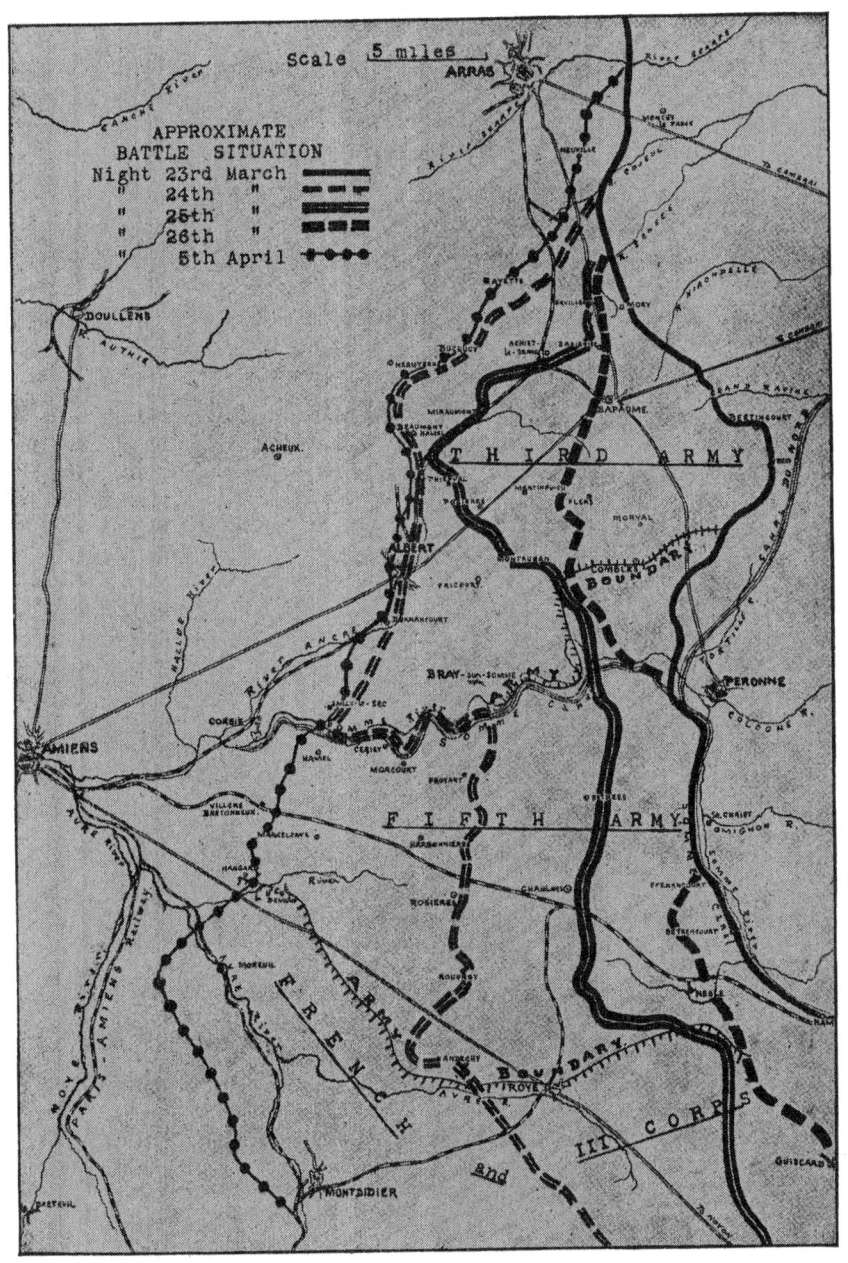

SECOND SOMME BATTLE;
Stages of Retreat.

THE GREAT GERMAN OFFENSIVE 197

The Northern Front Firm

27. Meanwhile, very heavy fighting had been taking place on the northern portion of the battle front. The enemy pressed closely upon our troops, as they withdrew to the line of the ridge running from north of Peronne to Nurlu and Equancourt. Heavy attacks developed at an early hour between these two places, and also between Le Bucquière and Beugny, and at Mory.

On the Third Army front, where our resources were greater, the enemy was held in check, though he gained possession of Le Bucquière and Beugny after a prolonged struggle. In this fighting the 9th Battalion, Welsh Regiment, 19th Division, greatly distinguished itself in the defence of Beugny, which it held till dusk, thereby enabling the other battalions of its brigade in position to the north of the village to extricate themselves successfully from what would otherwise have been a hopeless situation.

No less than six separate attacks, in two of which the enemy brought up cavalry and guns, were repulsed by the 124th Brigade of the 41st Division, Major-General Sir S. T. B. Lawford commanding the division, opposite Vaulx Vraucourt. The fighting in this sector of the front was very severe, but here and at all points north of the Bapaume-Cambrai Road our line was maintained. About 3.30 p.m. the enemy again attacked five times from the direction of Vaulx and five times from Beaumetz-lez-Cambrai, and on each occasion was repulsed. The 40th Division, under command of Major-General J. Ponsonby, regained Mory during the afternoon by successful counter-attacks, and the 31st Division, under command of Major-General R. J. Bridgford, drove off the attacks of two German divisions about St. Leger with heavy loss.

The Retreat to the Tortille

28. At the junction of the Third and Fifth Armies the situation was less satisfactory, and as the day wore on it became critical.

During the morning, the divisions of the V. Corps had proceeded with their withdrawal, and, covered by rearguards who were heavily engaged, had fallen back from the Metz-en-Couture salient to the defences of the third zone about Ytres. The left of the VII. Corps, however, had been withdrawn under orders during the morning from the Nurlu positions to the line of the Canal du Nord, north of Moislains. As the result of this movement a gap was formed between the flank divisions of the two Corps, and this gap the enemy rapidly exploited. Though vigorous efforts were made to re-establish touch both by the 47th Division, under command of Major-

General Sir G. F. Gorringe, and by a brigade of the 2nd Division, Major-General C. E. Pereira commanding the division, they were unsuccessful. The right of the V. Corps was forced back by pressure from the south-east, first to the neighbourhood of Four Winds Farm, south of Ytres, where troops of the 47th Division made a gallant stand in the open until nightfall, and later to a position east of Rocquigny.

The divisions of the VII. Corps, after heavy fighting during the afternoon, were forced back west of Peronne, and across the line of the River Tortille to the high ground about Bouchavesnes and Government Farm, south of Sailly-Saillisel. At dusk, however, the line was still in movement. Small parties of the enemy searched constantly for gaps, and, having found them, bodies of German infantry pressed through in force and compelled our troops to make further withdrawals.

The Extension of the French Front

29. From the time when the indications of an offensive on my front first became definite I had been in close touch with the Commander-in-Chief of the French Armies.[1] On different occasions, as the battle developed, I discussed with him the situation and the policy to be followed by the Allied Armies. As a result of a meeting held in the afternoon of the 23rd March, arrangements were made for the French to take over as rapidly as possible the front held by the Fifth Army south of Peronne, and for the concentration of a strong force of French divisions on the southern portion of the battle front.

For my own part, after consultation with the First and Second Army Commanders, General Sir H. S. Horne and General Sir H. C. O. Plumer, concerning the situation on the fronts of their Armies and the possibilities of attacks developing there also, I arranged for the formation from the troops under their command of a special force of reserve divisions for action as occasion might demand. Measures were also taken to permit of the employment of the Canadian Corps for counter-attack, in the event of the enemy succeeding in piercing my front.

In this connection I desire to express my deep appreciation of the complete unselfishness with which the needs of their own fronts were at all times subordinated by the Army Commanders to the more pressing demands of the battle. A variety of considerations made it necessary for me at this date to draw particularly heavily upon the resources of the Second Army. All my demands were

[1] General Petain.

THE GREAT GERMAN OFFENSIVE 199

met by the Second Army Commander in the most helpful and disinterested spirit.

The Retreat Across the Somme Battlefield

30. During the night of the 23rd/24th March the situation on the battle front remained unchanged as far south as the neighbourhood of Ytres. Beyond that point divisions and brigades had lost touch in the course of their frequent withdrawals, and under the constant pressure of the enemy the rearward movement continued. At dawn German infantry had already reached Bus, Lechelle and Le Mesnil-en-Arrouaise, and during the morning of the 24th March entered Saillisel, Rancourt and Cléry. It became necessary to order the evacuation of Bertincourt, and gradually to swing back the right of the Third Army in conformity with the movement farther south. To the north of Bertincourt, though the enemy gained possession of Mory in the early morning after continuous fighting throughout the night, our troops substantially maintained their positions, the Guards Division under the command of Major-General G. P. T. Feilding, and the 3rd and 31st Divisions in particular, beating off a succession of heavy attacks.[1]

The enemy's advance at the junction of the Third and Fifth Armies was not made without heavy sacrifice. In the retirement of our troops there was no panic of any sort. Units retreated stubbornly from one position to another as they found them turned and threatened with isolation; but at many points fierce engagements were fought, and wherever the enemy attempted a frontal attack he was beaten off with loss.

During the early part of the morning the troops of the 17th Division drove off four attacks east of Barastre, and the 47th Division held the village of Rocquigny from sunrise until well into the afternoon, beating off all attacks with rifle and machine gun fire, until the enemy worked round their flank between Rocquigny and Le Transloy and forced them to withdraw.

South of this point, however, the enemy pressed forward rapidly through the gap which he had made, and succeeded in isolating a part of the South African Brigade, 9th Division, near Marrières Wood, north of Cléry. These troops maintained a most gallant resistance until 4.30 p.m., when they had fired off all their ammunition and only about 100 men remained unwounded. Early in the afternoon German infantry entered Combles, and having gained

[1] After one of these attacks, 400 dead Germans were counted in front of one machine gun position west of Hénin. Ludendorff refers specially to the losses of Von Below's 17th Army on the Arras front, stating that by the 25th March that Army was quite exhausted.

the high ground at Morval were advancing towards Les Bœufs. Their continued progress threatened to sever the connection between the Fifth and Third Armies, and the situation was serious.

In view of this situation the V. and IV. Corps were ordered to fall back to the general line, Bazentin—Le Sars—Grévillers—Ervillers. Meanwhile the leading troops of the 35th Division, under command of Major-General G. McK. Franks, which was arriving at Bray-sur-Somme, and certain composite battalions composed of all available troops in the Albert area, and including tanks personnel with Lewis guns, were hurried forward along the north bank of the river to the support of the VII. Corps. During the afternoon, also, units of the 1st Cavalry Division[1] reached Montauban.

The enemy had already passed Cléry, and was pressing the remaining troops of the 9th and 21st Divisions hard when these various bodies of troops came into action. The 15th Battalion, Cheshire Regiment, and the 15th Battalion, Notts and Derby Regiment, of the 35th Division, checked the enemy by a successful counter-attack, and thereafter a line was taken up and held from the river at Ham to Trônes Wood and Longueval. For the moment the danger in this sector was averted.

The withdrawal of the right and centre of the Third Army was carried out during the afternoon and evening in circumstances of great difficulty, as on the right flank bodies of German infantry were already between our troops and the positions to which they were directed to fall back. In this withdrawal valuable service was rendered by twelve machine guns of the 63rd Division Machine Gun Battalion in Les Bœufs. These guns held up the enemy's advance from Morval at a critical period, firing 25,000 rounds into the enemy's advancing masses, and by their action enabling their division to reach the position assigned to it.

By nightfall the divisions of the V. Corps had taken up their line successfully between Bazentin, High Wood, Eaucourt l'Abbaye and Ligny-Thilloy. Before midnight the troops of the IV. Corps, who had carried out their withdrawal by stages in the face of constant attacks, were established on the line assigned to them west of Bapaume, between Le Barque and Ervillers. Touch between the several divisions of the V. Corps and between the V. and IV. Corps, however, was not properly established.

The Fight for the Somme Crossings

31. South of Peronne the night of the 23rd/24th March passed comparatively quietly; but with the dawn powerful attempts were

[1] These had been brought up from the battle south of the Somme.

made by the enemy to force the crossings of the Somme, and these attempts were by no means confined to the recognised points of passage. Owing to the dry weather, the river and marshes did not constitute a very formidable obstacle to infantry, while the trees and undergrowth along the valley afforded good cover to the enemy, and limited the field of fire of the defenders.

In the early morning, hostile forces which had crossed the river at St. Christ and Bethencourt, were attacked and driven back by troops of the 8th Division, under command of Major-General W. C. G. Heneker, and of the 20th Division: but at Pargny the enemy succeeded in maintaining himself on the west bank of the river, and the flanks of the 8th and 20th Divisions were no longer in touch. During the remainder of the day the enemy repeated his attacks at these and other points, and also exercised strong pressure in a westerly and south-westerly direction from Ham. Our troops offered vigorous resistance, and opposite Ham a successful counter-attack by the 1/5th (Pioneer) Battalion, Duke of Cornwall's Light Infantry, 61st Division, materially delayed his advance.

At nightfall the line of the river north of Epenancourt was still held by us, but the gap opposite Pargny had been enlarged, and the enemy had reached Morchain. South of that point the 20th Division, with its left flank in the air and having exhausted all reserves in a series of gallant and successful counter-attacks, fell back during the afternoon to the line of the Libermont Canal, to which position the great weight of the enemy's attacks from Ham had already pressed back the troops on its right.

The Retreat from Chauny

32. In the area between the Somme and the Oise the enemy's attacks had recommenced at dawn in thick fog, and were pressed with great energy. Troops of the 20th and 36th Divisions at Eaucourt and Cugny found their retreat endangered by the progress made by the enemy on their flanks, and extricated themselves with difficulty, falling back on Villeselve, and ultimately to the neighbourhood of Guiscard. The withdrawal of the troops at Cugny was made possible by a brilliant mounted charge by a squadron of the 6th Cavalry Brigade, which broke through the German line, taking over 100 prisoners and sabring a large number of the enemy.

Throughout the whole of the fighting in this area very gallant work was done, both mounted and dismounted, by units of the 2nd and 3rd Cavalry Divisions, Major-General A. E. W. Harman commanding the 3rd Cavalry Division, in support of our own and the French infantry. The work of the mounted troops, in particular, was invaluable, demonstrating in marked fashion the importance of the part which cavalry have still to play in modern war. So urgent was the demand for more mounted men that arrangements were made during the progress of the battle to provide with horses several regiments of Yeomanry who had but recently been dismounted for employment with other arms. In common with the rest of the cavalry, these Yeomanry did excellent service. Without the assistance of mounted troops, skilfully handled and gallantly led, the enemy could scarcely have been prevented from breaking through the long and thinly held front of broken and wooded ground before the French reinforcements had had time to arrive.

Though French troops were coming rapidly to the assistance of the III. Corps, which on this day passed under the command of the Third French Army, the Allied forces were not yet in sufficient strength to hold up the enemy's advance. After heavy fighting throughout the morning to the east and north of Chauny, our line was gradually forced back to the south and west of that town. In the course of the night the French and British troops immediately north of the Oise were withdrawn to the ridge above Crepigny, whence the line ran across the high ground covering Noyon to the neighbourhood of Guiscard and Libermont.

The Ancre Crossed

33. During the night of the 24th/25th March constant fighting took place on the northern portion of the battle front about Sapignies and Behagnies, where the enemy made determined but unsuccessful efforts to break through.

On the following day the enemy maintained great pressure on this front from Ervillers to the south. Shortly after dawn a very heavy attack on our positions east of the Arras-Bapaume road between Favreuil and Ervillers was repulsed with great loss, and a counter-attack by the 42nd Division, under command of Major-General A. Solly-Flood, drove the enemy out of Sapignies. Later in the morning the 2nd Division beat off an attack at Ligny-Thilloy, and our positions to the north of this point were maintained practically unchanged until midday.

At noon fresh attacks developed in great force, and under the weight of the assault the right of the IV. Corps, with which the divisions of the V. Corps were not in touch, was gradually pressed back. The enemy gained Grévillers, in which neighbourhood the 19th Division was hotly engaged, and also Bihucourt. North of this point our positions were substantially maintained, and at the end of the day our troops still held Ervillers, where the 1st/10th

THE GREAT GERMAN OFFENSIVE 203

Battalion, Manchester Regiment, 42nd Division, had repulsed eight attacks.

On the north bank of the Somme also, between the neighbourhood of Hem and Trônes Wood, all the enemy's attacks were held. Though their left flank was constantly in the air, the various forces operating in this sector maintained a gallant and most successful resistance all day, counter-attacking frequently. Prisoners from five German divisions were taken by us in the course of this fighting, and the enemy's casualties were stated by them to have been abnormally heavy.

Between Montauban and the neighbourhood of Grévillers, however, our troops had been unable to establish touch on the line to which they had withdrawn on the 24th March. After heavy fighting throughout the morning and the early part of the afternoon, in which the 63rd Division in particular, under command of Major-General C. E. Laurie, beat off a number of strong assaults, divisions commenced to fall back individually towards the Ancre, widening the gap between the V. and IV. Corps.

During the afternoon the enemy reached Courcelette, and was pressing on through the gap in our line in the direction of Pys and Irles, seriously threatening the flank of the IV. Corps. It became clear that the Third Army, which on this day had assumed command of all troops north of the Somme, would have to continue the withdrawal of its centre to the line of the River Ancre, already crossed by certain of our troops near Beaucourt. All possible steps were taken to secure this line, but by nightfall hostile patrols had reached the right bank of the Ancre north of Miraumont and were pushing forward between the flanks of the V. and IV. Corps in the direction of Serre and Puisieux-au-Mont. In view of this situation, the IV. Corps fell back by stages during the night and morning to the line Bucquoy-Ablainzevelle, in touch with the VI. Corps about Boyelles. On the right the remaining divisions of the Third Army were withdrawn under orders to the line Bray-sur-Somme—Albert, and thence took up positions along the west bank of the Ancre to the neighbourhood of Beaumont Hamel.

In spite of the dangerous gap about Serre the general position on the Third Army front, though still serious, gave less cause for anxiety. Considerable reinforcements had now come into line, and had shown their ability to hold the enemy, whose troops were becoming tired, while the transport difficulties experienced by him in the area of the old Somme battlefield were increasing. Other reinforcements were coming up rapidly, and there seemed every hope that the line of the Ancre would be secured and the enemy stopped north of the Somme.

The Situation South of the Somme

34. South of the Somme the situation was less satisfactory. The greater portion of the defensive line along the river and canal had been lost, and that which was still held by us was endangered by the progress made by the enemy north of the Somme. All local reserves had already been put into the fight, and there was no immediate possibility of sending further British troops to the assistance of the divisions in line.

On the other hand, the French forces engaged were increasing steadily, and on this day our Allies assumed responsibility for the battle front south of the Somme, with general control of the British troops operating in that sector. The situation still remained critical, however, for every mile of the German advance added to the length of front to be held, and, while the exhaustion of my divisions was hourly growing more acute, some days had yet to pass before the French could bring up troops in sufficient strength to arrest the enemy's progress.

The Enemy in Noyon

35. During the night the enemy had gained possession of Guiscard, and, in the early morning of the 25th March, strongly attacked the Allied positions on the wooded spurs and ridges east and north-east of Noyon. The position of the French and English batteries north of the Oise Canal became hazardous, and they were accordingly withdrawn across the canal at Appily. Dismounted troops of the Canadian Cavalry Brigade actively assisted in covering this withdrawal, which was successfully completed at 1.0 p.m. Shortly afterwards another heavy attack developed in this sector and was checked after hard fighting. At the close of this engagement, troops of the 18th Division retook the village of Babœuf by a brilliant counter-attack, capturing 150 prisoners. Early in the fight French armoured cars rendered valuable service and killed a number of the enemy.

Meanwhile the enemy's progress south and west of Guiscard had continued, and that night his troops entered Noyon. The French and British troops to the east of the town were therefore ordered to withdraw southwards across the Oise, and by the morning of the 26th March this had been successfully accomplished.

After this date, the troops of the III. Corps were gradually relieved by the French reinforcements and sent north to rejoin the Fifth Army.

THE GREAT GERMAN OFFENSIVE 205

The Retreat from the Somme

36. On the Fifth Army front, also, fighting had recommenced at an early hour. Hostile attacks at Licourt and to the south of it widened the gap between the XVIII. and XIX. Corps, and the enemy entered Nesle, forcing the French and British troops back to the high ground on the south bank of the Ingon River, southwest of the town. To the south of this point his troops crossed the Libermont Canal, while to the north the right of the XIX. Corps was slowly pushed back in the direction of Chaulnes. Marchélepot was burning, but our troops at midday were reported to be still holding the line of the canal east of Villers Carbonnel and Barleux.

In view, however, of the situation to the south and the progress made by the enemy on the right bank of the Somme west of Peronne, it was impossible for this position to be maintained. Accordingly, our troops were gradually withdrawn during the evening to the general line Hattencourt-Estrées-Frise, the 39th Division delivering a counter-attack south of Biaches to cover the withdrawal in that area.

A gap still existed between the XVIII. and XIX. Corps west of Nesle, and the Germans had already reached Liancourt Wood, when the 61st Brigade of the 20th Division, which had hitherto been engaged with the 36th Division farther south, was brought up in buses to the neighbourhood of Liancourt. Though reduced to some 450 rifles in its previous fighting, the brigade successfully held up the enemy's advance and made it possible for the remainder of its division to withdraw unmolested through Roye on the morning of the 26th March.

Carey's Force

37. The whole of the troops holding the British line south of the Somme were now greatly exhausted, and the absence of reserves behind them gave ground for considerable anxiety. As the result of a conference held by the Fifth Army Commander on the 25th March, a mixed force, including details, stragglers, schools personnel, tunnelling companies, Army troops companies, field survey companies, and Canadian and American engineers, had been got together and organised by General Grant, the Chief Engineer to the Fifth Army. On the 26th March these were posted by General Grant, in accordance with orders given by the Fifth Army Commander, on the line of the old Amiens defences between Mezières, Marcelcave and Hamel. Subsequently, as General Grant could ill be spared from his proper duties, he was directed to hand over command of his force to General Carey.[1]

[1] At this time General Carey was on his way back from England to take command of the 20th Division, and was therefore available.

Except for General Carey's force there were no reinforcements of any kind behind the divisions, which had been fighting for the most part continuously since the opening of the battle. In consideration of this fact and the thinness of our fighting line, the Fifth Army Commander did not deem it practicable for our troops to attempt to maintain the Hattencourt-Frise positions if seriously attacked. Accordingly, orders had been given on the night of the 25th March that, in the event of the enemy continuing his assaults in strength, divisions should fall back, fighting rearguard actions, to the approximate line Le Quesnoy-Rosières-Proyart. This line was intended to link up with the right of the Third Army at Bray.

The Attempt to Sever the Allied Armies

38. On the morning of the 26th March the enemy recommenced his attack in strength south-westwards and westwards from Nesle, in the double hope of separating the French and British Armies and interfering with the detraining arrangements of our Allies by the capture of Montdidier.

Heavy attacks developed also about Hattencourt, in the neighbourhood of the St. Quentin-Amiens Road, and at Herbécourt. Under the pressure of these assaults our divisions commenced to withdraw slowly in accordance with orders to the line indicated above. This was taken up successfully and maintained, a number of hostile attacks during the afternoon and evening being beaten off by counter-attacks in which local commanders displayed great energy and initiative.

As the British forces retired westwards, however, the French troops on their right were gradually forced back in a south-westerly direction beyond Roye, leaving a gap between the French and British Armies of which the enemy took immediate advantage. To fill this gap the 36th and 30th Divisions, which on the previous day had been withdrawn to rest, were put once more into the battle and speedily became involved in heavy fighting about Andechy and to the north of that place. Though the enemy had penetrated behind them and had taken Erches, the troops of the 36th Division at Andechy maintained a most gallant resistance until the afternoon of the 27th March, thereby playing no small part in preventing the enemy from breaking through between the Allied Armies.

On this part of the battle front a very gallant feat of arms was performed on this day by a detachment of about 100 officers and men of the 61st Brigade, 20th Division, at Le Quesnoy. The detachment was detailed to cover the withdrawal of their division, and under the command of their Brigade Major, Captain E. P. Combe, M.C.,

THE GREAT GERMAN OFFENSIVE   207

successfully held the enemy at bay from early morning until 6.0 p.m., when the eleven survivors withdrew under orders, having accomplished their task.

At the end of the day, although the enemy's thrust west of Roye had pressed back our right somewhat beyond the positions to which it had been intended to withdraw, the British forces south of the Somme were in touch with the French, and the general line, Guerbigny — Rouvroy-en-Santerre — Proyart, had been taken up successfully.

The Northern Advance Stopped

39. Meanwhile, north of the Somme the battle was entering upon its final stages; though the enemy's effort was not yet fully spent and his troops were still capable of powerful attacks.

During the morning of the 26th March our troops continued the taking up of the Ancre line without much interference from the enemy, but between Hamel and Puisieux the situation was not yet clear. A gap still existed in this area between the V. and IV. Corps, through which bodies of German infantry worked their way forward and occupied Colincamps with machine guns. These machine guns were silenced by a section of field artillery of the 2nd Division, which gallantly galloped into action and engaged them over open sights. Early in the afternoon troops of the New Zealand Division, under command of Major-General Sir A. H. Russell, retook Colincamps, while a brigade of the 4th Australian Division, Major-General E. G. Sinclair-Maclagan commanding the division, filled the gap between Hébuterne and Bucquoy. In the fighting in this area our light tanks [1] came into action for the first time and did valuable service.

With the arrival of fresh troops, our line on this part of the front became stable, and all attempts made by the enemy during the day to drive in our positions about Bucquoy and to the north were repulsed with great loss.

The Withdrawal from Bray-sur-Somme

40. Farther south, the Bray-sur-Somme—Albert line had been taken up successfully on the night of the 25th/26th March, and fighting of a minor character occurred during the morning, particularly at Méaulte, where troops of the 9th Division beat off a strong attack. Owing, however, to a misunderstanding, the Bray-sur-

[1] These light tanks, or "whippets," were mistaken by some of our troops for German machines, and gave rise to a local report that the enemy had broken through towards Souastre.

O

Somme—Albert line was regarded by the local commander as being merely a stage in a further retirement to the line of the Ancre, south of Albert. Accordingly, on the afternoon and evening of the 26th March, the withdrawal was continued, and when the higher command became aware of the situation the movement had already proceeded too far for our former positions to be re-established.

By the time the withdrawal had been stopped, the right of the Third Army rested on the Somme about Sailly-le-Sec; while the Fifth Army still held the south bank of the Somme north of Proyart, about five miles farther east. The left flank of the Fifth Army, therefore, was dangerously uncovered, being protected merely by the natural obstacle of the river and an improvised force of 350 men with Lewis guns and armoured cars which had been sent up to hold the crossings.

General Foch appointed to take Command of the Allied Forces

41. On this day, the 26th March, the Governments of France and Great Britain decided to place the supreme control of the operations of the French and British forces in France and Belgium in the hands of General Foch, who accordingly assumed control.[1]

The Enemy in Albert

42. During the night of the 26th/27th March, the enemy had gained possession of Albert after some fighting with our rearguards in the town, and obtained a footing in Aveluy Wood. His efforts to force our positions on the high ground west of the Ancre, however, met with no success, and several attempts made by him on the 27th March to debouch from Albert were driven back with heavy loss to his troops.

About midday, a series of strong attacks commenced all along our front from about Bucquoy to the neighbourhood of Hamelincourt, in the course of which the enemy gained possession of Ablainzevelle and Ayette. Elsewhere, all his assaults were heavily repulsed by troops of the 62nd Division, under command of Major-General W. P. Braithwaite, and of the 42nd and Guards Divisions. On the remainder of our front north of the Somme, save for minor readjustments of our line at certain points, in the course of which we captured a number of prisoners and machine guns, our positions remained unchanged.

[1] The appointment of a Generalissimo was made imperative by the immediate danger of the separation of the French and British Armies.

THE GREAT GERMAN OFFENSIVE 209

The Fight for the Rosières Line

43. South of the Somme, meanwhile, the enemy had recommenced his attacks at about 8.30 a.m. on the greater part of the Fifth Army front and against the French. The line occupied by our troops at this time, had it been maintained, would have preserved Amiens from serious bombardment, and orders were issued that every effort was to be made to hold our positions. In the fighting which followed, troops of all divisions, despite the weakness of their numbers, and the tremendous strain through which they had already gone, displayed a courage and determination in their defence for which no praise can be too high.

At 10.0 a.m. the 8th Division at Rosières had already repulsed a heavy attack, and the enemy was pressing hard against our positions in the neighbourhood of Proyart. The results of the unfortunate withdrawal from Bray now became apparent. The enemy was not slow to take advantage of the position held by him along the north bank of the Somme in the rear of our troops, and in spite of our efforts to destroy or hold the river crossings, began to pass strong parties of infantry to the south bank at Cérisy.

Being heavily attacked in front and with bodies of the enemy established south of the river in their immediate rear, our troops at Proyart and to the north were compelled to fall back. The enemy gained Framerville, Proyart and Morcourt, and endeavoured to advance southwards behind our line.

In view of the absence of reserves behind this front other than the composite force already referred to, the situation was serious. Troops of the 1st Cavalry Division were hurried across the river and occupied Bouzencourt, in which neighbourhood they had sharp fighting. A very gallant and successful counter-attack carried out with great dash by the 2nd Battalion Devon Regiment and the 22nd (Pioneer) Battalion Durham Light Infantry, both of the 8th Division (which was itself heavily engaged at the time at Rosières), supported by troops of the 50th Division, at this date under command of Major-General H. C. Jackson, held up the enemy a short distance south-west of Proyart. A counter-attack by the 66th Division restored the situation about Framerville, and at nightfall our troops were still east and north of Harbonnières, whence our line ran north-westwards to Bouzencourt.

South of Harbonnières, the 8th Division held the village of Rosières against all attacks and killed great numbers of the enemy. South of this point, as far as Arvillers, troops of the 24th, 30th and 20th Divisions maintained their positions substantially unchanged throughout the day, though beyond their right flank the enemy passed Davenscourt and captured Montdidier.

The Amiens Defences

44. During the night of the 27th/28th March, parties of the enemy worked their way southwards from Morcourt and Cérisy and entered Bayonvillers and Warfusée-Abancourt, astride the main Amiens road. Our troops east of these places were seriously endangered, and in the early morning of 28th March were directed to withdraw to the line Vrély-Marcelcave. Our line from Marcelcave to the Somme was manned by Carey's Force, with the 1st Cavalry Division in close support. During the evening, the enemy concentrated heavy artillery fire on Marcelcave and forced these troops to withdraw a short distance to the west of the village.

The position of our troops at Arvillers and Vrély, however, in the deep and narrow salient between the Avre and Luce Rivers, was rapidly becoming untenable. The enemy was pushing southwards from Guillaucourt, and beyond our right flank had entered Contoire and was pressing the French troops back upon Hangest-en-Santerre. A gallant attempt by troops of the 61st Division to regain Warfusée-Abancourt and lighten the pressure from the north proved unsuccessful, and in the course of the afternoon and evening our troops fell back through the 20th Division, which during the evening was disposed on the line Mezières-Démuin. At nightfall we held approximately the Amiens defence line on the whole front south of the Somme from Mezières to Ignaucourt and Hamel.

The nature of the fighting on the southern portion of the battle front, where our troops had been engaged for a full week with an almost overwhelming superiority of hostile forces, had thrown an exceptional strain upon the Fifth Army Commander and his Staff. In order to avoid the loss of efficiency which a continuance of such a strain might have entailed, I decided to avail myself of the services of the Staff of the Fourth Army, which was at this time in reserve. General Sir H. S. Rawlinson, Bt., who had but recently given up the command on appointment to Versailles, accordingly returned to his old Army, and at 4.30 p.m. on this day assumed command of the British forces south of the Somme. At the same time the construction of new defence lines made necessary by the enemy's advance called for the appointment of an able and experienced Commander and Staff to direct this work and extemporise garrisons for their defence. I accordingly ordered General Gough to undertake this important task.

A Break in the Clouds

The Attack on Arras

45. Meanwhile, between 7.0 and 8.0 a.m. on the morning of the 28th March, fighting of the utmost intensity had broken out north of the Somme from Puisieux to north-east of Arras. Finding himself checked on the northern flank of his attack, the enemy on this day made a determined effort to obtain greater freedom for the development of his offensive, and struck in great force along the valley of the Scarpe at Arras.

This development of the battle, which had been foreseen as early as the 23rd March, involved the right of the XIII. Corps, under command of Lieut.-General Sir H. de B. de Lisle, on the right of the First Army, and represented a considerable extension of the original front of attack. A German success in this sector might well have had far-reaching effects. There is little doubt that the enemy hoped to achieve great results by this new stroke, and that its failure was a serious set-back to his plans.[1]

After a bombardment of great violence three fresh German divisions advanced to the assault along the north bank of the Scarpe River against the positions held by the 4th and 56th British Divisions, under the command respectively of Major-General T. G. Matheson, and Major-General F. A. Dudgeon, and were supported in their attack by the two German divisions already in line. According to captured documents, the enemy's immediate object was to gain the general line Vimy—Bailleul—St. Laurent-Blangy, when three special assault divisions were to carry the Vimy Ridge on the following day. Immediately south of the Scarpe four German divisions were engaged, to two of which were assigned the tasks of capturing Arras and the heights overlooking the town. This assault, the weight of which fell on the 3rd and 15th British Divisions, Major-General H. L. Reed commanding the latter division, was supported by powerful attacks, in which eleven hostile divisions were engaged, along our whole front southwards to beyond Bucquoy. Still farther south, as far as Dernancourt, strong local attacks were delivered at different points. The methods followed by the enemy on this occasion were the same as those employed by him on the 21st March, but in this instance the thick fog which had played so decisive a part on that day was absent. In

---

[1] A German prisoner on the XVII. Corps front was found to be carrying six days' rations, two blankets and a new pair of boots. Ludendorff states that the capture of the Vimy Ridge was to have been followed by an attack by the German Sixth Army to carry the high ground east of Lens. He attached the highest importance to both these attacks.

consequence, our artillery and machine guns were given every opportunity to engage the German infantry both when assembling and while advancing to the attack, and the heaviest losses were inflicted on them by our fire.

Immediately prior to the assault, masses of German infantry with artillery in rear of them were observed drawn up in close formation on Greenland Hill, and were shelled by our artillery. North of the Scarpe, about Rœux, great execution was done at point-blank range by single guns which we had placed in forward positions close up to our front line.[1] The enemy's infantry in this sector are reported to have advanced almost shoulder to shoulder in six lines, and on the whole front our machine gunners obtained most favourable targets.

The weight and momentum of his assault and the courage of his infantry, who sought to cut their way through our wire by hand under the fire of our machine guns, sufficed to carry the enemy through the gaps which his bombardment had made in our outpost line. Thereafter, raked by the fire of our outposts, whose garrisons turned their machine guns and shot at the enemy's advancing lines from flank and rear, and met by an accurate and intense fire from all arms, his troops were everywhere stopped and thrown back with the heaviest loss before our battle positions.

A second attack launched late in the afternoon north of the Scarpe, after a further period of bombardment, was also repulsed at all points. At the end of the day our battle positions astride the Scarpe were intact on the whole front of the attack, and in the evening successful attacks enabled us to push out a new outpost line in front of them. Meanwhile, the surviving garrisons of our original outpost line, whose most gallant resistance had played so large a part in breaking up the enemy's attack, had fought their way back through the enemy; though a party of the 2nd Battalion, Seaforth Highlanders, 4th Division, remained cut off at Rœux until successfully withdrawn during the night.

On the southern portion of his attack, the enemy's repulse was, if possible, even more complete than on the new front east of Arras. Attacks on the Guards Division and on the 31st Division were defeated after all-day fighting. The 42nd Division drove off two attacks from the direction of Ablainzevelle, and the 62nd Division with an attached brigade of the 4th Australian Division also beat off a succession of heavy attacks about Bucquoy with great loss to the enemy.

[1] The detachments of certain forward 15-pounder guns, after firing all their ammunition and destroying their guns, got away safely on bicycles along the main Douai road to Arras.

THE GREAT GERMAN OFFENSIVE 213

Less important attacks at different points between Hébuterne and Dernancourt were in each case repulsed, and led to the capture of a number of prisoners by our troops.

The End of the First Stage

46. With this day's battle, which ended in the complete defeat of the enemy on the whole front of his attack, the first stage of the enemy's offensive weakened and eventually closed on the 5th April. During these days hostile pressure continued south of the Somme, and after much fierce and fluctuating fighting in this area, accompanied by a number of strong local attacks also on the northern portion of the battle front, the enemy on the 4th and 5th April made final unsuccessful efforts to overcome the resistance of the Allies. These attacks, however, though formidable, lacked the weight that had made his earlier successes possible, while the strength of the Allied positions increased from day to day.

During the night of the 28th/29th March, our outpost line between Arleux-en-Gohelle and Avion was withdrawn to conform to our positions farther south. Except at minor points, no further ground was gained by the enemy north of the Somme; while by successful local operations on the 30th March and the night of the 2nd/3rd April, the New Zealand Division advanced their line at Hébuterne, capturing 250 prisoners and over 100 machine guns, and the 32nd Division, under command of Major-General C. D. Shute, retook Ayette with 192 prisoners. A number of prisoners were taken by us also in local fighting at other points.

The Fighting in the Avre and Luce Valleys

47. During these latter days the problem south of the Somme was to disengage the divisions which had been fighting since the 21st March, and give them an opportunity to reorganise.[1] Profiting by the great weariness of our troops, the enemy was making

[1] A marked feature of almost all reports sent in by liaison officers during the battle was the good spirit of the men in the fighting line and their confidence that they had given a good account of themselves. The following passage from the report of an officer who visited the front south of the Somme on the 28th March is worth quoting, as giving a first-hand impression of the spirit prevailing at that time :—" From what I saw and from the people with whom I talked, there seems little doubt that although our men are dog-tired they have not lost heart, and I was told that they are all convinced that we are winning. During the earlier stages of the battle they fought exceedingly well, and killed large numbers of the enemy. Even now portions of the line are putting up a very good fight and even at times counter-attacking with success. Divisions are very much disorganised and have with them men of all sorts of divisions, and all Divisional Commanders with whom I have spoken have said that once they are able to re-organise they think they will find their divisions much stronger than they expect. . . . I have not heard any ' grousing ' from anybody."

progress by local attacks rather than by general attacks in force, and there is little doubt that, had it been possible to put in fresh troops a few days earlier, the enemy's advance could have been stopped and even turned back without much difficulty.

The divisions of the III. Corps, which had already been heavily engaged, were on their way to reinforce our line. These troops, however, had not yet arrived, and on the 29th March the greater part of the British front south of the Somme was held by Carey's Force, assisted by the 1st Cavalry Division and such troops of the divisions originally engaged as it had not yet been found possible to withdraw. In rear of these troops, a few of the divisions of the Fifth Army were given a brief opportunity to reassemble.

Hostile pressure recommenced during the morning of the 29th March from Démuin southwards, and in spite of vigorous counter-attacks our troops and the French were forced back from Mezières.

During the night the enemy established a footing in Moreuil Wood, and on the following morning attacked on both sides of the River Luce. Our line in Moreuil Wood was restored by a brilliant counter-attack carried out by the Canadian Cavalry Brigade, supported by the 3rd Cavalry Brigade, but the enemy gained possession of Démuin. North of the Luce also the enemy made some progress, but in the afternoon was held up and finally driven back into Aubercourt by counter-attacks carried out by troops of the 66th Division and the 3rd Australian Division, Major-General Sir J. Monash commanding the latter division. In this operation a squadron of the 2nd Cavalry Division co-operated very finely. In the evening a most successful counter-attack by troops of the 20th and 50th Divisions re-established our line south of the Luce and captured a number of prisoners.

Other hostile attacks on both banks of the Somme were repulsed with heavy loss to the enemy by the 1st Cavalry Division and the 3rd Australian Division, a battalion of United States Engineers rendering gallant service south of the river.

The fighting between the Avre and the Luce continued during the evening of this day, and in the afternoon of the 31st March developed into strong attacks between Moreuil and Démuin. Powerful assaults were delivered also on the French front as far south as Montdidier. In both cases the enemy made progress after heavy fighting, at the close of which troops of the 8th Division carried out a successful counter-attack, thereby considerably improving the situation west of Moreuil Wood. At the end of the day our line ran from Moreuil Station to Hangard, and thence to our old line west of Warfusée-Abancourt.

THE GREAT GERMAN OFFENSIVE 215

On the following morning troops of the 2nd Cavalry Division and of the 8th Division again attacked, and as the result of a very gallant action effected a further improvement in our positions in this neighbourhood. On the 2nd April, for the first time since the opening of the enemy's offensive, no attack took place on the British front south of the Somme.

The Final Effort

48. On the 4th and 5th April the enemy made a final effort to prevent the French and British line from becoming stable.

The principal attack on the 4th April was made south of the Somme, and involved the whole of the British front between the river and Hangard, where we joined the French, and also the French Army on our right. The first assault, delivered at 7.0 a.m., after a comparatively short bombardment, was completely repulsed on the right of our line, but on the left obliged our troops to fall back to the west of Hamel and Vaire Wood. During the afternoon the enemy again attacked heavily on the right, and caused our line to be withdrawn a short distance in the neighbourhood of Hangard Wood.

The enemy attacked in dense formation, and his infantry afforded excellent targets for our artillery and machine guns. Particularly heavy losses were inflicted on the enemy by the artillery of the 3rd Australian Division, on the north bank of the Somme, which engaged his troops across the river over open sights with excellent effect.

The attack on the French front succeeded in making some progress on both sides of the Avre River.

On the 5th April the principal German effort was made north of the Somme, the enemy attacking heavily on practically the whole front from Dernancourt to beyond Bucquoy. Strong local attacks were made also south of the Somme about Hangard, where the French and British troops had severe fighting until late in the day, and in the sector immediately south of the river, where the attacking German infantry were stopped by our artillery and machine gun fire.

North of the river, except for minor readjustments of our line at certain points, particularly in the neighbourhood of Bucquoy, where he gained the eastern portion of the village, the enemy's efforts were entirely without result. His troops, held or driven back at all points, lost heavily, and any hope that he may have entertained of opening the road to Amiens at the eleventh hour ended in an exceedingly costly repulse.

In the neighbourhood of Rossignol Wood the enemy's attack was entirely disorganised by a local attack carried out at a somewhat earlier hour by the 37th Division, under command of Major-General H. B. Williams, as the result of which our positions were improved and over 130 prisoners captured by us.

With the failure of his attacks on the 4th and 5th April the enemy's offensive on the Somme battle front ceased for the time being, and conditions rapidly began to approximate to the normal type of trench warfare, broken only by occasional local attacks on either side.

Reason for Retirement on the Right of the Battle Front

49. Though the enemy's progress had been stopped, this result had been obtained only by the sacrifice of a very considerable area of ground and by a great expenditure of reserves. This latter factor was to have a material influence upon the course of the subsequent fighting on the northern portion of the British front. Before passing, therefore, to the operations on the Lys, it will be convenient to give some account of the causes to which the retirement on the Fifth Army front and the right of the Third Army can be attributed.

(i) In the first place, the forces at the disposal of the Fifth Army were inadequate to meet and hold an attack in such strength as that actually delivered by the enemy on its front.

The reason for this state of affairs has already been pointed out in paragraph 9 of this report, in which the relative importance of the various portions of the line held by the British Army was explained. The extent of our front made it impossible, with the forces under my command, to have adequate reserves at all points threatened. It was therefore necessary to ensure the safety of certain sectors which were vital, and to accept risks at others.

In certain sectors, particularly in the northern and central portions of my front, it was of vital importance that no ground should be given up to the enemy. In the southern sector alone it was possible under extreme pressure to give ground to some extent without serious consequences, over the area devastated by the enemy in his retreat in the spring of 1917. The troops holding this latter part of the front could fall back to meet their reinforcements, which need not necessarily be pushed forward so far or so rapidly as elsewhere. Moreover, the southern sector could be reinforced with French troops more easily than any other portion of the British line. I therefore considered it unsound to maintain a considerable force of British reserves south of the River Somme, while it was yet unknown where and to what extent the enemy would commit his reserves.

The Fifth Army was instructed early in February to act accordingly, both in regard to defensive preparations on the ground and in the actual conduct of the defence.

(ii) The front south of the River Omignon was only taken over by the British some seven weeks before the enemy's attack, a period insufficient to ensure that the scheme of defence would be in an efficient state of preparation. During the winter it had been possible to hold the defences in this sector very lightly, and they were consequently in themselves inadequate to meet any serious form of attack.

Much work, therefore, had to be carried out by the Fifth Army, and strenuous efforts were made with such resources as were available to improve the defences as rapidly as possible. Great difficulties, however, were met with in the devastated area. The roads were in a bad condition, there was no light railway system, the broad gauge system was deficient, and there was a serious lack of accommodation for the troops. The amount of labour at our disposal being limited, all available labour units in rear of the forward defensive zones were allotted to the construction of the Peronne Bridgehead defences, which were considered of primary importance, with the result that practically no work had been carried out with the object of securing the line of the River Somme itself.

(iii) The thick fog which enveloped the battlefield on the mornings of the 21st and 22nd March undoubtedly masked the fire of artillery, rifles and machine guns. Where the troops on the ground were more numerous this was not of such extreme importance; but where the defences were more lightly held, as in the southern sector of the Fifth Army front, and depended for their maintenance on the cross fire of artillery and machine guns, the masking of our fire enabled the enemy to penetrate and turn the flanks of certain important localities.

(iv) On the extreme right, the valley of the River Oise, normally marshy and almost impassable during the early spring, was, owing to the exceptionally dry weather, passable for infantry almost everywhere, and formed no serious obstacle. This applies equally to the valley of the River Somme, which in the latter stage of the battle was easily negotiated by the hostile infantry between the recognised points of passage. A much larger number of troops would therefore have been required to render the defence of these rivers secure. These forces, however, were not available except at the expense of other and more vital portions of my front, and as the exceptional weather conditions could not have been foreseen by the enemy at the time when the preparations for his offensive were undertaken, there was a strong possibility that he would not be able to take advantage of them.

(v) For some time prior to the 21st March it was known that the enemy had been making extensive preparations for an offensive on the Reims front, and that these preparations were already far advanced. As pointed out above, the bombardment on the battle front had been accompanied by great artillery activity on both sides of Reims. It could not be determined with certainty that this was a feint until the attack upon the British had been in progress for some days. The enemy might have employed a portion of his reserves in this sector, and the knowledge of this possibility necessarily influenced the distribution and utilisation of the French reserves.

The Storm-Cloud in the North

The Situation on the Northern Front [1]

50. The possibility of a German attack north of the La Bassée Canal, for which certain preparations appeared to have been carried out, had been brought to my notice prior to the 21st March. Indications that preparations for a hostile attack in this sector were nearing completion had been observed in the first days of April, but its extent and force could not be accurately gauged.

There were obvious advantages for the enemy in such a course of action. In the first place, the depth of his advance on the southern portion of the battle front had left him with a long and dangerously exposed flank between Noyon and Montdidier. The absence of properly organised communications in the battle area made this flank peculiarly vulnerable to a counter-stroke by the French. To prevent this, and preserve the initiative in his hands, it was essential that he should renew his attack without delay.

In the second place, the heavy and prolonged struggle on the Somme had placed a severe strain on the forces under my command and had absorbed the whole of my reserves. Further, to meet the urgent demands of the battle, I had been forced to withdraw ten divisions from the northern portion of my line, and to replace them by divisions exhausted in the Somme fighting, which had only just been made up with reinforcements recently sent out from home. The divisions thus withdrawn had been chiefly taken from the Flanders front, where, in a normal year, the condition of the ground could be relied upon to make offensive operations on a large scale impossible before May at the earliest.

A strong additional reason for drawing these divisions principally from tne north was furnished by conditions on the central portion of my front between the Scarpe and the La Bassée Canal.

[1] *Vide* Map No. 7.

Should urgent necessity arise it would be possible to give ground to a limited extent in the north, while still preserving strong lines of defence, which could in part be covered by inundations.[1] On the other hand, a break through on our centre, about Vimy, would mean the realisation of the enemy's plan which had been foiled by our defence at Arras on the 28th March, namely, the capture of Amiens and the separation of the bulk of the British armies from the French and from those British forces acting under the direction of the latter.

The enemy's preparations for an offensive in this central sector, the extreme importance of which will readily be understood, had been complete for some time. The admirable and extensive railway system serving it made it possible for him to effect with great rapidity at any moment the concentration of troops necessary for an attack. My own forces in this sector, therefore, could not greatly be reduced.

In consequence of these different factors, the bulk of the divisions in front line in the northern battle, and in particular the 40th, 34th, 25th, 19th and 9th Divisions which on the 9th April held the portion of my front between the Portuguese sector and the Ypres-Comines Canal, had already taken part in the southern battle. It must be remembered that before the northern battle commenced forty-six out of my total force of fifty-eight divisions had been engaged in the southern area.

At the end of March, however, the northern front was rapidly drying up under the influence of the exceptionally rainless spring, and, in view of the indications referred to, the possibility of an early attack in this sector became a matter for immediate consideration. Arrangements for the relief of the Portuguese divisions, which had been continuously in line for a long period and needed rest, were therefore undertaken during the first week of April, and were to have been completed by the morning of the 10th April. Meanwhile, other divisions which had been engaged in the Somme fighting, and had been withdrawn to rest and reorganise, were moved up behind the Lys front. Arrangements had already been made for the evacuation of the salient at Passchendaele should circumstances require it, a measure which would both upset any preparations which the enemy might have made for an offensive there and economise a few troops for use elsewhere.

The steps which I could take, however, to meet a danger which I could foresee, were limited by the fact that, though the enemy's progress on the Somme had for the time being been stayed, the great mass of hostile divisions still concentrated on that front

[1] These lines included the Wieltje—Pilckem Ridge, the Ypres Canal line, the Vlamertinghe line, and the Ouderdom—Brandhoek line.

constituted a threat to the safety of the British Armies of an imperative character. The enemy was in a position to take immediate advantage of any weakening of my forces in that area.

The Lys Battle Opened

51. The persistence of unseasonably fine weather and the rapid drying up of the low-lying ground in the Lys Valley enabled the enemy to anticipate the relief of the 2nd Portuguese Division.

On the night of the 7th April, an unusually heavy and prolonged bombardment with gas shell was opened along practically the whole front from Lens to Armentières. At about 4.0 a.m. on the 9th April the bombardment recommenced with the greatest intensity with both gas and high explosive shell.

The enemy's attack in the first instance was launched on the northern portion of the front of General Sir H. S. Horne's First Army, held by the XI. and XV. Corps under command respectively of Lieut.-General Sir R. C. R. Haking, and Lieut.-General Sir J. P. Du Cane. On the 10th April the right of General Sir H. C. O. Plumer's Second Army, held by the IX. Corps under command of Lieut.-General Sir A. Hamilton Gordon, was also involved. In the early stages of the battle the XV. Corps was transferred to the Second Army, and at later dates the extension of the battle front led to the intervention of the I. Corps, under command of Lieut.-General Sir Arthur Holland, on the First Army front, and of the XXII. Corps, under command of Lieut.-General Sir A. J. Godley, on the Second Army front. Subsequently the II. Corps of the Second Army, under command of Lieut.-General Sir C. W. Jacob, became involved in the withdrawal from the Passchendaele salient.

At about 7.0 a.m. on the 9th April, in thick fog which again made observation impossible, the enemy appears to have attacked the left brigade of the 2nd Portuguese Division in strength and to have broken into their trenches. A few minutes afterwards, the area of attack spread south and north. Shortly after 7.0 a.m. the right brigade of the 40th Division reported that an attack had developed on their front and was being held, but that machine gunners near their right-hand post could see the enemy moving rapidly through the sector to the south of them.

Communication with the divisions in line was difficult, but during the morning the situation cleared up, and it became apparent that a serious attack was in progress on the front of the 55th Division, under command of Major-General H. S. Jeudwine, and of the 2nd Portuguese and 40th Divisions from the La Bassée Canal to Bois Grenier. Meanwhile, shortly after the opening of the bom-

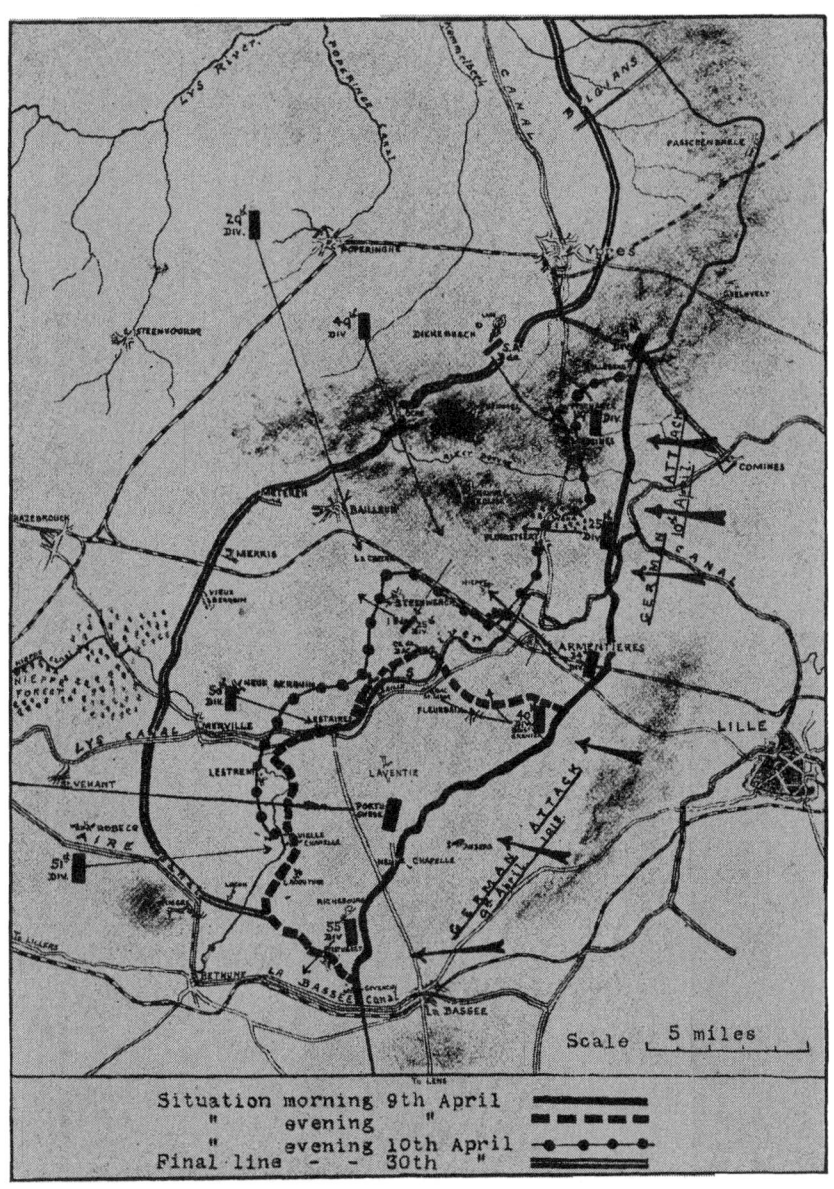

THE LYS BATTLE;
German Attacks of 9th & 10th April, 1918.

bardment, orders had been given to the 51st and 50th Divisions to move up behind Richebourg St. Vaast and Laventie and take up their positions in accordance with the pre-arranged defence scheme. Both these divisions had also been heavily engaged in the Somme battle, and had but recently arrived in the neighbourhood. The 1st King Edward's Horse and the 11th Cyclist Battalion had been sent forward at once to cover their deployment.

Between 8.0 a.m. and 9.0 a.m. the enemy succeeded in occupying the forward posts of the right battalion of the 40th Division and attacked northwards along the Rue Petillon and Rue de Bois. Our machine gun posts in this area continued to fight until all but one of their machine guns were destroyed, and by their fire greatly delayed his progress. At 10.15 a.m., however, his troops were already in Rouge de Bout, more than 2,000 yards in rear of the headquarters of the 40th Division's right battalion, which, at this hour, were still holding out at Petillon. Later in the morning, the 40th Division was pushed back by pressure on its front and flank to a position facing south between Bois Grenier, Fleurbaix and Sailly-sur-la-Lys, its right brigade in particular having lost heavily.

South of the Portuguese sector, the 55th Division was heavily attacked on its whole front, and by 10.30 a.m. its left brigade had been forced back from its outpost line. The main line of resistance was intact, and a defensive flank was formed facing north between Festubert and a strong point just south of Le Touret, where touch was established later with troops of the 51st Division.

Throughout the remainder of the day, the 55th Division maintained its positions against all assaults, and by successful counter-attacks captured over 750 prisoners. The success of this most gallant defence, the importance of which it would be hard to over-estimate, was due in great measure to the courage and determination displayed by our advanced posts. These held out with the utmost resolution though surrounded, pinning to the ground those parties of the enemy who had penetrated our defences, and preventing them from developing their attack. Among the many gallant deeds recorded of them, one instance is known of a machine gun which was kept in action although the German infantry had entered the rear compartment of the " pill-box " from which it was firing, the gun team holding up the enemy by revolver fire from the inner compartment.

To the north of the positions held by the 55th Division, the weight and impetus of the German attack overwhelmed the Portuguese troops, and the enemy's progress was so rapid that the arrangements for manning the rear defences of this sector with British troops could scarcely be completed in time.

The 1st King Edward's Horse and the 11th Cyclist Battalion, indeed, occupied Lacouture, Vieille Chapelle and Huit Maisons, and by their splendid defence of those places enabled troops of the 51st and 50th Divisions to come into action east of the Lawe River between Le Touret and Estaires. East of Estaires our troops found the enemy already in possession of the right bank of the river, and touch between the 50th and 40th Divisions could not be established. After heavy fighting the right of the 40th Division was forced back along the Lys, and early in the afternoon withdrew across the river at Bac St. Maur.

The remainder of the 40th Division, reinforced by troops of the 34th Division, established themselves in a position covering the approaches to Erquinghem and Armentières, between Fort Rompu on the Lys and our old front line north-east of Bois Grenier. Here they successfully maintained themselves, although the line was not readily defensible and was constantly attacked. In this fighting very gallant service was rendered by the 12th Battalion, Suffolk Regiment, 40th Division, who held out in Fleurbaix until the evening, though heavily attacked on three sides.

During the afternoon troops of the 51st and 50th Divisions (chiefly composed of drafts hurriedly sent up to join their regiments) were heavily engaged east of the Lawe River and were gradually pressed back upon the river crossings. The enemy brought up guns to close range, and in the evening crossed at Estaires and Pont Riqueul, but in both cases was driven back by counter-attacks. At the end of the day the bridgeheads were still held by us as far east as Sailly-sur-la-Lys.

In the course of the night our troops at Estaires and in the sector to the south were withdrawn to the left bank of the Lawe and Lys Rivers, after sharp fighting about Pont Riqueul. The bridges across both rivers were blown up, though, as had been the case in the Somme battle, in some instances their destruction was incomplete.

The Crossing at Bac St. Maur

52. East of Sailly-sur-la-Lys the enemy had followed closely the troops of the 40th Division who had crossed at Bac St. Maur and, though here also the bridge had been blown up, at about 3.0 p.m. succeeded in passing small parties across the river by an emergency bridge under cover of machine gun fire. During the remainder of the afternoon and evening the strength of his forces north of the river steadily increased, and pushing northwards they reached Croix du Bac. At this point they were counter-attacked early in the night by a brigade of the 25th Division, and pressed back. Our troops

were unable, however, to clear the German infantry completely from the village, and during the night the enemy established himself firmly on the north bank of the river.

The Struggle for Estaires

53. Early in the morning of the 10th April, the enemy launched heavy attacks covered by artillery fire about the river crossings at Lestrem and Estaires, and succeeded in reaching the left bank at both places; but in each case he was driven back again by determined counter-attacks by the 50th Division.

The enemy continued to exercise great pressure at Estaires, and fierce street fighting took place, in which both sides lost heavily. Machine guns, mounted by our troops in the upper rooms of houses, did great execution on his troops as they moved up to the attack, until the machine guns were knocked out by artillery fire. In the evening the German infantry once more forced their way into Estaires, and after a most gallant resistance the 50th Division withdrew at nightfall to a prepared position to the north and west of the town.

East of Estaires the enemy had already crossed the Lys in strength, with artillery in close support of his infantry, and by the evening had pressed back our troops to a position north of Steenwerck. Thereafter, the arrival of British reinforcements for the time being held up his advance.

The Attack at Messines

54. Meanwhile, after an intense bombardment of our front and support lines and battery areas between Frélinghien and Hill 60, strong hostile attacks had developed at about 5.30 a.m. in this sector also.

The outpost positions of the 25th and 19th Divisions in line north of Armentières and east of Messines were driven in, and during the morning the enemy worked his way forward under cover of mist along the valleys of the Warnave and Douve Rivers, on the flanks of our positions in Ploegsteert Wood and Messines. By midday he had gained Ploegsteert Village, together with the south-eastern portions of Ploegsteert Wood, and had captured Messines. North of that village the area of attack extended during the afternoon as far as the north bank of the Ypres-Comines Canal. In this new sector the enemy carried our forward positions as far as Hollebeke, pushing back our line to the crest of the Wytschaete Ridge.

Messines was retaken early in the afternoon by the South African

Brigade, 9th Division. During the night this division cleared Wytschaete of parties of German troops. North of Hollebeke our positions astride the Ypres-Comines Canal were substantially unchanged, and on this front the 9th Division killed great numbers of the enemy.

The Withdrawal from Armentières

55. The enemy's advance north of Armentières made the position of the 34th Division in that town very dangerous. Though it had not yet been attacked on its own front, its available reserves had already been heavily engaged in protecting its southern flank. As the northern flank also had now become exposed, it was decided to withdraw the division to the left bank of the Lys. The early stages of the movement were commenced shortly after midday. Though the operation was closely followed up by the enemy and pressed by him on all sides, it was carried out with great steadiness and in good order, and by 9.30 p.m. had been completed successfully. All the bridges across the river were destroyed.

The Fall of Merville

56. On the morning of the 11th April the enemy recommenced his attacks on the whole front, and again made progress. Between Givenchy and the Lawe River the successful resistance of the past two days was maintained against repeated assaults. Between Locon and Estaires the enemy, on the previous evening, had established a footing on the west bank of the river in the neighbourhood of Fosse. In this area and northwards to Lestrem he continued to push westwards, despite the vigorous resistance of our troops.

At Estaires, the troops of the 50th Division, tired and reduced in numbers by the exceptionally heavy fighting of the previous three weeks, and threatened on their right flank by the enemy's advance south of the Lys, were heavily engaged. After holding their positions with great gallantry during the morning, they were slowly pressed back in the direction of Merville.

The enemy employed large forces on this front in close formation, and the losses inflicted by our rifle and machine gun fire were unusually heavy. Our own troops, however, were not in sufficient numbers to hold up his advance, and as they fell back and their front gradually extended, gaps formed in the line. Through these gaps bodies of German infantry worked their way forward, and at 6.0 p.m. had reached Neuf Berquin. Other parties of the enemy pushed on along the north bank of the Lys Canal and entered Merville. As it did not appear possible to clear the town without fresh forces, which were not yet available, it was decided to withdraw behind the small stream which runs just west of the town. This withdrawal was successfully carried out during the evening.

The Withdrawal from Nieppe and Hill 63

57. Heavy fighting took place on the remainder of the front south of Armentières, and the enemy made some progress. In this sector, however, certain reinforcements had come into action, and in the evening a counter-attack carried out by troops of the 31st Division, recently arrived from the southern battlefield, regained the hamlets of Le Verrier and La Becque.

Meanwhile, north of Armentières strong hostile attacks had developed towards midday and were pressed vigorously in the direction of Nieppe and Neuve Église. In the afternoon, fierce fighting took place about Messines, which the enemy had regained. Beyond this his troops were not able to push their advance, being checked and driven back by a counter-attack by the South African Brigade. South of Hollebeke the 9th Division had again been heavily attacked during the morning, but had held their positions.

Owing to the progress made by the enemy in the Ploegsteert sector, the position of the 34th Division at Nieppe, where they had beaten off a determined attack during the morning, became untenable. Accordingly, in the early part of the night our troops at Nieppe fell back under orders to the neighbourhood of Pont d'Achelles. Still further to shorten our line and economise men, our troops between Pont d'Achelles and Wytschaete were withdrawn to positions about 1,000 yards east of Neuve Église and Wulverghem. This withdrawal involved the abandonment of Hill 63 and of the positions still held by us about Messines.

The Southern Flank Steady

58. Though our troops had not been able to prevent the enemy's entry into Merville, their vigorous resistance, combined with the maintenance of our positions at Givenchy and Festubert, had given an opportunity for reinforcements to build up our lines in this sector. As troops of the 3rd, 4th, 5th, 31st, 61st and 1st Australian Divisions began to arrive, the southern portion of the battle front gradually became steady. Time was still required, however, to complete our dispositions, and for the next two days the situation in this area remained critical.[1]

A sudden attack just before dawn on the 12th April broke through

[1] There is evidence that the German troops that had entered Merville got out of hand, and instead of pressing their advantage wasted valuable time in plundering the town. On the 12th the 5th Division arrived and secured this front.

the left centre of the 51st Division about Pacaut and Riez du Vinage, and, but for the gallantry and resource of two batteries of the 255th Brigade, R.F.A., commanded respectively by Major T. Davidson, D.S.O., and Major F. C. Jack, M.C., might have enabled the enemy to cross the La Bassée Canal. Each of these batteries as it retired left a gun within 500 yards of the canal and, assisted by a party of gunners who held the drawbridge with rifles, worked with them to such good purpose that the enemy's advance was stopped. The 3rd Division was already in action on the right of the 51st Division about Locon, where, though forced to fall back a short distance, our troops inflicted very heavy casualties upon an enemy greatly superior in numbers. On the left of the 51st Division, the 61st Division was coming into action about the Clarence River. Both the 3rd and the 61st Division had been engaged in many days of continuous fighting south of Arras; but with the arrival of these troops, battle-weary though they were, the enemy's progress in this sector of the front was definitely checked.

At Merville also, our troops, though compelled to give ground somewhat during the morning, thereafter maintained themselves successfully.

The Thrust towards Hazebrouck

59. Meanwhile, a situation which threatened to become serious had arisen north of Merville. At about 8.0 a.m. the enemy attacked in great strength on a front extending from south of the Estaires— Vieux Berquin Road to the neighbourhood of Steenwerck. After very heavy fighting, in the course of which the 1st Battalion Royal Guernsey Light Infantry, 29th Division, Major-General D. E. Cayley commanding the division, did gallant service, he succeeded in the afternoon in overcoming the resistance of our troops about Doulieu and La Becque, forcing them back in a north-westerly direction. As the result of this movement, a gap was formed in our line south-west of Bailleul, and bodies of the enemy who had forced their way through seized Outtersteene and Merris.

In the evening a brigade of the 33rd Division, Major-General R. J. Pinney commanding the division, with a body of cyclists, a Pioneer battalion, and every available man from schools and reinforcement camps, came into action in this sector. On their left, troops of the 25th, 34th and 49th Divisions, Major-General N. J. G. Cameron commanding the last-mentioned division, though heavily attacked, maintained their positions to the south and southeast of Bailleul, and before midnight our line had been re-formed.

Next day, the enemy followed up his attacks with great vigour, and the troops of the 29th and 31st Divisions, now greatly reduced

THE GREAT GERMAN OFFENSIVE   227

in strength by the severe fighting already experienced, and strung out over a front of nearly 10,000 yards east of the Forêt de Nieppe, were once more tried to the utmost. Behind them the 1st Australian Division, under command of Major-General Sir H. B. Walker, was in process of detraining, and the troops were told that the line was to be held at all costs, until the detrainment could be completed.

During the morning, which was very foggy, several determined attacks, in which a German armoured car came into action against the 4th Guards Brigade on the southern portion of our line, were repulsed with great loss to the enemy. After the failure of these assaults, he brought up field guns to point blank range, and in the northern sector with their aid gained Vieux Berquin. Everywhere except at Vieux Berquin, the enemy's advance was held up all day by desperate fighting, in which our advanced posts displayed the greatest gallantry, maintaining their ground when entirely surrounded, men standing back to back in the trenches and shooting in front and rear.[1]

In the afternoon the enemy made a further determined effort, and by sheer weight of numbers forced his way through the gaps in our depleted line, the surviving garrisons of our posts fighting where they stood to the last with bullet and bayonet. The heroic resistance of these troops, however, had given the leading brigades of the 1st Australian Division time to reach and organise their appointed line east of the Forêt de Nieppe. These now took up the fight, and the way to Hazebrouck was definitely closed.

The performance of all the troops engaged in this most gallant stand, and especially that of the 4th Guards Brigade, on whose front of some 4,000 yards the heaviest attacks fell, is worthy of the highest praise. No more brilliant exploit has taken place since the opening of the enemy's offensive, though gallant actions have been without number.

The action of these troops, and indeed of all the divisions engaged in the fighting in the Lys Valley, is the more noteworthy because, as already pointed out, practically the whole of them had been brought straight out of the Somme battlefield, where they had suffered severely and had been subjected to a great strain. All these divisions, without adequate rest and filled with young reinforcements which they had had no time to assimilate, were again hurriedly thrown into the fight and, in spite of the great disadvantages under which they laboured, succeeded in holding up the advance of greatly superior forces of fresh troops. Such an accomplishment reflects the greatest credit on the youth of Great Britain, as well as upon those responsible for the training of the young soldiers sent out from home at this time.

[1] The 5th Division were also attacked heavily, but held their ground.

The Struggle for Neuve Église

60. On the afternoon of the 12th April sharp fighting had taken place in the neighbourhood of Neuve Église, and during the night the enemy's pressure in this sector had been maintained and extended. By the morning of the 13th April his troops had forced their way into the village, but before noon were driven out by troops of the 33rd and 49th Divisions by a most successful counter-attack in which a number of prisoners were taken.

In the course of this day, also, a succession of heavy attacks were driven off with great loss to the enemy by the 33rd and 34th Divisions about Meteren and La Crèche. In the evening further attacks developed on this front and at Neuve Église. The pressure exercised by the enemy was very great, and bodies of German infantry, having forced their way in between La Crèche and Neuve Église, began a strong encircling movement against the left of the 34th Division north and east of the former village. During the early part of the night our troops maintained their positions, but before dawn on the 14th April withdrew under orders to a line in front of the high ground known as the Ravelsberg Heights between Bailleul and Neuve Église, the enemy having been too severely handled to interfere.

At Neuve Église the enemy again forced his way into the village, and heavy and confused fighting took place throughout the night. A party of the 2nd Battalion Worcestershire Regiment, 33rd Division, maintained themselves in the Mairie until 2.0 p.m. on the 14th April, and during the morning of this day other troops of the same division were reported to have cleared the village with bombs. The enemy persisted in his attacks, however, and by midnight Neuve Église was definitely in his possession. Other attacks delivered on the 14th April between Neuve Église and Bailleul and south-east of Meteren were repulsed.

Farther south, local fighting had taken place meanwhile both on the 13th and 14th April at a number of points between Givenchy and the Forêt de Nieppe. In these encounters the enemy had met with no success. On the other hand, a local operation carried out by the 4th Division on the evening of the 14th April resulted in the recapture of Riez du Vinage with 150 prisoners.

The Capture of Bailleul

61. On the morning of the 15th April the 19th Division repulsed hostile attacks about Wytschaete. Late in the afternoon fresh assaults in great strength, in which the Alpine Corps and two other fresh

THE GREAT GERMAN OFFENSIVE 229

German divisions were engaged, developed against Bailleul and the Ravelsberg Heights. After heavy fighting the enemy gained a footing on the eastern end of the high ground and, though driven back by a counter-attack, re-established his position there and worked west along the ridge. By 7.0 p.m. the whole of it was in his possession, and the retention of Bailleul itself became very difficult. Two hours later, hostile infantry forced their way into the town, and our troops, who were being heavily attacked from the east and south, were compelled to fall back to positions between Meteren and Dranoutre.

The Withdrawal at Passchendaele

62. In order to set free additional British troops for the battle and to delay the execution of any plans which the enemy might be entertaining for extending the flank of his attack to the north, I approved of putting into execution the scheme for the gradual evacuation of the Ypres salient. The first stage in this withdrawal had been carried out on the night of the 12th/13th April, since which date our positions on the Passchendaele Ridge had been held by outposts only.

On the night of the 15th/16th April the withdrawal was carried a stage further, our troops taking up positions along the line of the Steenbeek River and the Westhoek and Wytschaete Ridges.

The Arrival of French Troops

63. The constant and severe fighting on the Lys battle front, following so closely upon the tremendous struggle south of Arras, had placed a very serious strain upon the British forces. Many British divisions had taken part both in the northern and southern battles, while others had been engaged almost continuously from the outset of the German offensive. I had represented the state of affairs to General Foch, Commanding-in-Chief the Allied Forces, and had pointed out to him the necessity of relief for the British troops and their need of an opportunity to rest and refit. General Foch had complied with my request without delay. Certain French forces were moved to the north, and by this date were already in position close behind the British front in Flanders.

The First Attacks on Kemmel

64. At different times on the 16th April a number of strong local attacks were made by the enemy on the Meteren-Wytschaete front, which were for the most part repulsed with heavy loss to him by the 25th, 34th and 49th Divisions. At Meteren and Wytschaete,

however, he succeeded in penetrating our positions, and after much rather confused fighting established himself in both villages. Counter-attacks delivered during the evening by British and French troops failed to eject him, though at Wytschaete a battalion of the 9th Division reached the eastern edge of the village, and our line was ultimately established close up to its western and northern outskirts.

These attacks were followed on the morning of the 17th April by a determined attempt on the part of the enemy to capture the commanding feature known as Kemmel Hill. The assault was launched after a preliminary bombardment of great intensity, and was accompanied by strong attacks in the Meteren and Merris sectors.

The enemy's attacks in the Kemmel sector were pressed with great determination, but ended in his complete repulse at all points by troops of the 34th, 49th and 19th Divisions, his infantry being driven out by counter-attacks wherever they had gained a temporary footing in our line. The attacks at Meteren and Merris were also beaten off with heavy loss by the 33rd Division and the 1st Australian Division.

On this day also the enemy launched a strong assault upon the right of the Belgian Army about the Ypres-Staden Railway. This attack, the object of which was to capture Bixschoote and advance beyond the Yser Canal, ended in complete failure, and left over 700 prisoners in the hands of our Allies.

Operations North of Bethune

65. On the 18th April the enemy made a fresh effort to overcome our resistance on the southern flank of his attack. After a heavy bombardment, which at Givenchy is reported to have exceeded in intensity even the bombardment of the 9th April, his infantry attacked on nearly the whole front from Givenchy to west of Merville. At Givenchy and Festubert they succeeded at certain points in entering our positions, but after severe and continuous fighting, lasting throughout the day, the troops of the 1st Division, under command of Major-General E. P. Strickland, regained by counter-attacks practically the whole of their original positions. Elsewhere the enemy failed to obtain even an initial success, being repulsed with exceedingly heavy loss at all points by the 4th and 61st Divisions.

For nearly a week following the failure of these attacks the battle on the Lys front died down, though sharp fighting of a minor character took place from time to time at different points, particularly in the neighbourhood of Festubert, where a strong point, known as Route "A" Keep, changed hands more than once before

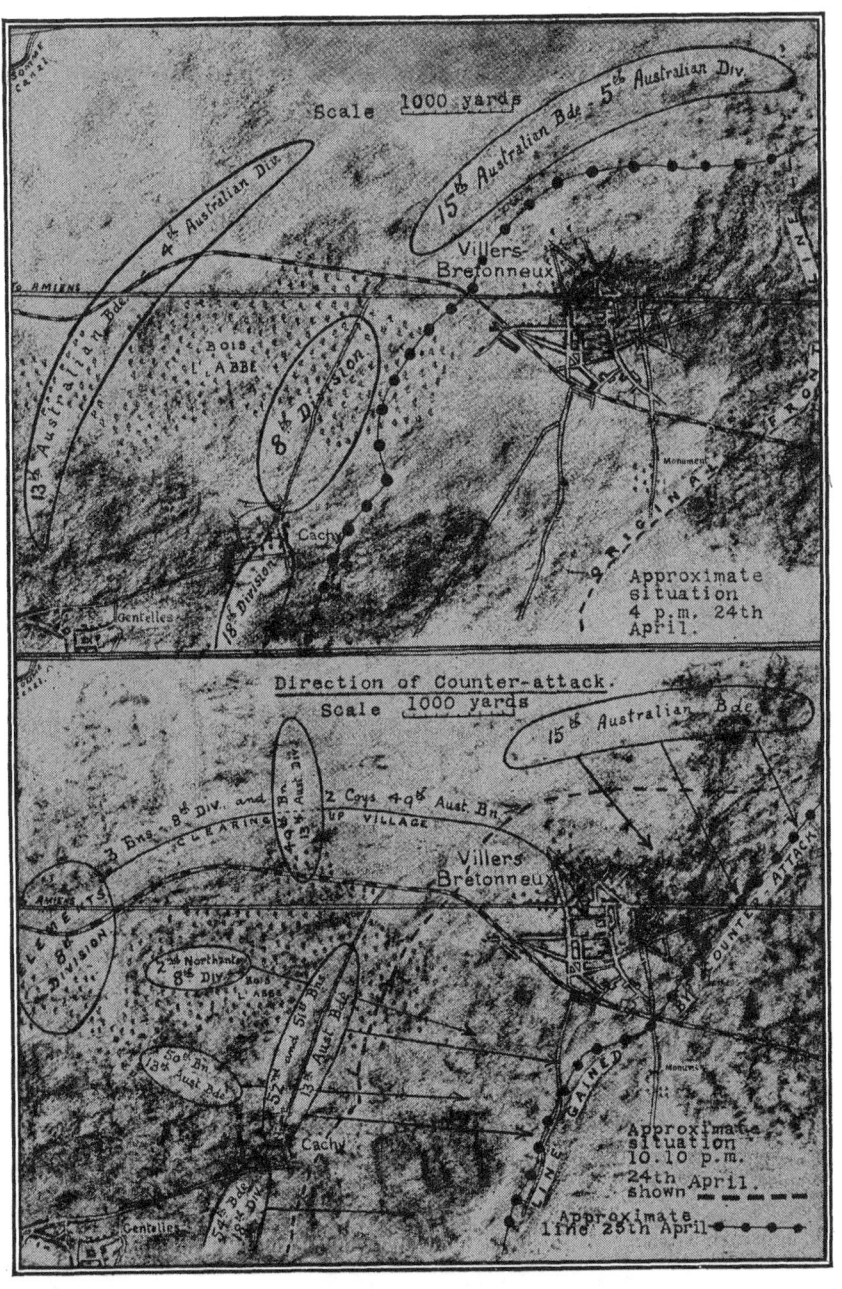

VILLERS BRETONNEUX;
23rd-25th April, 1918.

remaining finally in our possession. Further west, the 4th Division, in co-operation with the 61st Division, carried out a series of successful local operations north of the La Bassée Canal, resulting in the capture of some hundreds of prisoners and a considerable improvement of our positions between the Lawe and the Clarence Rivers.

During this period, also, the French troops which had already come into line in the neighbourhood of Meteren and opposite Spanbroekmolen gradually relieved the British troops between these two points, and by the morning of the 21st April had taken over the whole of the Kemmel sector.

THE STORM PASSES

The Attack on Villers Bretonneux

66. Local attacks, meanwhile, had taken place from time to time on both sides of the Somme battle front, particularly in the vicinity of Hangard, where our line linked up with the French, and about Aveluy Wood. On the 24th April a more serious attack, in which four German divisions were employed against the British forces alone and German and British tanks came into conflict for the first time, took place on the Allied front between the Somme and the Avre Valleys.

At about 6.30 a.m., after a heavy bombardment lasting about three hours, the enemy advanced to the assault on the whole British front south of the Somme, under cover of fog. In the ensuing struggle, German tanks broke through our line south-east of Villers Bretonneux, and turning to north and south, opened the way for their infantry. After heavy fighting, in which great losses were inflicted on his troops both by our infantry fire and by our light tanks, the enemy gained possession of Villers Bretonneux; but was held up on the edge of the wood just west of that place by a counter-attack by the 8th Division. South of Villers Bretonneux, some of our heavy tanks came into action and drove back the German tanks, with the result that the enemy's infantry were stopped some distance to the east of Cachy Village, which formed their objective. North of Villers Bretonneux, all attacks were repulsed.

At 10.0 p.m. on the night of the 24th/25th April, a counter-attack was launched by a brigade of the 18th Division and the 13th and 15th Brigades of the 4th and 5th Australian Divisions, Major-General Sir J. J. T. Hobbs commanding the latter division, and met with remarkable success. A night operation of this character, undertaken at such short notice, was an enterprise of great daring. The instant decision to seize the opportunity offered, and the rapid and thorough working out of the general plan and details of the attack on the part of the III. Corps Commander and divisional and subordinate commanders concerned, are most worthy of commendation, while the unusual nature of the operation called for the highest qualities on the part of the troops employed. It was carried out in the most spirited and gallant manner by all ranks. The 13th Australian Brigade, in particular, showed great skill and resolution in their attack, making their way through belts of wire running diagonally to the line of their advance, across very difficult country which they had no opportunity to reconnoitre beforehand.

At daybreak Villers Bretonneux was practically surrounded by our troops. During the morning two battalions of the 8th Division worked their way through the streets and houses, overcoming the resistance of such parties of the enemy as were still holding out. That afternoon Villers Bretonneux was again completely in our possession. In this well-conceived and brilliantly-executed operation nearly 1,000 prisoners were captured by our troops. A German tank was left derelict in our lines and was salved subsequently.

The Capture of Kemmel Hill

67. These operations on the southern front were followed on the 25th April by a renewal of the enemy's attacks in great strength north of the Lys.

Following upon a very violent bombardment, at about 5.0 a.m. the enemy attacked the French and British positions from Bailleul to the Ypres-Comines Canal with nine divisions, of which five were fresh divisions and one other had been but lightly engaged. The main object of the attack was the capture of Kemmel Hill by a direct assault upon the French, combined with an attack upon the British right south of Wytschaete, aimed at turning the British right flank and separating it from the French. At that date the British right flank lay on the Messines-Kemmel Road, at a point about half-way between Kemmel and Wytschaete.

After very heavy fighting, the German infantry worked their way round the lower slopes of the high ground, and at 10.0 a.m. had succeeded in capturing Kemmel Village and Hill; though elements of French troops held out until a late hour on the hill and in the village.

The weight of the attack in the British sector fell on the 9th Division and attached troops of the 49th Division, who at 7.0 a.m. were still holding their positions about Wytschaete intact, though heavily engaged. Fierce fighting continued in this neighbourhood

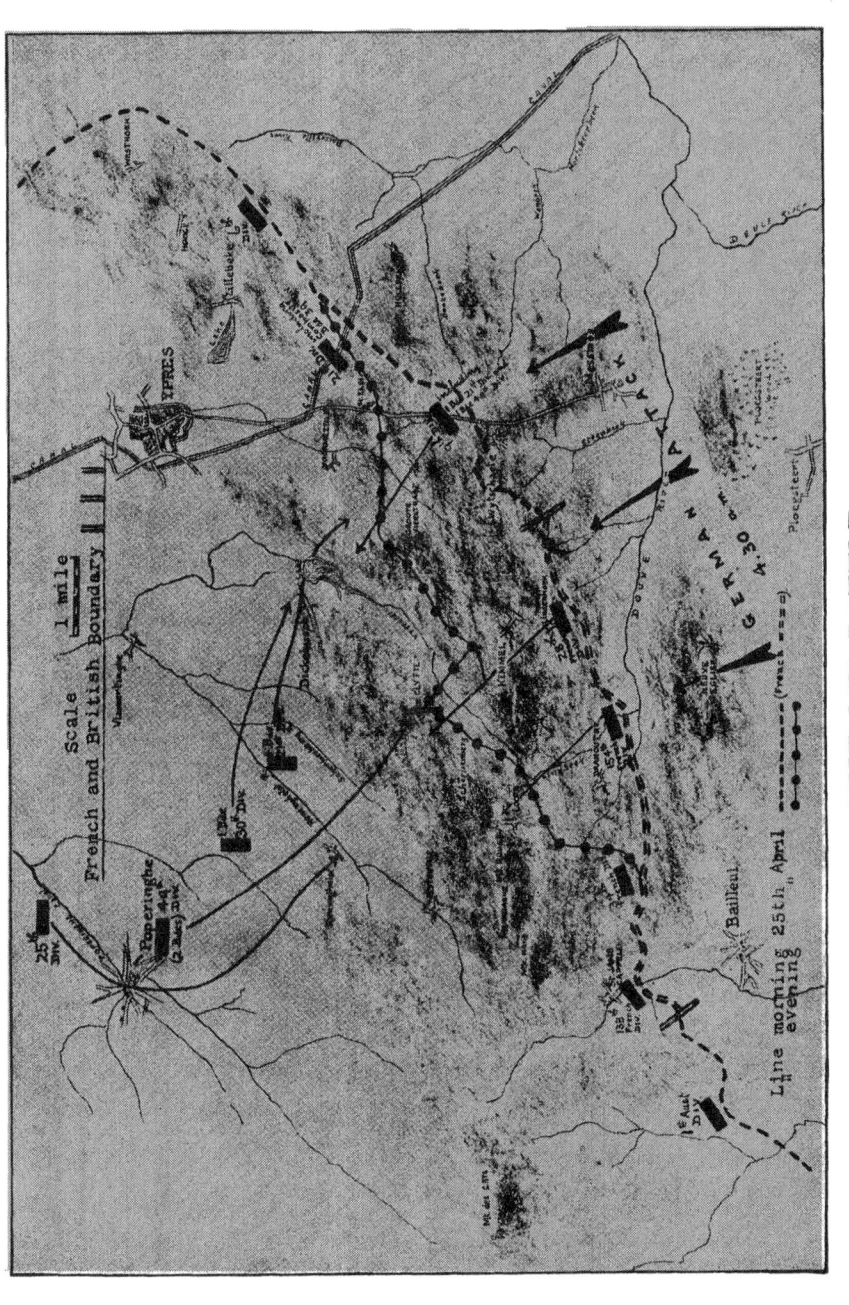

THE LYS BATTLE;
German Attack, 25th April, 1918.

THE GREAT GERMAN OFFENSIVE 233

for some hours later, and great numbers of Germans were killed by rifle and machine gun fire at short range. Later in the morning the right of the 9th Division was forced to fall back fighting stubbornly to Vierstraat, but at 1.0 p.m. our troops still held the Grand Bois north of Wytschaete.

In the afternoon the attack spread northwards along the front held by the 21st Division. By the evening our troops had been gradually pushed back from their forward positions, and held a line running from Hill 60 to Voormezeele, whence it passed north of Vierstraat to our junction with the French about La Clytte. The Allied line had not been broken, and reinforcements were hurrying up.

Next day fighting continued fiercely. In the early morning a very gallant counter-attack by the 25th Division, with attached troops of the 21st and 49th Divisions, undertaken in conjunction with the French, penetrated into Kemmel Village, taking over 300 prisoners. Our troops then found themselves exposed to heavy machine gun fire from the flanks, and were unable to maintain their positions.

Later in the morning the enemy renewed his attacks in strength, but, in spite of repeated efforts, was only able to make small progress at certain points. Troops of the 21st, 30th, 39th and 49th Divisions (Major-General C. A. Blacklock commanding the 39th Division), and the South African Brigade of the 9th Division, had heavy fighting, and made several gallant counter-attacks. It will not have been forgotten that each of the 21st, 30th and 39th Divisions had experienced severe and prolonged fighting in the battle of the Somme.

Successful counter-attacks were carried out also by the French, in the course of which the village of Locre was recaptured in a very gallant action.

The capture of Kemmel Hill seriously threatened our positions in the Ypres salient, the communications and southern defences of which were now under direct observation by the enemy, while his continued progress to the north-west in the Voormezeele sector would make the extrication of troops east of Ypres most hazardous. A further readjustment of our line in the salient was accordingly carried out on the night of the 26th/27th April, our troops withdrawing to the general line Pilckem—Wieltje—west end of Zillebeke Lake—Voormezeele.

The Enemy's Advance Stayed

68. On the 28th April local fighting took place in the neighbourhood of Locre and Voormezeele without material change in the situation; but on the following day, encouraged by the capture of

Kemmel Hill, the enemy made a determined effort to improve his success.

After a bombardment of exceptional intensity, which started at 3.10 a.m., a series of strong attacks were launched about 5.0 a.m. against the French and British positions from west of Dranoutre to Voormezeele. Very heavy fighting rapidly developed on the whole of this front, and ended in the complete repulse of the enemy with the heaviest losses to his troops.

At Locre and to the north of that village the enemy made desperate attempts to overcome the resistance of our Allies and gain possession of the high ground known as the Scherpenberg. At one time parties of his troops entered Locre, and penetrated to the cross roads between the Scherpenberg and Mont Rouge, but in both localities successful French counter-attacks drove him out after bitter fighting.

On the British front the positions held by the 21st, 49th and 25th Divisions were strongly attacked between 5.0 a.m. and 5.30 a.m. On the failure of these attacks bodies of German infantry advanced at 6.0 a.m. in mass formation, with bayonets fixed, against the 49th Division, and were repulsed with the heaviest losses. The 25th Division was again attacked at 8.35 a.m., and during the morning repeated attacks were made without result on this division and the 49th Division, as well as on the 21st Division and attached troops of the 30th and 39th Divisions. At all points the attack was pressed vigorously with massed bodies of troops, and the losses suffered by the German infantry were very great. Throughout the whole of the fighting our infantry and artillery fought magnificently, and in more than one instance our troops went out to meet the German attack and drove back the enemy with the bayonet.

At the end of the day, except for a small loss of ground about Voormezeele, our line was intact, and the enemy had undergone a severe and decided check.

In concert with this operation, the Belgian positions astride the Ypres-Staden Railway were again attacked, and once more vigorous counter-strokes by Belgian troops promptly ejected the German infantry from such ground as had been gained by them in their first assault. Here also the enemy's failure was complete.

On the 30th April the French retook Locre early in the morning, but beyond this no infantry action of importance took place, and the month closed with the enemy definitely held on both the southern and the northern battle fronts.

The Task of the British Armies

69. It has been seen that in the Somme battle, by the end of March, in addition to some ten German divisions engaged against

THE GREAT GERMAN OFFENSIVE 235

the French, a total of 73 German divisions were engaged and fought to a standstill by 42 British infantry divisions and three cavalry divisions. In order to complete the comparison between the forces engaged and to enable the nature of the task accomplished by our troops to be realised, it will be of value to give similar figures for the battle of the Lys.

In the Lys battle, prior to the 30th April the enemy engaged against the British forces a total of 42 divisions, of which 33 were fresh and 9 had fought previously on the Somme. Against these 42 German divisions 25 British divisions were employed, of which 8 were fresh and 17 had taken a prominent part in the Somme battle.

In the six weeks of almost constant fighting, from the 21st March to the 30th April, a total of 55 British infantry divisions and 3 cavalry divisions was employed on the battle fronts against a force of 109 different German divisions. During this period a total of 141 different German divisions were engaged against the combined British and French forces.

Our Troops

70. The splendid qualities displayed by all ranks and services throughout the Somme and Lys battles make it possible to view with confidence whatever further tests the future may bring.

On the 21st March the troops of the Fifth and Third Armies had the glory of sustaining the first and heaviest blow of the German offensive. Though assailed by a concentration of hostile forces which the enemy might well have considered overwhelming, they held up the German attack at all points for the greater part of two days, thereby rendering a service to their country and to the Allied cause the value of which cannot be over-estimated. Thereafter, through many days of heavy and continuous rearguard fighting, they succeeded in presenting a barrier to the enemy's advance until such time as the arrival of British and French reinforcements enabled his progress to be checked.

In the battle of the Lys, as has been pointed out above, many of the same divisions which had just passed through the furnace of the Somme found themselves exposed to the full fury of a second great offensive by fresh German forces. Despite this disadvantage they gave evidence in many days of close and obstinate fighting that their spirit was as high as ever and their courage and determination unabated. Both by them and by the divisions freshly engaged every yard of ground was fiercely disputed, until troops were overwhelmed or ordered to withdraw. Such withdrawals as were deemed necessary in the course of the battle were carried out successfully and in good order.

At no time, either on the Somme or on the Lys, was there anything approaching a breakdown of command or a failure of morale. Under conditions that made rest and sleep impossible for days together, and called incessantly for the greatest physical exertion and quickness of thought, officers and men remained undismayed, realising that for the time being they must play a waiting game, and determined to make the enemy pay the full price for the success which for the moment was his.

In the course of this Report it has been possible to refer to a very few of the many instances in which officers and men of all arms and services have shown courage and skill of the highest order. On countless other occasions officers and men, of whose names there is no record, have accomplished actions of the greatest valour, while the very nature of the fighting shows that on all parts of the wide battle fronts unknown deeds of heroism were performed without number.

Infantry

The British infantryman has always had the reputation of fighting his best in an uphill battle, and time and again in the history of our country, by sheer tenacity and determination of purpose, has won victory from a numerically superior foe. Thrown once more upon the defensive by circumstances over which he had no control, but which will not persist, he has shown himself to possess in full measure the traditional qualities of his race.

Artillery

The part of the artillery in a defensive battle is at once a most important and a most difficult one. The conditions under which guns are fought in trench warfare make a certain loss of material unavoidable when, in a defensive battle, a sudden change takes place to a war of movement. Yet, even in such circumstances, in which, moreover, the affording of artillery support to our infantry till the last moment is of paramount importance, much can be done and on countless occasions much was done, by swift and resolute action, to prevent guns falling into the hands of the enemy. The loss of artillery in the series of battles, though considerable, might well have been much greater but for the courage, skill and resource displayed by all ranks of the artillery, both heavy and field, and but for the constant efforts made to maintain close co-operation between artillery and infantry.

THE GREAT GERMAN OFFENSIVE

Of the courage and devotion of the artillery numerous instances could be given, but one example must suffice. On the occasion of the attack east of Arras on the 28th March, a six-inch howitzer battery was heavily engaged by the enemy's artillery. After all the gun detachments had been either killed or wounded and all the guns but one had been destroyed, the remaining four officers of the battery continued to serve their last gun, until two of them were killed and the other two wounded.

Cavalry

On the southern battle front, and particularly in the fighting about Noyon, cavalry were once more employed with great effect, and proved their extreme value in warfare of a more open nature. On more than one occasion they were able by rapid and successful action to restore a doubtful situation, while their appearance in the battle gave great encouragement to the infantry.

Royal Air Force

The work of the Royal Air Force, under command of Major-General J. M. Salmond, in co-operation with the other arms, has been brilliant. Throughout the period of active operations our airmen have established and maintained a superiority over the enemy's air forces without parallel since the days of the first Somme battle. Not content with destroying the enemy in the air, they have vigorously attacked his infantry, guns and transport with bombs and machine gun fire, and in the fighting south of the Somme in particular gave invaluable assistance to the infantry by these means on numerous occasions. In addition, the usual work of reconnaissance, photography, artillery co-operation and bombing has been carried out vigorously and with remarkable results.

Tank Corps

Reference has been made more than once in the body of this Report to the very valuable work accomplished by tanks and tank personnel in the course of the Somme battle. Throughout the whole of this fighting, tanks took part in numerous successful counter-attacks, many of which were instrumental in checking the enemy's progress at critical points. On these occasions tanks have shown that they possess capabilities in defence little, if at all, less than those which they have already proved in attack. In their first encounter with German tanks, officers and men of the Tank Corps displayed with success under conditions new in warfare the same energy and resource which have always characterised their action.

Machine Guns and Trench Mortars

The experience of the Somme and Lys battles has emphasised once more the great value of the machine gun in defensive warfare, when handled by brave, skilful and resolute men. In the course of the recent fighting officers and men of the Machine Gun Corps have furnished innumerable examples of the utmost resolution, courage and skill in the use of their weapons. They have been largely instrumental in defeating the enemy's determined efforts to break through, and have inflicted on him very severe losses.

The same conditions of warfare on the battle fronts which handicapped the work of the artillery affected trench mortars in an even greater degree. Despite the disadvantages under which they suffered, the personnel of trench mortar batteries of all natures have performed on numberless occasions the most valuable service in the defence of strong points and defended localities, serving their weapons with effect though surrounded by the enemy, and giving the greatest possible assistance to the infantry and machine gunners.

Royal Engineers

The work of the Royal Engineers, both during and subsequent to the retreat on the Somme and on the northern battle front, has been particularly arduous. In addition to the heavy demands made upon them in the destruction of roads and bridges and such-like matters during retreat, and the labour entailed in the construction of new positions, they have frequently been called upon to take their place in the firing line. On such occasions their various units have behaved with the greatest steadfastness and courage, and, in circumstances such as those in which the 251st Tunnelling Company greatly distinguished itself at Givenchy, have added to the high reputation of their service.

In this connection, a generous recognition is due to the gallant conduct of the various composite battalions which on different occasions took their place in the firing line.

During the long periods of active fighting the strain placed upon the Signal Service was immense. The frequent changes of headquarters and the shifting of the line entailed constant labour, frequently attended with great danger, in the maintenance of communications; while the exigencies of the battle on more than one occasion brought the personnel of the signal units into the firing line. The Signal Service met the calls upon it in a manner wholly admirable, and the efficient performance of its duties was of incalculable value.

THE GREAT GERMAN OFFENSIVE 239

On different occasions, and particularly on the Third Army front at the commencement of the German offensive, personnel of the Special Brigade (Gas Services) became involved in the infantry battle, and behaved with a like gallantry to that which they have always displayed in the performance of their special duties.

Other Services

The enormous amount of additional work thrown upon the different branches of my Staff and upon the Administrative Services and Departments by such fighting as that of March and April can readily be imagined. The evacuation of great masses of stores, hospitals, rolling-stock, agricultural implements, non-combatants, labour units and civilians from the battle area, and the supplying of the troops in constantly changing places with food and ammunition called for the highest powers of organisation, the most constant forethought and supervision, and the most devoted labour. That all this work was carried out so smoothly and successfully under circumstances of extraordinary difficulty, and that there was never any lack of food or ammunition for the troops reflects the very highest credit on all concerned.

Upon the Transportation Services, moreover, and particularly upon the Omnibus Park, the rapid movement of reserves placed a peculiarly heavy strain, which the different units concerned never failed to meet successfully.

Much additional work, also under circumstances of unusual difficulty and danger, has necessarily been thrown upon the medical and nursing services. The conduct of the Royal Army Medical Corps and Medical Corps of the Overseas Dominions has again been beyond all praise, while the efficient organisation of the medical services as a whole proved itself fully equal to the occasion. I take this opportunity to acknowledge the lasting debt due in this connection to Lieut.-General Sir A. T. Sloggett, until recently Director-General of Medical Services, with whom the work of the medical services has so long been identified.

Commanders and Staffs

I desire to express my deep appreciation of the loyal and devoted work of the Commanders and Staffs of all formations of the British Army serving under me in a period of exceptional stress. In defensive battles of such magnitude as those which have just been fought to a successful conclusion the part played by subordinate commanders and staffs is frequently of decisive importance, demanding great strength of character and a high standard of ability, while the physical and mental strain is correspondingly great. That mistakes should occur in such circumstances is almost inevitable. That they should have been so few as they were and that control should at all times have been so well maintained reflects the greatest credit upon the individuals concerned, upon the staff arrangements of all formations, and the Army as a whole.

The part played by the various Branches of the Staff of an Army in the organisation and control of battles such as those referred to in this Despatch is one of the utmost importance, and the strain thrown upon the individual officers composing them is very great.

I wish to thank the heads of the various Branches of the Staff and of Departments and Services for the essential share that they and their subordinates have taken in preventing the realisation of the enemy's plans.

I am glad to acknowledge the great assistance given me at all times by my Chief of the General Staff, Lieut.-General the Hon. Sir H. A. Lawrence, whose cool judgment, equable temperament and unfailing military insight were of the utmost value in circumstances demanding the exercise of such qualities in a peculiarly high degree.

The rapid incorporation of reinforcements and reorganisation of exhausted units without which the battle could scarcely have been maintained was most ably carried out by the Adjutant-General, Lieut.-General Sir G. H. Fowke, and his Branch.

The work of my Quartermaster-General's Branch under Lieut.-General Travers Clarke, in the provision and replacement of munitions and supplies of all kinds was of the highest importance, and was performed with the greatest ability and success.

The large and incessant demands made upon the Transportation Services in the course of the battle were met in the most admirable manner by my Director-General, Brigadier-General S. D'A. Crookshank, and those working under him.

My thanks are due also to the subordinate members of my Staff at General Headquarters, whose heavy and responsible duties were discharged throughout the period under review with most commendable smoothness and efficiency. In particular I desire to mention the services of my Artillery Adviser, Major-General Sir J. F. N. Birch; my Engineer-in-Chief, Major-General G. M. Heath; the head of the Operations Section, Major-General J. H. Davidson; the head of the Staff Duties Section, Major-General G. P. Dawnay; the head of my Intelligence Section, Brigadier-General E. W. Cox; and my Director of Army Signals, Major-General Sir J. S. Fowler.

THE GREAT GERMAN OFFENSIVE 241

Home Authorities and the Royal Navy

My thanks, and those of all ranks of the British Armies in France, are due also to the different authorities at home, whose prompt and energetic action enabled the unavoidable losses of personnel and material incurred during the battle to be replaced with such rapidity. We are glad also to place on record once again our deep appreciation of the work of the Royal Navy, upon whose unceasing efforts depends the maintenance of the British Forces in France.

Our Allies

71. I cannot close this Report without paying my personal tribute to the ready and effective assistance given me by the French and Belgian Higher Commands in the course of the Somme and Lys battles. Reference has already been made to the schemes for mutual co-operation and assistance between the French and British Armies which formed so important a part of the Allied plan for the year's campaign. These schemes have been carried out with absolute loyalty. The support rendered by French troops south of the Somme and north of the Lys, and by Belgian troops in taking over the responsibility for the greater part of the line previously held by British troops north of Ypres, has been of incalculable value.

I desire also to express my appreciation of the services rendered by the Portuguese troops who had held a sector of my front continuously throughout the winter months, and on the 9th April were called upon to withstand the assault of greatly superior forces.

Finally, I am glad to acknowledge the ready manner in which American Engineer Units have been placed at my disposal from time to time, and the great value of the assistance they have rendered. In the battles referred to in this Despatch, American and British troops have fought shoulder to shoulder in the same trenches, and have shared together in the satisfaction of beating off German attacks. All ranks of the British Army look forward to the day when the rapidly growing strength of the American Army will allow American and British soldiers to co-operate in offensive action.

> I have the honour to be,
> My Lord,
> Your Lordship's obedient Servant,
> D. HAIG, Field-Marshal,
> Commanding-in-Chief, British Armies in France.

THE ADVANCE TO VICTORY

THE ADVANCE TO VICTORY

21st December, 1918.[1]

MY LORD,—

I have the honour to submit the following Report on the operations of the forces under my command since the successful termination of the great defensive battles on the Somme and Lys Rivers, which were described in my last Despatch.

GENERAL INTRODUCTION

State of the British Armies

1. At the end of April, 1918, though the onrush of the German Armies had been stemmed for the time being, the situation on the Western Front, and particularly on the British portion of it, was still critical.

The immense weight of the enemy's first and heaviest onslaughts in March and April, and the unprecedented masses of men and material employed by him, had called for practically the whole strength of the British Armies to withstand them, and had left our forces greatly weakened. Although prompt steps had been taken by the home authorities to dispatch to France as rapidly as possible all reinforcements then available in England, as well as to recall considerable bodies of troops from other theatres of war, these reinforcements required time to arrive. A further period was needed to complete their training and equipment, to allow troops brought from abroad to become acclimatised, and to enable the new drafts to become assimilated within their various units.

Meanwhile it had become impossible to maintain at an effective strength the full number of our divisions. At the beginning of May no less than eight divisions [2] had been reduced to cadres and were temporarily written off altogether as fighting units. Two other divisions were holding positions in line with reduced cadres which it was not yet possible to bring up to establishment.

---

[1] This Despatch was signed by Sir Douglas Haig in England, and for this reason bears no address of origin. It was published as a Supplement dated the 7th January, 1919, to the *London Gazette* of the 3rd January, 1919.

[2] The 14th, 16th, 31st, 34th, 39th, 40th, 59th and 66th. The 30th and 61st were in line, but not made up to establishment.

Arrangements had been made at the end of April to hand over to the French for employment on a quiet part of their front a further five divisions, comprising the IX. Corps (see para. 10 below). These had only just been reconstituted, and, being badly in need of rest and training, were not yet considered fit to hold an active sector. In return for these five British divisions, and in accordance with Marshal Foch's views, presently explained, regarding the enemy's intentions, the French had dispatched a number of their divisions to be held in reserve in rear of the British right and to strengthen the Flanders front.

There remained available for operations on the British front forty-five British infantry divisions, most of which were below establishment. Fully three-fourths of them had been heavily engaged in one or other of the enemy's offensives, if not in both. All were urgently in need of rest; they contained a large number of young, partially trained and totally inexperienced recruits, and subordinate commanders had had little or no opportunity to become acquainted with their men.

The Position of our Allies

2. The French, though as yet they had been less heavily engaged than ourselves, had none the less been obliged to employ a substantial proportion of their reserves in the fighting south of the Somme and north of the Lys.

The American Army, though rapidly increasing in numbers and efficiency, was not yet ready to take the field in sufficient strength materially to affect the situation. In short, the German attacks, though they had failed to break the Allied line, had stretched the resources of the Allies to the uttermost; while before Amiens and Hazebrouck they had brought the enemy within a short distance of strategic points of great importance. In these circumstances, the possibility of an immediate renewal of the enemy's offensive could not but be viewed with grave anxiety.

The Enemy's Position

3. On the other hand, the enemy had undoubtedly paid heavily for his successes, and had used up a great number of divisions, among them his best and his most highly trained. The reserves which he was known to have had at his disposal at the beginning of the year would suffice, indeed, to make good his losses; but in his case, also, time would be required before the divisions which had suffered most would be fit to undertake a fresh attack against prepared positions.

THE ADVANCE TO VICTORY 247

At the commencement of the period under review the enemy was estimated to possess seventy-five divisions in reserve on the Western Front.[1] It was evident that further German attacks could not long be postponed if the enemy was to achieve a decision before the weight of the American Army was thrown into the scale.

The Enemy's Intentions

4. At this period, early in May, the Allied High Command repeatedly expressed the opinion that the enemy would renew his attack on a large scale on the front Arras-Amiens-Montdidier. The strategic results to be obtained by the capture of Amiens, the separation of the French and British Armies, and an advance towards the sea along the Valley of the Somme were very great, and might well have proved decisive. The enemy's opening offensive had already brought him within a measurable distance of success in this direction, and had carried his Armies through practically the whole of our organised lines of defence.

Since the conclusion of his attacks on this front in the first week of April, the enemy had had a considerable period of time in which to re-establish communications through the devastated area, and make his preparations for a fresh advance. This period of delay had also afforded us some opportunity, of which full use was being made with all the means and resources in our power, to lay out new trench lines and reconstruct such old systems as already existed. This work, however, was still far from complete, and our defences could not be compared with those which the enemy had already over-run.

The Policy of the British Armies

5. In short, the enemy still possessed a sufficient superiority of force to retain the initiative, and it was known that he would be compelled to act within a comparatively limited time if he were to turn his superiority to account before it passed from him. These were the two main factors which had to be taken into consideration when deciding the policy of the British Armies during the late spring and early summer. The common object of the French and ourselves was to tide over the period which must still elapse until the growth of the American Armies and the arrival of Allied reinforcements placed the opposing forces once more on a footing of equality.

The situation was an anxious one, but it was confidently expected that, if all measures open to us were undertaken promptly and

[1] This was probably rather an over-estimate.

executed with the energy and zeal demanded by the occasion, the enemy's future assaults would be met and overthrown as those had been which he had already made. If the Allies could preserve their front unbroken until August at the latest there was every hope that during the later portion of the year they would be able to regain the initiative, and pass to the offensive in their turn.

The period under review accordingly divides itself naturally into two main sections. During the first, the policy governing the action of the forces under my command was the maintenance of an active defence, whereby our line might be preserved unbroken, while every opportunity was taken to rest and train our sorely-tried divisions. As the strength and efficiency of our divisions were restored, minor operations of gradually increasing scope, but with limited objectives, could be carried out with greater frequency. These would serve to keep alive the fighting spirit of the troops, and could be used to effect local improvements in our line, where such improvement was considered necessary either for defence or for attack.

The second period arrived when the swelling list of German casualties and the steady influx of American and Allied reinforcements had produced an equilibrium of strength between the opposing forces. The complete success of the Allied counter-attack on the 18th July near Soissons marked this turning-point in the year's campaign, and commenced the second phase of the Allied operations. Thereafter the initiative lay with the Allies, and the growing superiority of their forces enabled them to roll back the tide of invasion with ever-increasing swiftness. At this point and in this connection I should like to pay my personal tribute to the foresight and determination of the French Marshal in whose hands the co-ordination of the action of the Allied Armies was placed.

PART I

The Period of Active Defence

Reorganisation

6. During the period following the breakdown of the German attacks on the Lys the military centre of gravity moved to the south, and, as regards the British front, the months of May, June and July, though full of incident of a minor character, in which the different troops concerned showed great gallantry and skill, can be dealt with comparatively shortly.

At the outset of this period, the most pressing need after that of filling up the gaps in our divisions, was to close the breaches which the German advances had made in our successive defensive systems. This work had been begun, indeed, in the early days of the Somme offensive, but much still remained to be accomplished before our positions could be regarded as reasonably secure.

Further, the depth to which the enemy had penetrated in the Somme and Lys Valleys had disrupted important lateral lines of railway, and had created a situation of extreme gravity with regard to the maintenance of communications in Northern France. At Amiens, Béthune and Hazebrouck much-used railway junctions had been brought under the effective fire of the enemy's guns, while the railway centre at St. Pol was threatened. To relieve the situation a comprehensive programme of railway construction was undertaken by us in conjunction with the French, so as to provide three separate routes for North and South traffic, which should be independent of Amiens. This involved extensive doublings and quadruplings of existing railways and the building of new lines, for which some 200 miles of broad gauge track was laid during the period April-July.

All these various constructional needs threw an immense amount of work upon the staff of the departments concerned, and called for the employment of great quantities of skilled and unskilled labour. All available resources of men and material were concentrated upon satisfying them, and by the time that the great change in the general military situation had taken place, the essential part had been satisfactorily accomplished. In particular, a complete series of new defensive lines had been built, involving the digging of 5,000 miles of trench.

Minor Operations in May and June

7. While intense activity prevailed behind the lines, our fighting troops were not idle. Full use was made of harassing tactics by all arms, and in the Lys salient in particular the German troops crowded into this exposed area were continually subjected to a most effective system of artillery harassing fire.

The losses suffered by the enemy in the Lys sector and the destruction caused to his artillery and material were very great. Convincing evidence of this was obtained from prisoners' statements and was furnished also by the extensive German graveyards [1] afterwards found in this area, by the condition of the roads, and the litter of all kinds found near them and near battery positions and dumps. These tactics undoubtedly postponed the renewal of the

---

[1] In a single vast graveyard near Sailly-sur-la-Lys over 5,000 Germans are buried.

German offensive on this front until the Allied counter-offensive made it impossible.

The chief centres of infantry activity during this period were on the fronts of the Fourth and Second Armies. Early in May small operations improved our line about Morlancourt. These were followed on the 19th May by an admirably executed operation in which the 2nd Australian Division (Major-General N. M. Smyth) took Ville-sur-Ancre with 400 prisoners. Later, on the 10th June, the same division in a highly successful night attack on a front of about two miles south of Morlancourt, effected a substantial advance, taking over 300 prisoners.

On the Second Army front, Locre Hospice and the small woods south-east of Dickebusch Lake, known as Scottish and Ridge Woods, were the scenes of very lively fighting, in which French forces took part. A successful minor operation by the French on the 20th May resulted in a valuable gain of ground in the neighbourhood of Locre Hospice and the capture of over 500 prisoners, though the Hospice itself was not secured by us till the first week in July. Ridge Wood changed hands several times prior to its final capture with 350 prisoners by the 6th Division (Major-General Sir T. O. Marden) and 33rd Division (Major-General Sir R. J. Pinney) on the 14th July.

A material improvement in our line was also effected by the capture on 3rd June of the small hill known as the Mont de Merris, west of Merris village, with nearly 300 prisoners, by the 1st Australian Division (Major-General Sir H. B. Walker) and troops of the 29th Division (Major-General D. E. Cayley). At other points there was much fighting of a minor character, notably about Aveluy Wood and in the neighbourhood of the Lawe River and Merville.

Operations in July ; Hamel Captured

8. Two months of comparative quiet worked a great change in the condition of the British Armies. The drafts sent out from England had largely been absorbed, many of the reinforcements from abroad had already arrived, and the number of our effective infantry divisions had risen from forty-five to fifty-two. In artillery we were stronger than we had ever been.

Though the general situation did not warrant the adoption of a definitely offensive policy, in view of the concentration of the bulk of the enemy's large reserves in Prince Rupprecht's Group of Armies opposite the British front, I now felt strong enough to undertake operations of a somewhat larger scope, which would at once strengthen our position for defence and fit in with future schemes.

The first of these, carried out at the end of June, east of Nieppe

THE ADVANCE TO VICTORY 251

Forest, aimed at establishing our main line of resistance farther in advance of the wooded ground, which was constantly being shelled with gas. The assault, launched at 6.0 a.m. on the 28th June by the 5th Division (Major-General R. B. Stephens) and 31st Division (Major-General J. Campbell), without preliminary bombardment, took the enemy by surprise and was completely successful; the German defences west of the Plate Becque stream, on a front of 6,000 yards from Pont Tournant to La Becque, being captured, together with some 450 prisoners.

A necessary preliminary to any operation to disengage Amiens was the recapture of our old positions east of Hamel and Vaire Wood and the clearing of the Villers Bretonneux Plateau. This was accomplished on the 4th July by the Australian Corps (Lieut.-General Sir J. Monash), with the aid of four companies of the 33rd American Division and sixty tanks.

The most striking characteristic of the attack was the close and effective co-operation between tanks and infantry. Moving up and down behind the barrage, the tanks either killed the enemy or forced him to take shelter in dug-outs, where he became an easy prey to the infantry. Hamel was taken by envelopment from the flanks and rear, the enemy was driven from Vaire Wood, and at the end of the day our troops had gained all their objectives and over 1,500 prisoners.

Our success at Hamel was followed by a series of admirably executed operations north of the Lys.

On the 11th July troops of the 1st Australian Division gave a striking example of their ascendancy over the German infantry opposite to them. At 11.0 a.m. on this day, four men went out on patrol near Merris and returned with between thirty and forty prisoners. Other patrols, pushed forward both by the 1st Australian and 31st Divisions, secured in two days no fewer than 223 prisoners and established a number of new posts well in advance of our former line.

Surprise played an important part in the successful attack by which the 9th Division (Major-General H. H. Tudor) took Meteren on the 19th July, with some 350 prisoners. The village stood on high ground close to our line, and its capture provided greater depth to our defence.

For some time prior to this attack gas was discharged, in conjunction with a smoke and high-explosive shell bombardment. When at 7.55 a.m. on the 19th July our infantry advanced behind a barrage of smoke and high explosive the enemy was expecting only a gas discharge, and had in many cases put on gas masks.

The capture of Meteren was followed shortly after midnight on the 28th/29th July by a boldly-conceived operation by the 1st

Australian Division, which resulted in the capture of Merris, with 187 prisoners.

Operations on the French Front

9. By the end of July the reconstitution of the British Armies had been completed. The spirit of the men was as high as ever, and the success of their various local operations had had a good effect. I had once more at my command an effective striking force, capable of taking the offensive with every hope of success when the proper moment should arrive.

Meanwhile, events of the utmost and most critical importance had been taking place on the French front.

The British General Staff had always held the opinion that before the resumption of the enemy's main offensive on the Arras-Amiens-Montdidier front the attack on our northern flank in Flanders would be followed by a similar attack on the southern flank of the Allied Armies. This view had proved correct. Though probably delayed by his unexpectedly extensive commitments in the Lys battle, at the end of May the enemy had developed his plan of operations on the lines which we had foreseen, and had launched a violent surprise attack on the Aisne front. In this attack certain British divisions which had been sent there to rest became involved from the outset.

Operations of the IX. Corps in the Aisne Battle

10. At the end of April and early in May the 8th, 21st, 25th and 50th Divisions, subsequently reinforced by the 19th Division, and constituting the IX. British Corps, under command of Lieut.-General Sir A. Hamilton Gordon, had been placed at Marshal Foch's disposal as noted above. These divisions had been dispatched by him to the French Sixth Army, to take the place of certain French divisions concentrated behind Amiens.

Of these divisions, the 19th (Major-General G. D. Jeffreys), 21st (Major-General D. G. M. Campbell), 25th (Major-General Sir E. G. Bainbridge) and 50th Divisions (Major-General H. C. Jackson) had taken part in both the Somme battle and the battle of the Lys. The 8th Division (Major-General W. C. G. Heneker) had been involved south of the Somme in some of the heaviest fighting of the year, and had behaved with distinguished gallantry. All these divisions had but lately been filled up with young drafts, and, despite their high spirit and gallant record, were in no condition to take part in major operations until they had had several weeks' rest. During the first fortnight in May three of these divisions—the 21st,

THE ADVANCE TO VICTORY

8th and 50th—were put into line on a front of about fifteen miles between Bermicourt and Bouconville, north-west of Reims.

About the 26th May, prisoners taken by the French gave the first definite information regarding the great offensive launched by the enemy on the Aisne front on the morning of the 27th May. This attack, delivered by twenty-eight German divisions supported by tanks, was directed against the Sixth French Army on a front of about thirty-five miles north-west of Reims. It involved the whole of the IX. British Corps, as well as the French Corps holding the Chemin des Dames on the left of the British sector.

Preceded by an artillery and trench mortar bombardment of great intensity, the German infantry broke into the battle positions of the Allied divisions. The enemy gained a footing on the Chemin des Dames at an early hour, and pressing on in the centre of his attack in overwhelming strength, forced the line of the Aisne on a wide front. By nightfall he had crossed the Vesle west of Fismes, and in the British sector, after very heavy and determined fighting, had compelled the left and centre of the IX. Corps, now reinforced by the 25th Division, to swing back to a position facing west and north-west between the Aisne and the Vesle.

On the 28th May and following days the enemy launched fresh attacks in great force on the whole battle front, pressing back our Allies to west of Soissons and south of Fère-en-Tardenois. The IX. British Corps, greatly reduced in numbers by severe and incessant fighting, was forced to withdraw across the Vesle, and thence gradually pressed back in a south-easterly direction between the Vesle and the Ardre. During the night of the 28th/29th May the 19th Division was brought up in buses, and put in to fill a gap in the French line across the Ardre Valley, deploying with great skill and steadiness. By the evening of the 30th May, at which date in the centre of his attack the enemy had reached the Marne, the rate of his advance in the British sector had begun to slacken.

During the next few days, however, fighting was still intense. On the southern and western portions of the battle front the enemy made deep progress, gaining the north bank of the Marne from Dormans to Château Thierry and advancing astride the Aisne to the outskirts of the Villers Cotterets Forest, and across the high ground north-east of Attichy. On the eastern flank of the salient created by the enemy's advance the British forces, at this date under command of the French Fifth Army, withdrew gradually to the line Aubilly-Chambrecy-Boujacourt, where they were able to consolidate. Though the enemy's attacks continued persistently for some time longer, and on the 6th June culminated in two determined attempts upon the important position known as the Montagne de

Bligny, which commands the valley of the Ardre, all these attacks were most gallantly repulsed, and the enemy's advance definitely stayed.

Throughout this long period of incessant fighting against greatly superior numbers the behaviour of all arms of the British forces engaged was magnificent. What they achieved is best described in the words of the French General [1] under whose orders they came, who wrote of them :—" They have enabled us to establish a barrier against which the hostile waves have beaten and shattered themselves. This none of the French who witnessed it will ever forget."

The Second Battle of the Marne

11. While our troops were still engaged in the fighting southwest of Reims a fresh battle had broken out on the 7th June on the French front between Noyon and Montdidier. In this case the enemy did not succeed in effecting a surprise, but the strain thrown upon the French Armies by these two attacks was considerable, and the situation was such that the German Command might reasonably be expected to endeavour to develop it with all the means at their disposal.

While, on the one hand, at the beginning of July it was known that Prince Rupprecht's reserve group of divisions about Douai and Valenciennes were still intact and opposite the British front, on the other hand, for a number of reasons it was believed at French General Headquarters that the Germans were about to attack in strength east and west of Reims. It was apprehended, indeed, that the attack might spread even farther east into the Argonne and might endanger a wide sector of the French position. Marshal Foch accordingly withdrew the whole of the French forces, some eight divisions, from Flanders, and transferred them southwards to the French front. In addition he asked that four British divisions might be moved, two of them to areas south of the Somme and two to positions astride that river, so as to ensure the connection between the French and British Armies about Amiens and to enable him to move four French divisions farther east to his right flank. After carefully weighing the situation, I agreed to this proposal, and immediate orders were given for the movement.

On the 13th July a further request was received from Marshal

[1] General Maistre. In a farewell letter to General Hamilton Gordon, dated the 3rd July, 1918, he wrote :—" Avec une ténacité, permettez-moi de dire, toute anglaise, avec les débris de vos divisions décimées, submergées par le flot ennemi, vous avez reformé, sans vous lasser, des unités nouvelles que vous avez engagées dans la lutte, et qui nous ont enfin permis de former la digue où ce flot est venu se briser. Cela aucun des témoins français ne l'oubliera ! "

THE ADVANCE TO VICTORY

Foch that these four British divisions might be placed unreservedly at his disposal, and that four other British divisions might be dispatched to take their places behind the junction of the Allied Armies. This request was also agreed to, and the 15th, 34th, 51st and 62nd British divisions, constituting the XXII. Corps, under command of Lieut.-General Sir A. Godley, were accordingly sent down to the French front.

Meanwhile, on the 15th July, the enemy had launched his expected attack east and south-west of Reims, and after making some progress at first and effecting the passage of the Marne, was held by the French, American and Italian forces on those fronts. On the 18th July Marshal Foch launched the great counter-offensive which he had long been preparing on the front between Château Thierry and Soissons, supporting this successful stroke by vigorous attacks also on other parts of the German salient. In this fighting the XXII. British Corps speedily became involved.

Operations by the XXII. Corps

12. On the 20th July the 51st and 62nd Divisions of the XXII. Corps, under command of Major-Generals G. T. C. Carter-Campbell and W. P. Braithwaite respectively, attacked in conjunction with the French on the eastern side of the salient south-west of Reims. The sector assigned to the British troops covered a front of 8,000 yards astride the Ardre River, and consisted of an open valley bottom, with steep wooded slopes on either side. Both valley and slopes were studded with villages and hamlets, which were for the most part intact and afforded excellent cover to the enemy.

On this front our troops were engaged for a period of ten days in continuous fighting of a most difficult and trying nature. Throughout this period steady progress was made, in the face of vigorous and determined resistance. Marfaux was taken on the 23rd July, and on the 28th July British troops retook the Montagne de Bligny, which other British troops had defended with so much gallantry and success two months previously. In these operations, throughout which French artillery and tanks rendered invaluable assistance, the 51st and 62nd Divisions took 1,200 prisoners from seven different German divisions and successfully completed an advance of over four miles.

Meanwhile, on the 23rd July, the 15th and 34th Divisions, under command of Major-Generals H. L. Reed and C. L. Nicholson respectively, attacked on the west side of the salient in the neighbourhood of Berzy-le-Sec and Parcy-Tigny, south-west of Soissons. These divisions also had many days of heavy and continuous fighting on different parts of this front until withdrawn during the first days of August, and acquitted themselves very gallantly side by side with their French comrades in arms. Many prisoners were taken by both divisions, and the 15th Division in particular earned distinction in the fierce struggle for Buzancy.[1]

PART II

THE PERIOD OF OFFENSIVE ACTION

The Situation at the End of July

13. The definite collapse of the ambitious offensive launched by the enemy on the 15th July, and the striking success of the Allied counter-offensive south of the Aisne, effected a complete change in the whole military situation. The German Army had made its effort and had failed. The period of its maximum strength had been passed, and the bulk of the reserves accumulated during the winter had been used up. On the other hand, the position of the Allies in regard to reserves had greatly improved. The fresh troops made available during the late spring and early summer had been incorporated and trained. The British Army was ready to take the offensive; while the American Army was growing rapidly and had already given convincing proof of the high fighting quality of its soldiers.

At a conference held on the 23rd July, when the success of the attack of the 18th July was well assured, the methods by which the advantage already gained could be extended were discussed in detail. The Allied Commander-in-Chief asked that the British, French and American Armies should each prepare plans for local offensives, to be taken in hand as soon as possible, with certain definite objectives of a limited nature. These objectives on the British front were the disengagement of Amiens and the freeing of the Paris-Amiens Railway by an attack on the Albert-Montdidier front. The rôle of the French and American Armies was to free other strategic railways by operations farther south and east.

In addition to the disengagement of Amiens, the situation on the British front presented strong arguments in favour of certain other schemes, such as the disengagement of Hazebrouck by the recapture of Kemmel Hill, combined with an operation in the

[1] The 17th French Division generously erected a monument to the 15th Division on the highest point of the Buzancy plateau, where was found the body of the Scottish soldier who had advanced the farthest in the attack of the 28th July.

THE ADVANCE TO VICTORY

direction of La Bassée. If successful, such an operation would have the effect of improving our position at Ypres and Calais. The Lys salient would be reduced and the safety of the Bruay coal mines become less threatened.

These different operations had already been the subject of correspondence between Marshal Foch and myself, as well as of the earnest consideration of the British General Staff. Ultimately, I had come to the conclusion that of the tasks assigned to the British forces the operation east of Amiens should take precedence, as being the most important and the most likely to give large results.

It would depend upon the nature of the success which might be obtained in these different Allied operations whether they could be more fully exploited before winter set in. It was subsequently arranged that attacks would be pressed in a converging direction towards Mézières by the French and American Armies, while at the same time the British Armies, attacking towards the line St. Quentin-Cambrai, would strike directly at the vital lateral communications running through Maubeuge to Hirson and Mézières, by which alone the German forces on the Champagne front could be supplied and maintained.

As a secondary result of the advance of the British Armies towards the all-important railway centres about Maubeuge, the group of German Armies in Flanders would find their communications threatened from the south, and any operations which it might be possible for the Allies to undertake in that theatre at a later date would be powerfully assisted thereby. It was obviously of vital importance to the enemy to maintain intact his front opposite St. Quentin and Cambrai, and for this purpose he depended on the great fortified zone known as the Hindenburg Line.

General Scheme of British Operations [1]

14. The brilliant success of the Amiens attack was the prelude to a great series of battles, in which, throughout three months of continuous fighting, the British Armies advanced without a check from one victory to another. The progress of this mighty conflict divides itself into certain stages, which themselves are grouped into two well-defined phases.

(A). During the first part of the struggle the enemy sought to defend himself in the deep belt of prepared positions and successive trench systems which extended from the spring-tide of the German advance, about Albert and Villers Bretonneux, to the Hindenburg

[1] *Vide* Maps No. 8 and 9.

Line between St. Quentin and the Scarpe. From these positions, scene of the stubborn battles of the two preceding years, the German Armies were forced back step by step by a succession of methodical attacks which culminated in the breaking through of the Hindenburg Line defences.

(B). Thereafter, during the second period of the struggle our troops were operating in practically open country against an enemy who endeavoured to stand, on such semi-prepared or natural defensive positions as remained to him, for a period long enough to enable him to organise his retreat and avoid overwhelming disaster. The final stages of our operations, therefore, are concerned with the breaking of the enemy's resistance on these lines.

Throughout this latter period, the violence of our assaults and the rapidity of our advance towards the enemy's vital centres of communication about Maubeuge threatened to cut the main avenue of escape for the German forces opposite the French and American Armies. The position of the German Armies in Flanders, themselves unable to withstand the attacks of the Allied forces operating under the King of the Belgians, was equally endangered by our progress behind their left flank. To the south and north of the area in which our victorious Armies were driving forward through his weakening defence, the enemy was compelled to execute hasty withdrawals from wide tracts of territory.

The second phase had already reached its legitimate conclusion when the signing of the Armistice put an end to hostilities. Finally defeated in the great battles of the 1st and 4th November, and utterly without reserves, the enemy at that date was falling back without coherent plan in widespread disorder and confusion.

FIRST PHASE: THE FIGHTING IN ENTRENCHED POSITIONS

THE BATTLE OF AMIENS (8th-12th August)

Plan of Operations

15. The plan of the Amiens operation was to strike in an easterly and south-easterly direction, using the Somme River to cover the left flank of our advance, with the object in the first place of gaining the line of the Amiens outer defences between Le Quesnel and Méricourt sur Somme, thereby freeing the main Paris-Amiens Railway. Having gained the Amiens defence line, the attack was to proceed without delay towards Roye, and to include the capture as

THE ADVANCE TO VICTORY

soon as possible of the important railway junction of Chaulnes, thereby cutting the communications of the German forces in the Lassigny and Montdidier areas. If all went well, French troops would be in readiness to co-operate by pressing the enemy south-east of Montdidier.

Preliminary instructions to prepare to attack east of Amiens at an early date had been given to the Fourth Army Commander, General Rawlinson, on the 13th July, and on the 28th July the French First Army, under command of General Debeney, was placed by Marshal Foch under my orders for this operation. Further to strengthen my attack, I decided to reinforce the British Fourth Army with the Canadian Corps, and also with the two British divisions which were then held in readiness astride the Somme.

In order to deceive the enemy and to ensure the maximum effect of a surprise attack, elaborate precautions were taken to mislead him as to our intentions and to conceal our real purpose.

Instructions of a detailed character were issued to the formations concerned, calculated to make it appear that a British attack in Flanders was imminent. Canadian battalions were put into line on the Kemmel front, where they were identified by the enemy. Corps headquarters were prepared, and casualty clearing stations were erected in conspicuous positions in this area. Great activity was maintained also by our wireless stations on the First Army front, and arrangements were made to give the impression that a great concentration of tanks was taking place in the St. Pol area. Training operations, in which infantry and tanks co-operated, were carried out in this neighbourhood on days on which the enemy's long-distance reconnaissance and photographic machines were likely to be at work behind our lines.

The rumour that the British were about to undertake a large and important operation on the northern front quickly spread. In the course of our subsequent advances convincing evidence was obtained that these different measures had had the desired effect, and that the enemy was momentarily expecting to be attacked in strength in Flanders.

Meanwhile, the final details for the combined British and French attack had been arranged early in August, and the date for the assault fixed for the morning of the 8th. The front held by the Australian Corps on the right of the British line was extended south-wards to include the Amiens-Roye Road,[1] and the Canadian Corps was moved into position by night behind this front. The assembly of

---

[1] This extension of the British front was discovered by the enemy, but was taken to indicate that the front was to become a quieter one.

tanks and of the Cavalry Corps was postponed until the last moment and carried out as secretly as possible.

Partly as the result of successful minor operations of the Allies, and partly in consequence of the change in the general situation, the enemy during the first days of August withdrew from the positions still held by him west of the Avre and Ancre rivers. These movements did not affect our plans, but, on the other hand, a strong local attack launched by the enemy on the 6th August south of Morlancourt led to severe fighting, and undoubtedly rendered the task of the III. Corps more difficult.

The Troops Employed

16. The front of attack of General Rawlinson's Fourth Army extended for a distance of over eleven miles from just south of the Amiens-Roye Road to Morlancourt exclusive. The troops employed were : On the right the Canadian Corps, under command of Lieut.-General Sir A. W. Currie, with the 3rd, 1st and 2nd Canadian Divisions in line, and the 4th Canadian Division in close support ; in the centre the Australian Corps, under command of Lieut.-General Sir J. Monash, with the 2nd and 3rd Australian Divisions in line and the 5th and 4th Australian Divisions in support ; on the left, north of the Somme, the III. Corps, under the command of Lieut.-General Sir R. H. K. Butler, with the 58th and 18th Divisions in line and the 12th Division in support.

The attack of the French First Army, under General Debeney, was timed to take place about an hour later than the opening of the British assault, and was delivered on a front of between four and five miles between Moreuil inclusive and the British right. As the Allied troops made progress, the right of the French attack was to be gradually extended southwards until the southern flank of the Allied battle front rested on Braches.

Behind the British front the British Cavalry Corps, consisting of three cavalry divisions under command of Lieut.-General Sir C. T. McM. Kavanagh, was concentrated at zero hour east of Amiens. A special mobile force of two motor machine gun brigades and a Canadian cyclist battalion, under command of Brigadier-General Brutinel, had orders to exploit success along the line of the Amiens-Roye Road.

The Battle Opened

17. At 4.20 a.m. on the 8th August our massed artillery opened intense fire on the whole front of attack, completely crushing the enemy's batteries, some of which never succeeded in coming into action. Simultaneously British infantry and tanks advanced to the

assault. The enemy was taken completely by surprise, and under cover of a heavy ground mist our first objectives, on the line Démuin, Marcelcave, Cérisy, south of Morlancourt, were gained rapidly.

After a halt of two hours on this line by the leading troops, infantry, cavalry and light tanks passed through and continued the advance, the different arms working in co-operation in the most admirable manner. At the close of the day's operations our troops had completed an advance of between six and seven miles. The Amiens outer defence line, including the villages of Caix, Harbonnières and Morcourt, had been gained on the whole front of attack, except at Le Quesnel itself. Cavalry and armoured cars were in action well to the east of this line, and before dawn on the 9th August Le Quesnel also had been taken. North of the Somme the enemy was more alert as the result of the recent engagements in this sector, and succeeded by heavy fighting in maintaining himself for the time being in the village of Chipilly.

East of the line of our advance the enemy at nightfall was blowing up dumps in all directions, while his transport and limbers were streaming eastwards towards the Somme, affording excellent targets to our airmen, who made full use of their opportunities. Over 13,000 prisoners, between 300 and 400 guns, and vast quantities of ammunition and stores of all kinds remained in our possession.

The brilliant and predominating part taken by the Canadian and Australian Corps in this battle is worthy of the highest commendation. The skill and determination of these troops proved irresistible, and at all points met with rapid and complete success. The fine performance of the cavalry throughout all stages of the operation also deserves mention. Having completed their assembly behind the battle-front by a series of night marches, on the first day of the attack they advanced 23 miles from their points of concentration, and by the dash and vigour of their action, both on this and subsequent days, rendered most valuable and gallant service. The general success of all arms was made possible by the good staff work of my own Staff at General Headquarters, and of the Staffs of the Armies concerned. Under the able and experienced direction of the Fourth Army Commander, General Rawlinson, the preparations for the battle, including detailed artillery arrangements of an admirable nature, were carried out with a thoroughness and completeness which left nothing to chance. Without this excellent staff work neither the rapid concentration of troops, unknown to the enemy, nor the success of our initial assault and its subsequent development could have been accomplished.

Meanwhile, at 5.5 a.m., the attack of the French First Army had been launched successfully, and gained the line Pierrepont, Plessier,

Fresnoy, all inclusive, in touch with Brutinel's Force on the Amiens-Roye Road west of Le Quesnoy. Three thousand three hundred and fifty prisoners and many guns were taken by the French forces on this day.

The Advance Continued

18. The sweeping character of this success, which in one day had gained our first objective and disengaged the Paris-Amiens Railway, opened a clear field for the measures of exploitation determined upon to meet such an event.

The attack was continued on the 9th August. After meeting with considerable opposition on the line Beaufort-Vrély-Rosières-Framerville, the enemy's resistance weakened under the pressure of our troops, and once more rapid progress was made. The 8th Hussars, 1st Cavalry Division (Major-General R. L. Mullens), took Méharicourt at a gallop;[1] the 2nd and 3rd Cavalry Divisions (Major-Generals T. T. Pitman and A. E. W. Harman) also passed through our advancing infantry, capturing a number of prisoners and gaining much ground. That night we held Bouchoir, Rouvroy, Morcourt and Framerville, and were on the western outskirts of Lihons and Proyart.

North of the Somme the III. Corps, including the 12th Division (Major-General H. W. Higginson) and a regiment of the 33rd American Division (Major-General G. Bell), attacked in the late afternoon and gained a line east of Chipilly, Morlancourt and Dernancourt.

During the following days our operations continued successfully in close co-operation with the French. By the evening of the 12th August our infantry had reached the old German Somme defences of 1916, on the general line west of Damery, east of Lihons, east of Proyart, having repulsed with severe loss determined counter-attacks in the neighbourhood of Lihons. North of the Somme we were on the western outskirts of Bray-sur-Somme.

Montdidier had fallen to the French two days earlier, and on the whole front from the Oise River to the Roye Road at Andechy our Allies had made deep and rapid progress.

On the night of the 12th August, as has been seen, our advance east of Amiens had reached the general line of the old Roye-Chaulnes defences. The derelict battle area which now lay before our troops, seared by old trench lines, pitted with shell holes, and crossed in all directions with tangled belts of wire, the whole covered by the wild vegetation of two years, presented unrivalled opportunities for stubborn machine gun defence.

---

[1] The capture of Méharicourt is claimed also by the 2nd Canadian Division. The report of the Cavalry Corps is as stated above.

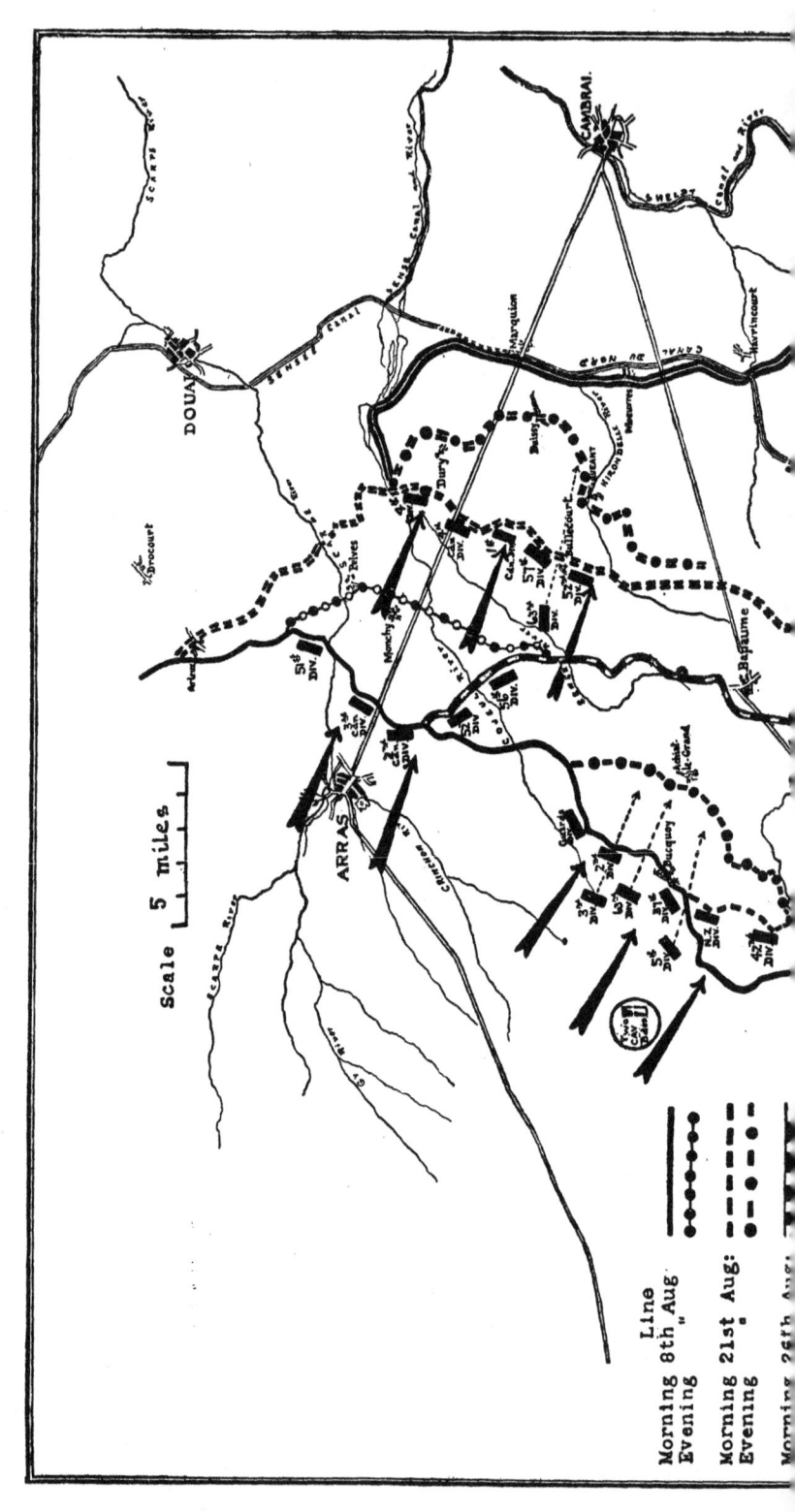

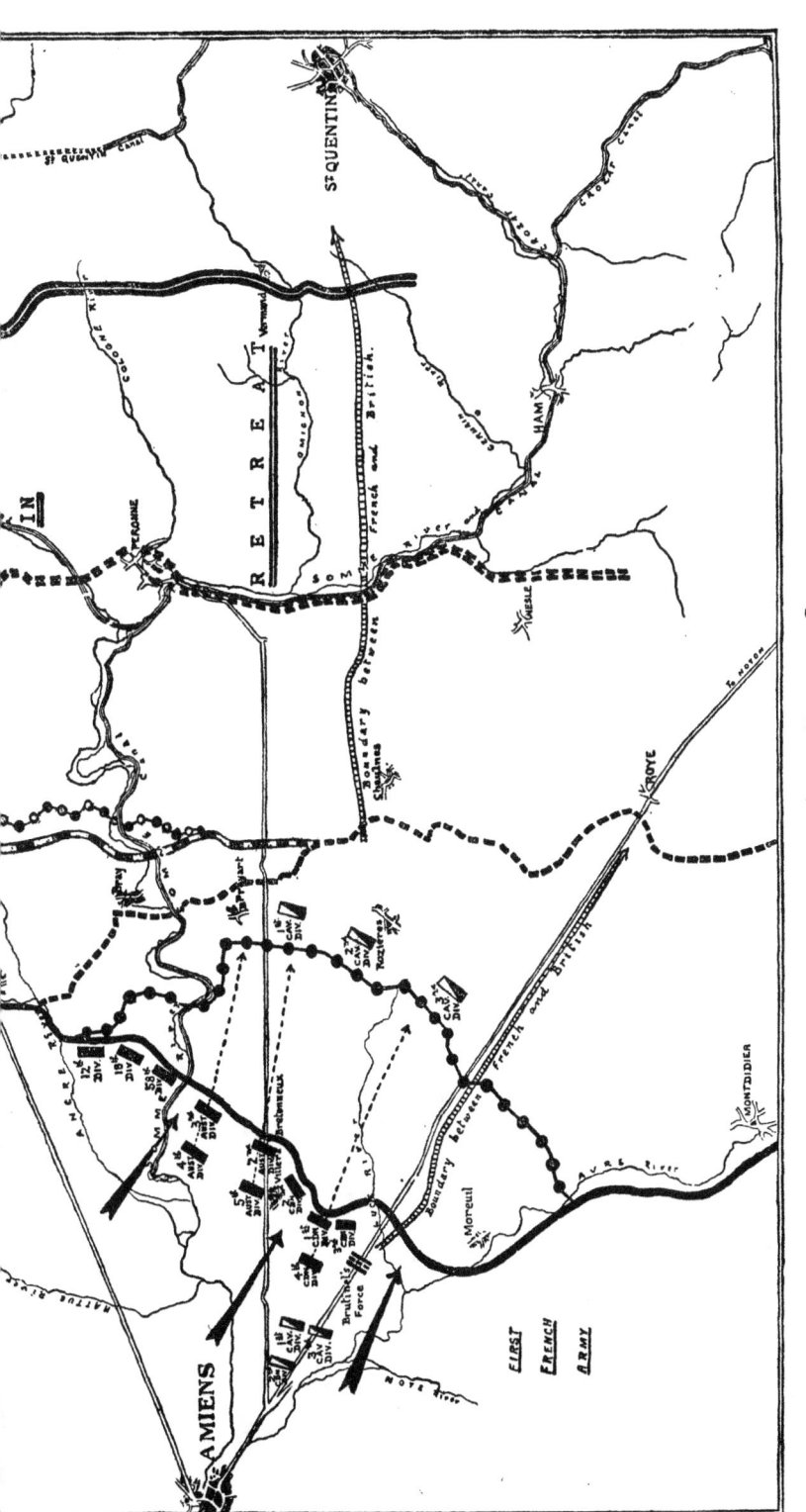

Opening of the Final British Offensive
8th August–9th September, 1918

THE ADVANCE TO VICTORY

Attacks carried out on the 13th August[1] proved the strength of these positions, and showed that the enemy, heavily reinforced, was ready to give battle for them. I therefore determined to break off the battle on this front, and transferred the front of attack from the Fourth Army to the sector north of the Somme, where an attack seemed unexpected by the enemy. My intention was for the Third Army to operate in the direction of Bapaume, so as to turn the line of the old Somme defences from the north. The French First Army now ceased to be under my command.

Meanwhile, south of the Somme, our pressure was to be maintained, so as to take advantage of any weakening on the part of the enemy and encourage in him the belief that we intended to persist in our operations on that front. During the succeeding days, local attacks gave us possession of Damery, Parvillers and Fransart, and made progress also at other points.

The Results of the Battle of Amiens

19. The results of the battle of Amiens may be summarised as follows. Within the space of five days the town of Amiens and the railway centring upon it had been disengaged. Twenty German divisions had been heavily defeated by thirteen British infantry divisions and three cavalry divisions, assisted by a regiment of the 33rd American Division and supported by some four hundred tanks. Nearly 22,000 prisoners and over four hundred guns had been taken by us and our line had been pushed forward to a depth of some twelve miles in a vital sector. Further, our deep advance, combined with the attacks of the French Armies on our right, had compelled the enemy to evacuate hurriedly a wide extent of territory to the south of us.

The effect of this victory, following so closely after the Allied victory on the Marne, upon the moral both of the German and British troops was very great. Buoyed up by the hope of immediate and decisive victory, to be followed by an early and favourable peace, constantly assured that the Allied reserves were exhausted, the German soldiery suddenly found themselves attacked on two fronts and thrown back with heavy losses from large and important portions of their earlier gains. The reaction was inevitable and of a deep and lasting character.[2]

[1] Already on the 10th August, in the course of a visit to the 32nd Division east of Le Quesnel, the Commander-in-Chief had personally satisfied himself that the enemy's opposition on this front had really stiffened.

[2] Ludendorff describes the 8th August as "the black day of the German Army in the history of this war." He ascribes directly to it the defection of Bulgaria and the general discouragement of Germany's Allies.

On the other hand, our own troops felt that at last their opportunity had come, and that, supported by a superior artillery and numerous tanks, they could now press forward resolutely to reap the reward of their patient, dauntless and successful defence in March and April. This they were eager to do, and as they moved forward during the ensuing months, from one success to another, suffering, danger and losses were alike forgotten in their desire to beat the enemy and their confidence that they could do so.

Meanwhile, as a further and immediate result of our successes, the enemy was thrown back definitely upon a defensive policy, and began to straighten out the salients in his line. Between the 14th and 17th August he withdrew from his positions about Serre, and farther north indications multiplied of an intention shortly to abandon the salient in the Lys valley. Our patrols were already beginning to push forward on this front, and on the night of the 13th/14th August established posts south and east of Vieux Berquin. On the 18th and 19th August the capture of Outtersteene village and ridge, with some 900 prisoners by the 31st, 29th and 9th Division of the Second Army, hastened the enemy's movements on the Lys.

The Battle of Bapaume (21st August—1st September)

Scheme of Operations

20. In deciding to extend the attack northwards to the area between the rivers Somme and Scarpe I was influenced by the following considerations.

The enemy did not seem prepared to meet an attack in this direction, and, owing to the success of the Fourth Army, he occupied a salient the left flank of which was already threatened from the south. A further reason for my decision was that the ground north of the Ancre River was not greatly damaged by shellfire, and was suitable for the use of tanks. A successful attack between Albert and Arras in a south-easterly direction would turn the line of the Somme south of Peronne, and gave every promise of producing far-reaching results. It would be a step forward towards the strategic objective St. Quentin-Cambrai.

This attack, moreover, would be rendered easier by the fact that we now held the commanding plateau south of Arras about Bucquoy and Ablainzevelle which in the days of the old Somme fighting had lain well behind the enemy's lines. In consequence we were here either astride or to the east of the intricate systems of trench lines which, in 1916, we had no choice but to attack

THE ADVANCE TO VICTORY 265

frontally, and enjoyed advantages of observation which at that date had been denied us.

It was arranged that on the morning of the 21st August a limited attack should be launched north of the Ancre to gain the general line of the Arras-Albert Railway, on which it was correctly assumed that the enemy's main line of resistance was sited. The day of the 22nd August would then be used to get troops and guns into position on this front and to bring forward the left of the Fourth Army between the Somme and the Ancre. The principal attack would be delivered on the 23rd August by the Third Army and the divisions of the Fourth Army north of the Somme, the remainder of the Fourth Army assisting by pushing forward south of the river to cover the flank of the main operation. Thereafter, if success attended our efforts, the whole of both Armies were to press forward with the greatest vigour and exploit to the full any advantage we might have gained.

As soon as the progress of the Third Army had forced the enemy to fall back from the Mercatel spur, thereby giving us a secure southern flank for an assault upon the German positions on Orange Hill and about Monchy-le-Preux, the moment arrived for the First Army to extend the front of our attack to the north. Using the River Sensée to cover their left, in the same way as the River Somme had been used to cover the left of the Fourth Army in the battle of Amiens, the right of the First Army attacked east of Arras, and by turning from the north the western extremity of the Hindenburg Line compelled the enemy to undertake a further retreat. It was calculated correctly that this gradual extension of our front of attack would mislead the enemy as to where the main blow would fall, and would cause him to throw in his reserves piecemeal.

Opening Attacks.—Albert

21. At 4.55 a.m. on the 21st August the IV. and VI. Corps of General Sir Julian Byng's Third Army, under command respectively of Lieut.-General Sir G. M. Harper and Lieut.-General Sir J. A. L. Haldane, attacked on a front of about nine miles north of the Ancre, from Miraumont to Moyenneville.

The opening assault was delivered by the divisions then in line [1] —namely, the 42nd, New Zealand and 37th Divisions of the IV. Corps, and the 2nd and Guards Divisions of the VI. Corps, supported by tanks, and carried the enemy's foremost defences rapidly and without difficulty. The 5th Division and 63rd Division (Major-General C. E. Lawrie) of the IV. Corps, and the 3rd Division

[1] See Sketch Map facing page 262 above.

(Major-General C. J. Deverell) of the VI. Corps then passed through, and continued the advance. During this stage the thick fog, which at first had favoured us, led to some loss of direction. None the less, after much hard fighting, particularly about Achiet-le-Petit and Logeast Wood, where the enemy counter-attacked vigorously, our troops reached the general line of the railway on practically the whole front, capturing the above-named village and wood, together with Courcelles and Moyenneville, east of which places they crossed the railway.

The 21st Division of the V. Corps assisted by clearing the north bank of the Ancre about Beaucourt, and as a result of the whole operation the positions we required from which to launch our principal attack were gained successfully, with over 2,000 prisoners.

Early next morning the III. Corps of the Fourth Army, assisted by a small number of tanks, attacked with the 47th, 12th and 18th Divisions, the 3rd Australian Division and the 38th Division co-operating on either flank. By this attack, in which the 18th Division (Major-General R. P. Lee) forced the passage of the River Ancre and captured Albert by a well-executed enveloping movement from the south-east, our line between the Somme and the Ancre was advanced well to the east of the Bray-Albert Road. The left of the Fourth Army was brought forward in conformity with the remainder of our line, and over 2,400 prisoners and a few guns were taken by us.

The Main Attack Launched

22. These preliminary attacks cleared the way for the main operation. This was opened on the 23rd August by a series of strong assaults on practically the whole front of thirty-three miles from our junction with the French north of Lihons to Mercatel, in which neighbourhood the Hindenburg Line from Quéant and Bullecourt joined the old Arras-Vimy defence line of 1916. About 100 tanks were employed by us on different parts of this front, and were of great assistance, particularly in overcoming the enemy's machine gunners. Many of these fought with great determination, continuing to fire until their guns were run over by the tanks.

On the eve of these operations I issued a Note of instructions to the forces under my command, in which I drew attention to the favourable change which had taken place in the conditions under which operations were being conducted, and emphasised the necessity for all ranks to act with the utmost boldness and resolution. Wherever the enemy was found to be giving way, there the pressure was to be increased.

To this appeal all ranks and all Services responded during the

THE ADVANCE TO VICTORY 267

strenuous fighting of the succeeding weeks with a whole-hearted and untiring devotion, for which no words of mine can adequately express my admiration and my gratitude. Divisions, which in the worst days of the March retreat had proved themselves superior to every hardship, difficulty and danger, once more rose to the occasion with the most magnificent spirit. Over the same ground that had witnessed their stubborn greatness in defence they moved forward to the attack with a persistent vigour and relentless determination which neither the extreme difficulty of the ground, nor the obstinate resistance of the enemy, could diminish or withstand.

At 4.45 a.m. the Australian Corps attacked south of the Somme, employing the 32nd Division (Major-General T. S. Lambert), composed of men of Lancashire, Dorset and Scotland, and the 1st Australian Division (Major-General T. W. Glasgow), and captured Herleville, Chuignolles and Chuignes, with over 2,000 prisoners. The fighting about Chuignolles, on the Australian front, was very heavy, and great numbers of the enemy were killed.

At the same hour the 18th Division and the right brigade of the 38th Division of the III. and V. Corps recommenced their attacks about Albert, and by a well-executed operation, entailing hard fighting at different points, captured the high ground east of the town known as Tara and Usna Hills. At the same time two companies of the Welsh Regiment, part of the left brigade of the 38th Division, waded the Ancre in the neighbourhood of Hamel, and with great gallantry maintained themselves all day east of the river against constant counter-attacks.

Meanwhile, at different hours during the morning, the other divisions of the V. Corps and the IV. and VI. Corps (comprising respectively the 17th and 21st Divisions ; the 42nd, New Zealand, 5th and 37th Divisions ; and the 2nd, 3rd, Guards, 56th and 52nd Divisions) attacked along the whole front north of Albert, directing the chief weight of their assault upon the sector Miraumont—Boiry Becquerelle.

Our troops met with immediate success. On the right, progress was made by light forces of the 17th and 21st Divisions along the left bank of the Ancre north of Thiepval, but in this sector no deep advance was attempted during the day.

North of the Ancre, the attack of the VI. Corps was opened at 4.0 a.m., at which hour the 3rd Division took Gomiecourt with 500 prisoners. During the morning the attack spread along the front of the IV. Corps also. The enemy's main line of resistance was stormed and, penetrating deeply beyond it, our troops captured Bihucourt, Ervillers, Boyelles and Boiry Becquerelle, together with over 5,000 prisoners and a number of guns. Under the continued pressure of our attacks the enemy was becoming disorganised, and showed signs of confusion.

Our troops were now astride the Arras-Bapaume Road, and closing down upon the latter town from the north and north-west. The position of the German divisions in the pronounced salient on the Thiepval Ridge was becoming perilous.

At 1.0 a.m. on the night of the 23rd/24th August the Third and Fourth Armies again attacked, and during the early morning the advance was resumed on the whole front from the Somme to Neuville Vitasse. On the right, the 3rd Australian Division took Bray-sur-Somme, and the 47th Division (Major-General Sir G. T. Gorringe), the 12th and 18th Divisions of the III. Corps carried our line forward across the high ground between Bray and La Boisselle. In the neighbourhood of the latter village and at certain other points heavy fighting took place, and a number of prisoners were taken.

On the front of the Third Army, the same divisions which had delivered the attacks on the previous day again moved forward against the beaten enemy and pressed him back rapidly. The German positions on the Thiepval Ridge were carried by a well-conceived and admirably executed concentric attack, directed upon the high ground about Pozières from the south-west and north-west. In this brilliant operation the brigade of the 38th Division attacking on the right crossed the Ancre at Albert during the early part of the night, and formed up close to the German lines on a narrow front between the Albert-Pozières Road and the marshes of the Ancre. The left brigade of the same division waded breast deep through the flooded stream opposite Hamel, under heavy fire, and formed up in the actual process of a German counter-attack along the line held by the two companies who had crossed on the previous morning. At the given hour, the brigades of the 38th Division advanced in concert with the other divisions of the V. Corps on their left, and drove the enemy from the high ground about Ovillers and Thiepval. Continuing their advance, the divisions of the V. Corps gained Pozières, Courcelette and Martinpuich. Miraumont, which for three days had resisted our attacks, was taken by the 42nd Division (Major-General A. Solly-Flood) with many prisoners, and pressing forward the same division seized Pys. The 5th Division (Major-General J. Ponsonby) having captured Irles, cleared Loupart Wood in co-operation with the New Zealand Division (Major-General Sir A. H. Russell), tanks rendering valuable assistance to our infantry in both localities. New Zealand troops having taken Grévillers, reached Avesnes-les-Bapaume, and assisted also in the capture of Biefvillers by the 37th Division (Major-General H. B. Williams). Strong opposition was encountered on the high ground between Sapignies

THE ADVANCE TO VICTORY 269

and Mory. Our troops pressed the enemy in these villages closely, and farther north the Guards Division (Major-General G. P. T. Feilding) gained possession of St. Leger. On the left, troops of the 56th Division (Major-General Sir C. P. A. Hull) had heavy fighting about Croisilles and on the high ground north-west of that village known as Henin Hill. Important progress was made, and on their left the 52nd Division (Major-General J. Hill) took Hénin-sur-Cojeul and gained a footing in St. Martin-sur-Cojeul.

Several thousand prisoners, many guns and great quantities of material of every kind were captured by us on this day.

Bapaume Taken

23. During the next five days our troops followed up their advantage hotly, and in spite of increasing resistance from the German rearguards, realised a further deep advance. The enemy clung to his positions in the later stages of this period with much tenacity. His infantry delivered many counter-attacks, and the progress of our troops was only won by hard and determined fighting.

During these days the 37th Division cleared Favreuil late in the evening of the 25th August, after much confused fighting. On the same day the 2nd Division captured Sapignies and Behagnies, taking a number of prisoners, and the 62nd Division drove the enemy from Mory.

On the 27th August the 18th Division secured possession of Trônes Wood, after an all-day struggle in the course of which troops of the 2nd Guard Division, fresh from reserve, made strong but unsuccessful counter-attacks. Next day the 12th Division and 58th Division (Major-General F. W. Ramsay) captured Hardecourt and the spur south of it, overcoming strong resistance. Both on the 27th and 28th August the 38th (Welsh) Division (Major-General T. A. Cubitt) was engaged in bitter fighting about Longueval and Delville Wood, and made progress in company with the 17th Division (Major-General P. R. Robertson) attacking towards Flers.

Yielding before the persistent pressure of our attacks, in the early morning of the 29th August the enemy evacuated Bapaume, which was occupied by the New Zealand Division. On the same day the 18th Division entered Combles, while to the north of Bapaume a gallant thrust by the 56th and 57th Divisions penetrated the enemy's positions as far as Riencourt-lez-Cagnicourt. Though our troops were unable at this time to maintain themselves in this village our line was established on the western and northern outskirts of Bullecourt and Hendecourt.

By the night of the 30th August the line of the Fourth and Third Armies north of the Somme ran from Cléry-sur-Somme past the western edge of Marrières Wood to Combles, Lesbœufs, Bancourt, Frémicourt and Vraucourt, and thence to the western outskirts of Ecoust, Bullecourt and Hendecourt. Any further advance would threaten the enemy's line south of Peronne along the east bank of the Somme, to which our progress north of the river had already forced him to retreat.

This latter movement had been commenced on the 26th August, on which date Roye was evacuated by the enemy, and next day had been followed by a general advance on the part of the French and British forces between the Oise and the Somme. By the night of the 29th August, Allied infantry had reached the left bank of the Somme on the whole front from the neighbourhood of Nesle, occupied by the French on the 28th August, northwards to Peronne. Farther south the French held Noyon.

The Fight for Mont St. Quentin and the Capture of Peronne

24. During these days an increase in hostile artillery fire and the frequency and strength of the German counter-attacks indicated that our troops were approaching positions on which the enemy intended to stand, at any rate for a period. In the face of this increased resistance, by a brilliant operation commenced on the night of the 30th/31st August, the 2nd Australian Division (Major-General C. Rosenthal) stormed Mont St. Quentin, a most important tactical feature commanding Peronne and the crossings of the Somme at that town. Being prevented by floods and heavy machine-gun fire from crossing the river opposite Mont St. Quentin, the 5th Australian Infantry Brigade was passed across the Somme at Feuillières, two miles farther west, by means of hastily constructed bridges. By 10.15 p.m. on the 30th August, the brigade had captured the German trenches east of Cléry, and was assembled in them ready for an assault which should turn the German positions from the north-west. At 5.0 a.m. on the 31st August the assault was launched, and, despite determined opposition, was completely successful. Both in the attack itself and in the course of repeated counter-attacks, delivered with great resolution by strong hostile forces throughout the remainder of the day and the greater part of the following night, fighting was exceptionally severe, and the taking of the position ranks as a most gallant achievement.

In this operation nearly 1,000 prisoners were taken, and great numbers of the enemy were killed. On the 1st September, as a direct consequence of it, Australian troops captured Peronne.

THE ADVANCE TO VICTORY 271

In support of the operation against Mont St. Quentin, on the morning of the 31st August the left of the Fourth Army (the 3rd Australian, 58th, 47th and 18th Divisions) attacked towards Bouchavesnes, Rancourt and Frégicourt, and by successful fighting on this and the following day captured these villages with several hundred prisoners. On the Third Army front also there was hard fighting on both of these days. At the close of it we held Sailly Saillisel, Morval, Beaulencourt and Riencourt-les-Bapaume, and were established on the ridges east of Bancourt, Frémicourt, Vaulx Vraucourt and Longatte. Troops of the XVII. Corps, under command of Lieut.-General Sir C. Fergusson, completed the capture of Bullecourt and Hendecourt, and, following up their advantage, during the night took Riencourt-lez-Cagnicourt with 380 prisoners.

The Results of the Battle of Bapaume

25. The 1st September marks the close of the second stage in the British offensive. Having in the first stage freed Amiens by our brilliant success east of that town, in the second stage the troops of the Third and Fourth Armies, comprising 23 British divisions, by skilful leading, hard fighting and relentless and unremitting pursuit, in ten days had driven 35 German divisions from one side of the old Somme battlefield to the other, thereby turning the line of the River Somme. In so doing they had inflicted upon the enemy the heaviest losses in killed and wounded, and had taken from him over 34,000 prisoners and 270 guns. For the remarkable success of the battle of Bapaume, the greatest credit is due to the excellence of the staff arrangements of all formations, and to the most able conduct of the operations of the Third Army by its Commander, General Byng.

In the obstinate fighting of the past few days the enemy had been pressed back to the line of the Somme River and the high ground about Rocquigny and Beugny, where he had shown an intention to stand for a time. Thereafter, his probable plan was to retire slowly, when forced to do so, from one intermediary position to another; until he could shelter his battered divisions behind the Hindenburg defences. The line of the Tortille River and the high Nurlu Plateau offered opportunities for an ordered withdrawal of this nature, which would allow him to secure his artillery as well as much of the material in his forward dumps.

On the other hand, the disorganisation which had been caused by our attacks on the 8th and 21st August had increased under the pressure of our advance, and had been accompanied by a steady deterioration in the moral of his troops. Garrisons left as rearguards to hold up our advance at important points had surrendered as soon as they found themselves threatened with isolation. The urgent needs of the moment, the wide extent of front attacked, and consequent uncertainty as to where the next blow would fall, and the extent of his losses had forced the enemy to throw in his reserves piecemeal as they arrived on the battle front. On many occasions in the course of the fighting elements of the same German division had been identified on widely separated parts of the battle front.

In such circumstances, a sudden and successful blow, of weight sufficient to break through the northern hinge of the defences to which it was his design to fall back, might produce results of great importance. At this date, as will be seen from the events described in para. 27, our troops were already in position to deliver such a stroke.

The Withdrawal from the Lys Salient

26. Meanwhile, during the process of the great events briefly recorded above and in immediate consequence of them, other events of different but scarcely less importance were taking place on the northern portion of our front.

The exhaustion of the enemy's reserves resulting from the Allied attacks made the shortening of the German line imperative. The obvious sector in which to effect such a shortening was the Lys front. The enemy had only maintained himself in the Lys salient under the constant fire of our guns at the expense of heavy casualties, not only to his infantry in line, but to his artillery and troops in back areas. With the abandonment of his projected offensive against the Channel Ports all reason had gone for remaining in so costly a salient, while the threat, carefully maintained by us, of a British attack provided an additional reason for withdrawing.

Accordingly, from about the 26th July the enemy had been actively employed in removing the ammunition and stores accumulated for his offensive, and as early as the 5th August he had begun to effect local withdrawals on the southern flank of the salient.

The development of our own and the French offensives hastened this movement, although immense quantities of ammunition still remained untouched. On the 18th August our patrols, whose activity had been constant, were able to make a considerable advance opposite Merville. Next day Merville itself was taken, and our line advanced on the whole front from the Lawe River to the Plate Becque.

During the following days, various other small gains of ground were made by us on the southern and western faces of the salient, but on the northern face the enemy as yet showed no signs of with-

THE ADVANCE TO VICTORY 273

drawal, the various local operations carried out by us meeting with strong resistance. On the night of the 29th/30th August, however, impelled alike by the pressure exerted without remission by our troops on the spot and by the urgency of events elsewhere, the enemy commenced an extensive retirement on the whole of the Lys front.

In the early morning of the 30th August our troops found Bailleul unoccupied, and by the evening of that day our advanced detachments had reached the general line Lacouture, Lestrem, Noote Boom, east of Bailleul.

Thereafter, the enemy's withdrawal continued rapidly. At certain points, indeed, his rearguards offered vigorous resistance, notably about Neuve Église and Hill 63, captured with a number of prisoners by the 36th and 29th Divisions; but by the evening of the 6th September the Lys salient had disappeared. Kemmel Hill was once more in our hands, and our troops had reached the general line Givenchy, Neuve Chapelle, Nieppe, Ploegsteert, Voormezeele.

THE BATTLE OF THE SCARPE (26th August—3rd September)

The Retaking of Monchy-le-Preux

27. By the 25th August our advance had formed a salient of the German positions opposite Arras,[1] and the proper moment had therefore come for the third stage of our operations, in which the First Army should extend the flank of our attack to the north. By driving eastwards from Arras, covered on the left by the Rivers Scarpe and Sensée, the First Army would endeavour to turn the enemy's positions on the Somme battlefield, and cut his system of railway communications which ran south-westwards across their front.

At 3.0 a.m. on the 26th August, the Canadian Corps, Lieut.-General Sir A. W. Currie commanding, on the right of General Horne's First Army, attacked the German positions astride the Scarpe River with the 2nd and 3rd Canadian Divisions (commanded by Major-Generals Sir H. E. Burstall and L. J. Lipsett) and the 51st Division. This attack, delivered on a front of about 5½ miles and closely supported by the left of the Third Army, was completely successful. By noon we had taken Wancourt and Guemappe, and had stormed the hill and village of Monchy-le-Preux. This latter position was one of great natural strength, well organised for defence, and commanded observation of much importance. Many prisoners were taken, and later in the day substantial progress was

[1] See Sketch Map facing page 262.

made to the east of these three villages, a strong counter-attack east of Monchy being successfully repulsed. North of the Scarpe the 51st Division pushed forward their line towards Rœux, so as to secure an easily defensible base of departure for this advance, and by a successful attack during the evening captured Greenland Hill.

Their opening success was followed up by the troops of the First Army with the greatest energy, and on the following day Chérisy, Vis-en-Artois, the Bois du Sart, Rœux and Gavrelle were taken. By the end of the month they had gained the high ground east of Chérisy and Haucourt, had captured Eterpigny, and cleared the area between the Sensée and Scarpe Rivers west of the Trinquis Brook. North of the Scarpe, Plouvain was held by us. Our progress brought our troops to within assaulting distance of the powerful trench system running from the Hindenburg Line at Quéant to the Lens defences about Drocourt, the breaking of which would turn the whole of the enemy's organised positions on a wide front southwards.

The Storming of the Drocourt-Quéant Line

28. On the 2nd September the Drocourt-Quéant Line was broken, the maze of trenches at the junction of that line and the Hindenburg System was stormed and the enemy was thrown into precipitate retreat on the whole front to the south of it. This gallant feat of arms was carried out by the Canadian Corps of the First Army, employing the 1st and 4th Canadian Divisions and the 4th English Division, and the XVII. Corps of the Third Army, employing the 52nd, 57th and 63rd Divisions.[1]

The assault of the Canadians was launched at 5.0 a.m. on a front of about 4½ miles south of the Trinquis Brook, our infantry being supported by 40 tanks of the 3rd Tank Brigade and assisted by a mobile force of motor machine gun units, Canadian Cavalry and armoured cars. The attack was a complete success, and by noon the whole of the elaborate system of wire, trenches and strong points constituting the Drocourt-Quéant Line on the front of our advance was in our hands.

On the right the attack of the XVII. Corps, launched at the same hour by the 52nd and 57th Divisions, directed its main force on the triangle of fortifications marking the junction of the Hindenburg and Drocourt-Quéant lines north-west of the village of Quéant. Pressed with equal vigour it met with success equally complete. There was stern fighting in the network of trenches both north and south of Quéant, in which neighbourhood the 52nd (Lowland) Division performed distinguished service and by the progress they

[1] See Sketch Map facing page 262.

THE ADVANCE TO VICTORY

made greatly assisted our advance farther north. Early in the afternoon our troops had cleared the triangle, and the 63rd Division (Major-General C. A. Blacklock) had passed through to exploit the success thus gained.

During the afternoon our further progress met with considerable resistance from machine gun nests sited in woods and villages and on the reverse slopes of the Dury Ridge. There was hard fighting until dusk, especially on the front of the 63rd Division and of the 4th Division (Major-General T. G. Matheson). By nightfall this opposition had been overcome, the 63rd Division had reached the railway east of Quéant, and the 57th Division, swinging to the right, was threatening that village and Pronville from the north. Our troops had pushed forward to a depth of over three miles along the Arras-Cambrai Road, and had reached the outskirts of Buissy. Cagnicourt, Villers-les-Cagnicourt and Dury were in our hands. During the day 8,000 prisoners had been taken and many guns.

Troops of the Third and Fourth Armies prolonged the line of attack as far south as Peronne. At all points important progress was made, though fighting was severe.

In the battle of the Scarpe, as in the battles of Amiens and Bapaume and the victories that followed them, staff work of a high order played an important part in our success. The greatest credit is due to the First Army Commander, General Horne, and his Staff for the excellence of their arrangements.

The Enemy in Retreat

29. The result of the battles of Amiens, Bapaume and the Scarpe now declared itself.

During the night of the 2nd/3rd September the enemy fell back rapidly on the whole front of the Third Army and the right of the First Army. By the end of the day he had taken up positions along the general line of the Canal du Nord from Peronne to Ytres and thence east of Hermies, Inchy-en-Artois and Ecourt St. Quentin to the Sensée east of Lecluse. On the following day he commenced to withdraw also from the east bank of the Somme south of Peronne, and by the night of the 8th September was holding the general line Vermand, Epéhy, Havrincourt and thence along the east bank of the Canal du Nord.

The withdrawal was continued on the front of the French forces on our right. On the 6th September French troops occupied Ham and Chauny, and by 8th September had reached the line of the Crozat Canal.

Throughout this hasty retreat our troops followed up the enemy closely. Many of his rearguards were cut off and taken prisoner; on numerous occasions our forward guns did great execution among his retiring columns, while our airmen took full advantage of the remarkable targets offered them. Great quantities of material and many guns fell into our hands.

In the battle of the Scarpe itself, in which ten British divisions attacked and overthrew thirteen German divisions, thereby giving the signal for this general retreat, our total captures amounted to over 16,000 prisoners and about 200 guns.

THE BATTLE OF HAVRINCOURT AND EPÉHY (12th-18th September)

30. North of Havrincourt, the Canal du Nord, behind which the enemy had taken shelter, with the open slopes leading down to it swept by the fire of the German positions on the east bank, could scarcely be taken except by a carefully organised attack.

From the neighbourhood of Havrincourt, southwards, the enemy's main line of resistance was the well-known Hindenburg Line, which, after passing through that village, ran south-east across the Beaucamp, La Vacquerie and Bonavis Ridges to the Scheldt Canal at Bantouzelle, whence it followed the line of the canal to St. Quentin. In front of this trench system strong German forces held formidable positions about Havrincourt and Epéhy, which had to be taken before a final attack on the Hindenburg Line could be undertaken. By successful operations carried out during the second and third weeks of September these different defences were secured and our line advanced to within assaulting distance of the enemy's main line of resistance.

On the 12th September the IV. and VI. Corps of the Third Army attacked on a front of about five miles in the Havrincourt sector, employing troops of the New Zealand, 37th, 62nd and 2nd Divisions. The villages of Trescault and Havrincourt were taken by the 37th and 62nd Divisions respectively, and positions were secured which were of considerable importance in view of future operations.

On the right of the British front the IX. and Australian Corps continued to push forward with light forces. By the evening of the 17th September, as the result of skilful manœuvring and well-executed local attacks, they had captured Holnon Village and wood and Maissemy, and were closely approaching Le Verguier and Templeux-le-Guérard.

Next day, at 7.0 a.m., on the 18th September, the Fourth and Third Armies attacked in heavy rain on a front of about seventeen miles from Holnon to Gouzeaucourt, the First French Army co-operating south of Holnon. A small number of tanks accompanied our infantry, and were of great assistance.[1]

In this operation, our troops penetrated to a depth of three miles through the deep, continuous and well-organised defensive belt formed by the old British and German lines. On practically the whole front our objectives were gained successfully, the 1st, 17th, 21st and 74th Divisions (Major-General E. S. Girdwood commanding the 74th Division), and the 1st and 4th Australian Divisions (the latter commanded by Major-General E. Sinclair-Maclagan) distinguishing themselves by the vigour and success of their attack. On the extreme right and in the left centre about Epéhy the enemy's resistance was very determined, and in these sectors troops of the 6th, 12th, 18th and 58th Divisions had severe fighting. Before nightfall, however, the last centres of resistance in Epéhy were reduced, and both in this area and on our right about Gricourt local actions during the succeeding days secured for us the remainder of the positions required for an attack on the main Hindenburg defences.

At the close of these operations, in which fifteen British divisions defeated twenty German divisions and completed the fourth stage of our offensive, we had captured nearly 12,000 prisoners and 100 guns.

The Development of the Allied Plan [2]

31. The details of the strategic plan outlined in para. 13 upon which future operations should be based were the subject of careful discussion between Marshal Foch and myself. Preparations were already far advanced for the successful attack by which, on the 12th September, the First American Army, assisted by certain French divisions, drove the enemy from the St. Mihiel salient and inflicted heavy losses upon him in prisoners and guns. Ultimately, it was decided that as soon as possible after this attack four convergent and simultaneous offensives should be launched by the Allies as follows:—

By the Americans west of the Meuse in the direction of Mézières;

By the French west of Argonne in close co-operation with the American attack and with the same general objectives;

By the British on the St. Quentin-Cambrai front in the general direction of Maubeuge;

By Belgian and Allied forces in Flanders in the direction of Ghent.

By these attacks, it was expected, as already indicated, that the important German forces opposite the French and Americans would be pressed back upon the difficult country of the Ardennes, while

---

[1] This was one of the occasions on which dummy tanks were used, with great success.
[2] See the folding map at the end of the book.

the British thrust struck at their principal lines of communication.[1] In Flanders, it was intended to take advantage of the weakening of the German forces on this front to clear the Belgian coast by a surprise attack. Success in any one of these offensives might compel the enemy to withdraw to the line of the Meuse.

The Rôle of the British Armies

32. The results to be obtained from these different attacks depended in a peculiarly large degree upon the British attack in the centre. It was here that the enemy's defences were most highly organised. If these were broken, the threat directed at his vital systems of lateral communication would of necessity react upon his defence elsewhere.

On the other hand, the long period of sustained offensive action through which the British Armies had already passed had made large demands both upon the troops themselves and upon my available reserves. Throughout our attacks from the 8th August onwards, our losses in proportion to the results achieved and the numbers of prisoners taken had been consistently and remarkably small. In the aggregate, however, they were considerable, and in the face of them an attack upon so formidably organised a position as that which now confronted us could not be lightly undertaken. Moreover, the political effects of an unsuccessful attack upon a position so well known as the Hindenburg Line would be large, and would go far to revive the declining moral not only of the German Army but of the German people.

These different considerations were present to my mind. The probable results of a costly failure, or, indeed, of anything short of a decided success, in any attempt upon the main defences of the Hindenburg Line were obvious; but I was convinced that the British attack was the essential part of the general scheme, and that the moment was favourable.[2]

Accordingly, I decided to proceed with the attack, and all preparatory measures, including the preliminary operations already recounted, were carried out as rapidly and as thoroughly as possible.

The Hindenburg Line

33. Between St. Quentin and the village of Bantouzelle the principal defences of the Hindenburg system lie sometimes to

[1] See Map No. 9.
[2] On a visit to England on the 9th September, the Commander-in-Chief had indicated that a change had taken place in the character of the war. A decision might be obtained in the very near future.

the west, but more generally to the east of the line of the Scheldt Canal.

The canal itself does not appear to have been organised as the enemy's main line of resistance, but rather as an integral part of a deep defensive system, the outstanding characteristic of which was the skill with which it was sited so as to deny us effective artillery positions from which to attack it. The chief rôle of the canal was that of affording cover to resting troops and to the garrisons of the main defensive trench lines during a bombardment. To this end the canal lent itself admirably, and the fullest use was made by the enemy of its possibilities.

The general configuration of the ground through which this sector of the canal runs produces deep cuttings of a depth in places of some sixty feet, while between Bellicourt and the neighbourhood of Vendhuille the canal passes through a tunnel for a distance of 6,000 yards. In the sides of the cuttings the enemy had constructed numerous tunnelled dug-outs and concrete shelters. Along the top edge of them he had concealed well sited concrete or armoured machine gun emplacements. The tunnel itself was used to provide living accommodation for troops, and was connected by shafts with the trenches above. South of Bellicourt the canal cutting gradually becomes shallow, till at Bellenglise the canal lies almost at ground level. South of Bellenglise the canal is dry.

On the western side of the canal south of Bellicourt two thoroughly organised and extremely heavily wired lines of continuous trench run roughly parallel to the canal, at average distances from it of 2,000 and 1,000 yards respectively. Except in the tunnel sector the double line of trenches known as the Hindenburg Line proper lies immediately east of the canal, and is linked up by numerous communication trenches with the trench lines west of it.

Besides these main features, numerous other trench lines, switch trenches and communication trenches, for the most part heavily wired, had been constructed at various points to meet local weaknesses or take advantage of local command of fire. At a distance of about 4,000 yards behind the most easterly of these trench lines lies a second double row of trenches known as the Beaurevoir-Fonsomme line, very thoroughly wired and holding numerous concrete shelters and machine gun emplacements. The whole series of defences, with the numerous defended villages contained in it, formed a belt of country varying from 7,000 to 10,000 yards in depth, organised by the employment of every available means into a most powerful system, well meriting the great reputation attached to it.

The Battle of Cambrai and the Hindenburg Line
(27th September—5th October)

34. The battle of Cambrai, which on the 5th October culminated in the capture of the last remaining sectors of the Hindenburg Line, was commenced by the First and Third Armies.

Between the neighbourhood of St. Quentin and the Scheldt the Fourth, Third and First Armies in the order named occupied on the evening of the 26th September a line running from the village of Selency (west of St. Quentin) to Gricourt and Pontruet and thence east of Villeret and Lempire to Villers Guislain and Gouzeaucourt, both exclusive. Thereafter the line continued northwards to Havrincourt and Mœuvres, and thence along the west side of the Canal du Nord to the floods of the Sensée at Ecourt St. Quentin.

On the First and Third Army fronts strong positions covering the approaches to Cambrai between the Nord and Scheldt canals, including the section of the Hindenburg Line itself north of Gouzeaucourt, were still in the enemy's possession. His trenches in this sector faced south-west, and it was desirable that they should be taken in the early stages of the operation, so as to render it easier for the artillery of the Fourth Army to get into position. On the Fourth Army front, where the heaviest blow was to fall, the exceptional strength of the enemy's position made a prolonged bombardment necessary. I therefore decided that a very heavy bombardment, opened during the night of the 26th/27th September along the whole front of all three armies, should be followed on the morning of the 27th September by an attack delivered only by the First and Third Armies. In this way the enemy might be deceived as to the main point of attack, the First and Third Armies would be enabled to get nearer to their final objective, and the task of the Fourth Army artillery would be simplified.

The Battle Opened

35. On the morning of the 26th September French and American forces attacked on both sides of the Argonne, between the Meuse and the Suippe rivers.

At 5.20 a.m. on the 27th September the Third and First Armies attacked with the IV., VI., XVII. and Canadian Corps in the direction of Cambrai on a front of about 13 miles from Gouzeaucourt to the neighbourhood of Sauchy Lestrée. The success of the northern part of the attack depended upon the ability of our troops to debouch from the neighbourhood of Mœuvres, and to secure the crossings of the Canal du Nord in that locality. The northern portion of the

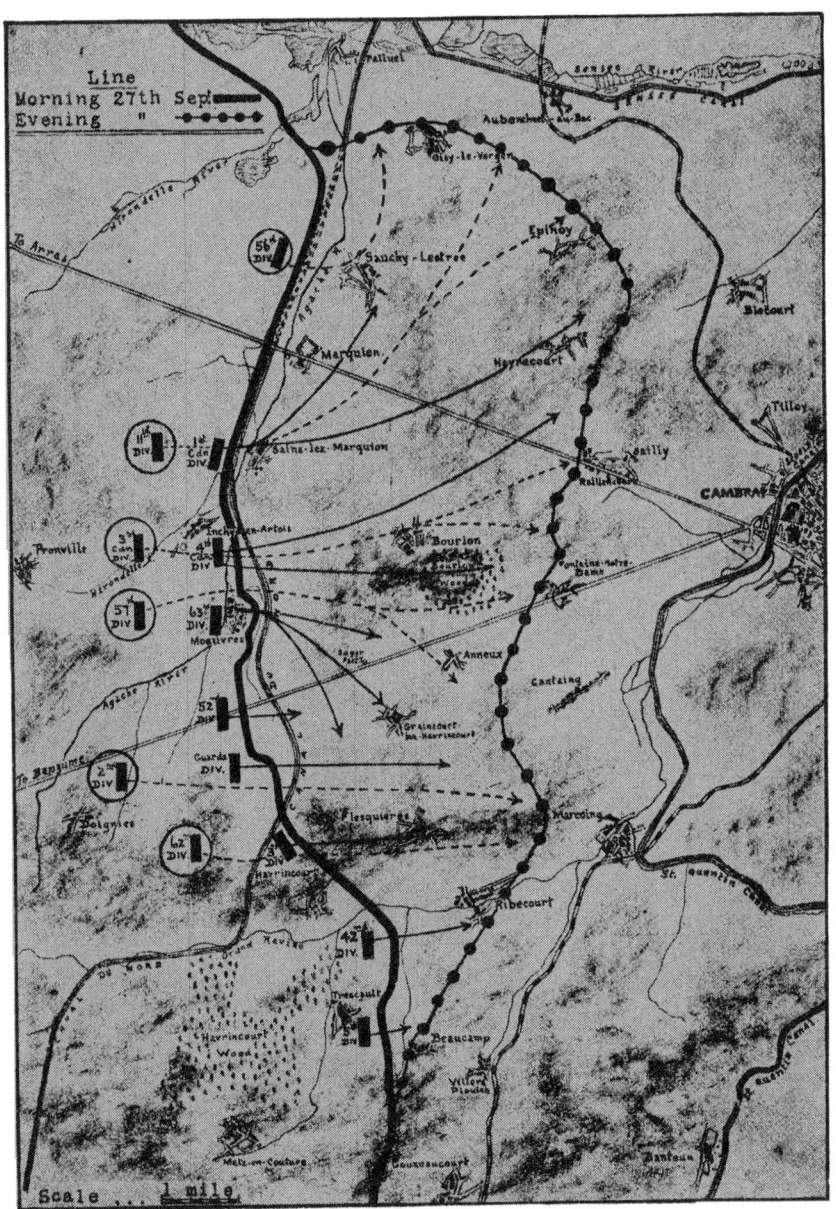

BATTLE OF CAMBRAI & THE HINDENBURG LINE
Cambrai Attack, 27th September, 1918.

THE ADVANCE TO VICTORY

canal was too formidable an obstacle to be crossed in the face of the enemy. It was therefore necessary for the attacking divisions to force a passage on a comparatively narrow front about Mœuvres, and thereafter turn the line of the canal farther north by a divergent attack developed fan-wise from the point of crossing. This difficult manœuvre was carried out successfully, and on the whole front of attack our infantry, assisted by some sixty-five tanks, broke deeply into the enemy's position.

The attack proceeded according to plan from the commencement. On the right strong resistance was encountered at Beaucamp. Several strong counter-attacks were made during the day in this neighbourhood, but in spite of them troops of the 5th and 42nd Divisions successfully established the right flank of our attack between Beaucamp and Ribécourt. The 3rd Division moved forward with the Guards, forcing the crossings of the canal in face of heavy fire from machine guns and forward field guns, and captured Ribécourt and Flesquières. The Guards Division (Major-General T. G. Matheson) took Orival Wood and reached the neighbourhood of Prémy Chapel, where the 2nd Division (Major-General C. E. Pereira) took up the advance.

In the centre the 52nd Division (Major-General F. J. Marshall), passing its troops across the canal by bridgeheads previously established by the 57th Division,[1] on the opening of the assault carried the German trench lines east of the canal and gained the high ground overlooking Graincourt. On their left the 63rd Division and the 4th and 1st Canadian Divisions (under command of Major-Generals Sir D. Watson and A. C. MacDonell) moved under cover of darkness down the west bank of the canal between Mœuvres and Sains-lez-Marquion. In the half light of dawn these three divisions stormed the line of the canal itself, and advanced on Graincourt, Anneux, Bourlon and the slopes to the north of the latter village.

As soon as the line of the canal had been secured our engineer troops commenced the construction of bridges, completing their task with remarkable speed and working with great gallantry under the fire of the German guns. Greatly assisted by their efforts our advance continued. Obstinate resistance was met with at Graincourt, and it was not until late in the day that the village was finally surrounded and captured by the 63rd Division. The 57th Division (Major-General R. W. R. Barnes) meanwhile had passed through and carried the line forward east of Anneux to Fontaine-Notre-Dame. Bourlon had been carried by the 4th Canadian Division, and the 3rd Canadian Division (Major-General F. O. W. Loomis)

---

[1] This is incorrect. There were no bridgeheads at this time and the crossings were forced by the 52nd Division at the opening of their attack.

had passed through at Bourlon Wood, which was wholly in our possession.

On the left the 1st Canadian Division, having seized Sains-lez-Marquion early in the attack, advanced with the 11th Division (Major-General H. R. Davies) and took Haynecourt, while the latter division captured Epinoy and Oisy-le-Verger. On the extreme left the 56th Division of the XXII. Corps crossed the canal and having cleared Sauchy Lestrée and Sauchy Cauchy, moved northwards towards Palluel.

At the end of the day our troops had reached the general line Beaucamp—Ribécourt—Fontaine-Notre-Dame—east of Haynecourt—Epinoy—Oisy-le-Verger, and had taken over 10,000 prisoners and 200 guns.

Next day the advance on this front was continued, and Gouzeaucourt, Marcoing, Noyelles-sur-l'Escaut, Fontaine-Notre-Dame, Sailly and Palluel were taken. At Marcoing our troops established themselves on the east bank of the Scheldt Canal and on the northern flank entered Aubencheul-au-Bac.

The Hindenburg Line Broken

36. The heavy and continuous bombardment opened on the morning of the 27th September, had been maintained by the Fourth Army along its whole front without intermission for two days. The intensity of our fire drove the enemy's garrisons to take refuge in their deep dug-outs and tunnels, and made it impossible for his carrying parties to bring up food and ammunition.

At 5.50 a.m. on the 29th September, under an intense artillery barrage, General Rawlinson's Fourth Army attacked on a front of 12 miles, between Holnon and Vendhuille, with the IX., II. American (General G. W. Read commanding) and III. Corps, a strong force of tanks, manned by British and American crews, accompanying the infantry. On the right of the Fourth Army the French First Army continued the line of attack in the St. Quentin sector. On the left the V. and IV. Corps of the Third Army had attacked at an earlier hour between Vendhuille and Marcoing, and had heavy fighting about Villers Guislain, Gonnelieu and Welsh Ridge.

On the Fourth Army front, the 46th Division (Major-General G. F. Boyd) greatly distinguished itself in the capture of Bellenglise. The village is situated in the angle of the Scheldt Canal, which, after running in a southerly direction from Bellicourt, here bends sharply to the east towards the Le Tronquoy Tunnel. Equipped with lifebelts, and carrying mats and rafts, the 46th Division stormed the western arm of the canal at Bellenglise and to the north of it, some

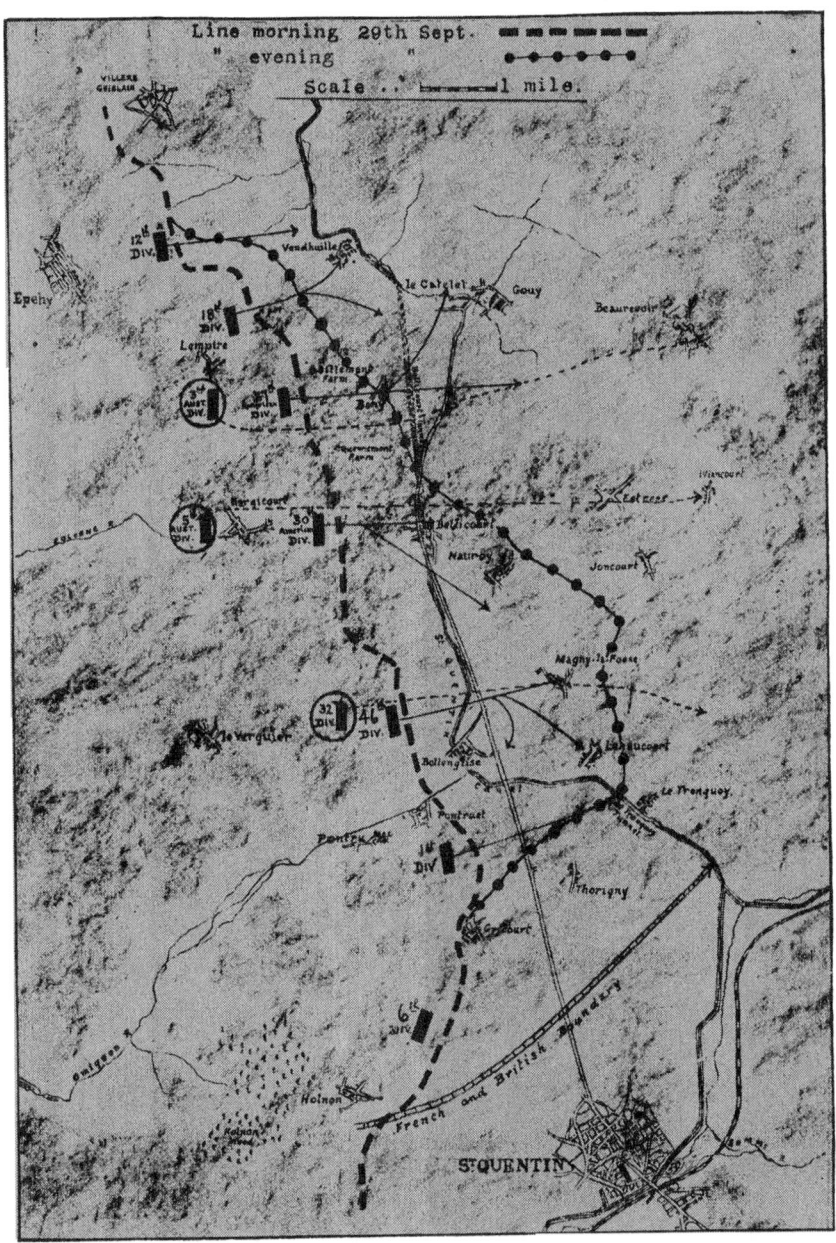

BATTLE OF CAMBRAI & THE HINDENBURG LINE
Hindenburg Line Attack, 29th September, 1918.

crossing the canal on footbridges which the enemy was given no time to destroy, others dropping down the sheer sides of the canal wall, and, having swum or waded to the far side, climbing up the farther wall to the German trench lines on the eastern bank. Having captured these trenches, the attacking troops swung to the right and took from flank and rear the German defences along the eastern arm of the canal and on the high ground south of the canal, capturing many prisoners and German batteries in action before the enemy had had time to realise the new direction of the attack. So thorough and complete was the organisation for this attack, and so gallantly, rapidly and well was it executed by the troops, that this one division took on this day over 4,000 prisoners and 70 guns.

On the remainder of the front, also, our attack met with remarkable success. South of Bellenglise, the 1st Division (Major-General E. P. Strickland), with the 6th Division covering their flank, crossed the ridge north-west of Thorigny and reached the west end of the Le Tronquoy Tunnel. Here they gained touch with the 32nd Division, who had passed through the 46th Division and taken Lehaucourt and Magny la Fosse.[1] North of Bellenglise, the 30th American Division (Major-General E. M. Lewis) having broken through the deep defences of the Hindenburg Line, stormed Bellicourt and seized Nauroy. On their left the 27th American Division (Major-General J. F. O'Ryan) met with very heavy enfilade machine gun fire, but pressed on with great gallantry as far as Bony, where a bitter struggle took place for the possession of the village.

Fighting on the whole front of the II. American Corps was severe, and in Bellicourt, Nauroy, Gillemont Farm, and at a number of other points amid the intricate defences of the Hindenburg Line, strong bodies of the enemy held out with great obstinacy for many hours. These points of resistance were gradually overcome, either by the support troops of the American divisions or by the 5th and 3rd Australian Divisions (Major-Generals Sir J. J. T. Hobbs and J. Gellibrand), which, moving up close behind the American troops, were soon heavily engaged.[2] On the left of the attack the 12th and 18th Divisions cleared the slopes above Vendhuille.

Meanwhile the Third Army captured Masnières and secured the crossings of the Scheldt Canal between that village and the outskirts of Cambrai, while the Canadian Corps made progress northwest of that town, taking St. Olle and Sancourt.

For the next two days our attacks continued on all fronts. On

[1] Both these villages were taken by the 46th Division. The 32nd Division continued the attack upon Levergies and captured Le Tronquoy on this day, not the 30th as stated in the text. The Sketch Map is also incorrect in this particular.

[2] The original plan was for the Australian divisions to go through the Americans to secure more distant objectives. This became impossible.

the 30th September the gap in the Hindenburg Line was enlarged by the capture of Thorigny and Le Tronquoy by the 1st and 32nd Divisions, thus securing possession of the Le Tronquoy Tunnel. On this day the enemy abandoned Villers Guislain and Gonnelieu, being threatened with envelopment, and withdrew behind the Scheldt Canal.

Next day, the IX. and Australian Corps attacked in conjunction with the French First Army, who occupied St. Quentin. Levergies was taken by the 32nd Division and Australian troops captured Joncourt, Estrées and Bony, establishing our line well to the north and east of the latter village.

In the Cambrai sector, the New Zealand and 3rd Divisions took Crèvecœur and Rumilly, while north of Cambrai the Canadian Corps cleared the high ground west of Ramillies and entered Blécourt. The fighting on the Canadian front at this period was particularly severe, and our troops displayed great courage and determination. The enemy employed large forces, amounting to at least eleven divisions in the space of five days, in his attempt to check our advance, and counter-attacked frequently and in strength.

Montbrehain and Beaurevoir

37. During the first week of October the Cambrai battle was completed by a series of successful minor operations, in which the breach driven through the Hindenburg Line, and such prepared defences as lay behind it, was widened.

On the 3rd October the Fourth Army attacked between Sequehart and Le Catelet and captured those villages and Ramicourt, together with the Beaurevoir-Fonsomme line on that front. In this operation the 50th Division took Gouy and Le Catelet after heavy and prolonged fighting, in which a number of counter-attacks were beaten off.

In the course of the next two days, other local improvements were effected in our line in this sector, and the villages of Montbrehain and Beaurevoir were captured after hard fighting, in which tanks did good service. Our advance compelled the enemy to evacuate the high ground about La Terrière, in the bend of the Scheldt Canal between La Catelet and Crèvecœur, with the result that on the 5th October the right of the Third Army was able to cross the Scheldt Canal and occupy the Hindenburg Line east of it, thereby greatly simplifying our arrangements for our next attack.

Results of Breaking the Hindenburg Line

38. The great and critical assaults in which during these nine days of battle the First, Third and Fourth Armies stormed the line

THE ADVANCE TO VICTORY

of the Canal du Nord and broke through the Hindenburg Line mark the close of the first phase of the British offensive. The enemy's defence in the last and strongest of his prepared positions had been shattered. The whole of the main Hindenburg defences had passed into our possession, and a wide gap had been driven through such rear trench systems as had existed behind them. The effect of the victory upon the subsequent course of the campaign was decisive. The threat to the enemy's communications was now direct and instant, for nothing but the natural obstacles of a wooded and well-watered country-side lay between our Armies and Maubeuge.

In the fighting of these days, in which thirty British and two American infantry divisions and one British cavalry division were engaged against thirty-nine German divisions, over 36,000 prisoners and 380 guns had been captured. Great as were the material losses the enemy had suffered, the effect of so overwhelming a defeat upon a moral already deteriorated was of even larger importance.

Combined with the events in Flanders presently narrated, the advance we had made opened a new threat to the German positions on the Lys front.

The Battle in Flanders

39. As indicated above in para. 13, the general strategic plan of the Allies contemplated the development of operations on the Flanders front. The details of these operations were settled at a conference held by the Commander-in-Chief of the Allied Armies at Cassel on the 9th September. The force to be engaged was to be placed under the command of His Majesty the King of the Belgians, and was to consist of the Belgian Army, some French divisions, and all the artillery and a certain number of divisions of the Second British Army, commanded by General Sir H. Plumer. To the definite plan then laid down I gladly gave my assent.

Accordingly at 5.30 a.m. on the 28th September the XIX. and II. Corps of the Second Army attacked without preliminary bombardment on a front of some $4\frac{1}{2}$ miles south of the Ypres-Zonnebeke Road. The 14th Division (Major-General P. C. B. Skinner), 35th Division (Major-General A. H. Marindin), 29th and 9th Divisions delivered the initial assault, being supported in the later stages of the battle by the 41st Division (Major-General Sir S. T. B. Lawford) and the 36th Division (Major-General C. Coffin). On the left of the II. Corps the Belgian Army continued the line of attack as far as Dixmude.

On both the British and Belgian fronts the attack was a brilliant success. The enemy, who was attempting to hold his positions with less than five divisions, was driven rapidly from the whole of the high ground east of Ypres, so fiercely contested during the battles of 1917. By the end of the day the British divisions had passed far beyond the farthest limits of the 1917 battles, and had reached and captured Kortewilde, Zandvoorde, Kruiseecke and Becelaere. On their left Belgian troops had taken Zonnebeke, Poelcapelle and Schaap Baillie, and cleared the enemy from Houthulst Forest.

South of the main attack, successful minor enterprises by the 31st, 30th (Major-General W. de L. Williams) and 34th British Divisions carried our line forward to St. Yves and the outskirts of Messines. Wytschaete was captured, and after sharp fighting our troops established themselves along the line of the ridge between Wytschaete and the canal north of Hollebeke.

During the succeeding days, despite continuous rain and great difficulties from the scarcity of practicable roads, the British and Belgian forces followed up the defeated enemy with the utmost vigour. On the 29th September our troops drove the German rearguards from Ploegsteert Wood and Messines and captured Terhand and Dadizeele. By the evening of the 1st October they had cleared the left bank of the Lys from Comines southwards, while north of that town they were close up to Wervicq, Gheluwe and Ledeghem. On their left the Belgian Army had passed the general line Moorslede-Staden-Dixmude.

In these most successful operations and their subsequent developments the British forces alone captured at light cost over 5,000 prisoners and 100 guns.

The Withdrawal from Lens and Armentières

40. Once more the effect of our successes showed itself rapidly.

At the beginning of September the enemy had withdrawn from his outpost positions astride the La Bassée Canal, and the activity of our patrols led to sharp fighting, in which the 16th (Major-General A. B. Ritchie), 55th (Major-General Sir H. S. Jeudwine) and 19th Divisions advanced our line close up to the outskirts of La Bassée. Thenceforward the situation on the Lys front had remained practically unchanged until the 30th September, when the divisions of General Sir W. R. Birdwood's Fifth Army made certain small advances south of the Lys. On the 2nd October, however, the enemy once more began an extensive withdrawal, falling back on the whole front from south of Lens to Armentières. In the sector south of Lens, indeed, patrols of the 20th Division (Major-General G. G. S. Carey) met with considerable resistance on this day about Acheville and Méricourt, but progress was made. During the next two days the movement continued, under vigorous pressure from

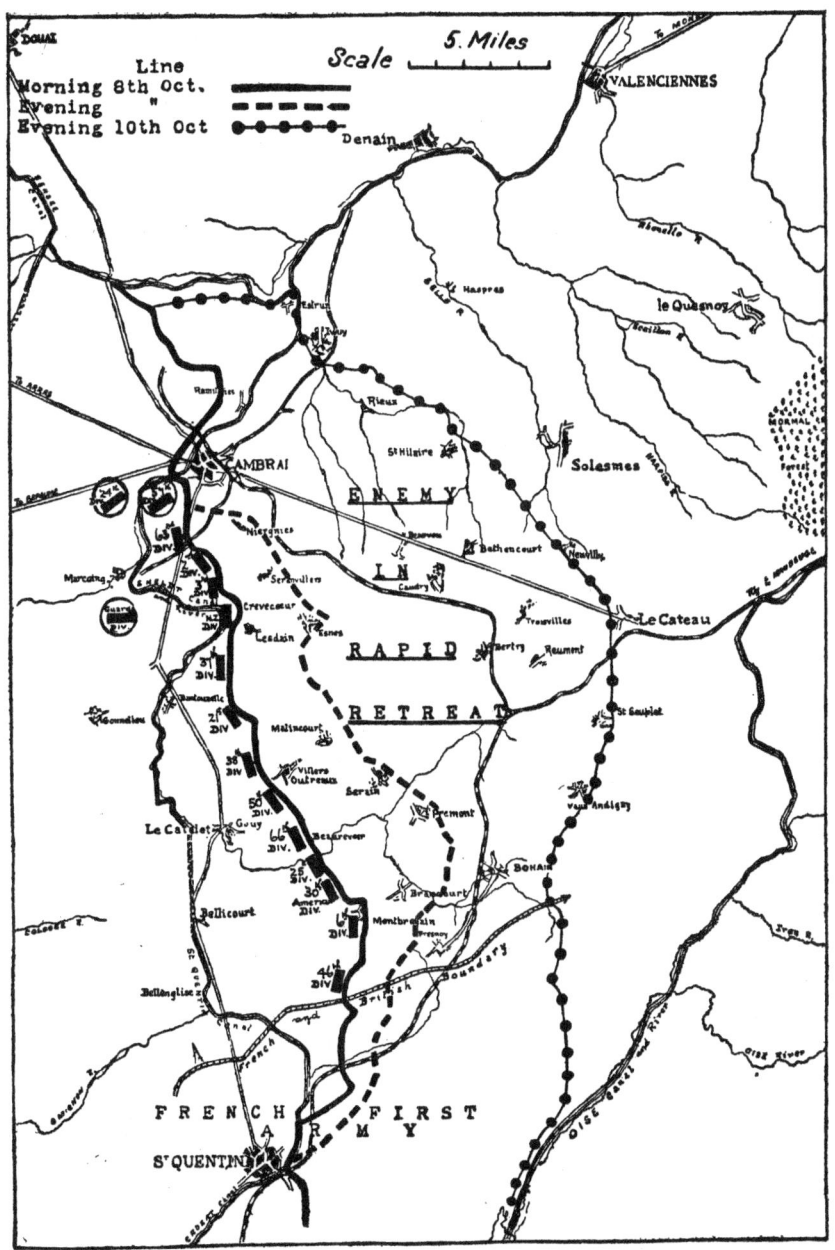

FINAL BRITISH OFFENSIVE—SECOND BATTLE OF LE CATEAU
8th October, 1918

THE ADVANCE TO VICTORY 287

our troops. By the evening of the 4th October north of Lens we had reached the general line Vendin le Vieil-Wavrin-Erquinghem-Houplines, where the increasing strength of the enemy's resistance indicated that he intended to stand at any rate for a time. South of Lens the withdrawal slackened about this date on the general line Fresnoy-Sallaumines-Vendin le Vieil, but shortly afterwards the development of our operations on the St. Quentin-Cambrai front forced upon the enemy a further retreat in this sector.

SECOND PHASE: THE FIGHTING IN OPEN COUNTRY

The Second Battle of Le Cateau (8th-12th October)

41. The second and concluding phase of the British offensive now opened, in which the Fourth and Third Armies and the right of the First Army moved forward with their left flank on the canal line which runs from Cambrai to Mons, and their right covered by the French First Army. This advance, by the capture of Maubeuge and the disruption of the German main lateral system of communications, forced the enemy to fall back upon the line of the Meuse and realised the strategic plan of the Allied operations.

The fighting which took place during this period, being in effect the development and exploitation of the Hindenburg Line victory, falls into three stages, the breaks between the different battles being due chiefly to the depth of our advances and the difficulties of re-establishing communications.

In the first of these stages, the battle of Le Cateau, certain incomplete defences still held by the enemy were captured, and his troops compelled to evacuate Cambrai and fall back behind the line of the Selle River. In the second stage, the Selle River was forced, and by a development of this operation our front pushed forward to the general line Sambre Canal—west edge of the Mormal Forest—Valenciennes, where we were in position for the final assault upon Maubeuge.

42. Having completed their arrangements, at 4.30 a.m. and 5.10 a.m. respectively on the 8th October the Third and Fourth Armies attacked on a front of over 17 miles from Sequehart to south of Cambrai. French troops continued the line of attack on our right as far south as St. Quentin. Farther south, French and American troops attacked on this day east of the Meuse and in Champagne, and made important progress.

On the British battle front our infantry and tanks penetrated the enemy's positions to a depth of between three and four miles, passing rapidly over the incomplete trench lines above referred to and gaining the open country beyond. Strong at the outset of our attack, during the later stages opposition weakened. Brancourt and Prémont were taken by the 30th American Division, while to the north of them the 66th Division (Major-General H. K. Bethell), attacking beside the 25th Division (Major-General J. R. E. Charles), captured Serain. Villers Outréaux was cleared by the 38th Division with the assistance of tanks after heavy fighting, and late in the afternoon Malincourt was captured. The New Zealand Division passed through Lesdain and took Esnes, while on the left of the attack, the 3rd, 2nd and 63rd Divisions captured Seranvillers, Forenville and Niergnies after very heavy fighting, in the course of which the enemy counter-attacked with tanks. On the extreme left the 57th Division made progress in the southern outskirts of Cambrai.

As the result of this attack the enemy's resistance temporarily gave way. His infantry became disorganised and retired steadily eastwards, while our airmen reported that the roads converging on Le Cateau were blocked with troops and transport. Several thousand prisoners and many guns fell into our hands. During the following night the Canadian Corps captured Ramillies and crossed the Scheldt Canal at Pont d'Aire. Canadian patrols entered Cambrai from the north and joined hands with patrols of the 57th Division working through the southern portion of the town. Next morning at 5.20 a.m. the Fourth and Third Armies resumed the attack on the whole front, cavalry assisting in the advance. By nightfall our troops were within two miles of Le Cateau, had captured Bohain, and were attacking Caudry from the south. Cambrai was in our hands, and our troops were three miles to the east of the town.

In this day's fighting cavalry again did valuable and gallant work, hurrying the enemy in his retreat and preventing him from completing the destruction of the railway which runs from St. Quentin to Busigny and Cambrai. When our infantry were held up by heavy machine gun fire from Cattigny Wood and Clary, a dashing charge by the Fort Garry Horse gained a footing in Cattigny Wood and assisted our infantry to press forward. Farther east, Dragoon Guards and Canadian Cavalry were instrumental in the capture of Honnechy, Reumont and Troisvilles.

On the 10th October our progress continued, though the enemy's resistance gradually stiffened as our troops approached the line of the river Selle, and attempts made by the cavalry to cross that stream had to be abandoned. That night we had reached the outskirts of Riqerval Wood, and held the west bank of the Selle river thence as far as Viesly, whence our line ran past St. Hilaire and

THE ADVANCE TO VICTORY 289

Avesnes, taken by the Guards and 24th Divisions, to the Scheldt at Thun St. Martin.

During these days the French First Army on our right advanced its line east of St. Quentin, clearing the west bank of the Oise-Sambre Canal as far north as Bernot.

The Withdrawal from Laon

43. By this advance, in which 20 British infantry divisions, two British cavalry divisions, and one American infantry division routed 24 German divisions and took from them 12,000 prisoners and 250 guns, we gained full possession of the important lateral double line of railway running from St. Quentin through Busigny to Cambrai. During the repair of such portions of it as had been destroyed and the removal of delay action mines left by the enemy, our line was carried forward by local operations. By the 13th October we had reached the Selle river at all points south of Haspres, and had established bridgeheads at a number of places.

Meanwhile, on the 7th October, under close pressure from our troops, the enemy had extended the flank of his withdrawal south of Lens, and on that day the 8th Division had captured Biache St. Vaast and Oppy, with some hundreds of prisoners. After the launching of our attack on the 8th October, this movement continued with increased rapidity. By the evening of the 13th October, our troops had reached the western suburbs of Douai, and were close up to the west banks of the Sensée Deviation and Haute Deule Canals on the whole front from Arleux (south of Douai) to Vendin le Vieil.

During this period also our Allies had been pushing forward steadily on both sides of the Argonne. Held by their attacks on his southern flank, while to the north the British offensive was driving forward rapidly behind his right, the enemy was forced to evacuate his positions in the Laon salient. Signs of a widespread German withdrawal were reported on the 11th October, and by the evening of the 13th October Laon was in French hands.

The Advance in Flanders Resumed

44. While these great events were taking place to the south of them, the Allied Forces in Flanders were busily engaged in re-establishing adequate communications in the area of the old Ypres battles. By dint of great exertions, and the most careful organisation of traffic routes, by the end of the second week in October the restoration of the Allied systems of communications was sufficiently far advanced to permit of a resumption of the offensive.

Accordingly, at 5.35 a.m. on the 14th October, the British, Belgian and French forces under command of His Majesty the King of the Belgians, attacked on the whole front between the Lys River at Comines and Dixmude.

The British sector extended for a distance of between nine and ten miles from Comines to the hamlet of St. Pieter, on the Menin-Roulers Road. The assault was launched by the X., XIX., and II. Corps of General Plumer's Second Army, under command respectively of Lieut.-General R. B. Stephens, Lieut.-General Sir H. E. Watts and Lieut.-General Sir C. W. Jacob, employing respectively the 30th and 34th Divisions, the 41st and 35th Divisions, and the 36th, 29th and 9th Divisions.

The Allied attack was again attended by complete success. The two southern British Corps advanced their line according to programme to the southern edge of the rising ground overlooking Wervicq, Menin and Wevelghem, in spite of very considerable resistance. Meanwhile, the II. Corps, after heavy fighting, penetrated to a depth of between three and four miles eastwards, capturing Moorseele and making progress beyond it to within a short distance of Gulleghem and Steenbeek. On our left Belgian troops reached Iseghem, French troops surrounded Roulers, while farther north other Belgian divisions took Cortemarck.

During the ensuing days our success was vigorously exploited. By the afternoon of the 16th October we held the north bank of the Lys from Frélinghien to opposite Harlebeke, and had crossed the river at a number of points. To the north of us our Allies also had made striking progress. Before nightfall on the 15th October Thourout was surrounded, and next day the enemy retired rapidly. Ostend fell on the 17th October, and three days later the northern flank of the Allied line rested on the Dutch frontier.

In these operations and others of a lesser nature, carried out on the last day of the month after the withdrawal next mentioned, the British forces operating on this battle front captured over 6,000 prisoners and 210 guns.

The Evacuation of Lille

45. Our advance north of the Lys had brought our troops far to the east of the Lille defences on the northern side, while our progress on the Le Cateau front had turned the Lille defences from the south. The German forces between the Sensée and the Lys were once more compelled to withdraw, closely followed by our troops, who constantly drove in their rearguards and took a number of prisoners. The enemy was given no opportunity to complete the

THE ADVANCE TO VICTORY

removal of his stores and the destruction of roads and bridges, or to evacuate the civil population.

The movement began on the 15th October, when, in spite of considerable opposition, our troops crossed the Haute Deule Canal on a wide front north of Pont-à-Vendin. By the evening of the 17th October the 8th Division of General Sir A. Hunter Weston's VIII. Corps had entered Douai and the 57th and 59th Divisions (Major-General N. M. Smyth) of Lieut.-General Sir R. C. B. Haking's XI. Corps were on the outskirts of Lille. At 5.50 a.m. on the 18th October our troops had encircled Lille, which was clear of the enemy. During the day our line was carried far to the east of these towns and east of Roubaix and Tourcoing, occupied by the 40th and 31st Divisions (Major-General Sir W. E. Peyton commanding 40th Division) of Lieut.-General Sir H. de B. de Lisle's XV. Corps. Thereafter our troops pressed forward steadily, until by the evening of the 22nd October they had reached the general line of the Scheldt on the whole front from Valenciennes to the neighbourhood of Avelghem.

THE BATTLE OF THE SELLE RIVER (17th-25th October)

The Forcing of the River Crossings

46. Meanwhile, communications on the Le Cateau front were improving, and it was possible to recommence operations of a more than local character for the forcing of the Selle positions and the attainment of the general line Sambre et Oise Canal—west edge of the Forêt de Mormal—Valenciennes. This advance would bring the important railway junction at Aulnoye within effective range of our guns.[1]

Our operations were opened on the 17th October by an attack by the Fourth Army on a front of about ten miles from Le Cateau southwards, in conjunction with the French First Army operating west of the Sambre et Oise Canal. The assault launched at 5.20 a.m. was delivered by the IX., II. American and XIII. Corps, employing respectively the 46th, 1st and 6th Divisions, the 30th and 27th American Divisions, and the 50th and 66th Divisions.

The enemy was holding the difficult wooded country east of Bohain and the line of the Selle north of it in great strength, his infantry being well supported by artillery. During the first two days his resistance was obstinate; but the attacking British and American troops made good progress. By the evening of the 19th

[1] At Aulnoye the main line from Mézières and Hirson links up with the main line to Maubeuge, Charleroi and Germany.

October, after much severe fighting, the enemy had been driven across the Sambre et Oise Canal at practically all points south of Catillon, whence our line followed the valley of the Richemont east and north of Le Cateau.

This success was followed at 2.0 a.m. on the 20th October by an attack upon the line of the Selle river north of Le Cateau. The troops employed were the 38th, 17th, 5th, 42nd, 62nd, Guards and 19th Divisions of the Third Army, and the 4th Division on the right of the First Army in that order from right to left.

On this occasion also the enemy's resistance was serious, and he had been able to erect wire entanglements along the greater part of the line. Our advance was strongly contested at every point, frequent counter-attacks being made. Supported by a number of tanks which had successfully crossed the river, our infantry, after severe fighting about Neuvilly, Amerval, Solesmes and Haspres, gained their objectives on the high ground east of the Selle, pushing out patrols as far as the river Harpies. North of Haspres other troops of the First Army continued to make progress on both sides of the Scheldt Canal, reaching the slopes overlooking the left bank of the Écaillon River and occupying Denain.

47. The capture of the Selle positions was followed almost immediately by the larger operation for the attainment of the required general line above-mentioned running from the Sambre Canal along the edge of the Mormal Forest to the neighbourhood of Valenciennes.

The original front of attack stretched from east of Mazinghien to Maison Bleue, north-east of Haussy, a distance of some fifteen miles. The assault was opened by the Fourth Army at 1.20 a.m. on the 23rd October and was delivered by the IX. and XIII. Corps, employing respectively the 1st and 6th Divisions and the 25th and 18th Divisions. The Third Army again attacked with the V., IV., VI. and XVII. Corps, employing respectively the 33rd and 21st Divisions, the 5th, 42nd, 37th and New Zealand Divisions, the 3rd and 2nd Divisions and the 19th Division. On the second day the 61st Division of the XVII. Corps and the 4th Division and 51st Division of the XXII. Corps, First Army, extended the line of attack for a further five miles northwards to the Scheldt.

The unfavourable weather of the preceding day had made it difficult to locate the enemy's batteries, and during the earlier stages of the battle hostile artillery fire was heavy. Despite this, and in spite of determined opposition at many points from the German machine gunners, in two days our infantry and tanks realised an advance of six miles over difficult country. About many of the woods and villages which lay in the way of our attack there was severe fighting, particularly in the large wood known as the Bois l'Évêque and at Pommereuil, Bousies Forest and Vendegies-sur-Écaillon. This latter village held out till the afternoon of the 24th October, when it was taken by an enveloping attack by troops of the 19th Division and 61st Division.

At the end of that day the western outskirts of the Forêt de Mormal had been reached, our troops were within a mile of Le Quesnoy and to the north-west of that town had captured the villages of Ruesnes and Maing. Local operations during the following three days gave us Englefontaine and established our line well to the north and east of the Le Quesnoy-Valenciennes railway, from the outskirts of Le Quesnoy, past Sepmeries and Artres to Famars.

The Enemy's Position at the End of October

48. By this time the rapid succession of heavy blows dealt by the British forces had had a cumulative effect, both moral and material, upon the German Armies. The difficulty of replacing the enemy's enormous losses in guns, machine guns and ammunition had increased with every fresh attack, and his reserves of men were exhausted. In the Selle battle the twenty-four British and two American divisions engaged had captured a further 20,000 prisoners and 475 guns from the thirty-one German divisions opposed to them, and had advanced to a great depth with certainty and precision. Though troops could still be found to offer resistance to our initial assault, the German infantry and machine gunners were no longer reliable, and cases were being reported of their retiring without fighting in front of our artillery barrage.

The capitulation of Turkey and Bulgaria and the imminent collapse of Austria—consequent upon Allied successes which the desperate position of her own armies on the western front had rendered her powerless to prevent—had made Germany's military situation ultimately impossible. If her armies were allowed to withdraw undisturbed to shorter lines, the struggle might still be protracted over the winter. The British Armies, however, were now in a position to prevent this by a direct attack upon a vital centre, which should anticipate the enemy's withdrawal and force an immediate conclusion.

THE BATTLE OF THE SAMBRE (1st-11th November)

49. The principal British attack was to take place at the beginning of November, as soon as possible after the capture of Valenciennes,

which I regarded as a necessary preliminary. In view of the likelihood of fresh withdrawals, time was of importance. Accordingly, at 5.15 a.m. on the 1st November, the XVII. Corps of the Third Army and the XXII. and Canadian Corps of the First Army attacked on a front of about six miles south of Valenciennes, and in the course of two days of heavy fighting inflicted a severe defeat on the enemy. During these two days the 61st Division (Major-General F. J. Duncan), 49th Division (Major-General N. J. G. Cameron) and 4th Division (Major-General C. H. T. Lucas) crossed the Rhonelle river, capturing Maresches and Preseau after a stubborn struggle, and established themselves on the high ground two miles to the east of it. On their left the 4th Canadian Division captured Valenciennes and made progress beyond the town.

As a consequence of this defeat the enemy on the 3rd November withdrew on the Le Quesnoy-Valenciennes front and our line was advanced. There were indications that a further withdrawal was contemplated both in the Tournai salient, where the line of the Scheldt was turned by our progress on the battle front, and also in the area to the south of us, where the enemy's positions were equally threatened by our advance. Our principal attack was ready.

50. The front of the decisive attack delivered by the Fourth, Third and First Armies on the 4th November extended for a distance of about thirty miles from the Sambre, north of Oisy, to Valenciennes.

The nature of the country across which our advance was to be made was most difficult. In the south the river had to be crossed almost at the outset. In the centre the great Forest of Mormal, though much depleted by German wood-cutting, still presented a formidable obstacle. In the north the fortified town of Le Quesnoy, and several streams which ran parallel to the line of our advance, offered frequent opportunities for successful defence. On the other hand our troops had never been so confident of victory or so assured of their own superiority.

After an intense bombardment our troops moved forward to the assault at about dawn, under a most effective artillery barrage, and very soon had penetrated the enemy's positions on the whole battle front. Throughout the day their pressure was never relaxed, and by the evening they had advanced to a depth of five miles, reaching the general line Fesmy—Landrecies—centre of Forêt de Mormal—Wargnies-le-Grand—five miles east of Valenciennes—Onnaing—Scheldt Canal opposite Thiers.

On the right of the attack the 1st Division of the IX. Corps, under the command of Lieut.-General Sir W. P. Braithwaite,

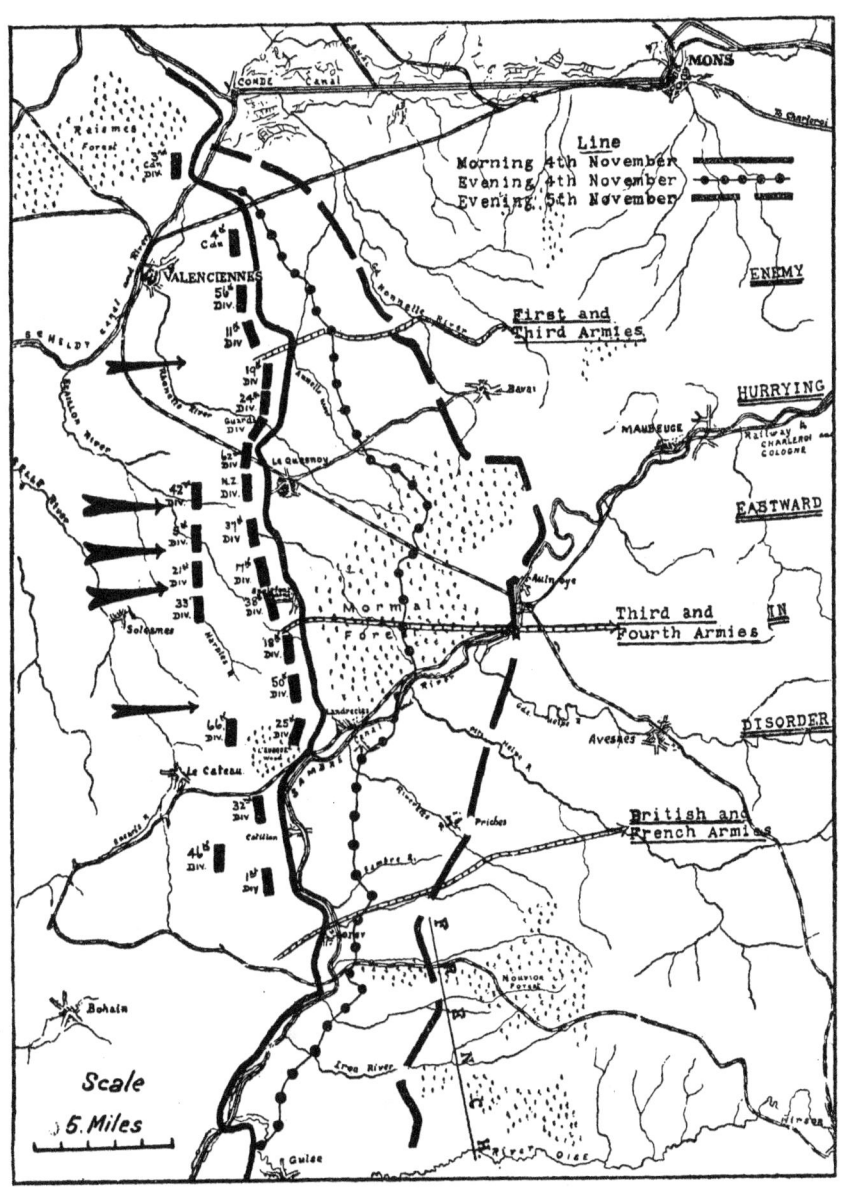

BATTLE OF THE SAMBRE
4th November, 1918

starting at 5.45 a.m., captured Catillon, and proceeded to pass troops across the Sambre at this place and at the lock some two miles to the south of it. This difficult operation was accomplished with remarkable rapidity and skill, and by 7.45 a.m. the 1st Battalion Cameron Highlanders and the 1st Battalion Northampton Regiment were east of the river. Bois l'Abbaye, Hautrève and La Groise were captured in turn, and though held up for a time at Fesmy, our troops took this place also in a renewed attack at 4.0 p.m., subsequently advancing well to the east of it.

The 32nd Division on the left of the IX. Corps met strong resistance all along the river line. By hard fighting they forced a crossing at Ors, and, pushing forward, took Mézières and Heurtebise, reaching the outskirts of La Folie. Later in the day other troops of this division, having crossed the river south of Landrecies, moved against La Folie from the north, and the village was captured.

Meanwhile the XIII. Corps, under command of Lieut.-General Sir T. L. N. Morland, had attacked at 6.15 a.m. with the 25th, 50th and 18th Divisions, and quickly over-ran the enemy's positions, despite strong opposition, which at Preux-au-Bois was maintained until the village was completely surrounded by our infantry and tanks. Severe fighting took place also about Landrecies, where a battalion of the 1st Guard Reserve Division had been specially detailed to hold the bridgehead. Troops of the 25th Division, having overcome this resistance, crossed the Sambre north and south of Landrecies by means of rafts, and captured the town.

The divisions of the Third Army in the centre of the attack also encountered stiff resistance at first, but when this was overcome made rapid progress. The 38th and 17th Divisions of the V. Corps, under command of Lieut.-General C. D. Shute, pushed far into the Forest of Mormal. Before dawn on the 5th November, the 38th Division had reached the eastern edge of the forest, while the 17th Division, after sharp fighting about Locquignol, had penetrated a mile to the east of that village.

On the IV. Corps front the 37th and New Zealand Divisions repulsed a counter-attack north of Ghissignies early in the battle with great loss to the enemy. Thereafter the 37th Division took Louvignies and Jolimetz, with over 1,000 prisoners, and during the late afternoon and evening pushed on to the centre of the forest. By 8.0 a.m. the New Zealand Division had already surrounded Le Quesnoy. Without attempting to take the town by direct assault, the New Zealand troops swept past and far to the east of it, capturing Herbignies by the evening. Meanwhile we had gained a footing on the ramparts surrounding Le Quesnoy, and at 4.0 p.m. the German garrison over 1,000 strong surrendered.

Opposite Orsinval the 62nd Division of the VI. Corps attacked at 5.20 a.m., and as soon as that village had been taken the Guards Division of the same corps attacked on the left of them. Both divisions had hard fighting, but made good progress, capturing Frasnoy and Preux-au-Sart, and reaching the western outskirts of Commegnies. On the front of the XVII. Corps on the left of the Third Army the enemy's resistance was less vigorous, though sharp fighting took place about Wargnies-le-Petit. This village and Wargnies-le-Grand were taken by the 24th Division (Major-General A. C. Daly) during the afternoon, while the 19th Division captured Bry and Eth.

On the front of the First Army the XXII. Corps and the Canadian Corps advanced against little opposition, except on their right. Here the 11th and 56th Divisions, having crossed the Aunelle River and captured the villages of Le Triez, Sebourg and Sebourquiaux, were counter-attacked on the high ground east of the Aunelle and pressed back slightly. The 4th and 3rd Canadian Divisions on their left reached the outskirts of Rombies, and the eastern side of the marshes north of Valenciennes.

In these operations and their developments twenty-six British divisions utterly defeated thirty-two German divisions, and captured 19,000 prisoners and more than 450 guns. On our right the French First Army, which had continued the line of attack southwards to the neighbourhood of Guise, kept pace with our advance, taking 5,000 prisoners and a number of guns.

The Return to Mons

51. By this great victory the enemy's resistance was definitely broken. On the night 4th/5th November his troops began to fall back on practically the whole battle front. Throughout the following days, despite continuous rain which imposed great hardships on our troops, infantry and cavalry pressed forward with scarcely a check, maintaining close touch with the rapidly retreating Germans.

On the 5th November the troops of the Fourth Army realised a further advance of some four miles, penetrating beyond Prisches and Maroilles. On the Third Army front the 5th, 21st and 33rd Divisions pushed forward well to the east of Mormal Forest, while farther north by the evening we were approaching Bavai. Only on the First Army front was the resistance encountered at all serious. Here, after regaining during the morning the ridge east of the Aunelle, and capturing Roisin, Meaurain and Angreau, the divisions of the XXII. Corps were held up for a time in front of Angre and along the line of the Honnelle River.

THE ADVANCE TO VICTORY

Throughout the day the roads packed with the enemy's troops and transport afforded excellent targets to our airmen, who took full advantage of their opportunities, despite the unfavourable weather. Over thirty guns, which bombs and machine gun fire from the air had forced the enemy to abandon, were captured by a battalion of the 25th Division in the fields near Le Preseau.

On the 6th November considerable opposition was again encountered on the front of the First Army, as well as on the left of the Third Army. Angre, however, was captured, and the Honnelle River crossed, while Canadian troops took Baisieux and Quiévrechain. During the night of the 6th/7th November the enemy's resistance again weakened, and early on the morning of the 7th November the Guards Division entered Bavai. Next day Avesnes fell into our hands, Hautmont was captured, and our troops reached the outskirts of Maubeuge.

Meanwhile to the north of the Mons-Condé Canal our success was bearing fruit. During the night of the 7th/8th November numerous explosions were observed behind the German lines, and on the following morning the VIII. Corps and I. Corps (Lieut.-General Sir Arthur Holland) of the First and Fifth Armies were able to move forward, occupying Condé and crossing the Scheldt on a considerable front south of Antoing. Farther north the enemy abandoned his bridgehead at Tournai, and the western portion of the town was occupied by our troops.

On the 9th November the enemy was in general retreat on the whole front of the British Armies. The fortress of Maubeuge was entered by the Guards Division and the 62nd Division (Major-General Sir R. D. Whigham), while the Canadians were approaching Mons. The progress of the Fifth Army was accentuated, and Peruwelz, Antoing and Tournai captured. The Second Army crossed the Scheldt on its whole front and reached the outskirts of Renaix.

Next day, the advance of the five British Armies continued, cavalry and cyclists operating in advance of the infantry. Only in the neighbourhood of Mons was any substantial opposition met with. Here the Canadians advancing towards the town from south and west, and working round it on the north, encountered an organised and tenacious machine gun defence. Farther north our cavalry were on the outskirts of Ath, and our line was far to the east of Tournai. Renaix had been captured and our troops were approaching Grammont.

In the early morning of the 11th November the 3rd Canadian Division captured Mons, the whole of the German defending force being killed or taken prisoners.

The Armistice

52. At 11.0 a.m. on the 11th November, in accordance with instructions received from the Commander-in-Chief of the Allied Armies, hostilities were suspended. At that hour the right of the Fourth Army was east of the Franco-Belgian frontier and thence northwards our troops had reached the general line Sivry—Erquelinnes — Boussoit—Jurbise — Herchies — Ghislenghien — Lessines—Grammont.

The military situation on the British front on the morning of the 11th November can be stated very shortly. In the fighting since the 1st November our troops had broken the enemy's resistance beyond possibility of recovery, and had forced on him a disorderly retreat along the whole front of the British Armies. Thereafter, the enemy was capable neither of accepting nor refusing battle. The utter confusion of his troops, the state of his railways congested with abandoned trains, the capture of huge quantities of rolling stock and material, all showed that our attack had been decisive. It had been followed on the north by the evacuation of the Tournai salient, and to the south, where the French forces had pushed forward in conjunction with us, by a rapid and costly withdrawal to the line of the Meuse.

The strategic plan of the Allies had been realised with a completeness rarely seen in war. When the armistice was signed by the enemy his defensive powers had already been definitely destroyed. A continuance of hostilities could only have meant disaster to the German Armies and the armed invasion of Germany.[1]

The Work of the Troops

53. In three months of epic fighting the British Armies in France have brought to a sudden and dramatic end the great wearing-out battle of the past four years.

In our admiration for this outstanding achievement, the long years of patient and heroic struggle by which the strength and spirit of the enemy were gradually broken down cannot be forgotten. The strain of those years was never ceasing, the demands they made upon the best of the Empire's manhood are now known. Yet throughout all those years, and amid the hopes and disappointments they brought

---

[1] The reasons which decided the Allies not to continue hostilities are referred to in the final Despatch, page 316 below. Supply difficulties would have very greatly delayed our advance. Widespread damage would have been caused to the country through which we passed, and further casualties must have been incurred. On the other hand, the Armistice in effect amounted to complete surrender by the enemy, and all that could have been gained by fighting came into our hands more speedily and at less cost.

with them, the confidence of our troops in final victory never wavered. Their courage and resolution rose superior to every test, their cheerfulness never failing, however terrible the conditions in which they lived and fought. By the long road they trod with so much faith and with such devoted and self-sacrificing bravery we have arrived at victory, and to-day they have their reward.

The work begun and persevered in so steadfastly by those brave men has been completed during the present year with a thoroughness to which the event bears witness, and with a gallantry which will live for all time in the history of our country. The annals of war hold record of no more wonderful recovery than that which, three months after the tremendous blows showered upon them on the Somme and on the Lys, saw the undefeated British Armies advancing from victory to victory, driving their erstwhile triumphant enemy back to and far beyond the line from which he started, and finally forcing him to acknowledge unconditional defeat.

The great series of victories won by the British forces between the 8th August and the 11th November is the outstanding feature of the events described in this Despatch. At Amiens and Bapaume, in the breaking of the Drocourt-Quéant and Hindenburg systems, before Le Cateau and on the Selle, in Flanders and on the Sambre, the enemy was again and again brought to battle and defeated.

In the decisive contests of this period, the strongest and most vital parts of the enemy's front were attacked by the British, his lateral communications were cut and his best divisions fought to a standstill. On the different battle fronts 187,000 prisoners and 2,850 guns were captured by us, bringing the total of our prisoners for the present year to over 201,000. Immense numbers of machine guns and trench mortars were taken also, the figures of those actually counted exceeding 29,000 machine guns and some 3,000 trench mortars. These results were achieved by 59 fighting British divisions, which in the course of three months of battle engaged and defeated 99 separate German divisions.

This record furnishes the proof of the skill of our commanders and their staffs, as well as of the fine fighting qualities of the British regimental officer and soldier. It is a proof also of the overwhelmingly decisive part played by the British Armies on the western front in bringing the enemy to his final defeat.

It is an accepted military doctrine that in good defensive positions any given force can hold up an attacking force of considerably greater numbers. This doctrine was proved in the fighting of March and April of this year, when, despite the enormous superiority of force which the enemy was able to concentrate against the right of the British Armies, all his efforts to effect a definite break-through were frustrated by our defence. Yet, as has been seen, when the tide of battle turned and the British Armies advanced to the attack, throughout practically the whole of the long succession of battles which ended in the complete destruction of the German powers of resistance, the attacking British troops were numerically inferior to the German forces they defeated.

It would be impossible to devise a more eloquent testimony to the unequalled spirit and determination of the British soldier, of all ranks and Services. We have been accustomed to be proud of the great and noble traditions handed down to us by the soldiers of bygone days. The men who form the Armies of the Empire to-day have created new traditions which are a challenge to the highest records of the past and will be an inspiration to the generations who come after us.

Infantry

Despite the enormous development of mechanical invention in every phase of warfare, the place which the infantryman has always held as the main substance and foundation of an army is as secure to-day as in any period of history. The infantryman remains the backbone of defence and the spearhead of the attack. At no time has the reputation of the British infantryman been higher, or his achievement more worthy of his renown. During the past three months, the same infantry divisions have advanced to the attack day after day and week after week with an untiring irresistible ardour which refused to be denied. No praise can be too high for the valour they have shown, no gratitude too deep for the work they have accomplished.

Artillery

Four years of scientific warfare have seen a consistent and progressive development in the power and influence of artillery, both in the actual infantry battle and in all the stages which lead up to it. Despite the handicap under which we started the war, British artillery has played a large part in that development and of late has dominated the enemy's artillery to an ever-increasing degree. The influence of this fact upon the moral both of our own and the enemy's troops could scarcely be exaggerated.

During the present year the greater number of guns available for our use and the amount and regularity of our ammunition supply, combined with the enemy's weakened powers of resistance, due to the bitter fighting of the past two years, have for the most part led to the substitution of sudden and intense outburst of fire for the prolonged destructive bombardments which preceded our attacks

THE ADVANCE TO VICTORY

in 1917. All ranks of the artillery have adapted themselves to these new conditions with complete success, and in the rapid movements of the latter stages of our advance have shown the highest technical skill and most indefatigable energy. The accuracy and intensity of our barrages, frequently arranged at short notice and with little opportunity being given for ranging or previous reconnoitring of the ground, have contributed largely to the success of our infantry attacks. The intimate co-operation between artillery and infantry, which is the first requisite in modern war, has been a marked feature of our operations.

Cavalry

The more open character of the recent fighting at once brought prominently to notice the fact that cavalry is still a necessary arm in modern war. On a number of occasions, to some of which short reference has been made in this Report, important results have been obtained by the use of cavalry, particularly in combination with light tanks and mobile machine gun units. Such increased opportunities as have been offered them have been seized and utilised by the cavalry with promptness and effect. Both in the development of the successes of our infantry attacks and in following up the various withdrawals thereby forced upon the enemy, the different cavalry units have performed work of the highest value.

Royal Air Force

During the past year the work of our airmen in close co-operation with all fighting branches of the Army, has continued to show the same brilliant qualities which have come to be commonly associated with that Service; while the ever-increasing size of the Royal Air Force and the constant improvement in the power and performance of machines, combined with the unfailing keenness of pilots and observers, have enabled intense activity to be maintained at all times.

Some idea of the magnitude of the operations carried out can be gathered from the fact that from the beginning of January, 1918, to the end of November, nearly 5,500 tons of bombs were dropped by us, 2,953 hostile aeroplanes were destroyed, in addition to 1,178 others driven down out of control, 241 German observation balloons were shot down in flames, and an area of over 4,000 square miles of country has been photographed, not once but many times.

The assistance given to the infantry by our low-flying aeroplanes during the battles of March and April was repeated during the German offensives on the Aisne and Marne, on both of which occasions British squadrons were despatched to the French battle front and did very gallant service. During our own attacks, hostile troops and transport have been constantly and heavily attacked with most excellent results.

Both by day and night our bombing squadrons have continually attacked the enemy's railway junctions and centres of activity, reconnaissance machines have supplied valuable information from both far and near, while artillery machines have been indefatigable in their watch over German batteries and in accurate observation for our own guns. In these latter tasks our balloons have done most valuable work and have kept pace with admirable energy and promptness with the ever-changing battle line.

Tanks

Since the opening of our offensive on 8th August, tanks have been employed in every battle, and the importance of the part played by them in breaking the resistance of the German infantry can scarcely be exaggerated. The whole scheme of the attack of the 8th August was dependent upon tanks, and ever since that date on numberless occasions the success of our infantry has been powerfully assisted or confirmed by their timely arrival. So great has been the effect produced upon the German infantry by the appearance of British tanks that in more than one instance, when for various reasons real tanks were not available in sufficient numbers, valuable results have been obtained by the use of dummy tanks painted on frames of wood and canvas.

It is no disparagement of the courage of our infantry, or of the skill and devotion of our artillery, to say that the achievements of those essential arms would have fallen short of the full measure of success achieved by our Armies had it not been for the very gallant and devoted work of the Tank Corps, under the command of Major-General H. J. Elles.

Trench Mortars

Throughout the period under review the personnel of the trench mortar batteries, both heavy, medium and light, have continued to discharge their duties with skill and efficiency whenever opportunity offered for the effective use of their arms. During the period of trench warfare the heavier types of trench mortars well maintained their superiority over the enemy, while during the war of movement later in the campaign numerous instances were reported when the lighter types have been used with effect well forward in the attack in overcoming the resistance of hostile strong points.

Machine Gun Corps

The high reputation earned by the different units of the Machine Gun Corps during the defensive battles of the spring has been well maintained under the changed conditions of the latter part of the year. The great value of the machine gun in the attack, when handled with energy and decision, has been proved again and again. The consistent failure of the enemy's frequent counter-attacks has been due in no small degree to the skilful use of these weapons.

Royal Engineers

Reference has already been made to the vast amount of work carried out on new defences during the earlier part of the period under review. In the construction of the 5,000 miles of new trench 20 million cubic yards of earth were shifted, while the wire entanglements erected in front of the trench lines consumed 23,500 tons of barbed wire and 15 million wooden or steel pickets.

During the period of our offensive all branches of the Royal Engineers and the Engineer units of the Dominions have shown the greatest energy and skill in the discharge of their different tasks. On many occasions, particularly in the construction of bridges under fire and in the removal of mines, they have shown courage of the highest order. In the course of our advance some 700 road bridges, exclusive of pontoon bridges, were constructed. Many of these, and in addition a large number of foot-bridges for infantry assault, were constructed under heavy shell and machine gun fire. Notable instances of the cool pluck and determination displayed in this work were furnished by a field company of the 38th Division, which in the crossing of the Selle River lost 50 per cent. of its effectives, yet completed its bridge, and by the fine performance of Engineer troops of the 1st Division at the crossing of the Sambre on the 4th November.

The work of the tunnelling companies has demanded equally with that of the field companies great courage and skill. In the period from the 8th August to the termination of hostilities nearly 14,000 German mines and traps of various descriptions, totalling over 540 tons of explosives, had been discovered and rendered harmless by the different tunnelling companies, while a further amount of nearly 300 tons of explosives had been withdrawn from our own demolition charges and minefields.

The provision of water for the troops presented a problem of great difficulty, which was met with equal energy and success. Many miles of new water mains were laid, and over 400 mechanical pumping plants, giving a daily yield of some 20 million gallons of water, were installed as our troops advanced. In addition to work of the kind performed by the transportation services, Engineer troops were responsible also for the repair of some 3,500 miles of roads, including the filling in of some 500 road craters.

Gas Services

Prior to the commencement of the advance several important gas operations, in which large quantities of gas were discharged, were carried out successfully by the Special Brigade. After our advance had begun, immediate advantage was taken of any temporary stabilisation of the line to carry out a large number of useful operations of a lesser character, wherever it was possible to do so without danger to the lives of French civilians.

Some idea of the magnitude of the work performed and of the energy and zeal displayed by all ranks can be gained from the fact that the 21 Special Companies, with the assistance of two American companies attached for instruction, discharged during the period March-November a total of over 2,250 tons of gas. Between the 11th March and the 7th October gas was discharged on 119 nights out of 210, and no less than 301 separate operations were successfully carried out, in addition to a large number of others, which, when all preparations had been completed, had to be abandoned in consequence of changes in the tactical situation. In all these different operations all ranks of the Gas Services have shown their accustomed courage and devotion to duty.

Signal Services

The constant movement of the line and the shifting of headquarters has again imposed an enormous strain upon all ranks of the Signal Service. The depth of our advance, and the fact that during the latter part of it the whole of the British Armies were simultaneously involved, made the maintenance of signal communications most difficult. The fact that in such circumstances the needs of the Army were met reflects the highest credit upon the zeal and efficiency of all ranks.

Transportation Services

Attention has already been drawn to the work thrown upon the Transportation Services as the result of the German advances during the early part of the year. From the commencement of the British offensive in August the situation became reversed. Defensive measures were abandoned, and the energies of all concerned were

THE ADVANCE TO VICTORY 305

centred upon the reconstruction of the railway system recaptured from the enemy. In spite of the fact that the enemy, as he withdrew, used every modern artifice for the destruction of railways, roads, bridges and water supplies, the Railway Construction troops were able to meet all demands and accomplished successfully an unparalleled programme of railway reconstruction. By the end of October no less than 1,050 miles of line, much of which had been destroyed, had been brought into service for our Armies. This included 485 miles of new track and some 4,000 feet of bridging.

The following is an instance of the speed with which the work of reconstruction was carried out. On the 17th October, Lille was evacuated by the enemy. On the 25th October the first train of supplies for the civil population entered the city, the railway having been carried across the Lys River at Armentières by a bridge constructed in the short space of four days. Some idea of the extent of the traffic dealt with can be gathered from the fact that in a period of six months nearly seven million officers and other ranks were carried by the broad and metre gauge railways. The number of ton miles worked by the light railway systems during a similar period amounted to over 21 millions.

The troops engaged upon this work have been drawn from the British Railway Companies and from Canada. They have worked continuously for months under great pressure. The energy and efficiency displayed in administration and execution are beyond all praise. I desire to acknowledge the great assistance rendered by the British railways and local authorities at home in supplying personnel, locomotives, wagons and plant, the valuable service of Canadian railway troops, and the loyal co-operation and assistance of the French railways.

A similar expansion is to be noticed in the work of the Roads Directorate. In June, 1917, the mileage of roads maintained was 1,640; in October of 1918 it was 4,412. During a period of six months of the present year 1,500,000 tons of road stone and 685,000 sleepers and pit props were used upon the roads. The enormous demand for material is reflected in a greatly increased output from the quarries and forests worked by us.

The work at the Base Ports has been discharged during the past year with an efficiency and dispatch undiminished by the fact that the ports have been persistently and heavily attacked by hostile aircraft. During the period under review the Channel Train Ferry Service, opened in February last, has proved of inestimable value.

As the result of the enemy's advance in the spring, the length of Inland Waterways operated by the British fell to less than 250 miles. By October, however, the mileage operated had risen to 464 miles, and, throughout our advance, every effort has been made to open up for navigation the waterways uncovered by the enemy's retreat. Very satisfactory results have been obtained and very valuable and important service has been rendered by the personnel concerned.

Supply Services

The demands made by our Armies upon the Supply Services throughout the period under review were great and increasing. Every advance made supply more difficult, and during the later stages of our offensive the work was complicated by the necessity of feeding many thousands of liberated civilians in the reconquered territories. Despite the magnitude of their task, these services rose magnificently to the demands made upon them. It is in no small degree due to their excellent organisation and administration that our Armies in the Field have never lacked food, clothing, equipment, guns or munitions. The greatest testimony to the efficiency of these services is the rapidity of our advances, which otherwise would have been impossible. Their work was unostentatious, but its effect was far reaching.

Forestry

During the twelve months ended on the 31st October, 1918, over two and a half million tons of timber have been cut for the use of the British and French Armies by the different units under the control of the Forestry Directorate. The work has been carried out with admirable thoroughness and efficiency in close co-operation with the Forestry Authorities of other Allied Armies, and has resulted in a very material saving of transport.

The Omnibus Park

In my last Despatch I referred to the invaluable work performed by the Auxiliary Omnibus Park throughout the German offensive. During the period under review further heavy calls have been made upon it in connection with our advance. In all, a total of nearly 800,000 troops have been carried and over 2,500,000 miles have been run by the Omnibus Park. In accomplishing this task all ranks concerned have once more shown the same zeal and devotion to duty which distinguished their previous conduct.

The Labour Corps

Throughout the period under review the demands upon the Labour Corps were incessant. The British labour companies were

THE ADVANCE TO VICTORY 307

composed entirely of men medically unfit for active operations, and more than half their number owed their incapacity to wounds or sickness incurred while serving with fighting units. The men of the Corps, however, made light of their disabilities. Many companies worked for months on end under shell fire, long marches were willingly undertaken, and the essential work entrusted to them was cheerfully performed often under conditions entailing all the hardship and strain without the excitement of actual fighting. The successive British advances imposed upon all ranks daily increasing work and responsibilities. It is to the credit of the Corps and of the excellent system of command and administration developed in it during the earlier part of the year that the labour companies have invariably answered all demands made upon them.

Medical Services

During the period under review the Medical Services, under the direction of Lieut.-General C. H. Burtchaell, deserve special commendation for the initiative, energy and success which have characterised all branches of their work. The rapid advance of the troops and the extended front on which operations were carried out during the final stages of the offensive created problems in connection with the collection, evacuation and treatment of wounded which had not been met with in the earlier phases of the war. These difficulties were met with the most admirable promptness and efficiency.

My thanks are due to the consulting surgeons and physicians for the invaluable assistance given by them in the application of new methods to the treatment of wounds and disease; to the R.A.M.C. Officers and Permanent Staffs of the Convalescent Depôts for work which enabled many thousands of men to be restored to the fighting ranks; to the untiring and devoted work of the British Red Cross Society, the Order of St. John and all members of the Nursing Services, whose unremitting kindness and constancy has done much to alleviate the sufferings of the sick and wounded; and finally for the very valuable services rendered by the Base Hospital Units and by individual officers of the Medical Corps of the United States of America, attached to the British Army.

The Chaplains' Department

Under the direction of the Principal Chaplain, the Rev. J. M. Simms, and the Deputy Chaplain-General, The Right Rev. Bishop Gwynne, the clergy of all denominations ministering to the Army have earned the admiration and affection of all ranks. I desire once more to express on behalf of all officers and men my profound appreciation of their unfailing devotion and self-sacrifice.

Administrative Services and Departments

To all other Administrative Services and Departments I desire to express the thanks of the fighting forces for the loyal and efficient manner in which they have carried out their essential tasks. During a period of great strain and incessant work they have contributed in their various spheres to the smooth working of the Army machine and are entitled to a full share in the victory of our arms.

The Navy and Home Authorities

The thanks of all ranks of the British Armies in France and Flanders are once more due to the Royal Navy and Mercantile Marine for their magnificent work, which throughout the heavy demands of the past year has at all times enabled our needs to be supplied.

We thank also the different Home Authorities and the workers in the great munition factories, both men and women, for the magnificent support they have given us through all stages of the war. We understand and appreciate the value of the work they have done.

Our Allies

At the moment when the final triumph of the Allied cause is assured, we and all others of the Allied and Associated Armies can look back on the years that have gone with a satisfaction undimmed by any hint of discord or conflict of interest and ideals. Few alliances of the past can boast such a record. Few can show a purpose more tenaciously and faithfully pursued, or so fully and gloriously realised. If the complete unity and harmony of our action is to be ascribed in part to the justice of our cause, it is due also to the absolute loyalty with which that cause has been pursued by all those entrusted with the control of the different Allied Armies that have fought side by side with ours.

I propose to submit at a later date a further and final Despatch dealing with the advance of the British Armies to the Rhine and the occupation of the Cologne Bridgehead.

I have the honour to be,
   my Lord,
     Your Lordship's obedient servant,
       D. HAIG, Field-Marshal,
        Commanding-in-Chief, British Armies in France.

THE FINAL DESPATCH

THE FINAL DESPATCH

General Headquarters,[1]
British Armies in France,
21st March, 1919.

SIR,—

I have the honour to submit the following final Despatch in which is described the advance of the British Forces into Germany and the occupation of the bridgehead east of the Rhine at Cologne. I include in this Despatch a brief review of the chief features of military interest which stand out among the operations of the British Armies on the Western front during the time I have been in command of them. I take this last opportunity also to refer by name to some few of the many able and gallant officers who have assisted me in my task, and to thank them personally.

PART I

THE ADVANCE INTO GERMANY

(11th November, 1918—31st December, 1918)

Arrangements for the Advance

1. At 11.00 on the 11th November, 1918, at which hour and date the Armistice granted to Germany by the Allies took effect, the British front extended over a distance of about 60 miles from the neighbourhood of Montbliart, east of Avesnes, to just north of Grammont (*vide* Map No. 10). This front from south to north was held by troops of the Fourth, Third, First, Fifth and Second British Armies, all of whom were in hot pursuit of the enemy at the moment when the armistice came into operation.

The provisions of the Armistice had settled in general terms the course to be followed subsequently by the belligerent groups of Armies. To co-ordinate the action of the Allied Armies, instructions of a more detailed character were issued by Marshal Foch to all concerned, and these formed the basis of the orders given by me during the period covered by this Despatch.

Troops were at once directed not to advance east of the line

---

[1] This Despatch was published as a Supplement, dated the 10th April, 1919, to the *London Gazette* of the 8th April, 1919.

reached by them at the time when hostilities ceased, and certain parties of Germans taken prisoner after that hour were returned to the enemy. Outposts were established along this line both for the sake of military security and in order to prevent all possibility of fraternisation. Behind these outposts the remainder of our forces were grouped and concentrated.

It was arranged that the forward movement of the different Allied Armies should be carried out by certain definite stages, through separate zones of action. The zone allotted to the British Armies extended from the front then held by us in an easterly direction as far as the German frontier, whence it continued in a north-easterly direction to the Cologne Bridgehead. The boundaries of this zone and the stages of the advance are shown on the attached map.[1]

In order to permit the enemy to withdraw his troops from the area immediately in front of us, our positions were maintained unchanged until the morning of the 17th November. Thereafter, to avoid all possibility of collision between the opposing forces, the movement of troops towards the frontier was regulated so as to preserve a safety zone of 10 kilometres in depth between our advanced detachments and the enemy's rearguards.

The general advance into Germany was directed to begin on the 1st December. On the 12th December, French, American and British forces would cross the Rhine at Mayence, Coblentz and Cologne, and commence the occupation of bridgeheads having a radius of 30 kilometres from the crossings at those towns. By that date, the enemy was bound by the terms of the Armistice to have withdrawn his military forces a distance of 10 kilometres from the right bank of the Rhine and from the perimeter of the Rhine Bridgeheads.

Re-adjustment of the British Forces

2. As we progressed eastwards, the front held by the British Armies, already short, would automatically be decreased. On the other hand, the maintenance of supply across and beyond the battle areas presented difficulties which would grow rapidly as our communications lengthened. These two considerations made it both feasible and necessary to effect a redistribution of troops, so that the extent of the forces advancing into Germany should be no more than was absolutely necessary to meet military requirements.

I decided that the opening stages of our advance should be carried out by the Second and Fourth Armies, under command of the two senior Army Commanders General Plumer and General

[1] Map No. 10.

Rawlinson, and that each Army should consist of four Corps each of four divisions. To ensure rapidity of movement and to facilitate supply, the artillery and auxiliary arms and services accompanying these Armies were cut down to a minimum, and all surplus units then attached to them were transferred to the First, Third and Fifth Armies. Arrangements were made for reorganising these last mentioned Armies and for withdrawing them to areas farther west.

The Advance to the German Frontier

3. At 05.00 on the morning of the 17th November the 2nd Cavalry Division covering the front of the Fourth Army, and the 1st and 3rd Cavalry Divisions covering the front of the Second Army crossed the line reached on the 11th November and commenced the march to the German Frontier. The leading infantry divisions moved forward on the following day.

The advance was carried out under active service conditions, cavalry leading and all military precautions being taken. Among all arms, the general bearing, smartness and march discipline of the troops were of a high order, reflecting credit on the Army and the nation. All traces of the desperate fighting and forced marches of the previous months had been removed, and men, horses, guns and vehicles appeared as though turned out for parade. Throughout the advance, despite long distances covered under difficult conditions, indifferent billets and the absence of the usual opportunities for bathing or renewing clothes, the same general standard of excellence was maintained in a remarkable degree.

The first troops to complete the portion of our advance which lay through Belgium were patrols of the 2nd Cavalry Division, who arrived on the German Frontier in the neighbourhood of Beho on the night of the 28/29th November. Next day the frontier was reached by the 1st Cavalry Division along the whole front of our advance. The infantry, who had been marching steadily in rear of the cavalry, closed up behind them in readiness for the advance into Germany.

During this part of our march the various stages above referred to were strictly observed, except that in front of our general advance detachments of cavalry had been sent forward to keep order in Charleroi and Namur in response to requests received from the local authorities.[1] Everywhere our troops were received with the utmost enthusiasm by the population of the liberated districts.

In every town and village streets were festooned with flags and spanned by triumphal arches bearing messages of welcome. Men,

---
[1] These detachments were not required to take any action.

women and children thronged to meet our troops and exchange greetings in French and English. Nor was their gratitude confined to demonstrations such as these. Wherever our men were billeted during their advance everything possible was done for their comfort. In many cases refreshment was pressed upon them without payment, and on all sides, despite the shortage of food from which the occupied districts of Belgium had long suffered, the generosity of the civil population found means to supplement the rations of our troops.

During this period large numbers of released prisoners of war, French and British, came through our lines and were passed back to collecting stations. The enemy seems to have liberated the majority of the Allied prisoners west of the Rhine without making any provision for their feeding and conveyance. The result was that much unnecessary suffering was caused to these unfortunate individuals, while a not inconsiderable additional burden was placed upon our own transport and supplies.

Supply Difficulties

4. Throughout the whole of the advance, and especially in the stage which followed the crossing of the German frontier, very great, but unavoidable, difficulties were encountered in connection with supply.

At the time of the Armistice railheads were on the general line Le Cateau, Valenciennes, Lille, Courtrai, and for many miles in front of them bridges had been broken and track torn up or destroyed by mines. Even after the cessation of hostilities delay-action mines, which the enemy had laid in the course of his retreat without preserving exact record of their location, went up from time to time, causing serious interruption to traffic. The clearing of these mines was a work of considerable risk, and the fact that comparatively so few mines exploded after trains had begun to run is entirely due to the great courage and skill with which officers, non-commissioned officers and men of the Tunnelling Companies performed the difficult and dangerous task of detecting them and rendering them harmless. The work of reconstruction, therefore, was most arduous, continuing day and night. The speed with which it was completed reflects great credit upon all ranks of the British Railway Companies and the Canadian Railway Troops Corps, as well as on the Railway Construction Engineers who controlled their work. Credit is due also to the personnel of the Railway Operating Division, who were called upon to keep traffic open with scarcely any of the ordinary traffic facilities.

Though roads had been pushed farther ahead, the same general conditions applied to them, while the extraordinary amount of traffic which it was necessary to direct along them made maintenance very difficult. Up to the night of the 25/26th November, on which date the railway was carried across the gap between Valenciennes and Mons, the Corps of the Second Army were still based on the railheads west of the River Scheldt, and supplies had to be brought forward by double and treble echelons of lorries. At the close of this period divisions were being fed by means of narrow one-way roads at distances of from 80 to 100 miles from their railheads. This imposed a great strain on the personnel of the Motor Transport Units and Mobile Repair Shops, who were compelled to work long hours under very trying and anxious conditions. I am glad to express my deep appreciation of the devoted service rendered by all ranks.

Until roads and railways could be got through to the areas which the enemy had not damaged, the progress of our troops was necessarily limited by our ability to supply them. Only by the greatest effort on the part of the departments concerned with reconstruction and supply, and at the expense of considerable hardship to the leading troops of the Fourth and Second Armies, and in particular the cavalry, could the programme of our advance be maintained. Troops were denied frequently and for long periods comforts which they had been accustomed to obtain even under battle conditions. Nothing beyond bare necessities could be got forward to them. Even these were at times short in some units, and on more than one occasion the only available supplies of food were the current day's issues carried on the man.

Many other causes conspired to render the problem of supply one of serious difficulty throughout our advance. At the date of the Armistice the amount of available rolling stock had been no more than sufficient to meet the requirements of our Armies. The advance to the Rhine added over 200 miles to the distances to be covered, and greatly reduced the amount of rolling stock available by largely increasing the time required for each train to complete its journey. The necessity for supplying the civil population of the territories through which the Allied Armies were advancing and the resumption of French civilian traffic put an additional strain upon our pooled resources. This strain was not met by rolling-stock taken over from the enemy, which came in very slowly, and was much of it unfit for immediate service.

In this connection it is not out of place to refer to the work done by the British Army in providing food and medical attendance for the civil population of the liberated districts through which we passed, a population which in France alone amounted to nearly 800,000 persons. This duty, though very willingly accepted by us, none the less made no small demands upon both rail and road transport. In France it entailed the supply and distribution of more than 5,000,000 rations during a period exceeding six weeks, until the French were able to complete their arrangements for relieving us of the task. The service we were able to render in the name of humanity has been most generously acknowledged by the French Authorities.

The fulfilment of our programme under such conditions would have been impossible without the exercise of great patience and whole-hearted co-operation on the part of the troops. Nor was it less dependent upon the untiring energy and efficiency displayed by commanders and staffs, in the methodical arrangement of the details of our advance and the concentration of our resources. I desire to place on record my appreciation of the careful forethought of the Staff and of the excellent conduct of all ranks under very trying conditions.

It will readily be understood from the foregoing that had our advance been conducted against active opposition, even from a beaten and demoralised enemy, our progress must have been greatly delayed. The difficulties of supply would have been enormously increased in many ways, among which would have been the necessity of bringing forward large quantities of ammunition. Bridges, railways and roads would have been destroyed in front of us, or blown up after we had passed by delay-action mines. Immense loss would have been caused to property of all descriptions and incalculable suffering inflicted upon the inhabitants of the invaded districts of Belgium, France and Luxembourg.

Further Re-adjustment of Troops

5. Towards the close of the advance to the German frontier, a further re-adjustment was effected in the disposition of my troops.

The sector allotted to the British Forces in the general scheme for the occupation of the Rhine Provinces was too narrow to admit of the employment of more than a single Army Command. I therefore directed that the German territory to be occupied by us should be held by General Plumer's Second Army, which for this purpose should be composed as follows :—The II. Corps (9th, 29th and New Zealand Divisions), the VI. Corps (Guards, 2nd and 3rd Divisions), the IX. Corps (1st, 6th and 62nd Divisions), the Canadian Corps (1st and 2nd Canadian Divisions), and the 1st Cavalry Division. The various changes and transfers necessary to give effect to this arrangement involved the taking over by the Second Army of the whole of the British front of advance, and the gradual withdrawal of the troops of the Fourth Army to the area west of the frontier and about Namur.

The Advance into Germany

6. On the morning of the 1st December, a date for ever memorable as witnessing the consummation of the hopes and efforts of $4\frac{1}{2}$ years of heroic fighting, the 1st Cavalry Division crossed the frontier between Belgium and Germany. On the same day the 2nd and 1st Canadian Divisions of the Canadian Corps and the 29th and 9th Divisions of the II. Corps resumed their march towards the frontier.

On this date, however, the supply situation became critical, trains due on the 30th November failing to arrive until the night of the 1st/2nd December. In consequence for two days the Army remained practically stationary, and it was not until the 4th December that progress was resumed.

In this stage of our march the line of our advance traversed the northern portion of the Ardennes, and, particularly on the right in the Canadian Corps area, the country through which our troops were passing was of a most difficult character. Practicable roads were few, villages were far apart, and facilities for billeting very limited. Our way lay across a country of great hills rising to over 2,000 feet, covered by wide stretches of forest, and cut by deep and narrow valleys, along the steep sides of which the roads wound in countless sudden curves. Marches were long, while the surface of the roads which had already borne the traffic of the retreating German Armies suffered anew under the passage of our columns. Even under conditions approximating to those of peace, severe demands were made upon the spirit and endurance of the troops.

British Troops in Cologne

7. On the 6th December, in response to a request previously made by the German authorities, and in order that the town might not be left without troops after the withdrawal of the enemy's military forces, the 2nd Brigade of the 1st Cavalry Division was sent forward to Cologne. A detachment of armoured cars of the 17th (A.C.) Battalion, Tank Corps, escorted the General Officer Commanding 1st Cavalry Division into Cologne, and thereafter picketed the bridges, being the first British troops to cross the Rhine. A great concourse of people thronged the streets of the city to watch the arrival of our troops. Next day, the 28th Infantry Brigade of the 9th Division arrived at Cologne by rail, and on the 8th December the 1st Cavalry Division reached the Rhine on the whole British front, securing the crossings of the river.

While during the following days our infantry continued their movement, on the 11th December the Military Governor, Lieut.-General Sir Charles Fergusson, arrived by train at Cologne. Accompanied by an escort of the 9th Lancers, he proceeded through crowded streets to the Hôtel Monopol, where he took up the duties of his office. As the Military Governor reached the entrance to the hotel, the Union Jack was hoisted above the building and floated out for the first time over the roof-tops of the city.

The Occupation of the Cologne Bridgehead

8. On the 12th December, the day fixed for that event by the general scheme of advance, the 1st Cavalry Division crossed the Rhine and commenced the occupation of the Cologne Bridgehead, the perimeter of which they reached on the following day.

On the 13th December the 2nd and 1st Canadian Divisions and the 29th and 9th Divisions of the Canadian and II. Corps passed across the Rhine at Cologne and Bonn respectively in four columns, each of the strength of a division. During the following three days they pushed forward to the bridgehead perimeter, gradually relieving the cavalry, and by the evening of the 16th December had completed the occupation of the bridgehead.

Before Christmas Day the troops of the Second Army had reached their final areas in the occupied territories of Germany. The military organisation of the bridgehead, so as to secure the crossing of the Rhine and render possible the rapid deployment of troops for action east of it, had been commenced, and was proceeded with steadily during the remainder of the year. In the course of this work, on the 28th December the perimeter of the bridgehead was slightly amended (*vide* Map No. 10), so as to accord with the boundaries of the German Communal Districts and thus simplify the work of administration.

Conduct of the Troops

9. In concluding this part of my Despatch, I desire to acknowledge with gratitude and pride the exemplary conduct of the troops, both throughout the different stages of their arduous advance and since its successful completion.

Among all Services and in all Armies, both those which took part in the advance and those which remained behind, the period following the armistice has indeed been one of no little difficulty. For those that went forward, the real hardships of the long marches, poor billets, and indifferent food constituted a strange contrast to ideas which had been formed of victory. For all, the sudden relaxation of the enduring tension of battle, and the natural desire of the great majority for an early return to civil life, could not but lead at times to a certain impatience with delays, and with the continuance, under conditions of apparent peace, of restrictions and routine duties gladly borne while the future of their country was at stake. Despite these disturbing factors, and the novelty of finding themselves masters in a conquered country, instances of misbehaviour have been remarkably few, and chiefly of a minor character. The inborn courtesy and good temper of the British soldier have guided them in their attitude towards the inhabitants of the occupied districts. The spreading of a better understanding of the causes of the temporary shortage of supplies, of the difficulties of demobilisation and of the continued necessity for keeping a strong Army in the field, has generally dispelled any incipient feelings of discontent.

The discipline, self-respect and strong sense of responsibility which carried our men through to victory, have in general been fully maintained amid changed conditions and new surroundings.

PART II

FEATURES OF THE WAR

A Single Great Battle

10. In this, my final Despatch, I think it desirable to comment briefly upon certain general features which concern the whole series of operations carried out under my command. I am urged thereto by the conviction that neither the course of the war itself nor the military lessons to be drawn therefrom can properly be comprehended, unless the long succession of battles commenced on the Somme in 1916 and ended in November of last year on the Sambre are viewed as forming part of one great and continuous engagement.

To direct attention to any single phase of that stupendous and incessant struggle and seek in it the explanation of our success, to the exclusion or neglect of other phases possibly less striking in their immediate or obvious consequences, is in my opinion to risk the formation of unsound doctrines regarding the character and requirements of modern war.

If the operations of the past $4\frac{1}{2}$ years are regarded as a single continuous campaign, there can be recognised in them the same general features and the same necessary stages which between forces of approximately equal strength have marked all the conclusive battles of history. There is in the first instance the preliminary stage of the campaign in which the opposing forces seek to deploy and manœuvre for position, endeavouring while doing so to gain some early advantage which might be pushed home to quick decision. This phase came to an end in the present war with the creation of continuous trench lines from the Swiss frontier to the sea.

Battle having been joined, there follows the period of real struggle in which the main forces of the two belligerent Armies are pitted against each other in close and costly combat. Each commander seeks to wear down the power of resistance of his opponent and to pin him to his position, while preserving or accumulating in his own hands a powerful reserve force with which he can manœuvre, and, when signs of the enemy becoming morally and physically weakened are observed, deliver the decisive attack. The greatest possible pressure against the enemy's whole front must be maintained, especially when the crisis of the battle approaches. Then every man, horse and gun is required to co-operate, so as to complete the enemy's overthrow and exploit success.

In the stage of the wearing-out struggle losses will necessarily be heavy on both sides, for in it the price of victory is paid. If the opposing forces are approximately equal in numbers, in courage, in moral and in equipment, there is no way of avoiding payment of the price or of eliminating this phase of the struggle.

In former battles this stage of the conflict has rarely lasted more than a few days, and has often been completed in a few hours. When Armies of millions are engaged, with the resources of great Empires behind them, it will inevitably be long. It will include violent crises of fighting which, when viewed separately and apart from the general perspective, will appear individually as great indecisive battles. To this stage belong the great engagements of 1916 and 1917 which wore down the strength of the German Armies.

Finally, whether from the superior fighting ability and leadership of one of the belligerents, as the result of greater resources or tenacity, or by reason of higher moral, or from a combination of all these causes, the time will come when the other side will begin to weaken and the climax of the battle is reached. Then the commander of the weaker side must choose whether he will break off the engagement, if he can, while there is yet time, or stake on a supreme effort what reserves remain to him. The launching and destruction of Napoleon's last reserves at Waterloo was a matter of minutes. In this World War the great sortie of the beleaguered German Armies, commenced on the 21st March, 1918, lasted for four months, yet it represents a corresponding stage in a single colossal battle.

The breaking down of such a supreme effort will be the signal for the commander of the successful side to develop his greatest strength, and seek to turn to immediate account the loss in material and moral which their failure must inevitably produce among his opponent's troops. In a battle joined and decided in the course of a few days or hours, there is no risk that the lay observer will seek to distinguish the culminating operations by which victory is seized and exploited from the preceding stages by which it has been made possible and determined. If the whole operations of the present war are regarded in correct perspective, the victories of the summer and autumn of 1918 will be seen to be as directly dependent upon the two years of stubborn fighting that preceded them.

The Length of the War

11. If the causes which determined the length of the recent contest are examined in the light of the accepted principles of war, it will be seen that the duration of the struggle was governed by and bore a direct relation to certain definite factors which are enumerated below.

In the first place, we were unprepared for war, or at any rate for a war of such magnitude. We were deficient in both trained men and military material, and, what was more important, had no machinery ready by which either men or material could be produced in anything approaching the requisite quantities. The consequences were two-fold. Firstly, the necessary machinery had to be improvised hurriedly, and improvisation is never economical and seldom satisfactory. In this case the high-water mark of our fighting strength in infantry was only reached after $2\frac{1}{2}$ years of conflict, by which time heavy casualties had already been incurred. In consequence, the full man power of the Empire was never developed in the field at any period of the war.

As regards material, it was not until midsummer, 1916, that the artillery situation became even approximately adequate to the conduct of major operations. Throughout the Somme Battle the expenditure of artillery ammunition had to be watched with the greatest care. During the battles of 1917, ammunition was plentiful, but the gun situation was a source of constant anxiety. Only in 1918 was it possible to conduct artillery operations independently of any limiting considerations other than that of transport.

The second consequence of our unpreparedness was that our Armies were unable to intervene, either at the outset of the war or until nearly two years had elapsed, in sufficient strength adequately to assist our Allies. The enemy was able to gain a notable initial advantage by establishing himself in Belgium and northern France, and throughout the early stages of the war was free to concentrate an undue proportion of his effectives against France and Russia. The excessive burden thrown upon the gallant Army of France during this period caused them losses, the effect of which has been felt all through the war and directly influenced its length. Just as at no time were we as an Empire able to put our own full strength into the field, so at no time were the Allies as a whole able completely to develop and obtain the full effect from their greatly superior man power. What might have been the effect of British intervention on a larger scale in the earlier stages of the war is shown by what was actually achieved by our original Expeditionary Force.

It is interesting to note that in previous campaigns the side which has been fully prepared for war has almost invariably gained a rapid and complete success over its less well prepared opponent. In 1866 and 1870, Austria and then France were overwhelmed at the outset by means of superior preparation. The initial advantages derived therefrom were followed up by such vigorous and ruthless action, regardless of loss, that there was no time to recover from the first stunning blows. The German plan of campaign in the present war was undoubtedly based on similar principles. The margin by which the German onrush in 1914 was stemmed was so narrow, and the subsequent struggle so severe, that the word "miraculous" is hardly too strong a term to describe the recovery and ultimate victory of the Allies.

A further cause adversely influencing the duration of the war on the Western front during its later stages, and one following indirectly from that just stated, was the situation in other theatres. The military strength of Russia broke down in 1917 at a critical period when, had she been able to carry out her military engagements, the war might have been shortened by a year. At a later date, the military situation in Italy in the autumn of 1917 necessitated the transfer of five British divisions from France to Italy at a time when their presence in France might have had far-reaching effects.

Thirdly, the Allies were handicapped in their task and the war thereby lengthened by the inherent difficulties always associated with the combined action of Armies of separate nationalities, differing in speech and temperament, and, not least important, in military organisation, equipment and supply.

Finally, as indicated in the opening paragraph of this part of my Despatch, the huge numbers of men engaged on either side, whereby a continuous battle front was rapidly established from Switzerland to the sea, out-flanking was made impossible and manœuvre very difficult, necessitated the delivery of frontal attacks. This factor, combined with the strength of the defensive under modern conditions,

THE FINAL DESPATCH

rendered a protracted wearing out battle unavoidable before the enemy's power of resistance could be overcome. So long as the opposing forces are at the outset approximately equal in numbers and moral and there are no flanks to turn, a long struggle for supremacy is inevitable.

The Extent of our Casualties

12. Obviously, the greater the length of a war the higher is likely to be the number of casualties incurred in it on either side. The same causes, therefore, which served to protract the recent struggle are largely responsible for the extent of our casualties. There can be no question that to our general unpreparedness must be attributed the loss of many thousands of brave men whose sacrifice we deeply deplore, while we regard their splendid gallantry and self-devotion with unstinted admiration and gratitude.

Given, however, the military situation existing in August, 1914, our total losses in the war have been no larger than were to be expected. Neither do they compare unfavourably with those of any other of the belligerent nations, so far as figures are available from which comparison can be made. The total British casualties in all theatres of war, killed, wounded, missing and prisoners, including native troops, are approximately three millions (3,076,388). Of this total, some two and a half millions (2,568,834) were incurred on the Western front. The total French losses, killed, missing, and prisoners, but exclusive of wounded, have been given officially as approximately 1,831,000. If an estimate for wounded is added, the total can scarcely be less than 4,800,000,[1] and of this total it is fair to assume that over four millions were incurred on the Western front. The published figures for Italy, killed and wounded only, exclusive of prisoners, amount to 1,400,000, of which practically the whole were incurred in the Western theatre of war.

Figures have also been published for Germany and Austria. The total German casualties, killed, wounded, missing and prisoners, are given at approximately six and a half millions (6,485,000), of which the vastly greater proportion must have been incurred on the Western front, where the bulk of the German forces were concentrated and the hardest fighting took place. In view of the fact, however, that the number of German prisoners is definitely known to be considerably understated, these figures must be accepted with

[1] The number of French wounded is now shown to be 2,560,000, making the total French casualties 4,291,800. It may be noted that the proportion of wounded to killed shown by the French casualty figures is considerably lower than the proportion in our own Army.

reserve. The losses of Austria-Hungary in killed, missing and prisoners are given as approximately two and three-quarter millions (2,772,000). An estimate of wounded would give a total of over four and a half millions.

The extent of our casualties, like the duration of the war, was dependent on certain definite factors which can be stated shortly.

In the first place, the military situation compelled us, particularly during the first portion of the war, to make great efforts before we had developed our full strength in the field or properly equipped and trained our Armies. These efforts were wasteful of men, but in the circumstances they could not be avoided. The only alternative was to do nothing and see our French Allies overwhelmed by the enemy's superior numbers.

During the second half of the war, and that part embracing the critical and costly period of the wearing-out battle, the losses previously suffered by our Allies laid upon the British Armies in France an increasing share in the burden of attack. From the opening of the Somme Battle in 1916 to the termination of hostilities the British Armies were subjected to a strain of the utmost severity which never ceased, and consequently had little or no opportunity for the rest and training they so greatly needed.

In addition to these particular considerations, certain general factors peculiar to modern war made for the inflation of losses. The great strength of modern field defences and the power and precision of modern weapons, the multiplication of machine guns, trench mortars and artillery of all natures, the employment of gas and the rapid development of the aeroplane as a formidable agent of destruction against both men and material, all combined to increase the price to be paid for victory.

If only for these reasons, no comparisons can usefully be made between the relative losses incurred in this war and any previous war. There is, however, the further consideration that the issues involved in this stupendous struggle were far greater than those concerned in any other war in recent history. Our existence as an Empire and civilisation itself, as it is understood by the free Western nations, were at stake. Men fought as they have never fought before in masses.

Despite our own particular handicaps and the foregoing general considerations, it is satisfactory to note that, as the result of the courage and determination of our troops, and the high level of leadership generally maintained, our losses even in attack over the whole period of the battle compare favourably with those inflicted on our opponents. The approximate total of our battle casualties in all arms, and including Overseas troops, from the commencement

THE FINAL DESPATCH 325

of the Somme Battle in 1916 to the conclusion of the Armistice is 2,140,000. The calculation of German losses is obviously a matter of great difficulty. It is estimated, however, that the number of casualties inflicted on the enemy by British troops during the above period exceeds two and a half millions. It is of interest, moreover, in the light of the paragraph next following, that more than half the total casualties incurred by us in the fighting of 1918 were occasioned during the five months March-July, when our Armies were on the defensive.

Why we Attacked whenever Possible

13. Closely connected with the question of casualties is that of the relative values of attack and defence. It is a view often expressed that the attack is more expensive than defence. This is only a half statement of the truth. Unquestionably, unsuccessful attack is generally more expensive than defence, particularly if the attack is pressed home with courage and resolution. On the other hand, attack so pressed home, if skilfully conducted, is rarely unsuccessful, whereas in its later stages especially, unsuccessful defence is far more costly than attack.

Moreover, the object of all war is victory, and a purely defensive attitude can never bring about a successful decision, either in a battle or in a campaign. The idea that a war can be won by standing on the defensive and waiting for the enemy to attack is a dangerous fallacy, which owes its inception to the desire to evade the price of victory. It is an axiom that decisive success in battle can be gained only by a vigorous offensive. The principle here stated has long been recognised as being fundamental, and is based on the universal teaching of military history in all ages. The course of the present war has proved it to be correct.

To pass for a moment from the general to the particular, and consider in the light of the present war the facts upon which this axiom is based.

A defensive rôle sooner or later brings about a distinct lowering of the moral of the troops, who imagine that the enemy must be the better man, or at least more numerous, better equipped with and better served by artillery or other mechanical aids to victory. Once the mass of the defending infantry become possessed of such ideas, the battle is as good as lost. An Army fighting on enemy soil, especially if its standard of discipline is high, may maintain a successful defence for a protracted period, in the hope that victory may be gained elsewhere or that the enemy may tire or weaken in his resolution and accept a compromise. The resistance of the German Armies was undoubtedly prolonged in this fashion, but in the end the persistence of our troops had its natural effect.

Further, a defensive policy involves the loss of the initiative, with all the consequent disadvantages to the defender. The enemy is able to choose at his own convenience the time and place of his attacks. Not being influenced himself by the threat of attack from his opponent, he can afford to take risks, and by greatly weakening his front in some places can concentrate an overwhelming force elsewhere with which to attack. The defender, on the other hand, becomes almost entirely ignorant of the dispositions and plans of his opponent, who is thus in a position to effect a surprise. This was clearly exemplified during the fighting of 1918. As long as the enemy was attacking, he obtained fairly full information regarding our dispositions. Captured documents show that, as soon as he was thrown once more on the defensive and the initiative returned to the Allies, he was kept in comparative ignorance of our plans and dispositions. The consequence was that the Allies were able to effect many surprises, both strategic and tactical.

As a further effect of the loss of the initiative and ignorance of his opponent's intentions, the defender finds it difficult to avoid a certain dispersal of his forces. Though for a variety of reasons, including the fact that we had lately been on the offensive, we were by no means entirely ignorant of the enemy's intentions in the spring of 1918, the unavoidable uncertainty resulting from a temporary loss of the initiative did have the effect of preventing a complete concentration of our reserves behind the point of the enemy's attack.

An additional reason, peculiar to the circumstances of the present war, which in itself compelled me to refuse to adopt a purely defensive attitude so long as any other was open to me, is to be found in the geographical position of our Armies. For reasons stated by me in my Despatch of the 20th July, 1918, we could not afford to give much ground on any part of our front.[1] The experience of the war has shown that if the defence is to be maintained successfully, even for a limited time, it must be flexible.

The End of the War

14. If the views set out by me in the preceding paragraphs are accepted, it will be recognised that the war did not follow any unprecedented course, and that its end was neither sudden nor should it have been unexpected. The rapid collapse of Germany's military powers in the latter half of 1918 was the logical outcome of the fighting of the previous two years. It would not have taken place but for that period of ceaseless attrition which used up the reserves

[1] See page 183 above.

of the German Armies, while the constant and growing pressure of the blockade sapped with more deadly insistence from year to year at the strength and resolution of the German people. It is in the great battles of 1916 and 1917 that we have to seek for the secret of our victory in 1918.

Doubtless, the end might have come sooner had we been able to develop the military resources of our Empire more rapidly and with a higher degree of concentration, or had not the defection of Russia in 1917 given our enemies a new lease of life.

So far as the military situation is concerned, in spite of the great accession of strength which Germany received as the result of the defection of Russia, the battles of 1916 and 1917 had so far weakened her Armies that the effort they made in 1918 was insufficient to secure victory. Moreover, the effect of the battles of 1916 and 1917 was not confined to loss of German man power. The moral effects of those battles were enormous, both in the German Army and in Germany. By their means our soldiers established over the German soldier a moral superiority which they held in an ever-increasing degree until the end of the war, even in the difficult days of March and April, 1918.

The Value of Cavalry in Modern War

15. From time to time as the war of position dragged on and the enemy's trench systems remained unbroken, while questions of man power and the shortage of shipping became acute, the wisdom or necessity of maintaining any large force of mounted men was freely discussed. In the light of the full experience of the war the decision to preserve the Cavalry Corps has been completely justified. It has been proved that cavalry, whether used for shock effect under suitable conditions or as mobile infantry, have still an indispensable part to play in modern war. Moreover, it cannot safely be assumed that in all future wars the flanks of the opposing forces will rest on neutral States or impassable obstacles. Whenever such a condition does not obtain opportunities for the use of cavalry must arise frequently.

Throughout the great retirement in 1914, our cavalry covered the retirement and protected the flanks of our columns against the onrush of the enemy, and on frequent occasions prevented our infantry from being over-run by the enemy's cavalry. Later in the same year at Ypres, their mobility multiplied their value as a reserve, enabling them rapidly to reinforce threatened portions of our line.

During the critical period of position warfare, when the trial of strength between the opposing forces took place, the absence of room to manœuvre made the importance of cavalry less apparent.

Even under such conditions, however, valuable results may be expected from the employment of a strong force of cavalry when, after there has been severe fighting on one or more fronts, a surprise attack is made on another front. Such an occasion arose in the operations before Cambrai at the close of 1917, when the cavalry were of the greatest service; while throughout the whole period of trench fighting they constituted an important mobile reserve.

At a later date, when circumstances found us operating once more in comparatively open country, cavalry proved themselves of value in their true rôle. During the German offensive in March, 1918, the superior mobility of cavalry fully justified their existence. At the commencement of the battle, cavalry were used under the Fifth Army over wide fronts. So great, indeed, became the need for mounted men that certain units which had but recently been dismounted were hurriedly provided with horses and did splendid service. Frequently, when it was impossible to move forward other troops in time, our mounted troops were able to fill gaps in our line and restore the situation. The absence of hostile cavalry at this period was a marked feature of the battle. Had the German command had at their disposal even two or three well-trained cavalry divisions, a wedge might have been driven between the French and British Armies. Their presence could not have failed to have added greatly to the difficulties of our task.

In the actions already referred to east of Amiens, the cavalry were again able to demonstrate the great advantage which their power of rapid concentration gives them in a surprise attack. Operating in close concert with both armoured cars and infantry, they pushed ahead of the latter and by anticipating the arrival of German reserves assisted materially in our success. In the battle of the 8th October, they were responsible for saving the Cambrai—Le Cateau—St. Quentin Railway from complete destruction. Finally, during the culminating operations of the war when the German Armies were falling back in disorganised masses, a new situation arose which demanded the use of mounted troops. Then our cavalry, pressing hard upon the enemy's heels, hastened his retreat and threw him into worse confusion. At such a time the moral effect of cavalry is overwhelming and is in itself a sufficient reason for the retention of that arm.

On the morning of the Armistice, two British cavalry divisions were on the march east of the Scheldt, and before the orders to stop reached them they had already gained a line ten miles in front of our infantry outposts. There is no doubt that, had the advance of the cavalry been allowed to continue, the enemy's disorganised retreat would have been turned into a rout.

The Value of Mechanical Contrivances

16. A remarkable feature of the present war has been the number and variety of mechanical contrivances to which it has given birth, or has brought to a higher state of perfection.

Besides the great increase in mobility made possible by the development of motor transport, heavy artillery, trench mortars, machine guns, aeroplanes, tanks, gas and barbed wire have in their several spheres of action played very prominent parts in operations, and as a whole have given a greater driving power to war. The belligerent possessing a preponderance of such mechanical contrivances has found himself in a very favourable position as compared with his less well provided opponent. The general superiority of the Allies in this direction during the concluding stages of the recent struggle undoubtedly contributed powerfully to their success. In this respect the Army owes a great debt to science, and to the distinguished scientific men who placed their learning and skill at the disposal of their country.

It should never be forgotten however that weapons of this character are incapable of effective independent action. They do not in themselves possess the power to obtain a decision, their real function being to assist the infantry to get to grips with their opponents. To place in them a reliance out of proportion to their real utility, to imagine, for example, that tanks and aeroplanes can take the place of infantry and artillery, would be to do a disservice to those who have the future of these new weapons most at heart by robbing them of the power to use them to their best effect.

Every mechanical device so far produced is dependent for its most effective use upon the closest possible association with other arms, and in particular with infantry and artillery. Aeroplanes must rely upon infantry to prevent the enemy from over-running their aerodromes, and, despite their increasing range and versatility of action, are clearly incapable in themselves of bringing about a decision. Tanks require the closest artillery support to enable them to reach their objectives without falling victims to the enemy's artillery, and are dependent upon the infantry to hold the position they have won.

As an instance of the interdependence of artillery and tanks, we may take the actions fought east of Amiens on the 8th August, 1918, and following days. A very large number of tanks were employed in these operations, and they carried out their tasks in the most brilliant manner. Yet a scrutiny of the artillery ammunition returns for this period discloses the fact that in no action of similar dimensions had the expenditure of ammunition been so great.

Immense as the influence of mechanical devices may be, they cannot by themselves decide a campaign. Their true rôle is that of assisting the infantryman, which they have done in a most admirable manner. They cannot replace him. Only by the rifle and bayonet of the infantryman can the decisive victory be won.

Close and Complete Co-operation between all Arms and Services

17. This war has given no new principles; but the different mechanical appliances above mentioned—and in particular the rapid improvement and multiplication of aeroplanes, the use of immense numbers of machine guns and Lewis guns, the employment of vast quantities of barbed wire as effective obstacles, the enormous expansion of artillery and the provision of great masses of motor transport —have introduced new problems of considerable complexity concerning the effective co-operation of the different arms and services. Much thought has had to be bestowed upon determining how new devices could be combined in the best manner with the machinery already working.

The development of the Air Service is a matter of general knowledge, and figures showing something of the work done by our airmen were included in my last Despatch.[1] The combining of their operations with those of the other arms, and particularly of the artillery, has been the subject of constant study and experiment, giving results of the very highest value. As regards machine guns, from a proportion of one gun to approximately 500 infantrymen in 1914, our establishment of machine guns and Lewis guns had risen at the end of 1918 to one machine gun or Lewis gun to approximately 20 infantrymen. This great expansion was necessarily accompanied by a modification of training and methods both for attack and defence, and resulted ultimately in the establishment of the Machine Gun Corps under an Inspector-General.

During the same period, the growth of our artillery was even more remarkable, its numbers and power increasing out of all proportion to the experience of previous wars. The 486 pieces of light and medium artillery with which we took the field in August, 1914, were represented at the date of the Armistice by 6,437 guns and howitzers of all natures, including pieces of the heaviest calibre.

This vast increase so profoundly influenced the employment of artillery and was accompanied by so intimate an association with other arms and services that it merits special comment.

In the first place, big changes were required in artillery organ-

[1] Page 301.

isation, as well as important decisions concerning the proportions in which the different natures of artillery and artillery ammunition should be manufactured. These changes and decisions were made during 1916, and resulted in the existing artillery organisation of the British Armies in France.

In order to gain the elasticity essential to the quick concentration of guns at the decisive point, to enable the best use to be made of them and to facilitate ammunition supply and fire control, Artillery Commanders, acting under Army and Corps Commanders, were introduced and Staffs provided for them. This enabled the large concentrations of guns required for our offensives to be quickly absorbed and efficiently directed. The proportions required of guns to howitzers and of the lighter to the heavier natures were determined by certain factors, namely, the problem of siting in the comparatively limited areas available the great numbers of pieces required for an offensive; the " lives " of the different types of guns and howitzers, that is the number of rounds which can be fired from them before they become unserviceable from wear; and questions of relative accuracy and fire effect upon particular kinds of targets.

The results attained by the organisation established in 1916 are in themselves strong evidence of the soundness of the principles upon which it was based. It made possible a high degree of elasticity, and by the full and successful exploitation of all the means placed at its disposal by science and experience, ensured that the continuous artillery battle which began on the Somme should culminate, as it did, in the defeat of the enemy's guns.

The great development of air photography, sound ranging, flash spotting, air-burst ranging [1] and aerial observation brought counter-battery work and harassing fire both by day and night to a high state of perfection. Special progress was made in the art of engaging moving targets with fire controlled by observation from aeroplanes and balloons. The work of the Field Survey Sections, in the location of hostile battery positions by re-section and the employment of accurate maps, was brought into extended use. In combination with the work of the Calibration Sections in the accurate calibration of guns, and by careful calculation of corrections of range required to compensate for weather conditions, it became possible to a large extent to dispense with registration, whereby the chance of effecting

[1] " Sound ranging " is an electro-mechanical means of recording the sound waves set up by the discharge of a gun and so computing its position. " Flash spotting " aims at the same result by taking cross bearings of a gun flash. " Air-burst ranging " is a method of bringing fire to bear upon concealed targets already located. Ranging shells are burst high above the target and the position of the burst ascertained by cross observation. From this is calculated the small correction necessary to bring fire to bear accurately upon the target.

Y

surprise was greatly increased. In the operations east of Amiens on the 8th August, 1918, in which over 2,000 guns were employed, practically the whole of the batteries concentrated for the purpose of the attack opened fire for the first time on the actual morning of the assault.

The use of smoke shell for covering the advance of our infantry and masking the enemy's positions was introduced and employed with increasing frequency and effect. New forms of gas shell were made available, and their combination with the infantry attack carefully studied. The invention of a new fuze known as "106," which was first used in the battle of Arras, 1917, enabled wire entanglements to be easily and quickly destroyed, and so modified our methods of attacking organised positions. By bursting the shell the instant it touched the ground and before it had become buried, the destructive effect of the explosion was greatly increased. It became possible to cut wire with a far less expenditure of time and ammunition, and the factor of surprise was given a larger part in operations.

Great attention was paid to the training of personnel, and in particular the Chapperton Down Artillery School, Salisbury Plain, was formed for training artillery brigade commanders and battery commanders, while Artillery Schools in France were organised for the training of subalterns and non-commissioned officers.

A short examination of our principal attacks will give a good idea of the increasing importance of artillery. On the first day of the Somme Battle of 1916 the number of artillery personnel engaged was equal to about half the infantry strength of the attacking divisions. On this one day a total of nearly 13,000 tons of artillery ammunition was fired by us on the Western front. Our attacks at Arras and Messines on the 9th April and 7th June, 1917, saw the total expenditure of artillery ammunition nearly doubled on the first days of those battles, while the proportion of artillery personnel to infantry steadily grew.

During the period following the opening of the Somme Battle, the predominance of our artillery over that of the enemy gradually increased, till at the time of the Arras Battle it had reached a maximum. In the course of the summer and autumn of 1917, however, the enemy constantly reinforced his artillery on our front, being enabled to do so owing to the relaxation of pressure elsewhere.

The battle of Ypres in the autumn of 1917 was one of intense struggle for artillery supremacy. By dint of reducing his artillery strength on other parts of the Western front, and by bringing guns from the East, the enemy definitely challenged the predominance of our artillery. In this battle, therefore, the proportion of our artillery to infantry strength was particularly large. In the opening attack on the 31st July our artillery personnel amounted to over

80 per cent. of the infantry engaged in the principal attack on our front, and our total expenditure of artillery ammunition on this day exceeded 23,000 tons. During the succeeding weeks the battle of the rival artilleries became ever more violent. On the two days 20th and 21st September, about 42,000 tons of artillery ammunition were expended by us, and in the successful attack of the 4th October, which gave us the main ridge about Broodseinde, our artillery personnel amounted to 85 per cent. of the infantry engaged in the assault.

During the winter of 1917-1918 the enemy so greatly added to his artillery strength by batteries brought from the Russian front that in his spring offensive he was able temporarily to effect a definite local artillery superiority. This state of affairs was short lived. Even before the breakdown of the German offensive, our guns had regained the upper hand. In the battles later in the year the superiority of our batteries once more grew rapidly, until the defeat of the German artillery became an accomplished fact. From the commencement of our offensive in August, 1918, to the conclusion of the Armistice, some 700,000 tons of artillery ammunition were expended by the British Armies on the Western front. For the fortnight from the 21st August to the 3rd September our average daily expenditure exceeded 11,000 tons, while for the three days of crucial battle on the 27th, 28th and 29th September nearly 65,000 tons of ammunition were fired by our artillery.

The tremendous growth of our artillery strength above described followed inevitably from the character of the wearing-out battle upon which we were engaged. The restricted opportunities for manœuvre and the necessity for frontal attacks made the employment of great masses of artillery essential.

The massing of guns alone, however, could not have secured success without the closest possible combination between our batteries and the infantry they were called upon to support, as well as with the other arms. The expansion was accompanied, therefore, by a constant endeavour to improve the knowledge of all ranks of both artillery, infantry and the air service concerning the work and possibilities of the other arms.

An intelligent understanding of "the other man's job" is the first essential of successful co-operation. To obtain the best results from the vast and complex machine composing a modern army, deep study of work other than one's own is necessary for all arms. For this study much time is needed, as well as much practical application of the principles evolved, and for reasons already explained, opportunity sufficient for adequate training could not be found. None the less, the best possible use was made of such opportunities as offered, and much was in fact accomplished.

The Signal Service

18. As a natural corollary to the general increase of our Forces, the Signal Service, required alike for the proper co-ordination of supply and for the direction and control of the battle, has grown almost out of recognition. From an original establishment of under 2,400 officers and men, trained and equipped chiefly for mobile warfare, at the end of 1918 the personnel of the Signal Service had risen to 42,000, fully equipped with all the latest devices of modern science to act efficiently under all conditions as the nervous system to the whole vast organism of our Army.

The commencement of trench warfare and the greater use of artillery led to a rapid development of the signal system which, as fresh units were introduced, became more and more elaborate. At the same time, the increase in the power and range of artillery made the maintenance of communications constantly more difficult. Many miles of deep trenches were dug, in which cables containing 50 to 100 circuits were buried to gain protection from shell fire. The use of wireless communication gradually became more widely spread and finally constituted part of the Signal establishment of all formations down to divisions. To provide an alternative method of communication with front line troops, in 1915 carrier pigeons were introduced and a special branch of the Signal Service was formed controlling ultimately some 20,000 birds. In 1917 a Messenger Dog Service was started for similar purposes and did good work on a number of occasions.

The expansion of the work of the Signal Service in the more forward areas was accompanied by a similar development on the Lines of Communication, at General Headquarters, Armies and Corps. Construction and Railway Companies were formed, and about 1,500 miles of main telegraph and telephone routes constructed in the Lines of Communication area alone, in addition to many miles in Army areas. Provision had to be made for communicating with London, Paris and Marseilles, as well as between the different Allied Headquarters. On the advance of our forces to the Rhine, telephone communication was established between General Headquarters at Montreuil and our troops at Cologne. Signal communication, entailing the putting up of many thousands of miles of wire, was provided also for the control of railway traffic; while to supplement electric communication generally a Despatch Rider Letter Service was maintained by motor cyclists.

The amount of Signal Traffic dealt with became very great, and on the Lines of Communication alone more than 23,000 telegrams have been transmitted in twenty-four hours. Similarly, at General

THE FINAL DESPATCH

Headquarters as many as 9,000 telegrams have been dealt with in twenty-four hours, besides 3,400 letters carried by Despatch Rider; an Army Headquarters has handled 10,000 telegrams and 5,000 letters in the same space of time, and a Corps 4,500 telegrams and 3,000 letters. In addition to telegrams and letters, there has been at all times a great volume of telephone traffic.

Something of the extent of the constructional work required, in particular to meet the constant changes of the battle line and the movement of Headquarters, can be gathered from the fact that as many as 6,500 miles of field cable have been issued in a single week. The average weekly issue of such cable for the whole of 1918 was approximately 3,300 miles.

Rearward Services and Personnel. Transportation

19. The immense expansion of the Army from 6 to over 60 infantry divisions, combined with the constant multiplication of auxiliary arms, called inevitably for a large increase in the size and scope of the services concerned in the supply and maintenance of our fighting forces.

As the Army grew and became more complicated the total feeding strength of our forces in France rose until it approached a total of 2,700,000 men. The vastness of the figures involved in providing for their needs will be realised from the following examples. For the maintenance of a single division for one day, nearly 200 tons dead weight of supplies and stores are needed, representing a shipping tonnage of nearly 450 tons. In an Army of 2,700,000 men, the addition of one ounce to each man's daily rations involves the carrying of an extra 75 tons of goods.

To cope with so great a growth, the number of existing directorates had gradually to be added to or their duties extended, with a corresponding increase in demands for personnel. The supervision of ports was entrusted to the Directorate of Docks which controlled special companies for the transhipping of stores. By the end of November, 1918, the number of individual landings in France at the various ports managed by us exceeded $10\frac{1}{2}$ million persons. During the 11 months January to November, 1918, the tonnage landed at these ports averaged some 175,000 tons per week.

To the Directorate of Transport, originally concerned with the administration of horse vehicles and pack animals, fell the further duty of exploiting mechanical road traction. Despite the employment of over 46,700 motor vehicles, including over 30,000 lorries, the number of horses and mules rose greatly, reaching a figure exceeding 400,000. The replacement, training and distribution of these animals was the duty of the Directorate of Remounts. The Directorate of Veterinary Services reduced losses and prevented the spread of disease, while the Inspector of Horse Feeding and Economies ensured that the utmost value was obtained from the forage and grain consumed.

To meet the requirements of mechanical and horse traffic, the upkeep or construction of a maximum of some 4,500 miles of roadway was entrusted to the Directorate of Roads. Some idea of the work involved may be obtained from the fact that for ordinary upkeep alone 100 tons of road material are required per fortnight for the maintenance of one mile of road. Under this Directorate were organised a number of Road Construction Companies, together with Quarry Companies to supply the necessary metal. In the month of October, 1918, over 85,000 tons of road material were conveyed weekly by motor transport alone, involving a petrol mileage of over 14,000,000 weekly. The total output of stone from the commencement of 1918 to the date of the Armistice amounted to some 3,500,000 tons.

For the working of the existing railways and for the construction or repair of many miles of track, both normal and narrow gauge, railway troops of every description, Operating Companies, Construction Companies, Survey and Reconnaissance Companies, Engine Crew Companies, Workshop Companies, Wagon Erecting Companies, and Light Railway Forward Companies had to be provided. Under the Directorate of Railway Traffic, the Directorate of Construction, and the Directorate of Light Railways, these and other technical troops during 1918 built or reconstructed 2,340 miles of broad gauge and 1,348 miles of narrow gauge railway. Throughout the whole period of their operation they guaranteed the smooth and efficient working of the railway system. In the six months May to October, 1918, a weekly average of 1,800 trains were run for British Army traffic, carrying a weekly average load of approximately 400,000 tons, while a further 130,000 tons were carried weekly by our light railways. The number of locomotives imported to deal with this traffic rose from 62 in 1916 to over 1,200 by the end of 1918, while the number of trucks rose from 3,840 to 52,600.

The Inland Water Transport section were organised under a separate Directorate for the working in France and Flanders of the canal and cross-channel barge traffic. On Inland waterways alone an average of 56,000 tons of material were carried weekly during 1918, the extent of waterways worked by us at the date of the Armistice being some 465 miles.

The wonderful development of all methods of transportation had an important influence upon the course of events. No war has been fought with such ample means of quick transportation as were available during the recent struggle. Despite the huge increase in the size of Armies, it was possible to effect great concentrations of troops with a speed which, having regard to the numbers of men and bulk of material moved, has never before been equalled. Strategic and tactical mobility has been the guiding principle of our transportation arrangements; but this was itself at all times vitally affected by questions of supply and by the necessity of providing for the evacuation and replacement on a vast scale of the sick and wounded.

The successful co-ordination and economic use of all the various kinds of transportation requires most systematic management, based on deep thought and previous experience. So great was the work entailed in the handling of the vast quantities of which some few examples are given above, so complex did the machinery of transport become and so important was it that the highest state of efficiency should be maintained, that in the autumn of 1916 I was forced to adopt an entirely new system for running our Lines of Communication. The appointment of Inspector General of Communications was abolished, and the services previously directed by that officer were brought under the immediate control of the Adjutant-General, the Quartermaster-General and the Director-General of Transportation. The last mentioned was a new office created with a separate Staff, composed for the greater part of civilian experts, to deal specifically with transportation questions. At the same time, the command and administration of the troops on the Lines of Communication were vested in a " General Officer Commanding the Lines of Communication Area."

The huge bulk of the supplies to be handled was due not merely to the size of our Army. It arose also from the introduction of new weapons and methods of war, and from the establishment of a higher standard of comfort for the troops. The incessant demands of the fighting forces for munitions were supplied by the Directorate of Ordnance Services, combined with a great expansion of Ordnance Workshops; while the Directorate of Engineering Stores provided on a vast scale the materials required for the construction of trench defences and kindred purposes. For the comfort and well-being of the troops, the Directorate of Supplies stored and distributed in sound condition fresh food, to take the place as far as possible of tinned rations. Through the agency of an Inspectorate of Messing and Economies, regular schools of cookery gave instructions to nearly 25,000 cooks, and careful measures were taken for the recovery of kitchen by-products. In August, 1918, over 860,000 lb. of dripping were received from Armies and consigned to England, while the cash value of the by-products disposed of from all sources has exceeded

£60,000 in a single month. Provision was made for baths, and a new Inspectorate supervised the running of Army laundries on up-to-date lines.

The Expeditionary Force Canteens made it possible to obtain additional comforts close up to the front. During 1918, the value of the weekly sales in the different canteens averaged 8½ million francs. These canteens were valuably supplemented by the various voluntary institutions ministering to the comfort and recreation of our troops, such as the Y.M.C.A., the Church Army, the Scottish Churches Huts, the Salvation Army, the Soldiers' Christian Association, the Catholic Women's League and Club Huts, the United Army and Navy Board, the Wesleyan Soldiers' Institute and the British Soldiers' Institute. In many cases these organisations carried on their work almost in the actual fighting line and did much to maintain the high moral of our Armies. To permit the troops to avail themselves of the opportunities so offered, methods devised by the Paymaster-in-Chief enabled soldiers to obtain money anywhere in the field. Parcels and letters from home have been delivered by the Army Postal Service with remarkable regularity.

As the effects of the enemy submarine warfare began to be felt and the shortage of shipping became more and more acute, so it became increasingly necessary for the Army in France to be more self-supporting. To meet this emergency vast hospitals and convalescent depôts, capable of accommodating over 22,000 men, were erected west of the Seine at Trouville. Additional General Hospitals with accommodation for over 7,000 patients were established in the neighbourhood of Boulogne, Étaples, and elsewhere. Between January, 1916, and November, 1918, the total capacity of hospitals and convalescent depôts in France grew from under 44,000 to over 157,000 persons.

Great installations were set up for the manufacture of gun parts and articles of like nature, for the repair of damaged material, as well as for the utilisation of the vast quantities of articles of all kinds collected from the battlefields by the organisation working under the direction of the Controller of Salvage. The Forestry Directorate, controlling over 70 Canadian and other Forestry Companies, worked forests all over France, in the North-West, Central and South-West Departments, the Vosges, Jura and Bordeaux country. As the result of its work our Armies were made practically independent of overseas imported timber. The Directorate of Agricultural Production organised farm and garden enterprises for the local supply of vegetables, harvested the crops abandoned by the enemy in his retreat and commenced the reclamation of the devastated area.

At the same time, a great saving of shipping was effected by the speeding up of work at the docks. The average tonnage discharged per hour in port rose from 12½ tons in January, 1917, to 34½ tons in July, 1918; while the average number of days lost by ships waiting berth at the ports fell from some 90 ship days per week at the beginning of 1917 to about 9 ship days per week in 1918.

For the accommodation of so wide a range of services, installations of all kinds, hutments, factories, workshops, storage for ammunition, clothing, meat and petrol, power houses and pumping stations, camps and hospitals, had to be planned and constructed by the Directorate of Works. Our business relations with the French, the obtaining of sites and buildings, called for the establishment of a Directorate of Hirings and Requisitions; while my Financial Adviser in France assisted in the adjustment of financial questions connected with the use of French railways and harbours, the exploitation of French forests and similar matters. The safe-guarding from fire of the great number of buildings erected or taken over by us and of the masses of accumulated stores was entrusted to a definite Staff under the supervision of a Fire Expert.

The creation and maintenance of the great organisation briefly outlined above made big demands upon our available supply of personnel. Though these demands so far as possible were met, under the supervision of the Controller of Labour, by imported labour or prisoners of war, it was not practicable at any time to supply more than a proportion of our needs in this manner. Many fit men who might otherwise have reinforced the fighting line had also to be employed, especially during the earlier stages of the war.

As, however, our organisation arrived at a greater state of completion and its working became smooth, so it began to be possible to withdraw considerable numbers of fit men from the rearward services. In many cases it was possible, where replacement was necessary, to fill the places of the fit men so withdrawn by women or unfit men. In this way when the man-power situation became acute a considerable saving was effected. During the great British attacks of 1918, of a total male feeding strength of a little over 2¼ millions, 1½ millions were in front of railhead. Even so, as has been found to be the case in the Armies of all other belligerents, so in our Army the number of fit men employed in the rearward services has at all times been large, and necessarily so.

It is hardly too much to assert that, however seemingly extravagant in men and money, no system of supply except the most perfect should ever be contemplated. To give a single example, unless our supply services had been fully efficient the great advance carried out by our Armies during the autumn of last year could not have been achieved.

Wars may be won or lost by the standard of health and moral of the opposing forces. Moral depends to a very large extent upon the feeding and general well being of the troops. Badly supplied troops will invariably be low in moral and an Army ravaged by disease ceases to be a fighting force. The feeding and health of the fighting forces are dependent upon the rearward services, and so it may be argued that with the rearward services rests victory or defeat. In our case we can justly say that our supply system has been developed into one of the most perfect in the world.

Replacement, Discipline and Welfare of the Troops

20. The preceding paragraph illustrates the demands which the conduct of operations made on the Staff and Directorates controlled by the Quartermaster-General. The parallel development of the Adjutant-General's Branch, while concerned with matters less patent to the casual observer has been no less remarkable. The problem of ensuring the supply of reinforcements at the times and places at which they will be required to replace casualties is present in all warfare, and is difficult in any circumstances. In operations conducted on the scale reached in this war it is exceedingly intricate. The successful solution of this problem alone entitles the Adjutant-General and his Staff to the greatest credit. It has formed, however, but a small part of their work.

Owing to the impossibility of foretelling what claims would be made on man-power by industry or by other theatres of war, it was necessary to prepare elaborate forecasts of the personnel likely to be required at various future dates, and to work out in advance the best manner of utilising reinforcements in the event of their being available in greater or less numbers. We were faced with an unexpected contraction in man-power in the winter of 1917 and an unexpected expansion in the summer of 1918. Both these developments were encountered with a success which could only have been attained by the greatest forethought and application on the part of the Staff concerned.

To reduce to cadre a depleted division, to fill it up when men became available, to break up a battalion and redistribute its personnel, to comb out a certain number of fit men from the rearward services, all sound simple operations. In reality each requires an immense amount of sympathetic treatment and clerical labour, the extent of the work involved being instanced by the fact that in the month of April, 1918, over 200,000 reinforcements were sent up to the fighting forces. The carrying out of measures of this nature was made more difficult by the continual formation of new types of unit

THE FINAL DESPATCH 341

to meet new requirements. It was necessary to find the personnel for those units with the least possible dislocation elsewhere, and with an eye to the most advantageous employment of the individual in regard to his medical category and special qualifications. The following figures will give some indication of the magnitude of the task. The Adjutant-General's office at the Base has prepared over 8 million records containing the military history of individual soldiers in France, and has received and dispatched over 22 million letters.

Whatever the quality of the troops, a just and efficient administration of military law is an indispensable adjunct to a high standard of discipline. I gratefully acknowledge the care with which officers of the Adjutant-General's Branch in all formations have ensured the observation of every safeguard which our law provides against injustice. They have seen to it that every plea which an accused or convicted soldier wishes to bring forward is heard, and that Commanders are advised as to the suitability of sentences. I take this opportunity of recording my satisfaction at the success which has attended the operation of the Suspension of Sentences Act. The number of men under suspended sentence, who by good conduct and gallant service in the field have earned remission of their sentence, has been most encouraging.

Closely related to the administration of military law is the work of the military police under the Provost-Marshal, and of the military prisons in the field. In the battle zone, where frequently they had to do duty in exposed positions under heavy fire and suffered severe casualties, the military police solved an important part of the problem of traffic control, by preventing the unavoidable congestion of troops and transport on roads in the vicinity of active operations from degenerating into confusion. In back areas, their vigilance and zeal have largely contributed to the good relations maintained between our troops and the civilian population.

Although the number of soldiers undergoing sentences of imprisonment in France has at no time amounted to 1 per thousand, the size of the Army has necessitated a considerable expansion of the Military Prisons in the field. The Director of Military Prisons, his Governors and warders have sought, not retribution, but to build up the self-discipline of the prisoner. They have been rewarded by seeing a large percentage of the men committed to their charge subsequently recover their characters as good soldiers.

Under the general control of the Adjutant-General, the Base Stationery Depôt, which went to France in 1914 with a personnel of ten, has expanded into the Directorate of Army Printing and Stationery Services, employing over 60 officers and 850 other ranks.

In addition to the printing and distribution of orders and instructions, it undertook the reproduction on a vast scale of aerial and other photographs, the number of which grew from 25,000 in 1916 to two and a quarter million in 1918. Other examples of administrative success are the Prisoners of War Section, and the Directorate of Graves Registration and Enquiries.

Of the care taken for the physical and moral welfare of the troops I cannot speak too highly.

In the former domain, the achievements of the Director-General of Medical Services and his subordinates have been so fully recorded by me in previous despatches that they need no further emphasis. It is sufficient to say that, in spite of the numbers dealt with, there has been no war in which the resources of science have been utilised so generously and successfully for the prevention of disease, or for the quick evacuation and careful tending of the sick and wounded.

In the latter sphere, the devoted efforts of the Army Chaplains of all denominations have contributed incalculably to the building up of the indomitable spirit of the Army. As the result of their teaching, all ranks came to know and more fully understand the great and noble objects for which they were fighting.

Under the immediate direction of the Adjutant-General in matters concerning military administration, the Principal Chaplain for members of all churches except the Church of England, and the Deputy Chaplain-General for members of the Church of England adminster in the greatest harmony a very complete joint organisation. Provided with a definite establishment for armies, corps and divisions, as well as for the principal base ports, base camps, hospitals and certain other units, they ensure that the benefit of religion is brought within the reach of every soldier.

In all the senior offices of this joint organisation, down to divisions, the Principal Chaplain and Deputy Chaplain-General have each their representatives, the appointments to those offices in the Principal Chaplain's section being apportioned between the different Churches, Protestant and Roman Catholic, in proportion to the numbers of their following in the Army as a whole. This organisation has worked for the common good in a manner wholly admirable and with a most noteworthy absence of friction. It has undoubtedly been much assisted, both in its internal economy and in its relations with commanders and troops, by being at all times in direct touch with the Adjutant-General's Branch.

No survey of the features of the war would be complete without some reference to the part played by women serving with the British Armies in France. Grouped also under the Adjutant-General's Branch of the General Staff, Queen Alexandra's Imperial Military

THE FINAL DESPATCH 343

Nursing Service, the Nursing Sisters of the Canadian Army Medical Corps and of the Australian, New Zealand, South African and Territorial Force Nursing Services, and the British Red Cross Society, have maintained and embellished a fine tradition of loyalty and efficiency. These services have been reinforced by members of Voluntary Aid Detachments from the British Isles, the Oversea Dominions and the United States of America, who have vied with their professional sisters in cheerfully enduring fatigue in times of stress and gallantly facing danger and death.

Women in the British Red Cross Society and other organisations have driven ambulances throughout the war, undeterred by discomfort and hardship. Women have ministered to the comfort of the troops in huts and canteens. Finally, Queen Mary's Auxiliary Army Corps, recruited on a wider basis, responded with enthusiasm to the call for drafts, and by the aid they gave to our declining manpower contributed materially to the success of our arms.

Training and Organisation

21. The experience gained in this war alone, without the study and practice of lessons learned from other campaigns, could not have sufficed to meet the ever-changing tactics which have characterised the fighting. There was required also the sound basis of military knowledge supplied by our Training Manuals and Staff Colleges.

The principles of command, Staff work, and organisation elaborated before the war have stood the test imposed upon them and are sound. The militarily educated officer has counted for much, and the good work done by our Staff Colleges during the past 30 years has had an important influence upon the successful issue of the war. In solving the various strategic and tactical problems with which we have been faced, in determining principles of training and handling of troops and in the control and elaboration of Army organisation generally, the knowledge acquired by previous study and application has been invaluable. Added to this have been the efficiency and smoothness of working resulting from standardisation of principles, assisted in many cases by the previous personal acquaintance at the Staff College of those called upon to work together in the field.

The course of the war has brought out very clearly the value of an efficient and well-trained High Command, in which I include not merely commanders of higher formations, but their Staffs also.

This has been the first time in our history that commanders have had to be provided for such large forces. Before the war, no one of our generals had commanded even an Army Corps such as has been used as a subsidiary formation in the battles of the last few years. In consequence, commanders have been faced with problems very different to those presented by the small units with which they had been accustomed to train in peace. That they exercised their commands with such success, as most of them did, shows, I venture to think, that their prior training was based on sound principles and conducted on practical lines.

Similarly as regards the Staff, the magnitude of our operations introduced a situation for which no precedent existed. The Staff Colleges had only produced a reserve of Staff officers adequate to the needs of our Army on a peace footing, and for the mobilisation of the Expeditionary Force of six divisions. Consequently, on the expansion of the Army during the war many officers had to be recruited for Staff appointments—from good regular officers chiefly, but also from officers of our new Armies—and trained for the new duties required of them. Though numbers of excellent Staff officers were provided in this way, it was found as a general rule that the relative efficiency in Staff duties of men who had passed through the Staff Colleges, as compared with men who had not had that advantage, was unquestionably greater.

Good Staff work is an essential to success in all wars, and particularly in a struggle of such magnitude as that through which we have just passed. No small part of the difficulty of achieving it lies in the possibility that officers on the Staff of higher formations may get out of touch with the fighting forces, and so lose sense of proportion and become unpractical. Every endeavour was made to avoid this by maintaining a constant interchange of such officers with others from the front, so that all might keep abreast with the latest ideas and experience both in the fighting line and elsewhere. In pursuance of this principle, in addition to 18 officers from Army or Corps Staffs and other officers from the Intelligence Corps or General List, there were brought in during the period of my command some 50 officers direct from active duty with divisions or smaller units to hold for longer or shorter periods appointments in the General Staff Branch at G.H.Q.

It may be accepted as a general rule that previous organisation should be upset as little as possible in war. As each war has certain special conditions, so some modification of existing ideas and practices will be necessary, but if our principles are sound these will be few and unimportant. In the present war, new organisations and establishments for dealing with the demands of both the fighting and the rearward services have been brought into being continually, and added to or absorbed by our existing organisation and establishment.

The constant birth of new ideas has demanded the exercise of the greatest care, not only to ensure that no device or suggestion of real value should be overlooked or discouraged, but also to regulate the enthusiasm of the specialist and prevent each new development assuming dimensions out of proportion to its real value. As the result of our own experience and that of the French during the fighting of 1915, all kinds of trench weapons were invented, bombs, bomb throwers, mortars, and even such instruments as trench daggers. In those days, the opinion was freely expressed that the war would be finished in the trenches and every effort was made to win victories in the trenches themselves. In consequence, rifle shooting was forgotten and was fast becoming a lost art. Similarly as regards artillery, the idea of dominating and defeating the hostile artillery before proceeding to the infantry attack was considered an impossibility.

Then followed the experience of the battle of the Somme in 1916, which showed that the principles of our pre-war training were as sound as ever. That autumn, a revival of old methods was inaugurated. Musketry shooting was everywhere carried out, and bayonet fighting was taught as the really certain way of gaining supremacy in hand-to-hand fighting. At the same time, as pointed out in para. 17 above, the greatest care was devoted to artillery shooting, as well as to the training of all arms for open fighting. The events of the next two years fully confirmed the lessons drawn from the battle of the Somme. In short, the longer the war has lasted the more emphatically has it been realised that our original organisation and training were based on correct principles. The danger of altering them too much, to deal with some temporary phase, has been greater than the risk of adjusting them too little.

22. Some idea of the extent of the organisation built up during the war for the training of our Armies can be gathered from a survey of the different schools actually established.

In the Armies important schools were maintained for the instruction of officers and non-commissioned officers of infantry and artillery in their several duties, for training in scouting, observation and sniping, in the use of trench mortars, in signalling, musketry and bayonet fighting, anti-gas precautions, mining and defence against tanks. The different Corps controlled a similar series of schools. Added to these were the special schools of the Cavalry Corps, including a School of Equitation; the Tank Corps Mechanical School; and the different courses instituted and managed by divisions, which were largely attended whenever the battle situation permitted.

Other schools under the direct supervision of General Headquarters provided instruction in the machine gun, Lewis gun and light mortar, in anti-aircraft gunnery, in observation for artillery, in sound ranging and flash spotting, wireless, bridging and other engineer duties, in firing and bombing from aeroplanes, and in physical and recreational training. At the Base depôts, big training and reinforcement camps were set up for infantry, artillery, cavalry, engineers, machine gunners, cyclists, Tank Corps, Signal and Gas personnel. Further, a regular succession of Staff officers and others were sent home to take part in the various schools and courses established in England.

In the course of the past year, it was found desirable to make provision for the more thorough co-ordination of effort among these various schools, and also for assisting commanders, especially during battle periods, in the training and instruction of such troops as might from time to time be in reserve. For this purpose an Inspectorate of Training was established. Training and organisation must always go hand-in-hand; for while tactical considerations dictate the organisation of units and methods of training, upon sound tactical organisation and training depend the development and effective employment of good tactics.

In the early spring of 1918, the foundations were laid of an educational scheme which might give officers and men throughout the Army an opportunity to prepare themselves for their return to civil life. Delayed in its application by the German offensive and the crowded events of the summer and autumn of that year, since the conclusion of the Armistice the scheme has been developed with most excellent results under the general direction of the training sub-section of my General Staff Branch, and generously supported in every possible way by the Educational Department at home. Divided into a general and a technical side, every effort has been made both to give opportunities for the improvement of general knowledge and to enable trained men to " get their hands in " before returning to civil life. In this way, between 400,000 and 500,000 persons have been brought under instruction, while the number of attendances at lectures has approached a million in the course of a month.

Our New Armies

23. The feature of the war which to the historian may well appear the most noteworthy is the creation of our new Armies.

To have built up successfully in the very midst of war a great new Army on a more than Continental scale, capable of beating the best troops of the strongest military nation of pre-war days, is an achievement of which the whole Empire may be proud. The total of over 327,000 German prisoners captured by us on the Western front is in striking contrast to the force of six divisions, comprising some 80,000 fighting men all told, with which we entered the war. That we should have been able to accomplish this stupendous task is due partly to the loyalty and devotion of our Allies and to the splendid work of the Royal Navy, but mainly to the wonderful spirit of the British race in all parts of the world.

Discipline has never had such a vindication in any war as in the present one, and it is their discipline which most distinguishes our new Armies from all similarly created armies of the past. At the outset the lack of deep-seated and instinctive discipline placed our new troops at a disadvantage compared with the methodically trained enemy. This disadvantage, however, was overcome, and during the last two years the discipline of all ranks of our new Armies, from whatever part of the Empire they have come, was excellent. Born from a widespread and intelligent appreciation of the magnitude of the issues at stake and a firm belief in the justice of our cause, it drew strength and permanence from a common-sense recognition of what discipline really means—from a general realisation that true discipline demands as much from officers as from men, and that without mutual trust, understanding, and confidence on the part of all ranks the highest form of discipline is impossible.

Drawn from every sphere of life, from every profession, department and industry of the British Empire, and thrust suddenly into a totally new situation full of unknown difficulties, all ranks have devoted their lives and energies to the service of their country in the whole-hearted manner which the magnitude of the issues warranted. The policy of putting complete trust in subordinate commanders and of allowing them a free hand in the choice of means to attain their object has proved most successful. Young officers, whatever their previous education may have been, have learnt their duties with enthusiasm and speed, and have accepted their responsibilities unflinchingly.

Our universities and public schools throughout the Empire proved once more, as they have proved time and again in the past, that in the formation of character, which is the root of discipline, they have no rivals. Not that universities and public schools enjoy a monopoly of the qualities which make good officers. The life of the British Empire generally has proved sound under the severest tests, and while giving men whom it is an honour for any officer to command, has furnished officers of the highest standard from all ranks of society and all quarters of the world.

Promotion has been entirely by merit, and the highest appointments were open to the humblest, provided he had the necessary qualifications of character, skill and knowledge. Many instances could be quoted of men who from civil or comparatively humble occupations have risen to important commands. A schoolmaster, a lawyer, a taxicab driver, and an ex-Serjeant-Major have commanded brigades; one editor has commanded a division, and another held successfully the position of Senior Staff Officer to a Regular division; the under-cook of a Cambridge College, a clerk to the Metropolitan Water Board, an insurance clerk, an architect's assistant, and a police inspector became efficient General Staff Officers; a Mess Serjeant, a railway signalman, a coal miner, a market gardener, an assistant secretary to a haberdashers' company, a Quartermaster-Serjeant, and many private soldiers have risen to command battalions; clerks have commanded batteries; a schoolmaster, a collier, the son of a blacksmith, an iron moulder, an instructor in tailoring, an assistant gas engineer, a grocer's assistant, as well as policemen, clerks and privates, have commanded companies or acted as adjutants.

As a body, and with few exceptions, new officers have understood that the care of their men must be their first consideration, that their men's comfort and well-being should at all times come before their own, that without this they cannot expect to win the affection, confidence, loyalty, and obedience of those they are privileged to command, or to draw the best from them. Moreover, they have known how to profit by the experience of others, and in common with their men they have turned willingly to the members of the old Regular Army for instruction and guidance in all branches of their new way of life.

On their part, officers, non-commissioned officers, and men of the old Regular Army have risen to the demands made upon them in a manner equally marvellous. Their leaven has pervaded the whole of the mighty force which in $4\frac{1}{2}$ years of war has gathered from all parts of the world round the small highly trained Army with which we entered the war. The general absence of jealousy and the readiness to learn, which in the field has markedly characterised all ranks of our new Armies, is proof both of the quality of our old Army and of the soundness of our pre-war training. If further proof were needed, it is found in the wonderful conduct and achievements of our Armies new and old, and in the general pride with which they are universally regarded.

In the earlier stages of the war the Regular Army was called on to provide instructors and cadres round which the new Armies could be formed. All that was best in the old Regular Army, its discipline, based on force of character, leadership and mutual respect, its traditions, and the spirit that never knows defeat, have been the foundations on which the new Armies have been built up. Heavy demands were necessarily made upon our establishment of trained regular officers, most regrettably depleted by the heavy sacrifices of the early days of the war. The way in which such demands have been met by those who survived those days have justified our belief in them.

Neither have the officers of the new Armies, whether drawn from the British Isles or the Dominions, risen with less spirit and success to the needs of the occasion. The great expansion of the Army, and the length of the war, necessitated an ever-increasing demand being made on them for filling responsible positions in command, staff and administrative appointments. The call has been met most efficiently. The longer the war continued, the greater became the part played in it by the new Armies of the Empire.

PART III

My Thanks to Commanders and Staffs

24. In the body of previous Despatches I have found a welcome opportunity to mention by name many distinguished officers, Commanders of Corps and Divisions, whose high soldierly qualities, powers of leadership and knowledge of men have largely influenced the course of the operations with which those Despatches have dealt. I have also been able to refer to some few of the many able and experienced Staff officers by whom I have at all times been so greatly assisted. It is not practicable, in the text of this Despatch, to set out the full list of those to whom I am indebted. I would say, however, of all those already mentioned, as well as of those whose names appear below and the many others whom the limits of space compel me to exclude, that no Commander has ever had or ever could wish for more loyal assistance given more ungrudgingly, or with a more complete devotion to the noble cause for which we have worked in common.

My thanks are especially due to the five Army Commanders—General Sir Herbert Plumer, General Sir Henry Rawlinson, General Sir Henry Horne, General the Hon. Sir Julian Byng and General Sir William Birdwood—whose names have become household words throughout the length and breadth of our Empire. I desire to associate with them the names of General Sir Charles Monro, who left the command of the First Army to assume the Chief Command in India; of General Sir Edmund Allenby, who, after conducting the operations of the Third Army in the battle of Arras, 1917, has since led our arms to victory in Palestine; and General Sir Hubert Gough, who, after distinguished service as a Brigade, Divisional and Corps Commander, commanded the Fifth Army (first known as the Reserve Army) during the Battles of the Somme and Ancre in 1916, east of Ypres in 1917, and finally in the great and gallant fight of March, 1918, the story of which is fresh in the minds of all.

To the heads of the Sections of my General Staff Branch at Headquarters, both past and present, I owe and readily acknowledge a great debt of gratitude for the energy, ability and loyalty with which they have discharged their important duties. Throughout the long and difficult period of the wearing-out battles of 1916 and 1917, my former Chief of the General Staff, Lieut.-General Sir Lancelot Kiggell, gave his great abilities and deep military learning to the services of his country with a loyalty and devotion which never spared himself, and in the end made demands upon his health which compelled him to retire under medical advice from the responsible position he had so ably held. His successor, Lieut.-General the Hon. Sir Herbert Lawrence, has continued his work with a like ability and with an unfailing insight, calm resolution and level judgment which neither ill-fortune nor good were able to disturb. My grateful thanks are due also to Lieut.-General Sir R. H. K. Butler, who acted as Deputy Chief of my General Staff until his appointment to the command of the III. Corps at the beginning of 1918.

Under the able, energetic and successful direction of Brigadier-General J. Charteris, the Intelligence Section of my General Staff Branch was developed into a far-reaching and most efficient organisation for the rapid collection, sifting and dissemination of information concerning the disposition, movements and intentions of the enemy. The activities of the Intelligence Section were incessant, and the knowledge obtained thereby of the utmost value. On the transfer of General Charteris to other duties, his work was carried on with great ability by Brig.-General E. W. Cox, and after the regrettable accident resulting in the death of that distinguished officer, by Brig.-General G. S. Clive.

Since the appointment of Lieut.-General Sir Nevil Macready to be Adjutant-General at home early in 1916, the work of my Adjutant-General's Branch has been most efficiently conducted under the direction of Lieut.-General Sir George Fowke. The problems of organising the supply of reinforcements to meet the needs of our Armies while active operations were in progress, of dealing with casualties and matters of discipline, have been succeeded or supplemented since the conclusion of the Armistice by the scarcely less difficult question of demobilisation. These different tasks have been performed by all ranks of the Adjutant-General's Branch with

THE FINAL DESPATCH 351

great ability and success, despite the fact that in each instance they were confronted by conditions without precedent in the history of our Army.

Throughout 1916 and 1917 the duties of the Quartermaster-General's Branch were ably directed during a period of constant expansion by Lieut.-General Sir Ronald Maxwell. Since his retirement the control of the vast organisation, some of the broad outlines of which are described in paragraph 19 of this Despatch, has been exercised by Lieut.-General Sir Travers Clarke, who has carried on the same task in the most efficient manner.

The Director-General of Transportation's Branch was formed under the brilliant direction of Major-General Sir Eric Geddes during the autumn of 1916, as above stated. To the large number of skilled and experienced civilians included by him on his Staff, drawn from the railway companies of Great Britain and the Dominions, the Army is deeply indebted for the general excellence of our transportation services. Since the transfer of Sir Eric Geddes to other duties his work has been ably conducted by his successors, Major-Generals Sir F. A. M. Nash and S. D'A. Crookshank.

The important work of the Military Secretary's Branch has been admirably carried out under the direction of Major-General Sir W. E. Peyton and his successor, Major-General H. G. Ruggles-Brise.

The steady increase of our strength in artillery and the development of the use of that important arm upon sound and successful lines has been due in great measure to the efforts of my artillery adviser, Lieut.-General Sir J. F. N. Birch and the able Staff working under him, among them Colonel J. T. Dreyer and Colonel S. W. H. Rawlins.

The wide range of services performed by the Royal Engineers were successfully directed during the battles of 1916 and 1917 by Major-General Sir S. R. Rice. Since that date they have been controlled with great efficiency by his successor in the post of Engineer-in-Chief, Major-General Sir G. M. Heath, formerly Chief Engineer of the First Army, assisted by my Deputy Engineers-in-Chief, Brig.-Generals J. E. Edmonds and H. Biddulph.

As indicated in a preceding paragraph, the activities of the Signal Service have expanded greatly during the period of my command. Under the direction of my Signal Officer-in-Chief, Major-General Sir J. S. Fowler, and my Deputy Signal Officer-in-Chief, Colonel E. V. Turner, the growing needs of the Army have been fully met.

The office of the Inspector-General of Training, established in the latter half of 1918, has been ably filled by Lieut.-General Sir Ivor Maxse, assisted by my Deputy Inspector-General of Training,

Major-General H. C. C. Uniacke, formerly commanding the artillery of the Fifth Army, as hereinafter mentioned.

Second only to the work of the Army Commanders and heads of Branches at General Headquarters in their influence upon the conduct of operations have been the parts played by the Senior General Staff officers of the several Armies. In their responsible and arduous tasks they have been most ably seconded by the general efficiency of the Army Staffs working with them, and in particular by the heads of the " A " and " Q " Branches of Army Staffs, the General Officers Commanding Royal Artillery within the Armies and the Chief Engineers of Armies.

From the commencement of the preparations for the first battle of the Somme and throughout all subsequent operations, the General Staff work of the Fourth Army Staff has been directed with great ability and success by Major-General Sir A. A. Montgomery. The admirable work done by the head of the Administrative Branch of the Staff, Major-General H. C. Holman, by Major-General C. E. D. Budworth who has controlled the work of the artillery of that Army with conspicuous success, and by the Chief Engineer of the Army, Major-General R. U. H. Buckland, has also contributed very materially to the success of the many brilliant operations undertaken by the Fourth Army.

The General Staff of the Army known during the Somme battle as the Reserve Army, and later as the Fifth Army, was well directed by Major-General N. Malcolm until the close of 1917. Major-General H. N. Sargent, head of the " A " and " Q " Branch of the Fifth Army Staff, Major-General Uniacke while commanding the artillery of the Army, and Major-Generals R. P. Lee and P. G. Grant, successively Chief-Engineers of the Army, have also filled their important and responsible positions with distinction and success. Subsequent to the appointment of Major-General Malcolm to the command of a division, the duties of senior General Staff Officer of the Fifth Army were efficiently discharged by Major-General J. S. J. Percy until his transfer to the Second Army, and thereafter by Major-General Sir C. B. B. White, with whom have been associated as head of the " A " and " Q " Branch and commander of the artillery of the Army respectively, Major-General P. O. Hambro and Major-General C. C. Van Straubenzee.

During the battle of Arras, the office of senior General Staff Officer of the Third Army was held by Major-General L. J. Bols. This able officer, who at a later date followed his Army Commander to Palestine, was succeeded by Major-General L. R. Vaughan (Indian Army), who has directed the work of the Third Army General Staff with great efficiency throughout the whole of the subsequent operations of that Army. The able manner in which have been performed the arduous duties devolving upon the head of the " A " and " Q " Branch, Major-General A. F. Sillem, upon Major-Generals R. St. C. Lecky and A. E. Wardrop, successively commanding the artillery of the Army, and Major-Generals E. R. Kenyon and W. A. Liddell, successive Chief Engineers of the Army, is also deserving of the highest commendation.

The work of the General Staff of the First Army in the attack and capture of the Vimy Ridge in 1917 and in all subsequent operations has been most ably directed by Major-General W. H. Anderson. Major-Generals P. G. Twining and A. W. Peck, the successive heads of the " A " and " Q " Branch of the Army Staff, Major-Generals Sir H. F. Mercer and E. W. Alexander, successively commanding the artillery of the Army, and Major-Generals G. M. Heath and E. H. de V. Atkinson, successively Chief Engineers of the Army, have also carried out their duties in a distinguished manner.

Throughout the operations of the Second Army at Messines and east of Ypres during the summer and autumn of 1917, the elaborate General Staff arrangements for that successful fighting were admirably directed by Major-General C. H. Harington. When at a later date General Harington was appointed Deputy Chief of the Imperial General Staff at the War Office, his work was undertaken by Major-General J. S. J. Percy, the present senior General Staff officer of the Second Army. Major-General A. A. Chichester, head of the " A " and " Q " Branch, Major-General G. McK. Franks and Major-General C. R. Buckle, successively commanding the artillery of the Army, and Major-General Sir F. M. Glubb, Chief Engineer of the Army, have also accomplished the arduous and responsible tasks associated with their respective appointments with great ability and success.

I recall with gratitude the magnificent work done during the fighting of 1916 and 1917 by Major-General Sir H. M. Trenchard, at that time commanding the Royal Flying Corps. The influence exerted by this able and distinguished officer upon the moral and the development of the British Air Service and in the creation of its splendid traditions can scarcely be exaggerated. Since his transfer to another but kindred field of activity, his work has been most ably and successfully carried on by Major-General Sir J. M. Salmond, commander of the Royal Air Force on the Western front.

The rapid development of the tank as a most potent instrument of war and the creation of the high traditions of the Tank Corps have been due in great measure to the energy and inspiration of their Commander, Major-General H. J. Elles.

The steady increase in the effectiveness of gas as a weapon of offence is largely to be attributed to the able work of my Director of Gas Services, Brigadier-General C. H. Foulkes.

Since the formation of the Machine Gun Corps and the creation of the office of Inspector of Machine Gun Units, held successively by Brigadier-Generals C. H. T. Lucas and L. F. Renny, the use of the machine gun has received a new impulse. Very gallant and efficient service has been rendered by all machine gun units, and not least by the battalions of the Guards Machine Gun Regiment, lately formed from personnel of the Household Cavalry Brigade and the Guards Division.

The development of bayonet fighting and the high standard generally attained by the troops in the use of this essential weapon are due in great measure to the teaching and enthusiasm of Col. R. B. Campbell, formerly Deputy Inspector of Physical and Bayonet Training.

The general efficiency of our Mining Services, and in particular the great success of the extensive mining operations carried out by us preparatory to the battle of Messines, is largely owed to the work of my former Inspector of Mines, Brigadier-General R. N. Harvey.

During the rapid and extensive troop movements of 1918 in particular, the constant work of the Auxiliary (Omnibus) Park was controlled with great ability by its commander, Lieut.-Colonel G. L. H. Howell.

Among others responsible for the efficient work of the various rearward services and Administrative Services and Departments, my thanks are especially due to Lieut.-General Sir J. J. Asser, under whose command a vast organisation with a numerous staff has been built up on the Lines of Communication, involving the control and administration of a wide extent of France, including the administrative areas of Abbeville, Étaples, Trouville and other places, and important bases at Dunkirk, Calais, Boulogne, Dieppe, Havre, Rouen, Cherbourg, Brest, and Marseilles; to my Directors of Medical Services past and present, namely, Surgeon-General Sir A. T. Sloggett and Lieut.-General C. H. Burtchaell, with their deputies, Surgeon-General Sir W. G. Macpherson and Major-General J. Thomson; my Deputy Adjutant-Generals, Major-Generals J. T. Burnett-Stuart and Sir E. R. C. Graham; my Deputy Quartermaster-Generals, Major-Generals R. Ford and R. S. May; the General Officer Commanding the Canadian Section at General Headquarters, Brigadier-General J. F. L. Embury; Lieut.-General Sir E. Locke Elliot, Commanding the Indian Contingent; my Provost-Marshal, Brigadier-General H. S. Rogers; my Director of Supplies, Major-General Sir E. E. Carter; my Director of Ordnance Services, Major-General Sir C. M. Mathew; my Director of

THE FINAL DESPATCH

Transport, Major-General Sir W. G. B. Boyce; my Director of Railway Traffic, Brigadier-General V. Murray; the Officer Commanding the Railway Operating Division, Lieut.-Colonel C. W. Paget; my Director of Light Railways, Brigadier-General G. H. Harrisson; my Director of Roads, Brigadier-General H. P. Maybury; my Director of Inland Water Transport, Brigadier-General C. M. Luck; my Director of Docks, Brigadier-General R. L. Wedgwood; my Director of Works, Major-General Sir A. M. Stuart; my Director of Engineering Stores, Brigadier-General J. W. S. Sewell; my Director of Remounts, Brigadier-General Sir F. S. Garratt; my Director of Veterinary Services, Major-General J. Moore; my Director of Army Postal Services, Brigadier-General W. Price; my Controller of Labour, Brigadier-General E. G. Wace; my Director of Military Prisons, Brigadier-General P. Umfreville, who with his Staff has performed very exacting duties with great firmness and tact; my Director of Agricultural Production, Brigadier-General J., Earl of Radnor; my Controller of Salvage, Brigadier-General E. Gibb; my Inspector of Quartermaster-General's Services, Horse Feeding and Economies, Major-General J. Vaughan; my Inspector of Quartermaster-General's Services, Messing and Economies, Lieut.-Colonel E. Larken; my Director of Forestry, Brigadier-General Lord Lovat; my Director of Army Printing and Stationery Services, Colonel S. G. Partridge; my Director of Graves Registration and Enquiries, Major-General Fabian Ware; my Financial Adviser, Brigadier-General H. G. Goligher; my Paymaster-in-Chief, Major-General Sir C. A. Bray; my Director of Hirings and Requisitions, Major-General the Right Hon. L. B. Friend; and my Deputy Controller of Expeditionary Force Canteens, Colonel E. Benson.

The duties of the Principal Chaplain and Deputy Chaplain-General have been discharged by the Reverend J. M. Simms and the Right Reverend Bishop L. H. Gwynne with a zeal and devotion for which I wish to express to them my sincere gratitude. My thanks are due also to Miss Lila Davy, the Chief Controller of the Women's Auxiliary Army Corps in France, for the very valuable assistance given by her and all ranks serving under her, and to Colonel the Hon. Sir Arthur Lawley, who as Commissioner has supervised the wonderful work done by the British Red Cross Society in France.

I desire also to take this last opportunity to record my personal appreciation of the very valuable help rendered, during the great events described in my Despatches, by other officers of my General Staff Branch at Headquarters, and in particular by Major-General Sir John Davidson, head of the Operations Section, and those who worked under him, among them Brigadier-General J. G. Dill,

Brigadier-General (at that time Lieut.-Colonel) E. Napper Tandy, Lieut.-Colonel W. G. S. Dobbie, and Major J. H. Boraston; by Major-General G. P. Dawnay, head of the Staff Duties Section; Brigadier-General K. Wigram, formerly head of the Operations (B) Section; Brigadier-General C. Bonham-Carter and Colonel H. F. Baillie for their work in connection with the formation and development of the scheme for General and Technical Education within the Army; and Lieut.-Colonel E. M. Jack, under whose direction the work of the Field Surveying battalions, in the preparation and supply of maps and the fixing of hostile battery positions, has been of the greatest value to our artillery and other arms and services.

My relations with the Allied and Associated Armies, the co-ordination of our operations, and the good feeling existing between all ranks of our Armies and the civil population of France and Belgium have been greatly assisted by the work of the different Inter-Allied Missions. In this connection I desire to refer gratefully to the help long given to me by Brigadier-General Clive in my dealings with French General Headquarters; to the valuable work done by Lieut.-General Sir J. P. Du Cane, the Senior British Military Representative at Marshal Foch's Headquarters; by the head of the British Mission with Belgian Headquarters, Brigadier-General the Earl of Athlone; by my present Representative at French General Headquarters, Brigadier-General F. W. L. S. H. Cavendish; by the head of the British Mission with the American Expeditionary Force, Brigadier-General C. M. Wagstaff; and by Brigadier-General C. A. Ker, head of the British Mission with the Portuguese Expeditionary Force.

I desire to refer also with deep gratitude to the invaluable assistance given to me by the able and gallant officers who in turn acted as Chief of the French Mission attached to my Headquarters, General des Vallières, who has since met a soldier's death, and his successors, Colonel de Bellaigue de Bughas and General de Laguiche. My thanks are due equally to Lieut.-General A. L. E. Orth, who as Chief of the Belgian Mission attached to my Headquarters has spared no pains to further the interests of our common cause; to Colonel C. Capello, Chief of the Italian Mission, and to Lieut.-Colonel Robert Bacon, who as Chief of the American Mission attached to my Headquarters has been able to give me advice and assistance of the greatest value on many occasions.

Finally, my thanks are due to the officers of my Personal Staff, and in particular to my Assistant Military Secretary, Lieut.-Colonel A. F. Fletcher; my Private Secretary, Major Sir Philip Sassoon, and Commandant E. A. Gemeau, by whose loyal and devoted assistance a great burden of work has been lifted from my shoulders.

25. I desire to conclude this Despatch with a very warm and sincere acknowledgment of the great debt owed by all ranks of the Armies in France to our kinsmen and kinswomen of the British Empire for the unfailing support they have given us by their thoughts, their prayers, and their work throughout the long years of war. In all those years their trust and confidence never wavered, their labours never ceased, and no sacrifices, hardships or privations were too great to be borne, provided that thereby the needs of the troops might adequately be supplied. The dauntless spirit of the people at home strengthened and sustained the invincible spirit of the Army, the while their incessant toil on land and sea, in the mine, factory and shipyard, placed in our hands the means with which to fight.

Neither do we forget the gratitude due from us to the various Home Authorities, and especially to the Ministry of Munitions, by whose efforts, in conjunction with those of the Governments of the Dominions, the working power and resources of the whole Empire were so rapidly developed and co-ordinated for the more vigorous prosecution of the war. The record of what they accomplished in the space of four and a half years is indeed stupendous. If the Army may justly be proud of a great victory, gallantly won at the end of an uphill fight, we have good reason to be thankful, too, for their devoted and patriotic work, which alone made it possible to continue the struggle until a successful conclusion had been reached.

    I have the honour to be,
        Sir,
        Your most obedient Servant,
            D. HAIG, Field-Marshal,
              Commanding-in-Chief, British Armies in France.

ORIGINAL TEXT

OF

MARSHAL FOCH'S INTRODUCTION

De tout temps, le Commandant en Chef des Armées Britanniques a adressé à son Gouvernement des Comptes-Rendus sommaires des périodes principales d'une campagne. Le Maréchal Sir Douglas Haig s'est conformé à cet usage. Il a rédigé, deux fois par an en moyenne, un aperçu des faits les plus saillants des opérations britanniques sur le front occidental. Les Comptes-Rendus embrassent la période où il commandait en Chef et s'étendent par suite de la fin de 1915 au début d'avril, 1919.

Ces rapports, établis avec un absolu souci de la vérité et scrupuleusement exacts dans les moindres détails, sont marqués d'une hauteur et d'une largeur de vue incontestables. Ils constituent des documents historiques de premier ordre, par les renseignements qu'ils apportent non seulement sur les opérations, mais aussi sur l'état des troupes, leur formation successive, les modifications apportées au cours de la guerre à leur instruction ; par les précisions qui mettent en relief avec leur valeur, les caractères propres à chaque contingent de l'Empire, les travaux incessants des États-Majors ; au total le labeur grâce auquel chacun augmente rapidement son expérience de la guerre et son savoir professionnel pour les adapter à une lutte pleine de nouveautés ; par le tableau de la tâche extraordinaire qui incomba aux différents services chargés de pourvoir aux besoins, grandissant sans cesse, d'une armée moderne.

Si parfois les rapports exposent les faits d'une touche légère et sans approfondir les raisons déterminantes ou certaines de leurs conséquences, c'est que, écrits au cours de la guerre et adressés au Gouvernement Britannique, ils vont à la nation elle-même dont ils doivent ménager les nerfs, comme ils doivent également éviter de fournir à l'ennemi une documentation utile.

Néanmoins, on dégage de leur lecture la remarquable continuité de vues qui, appliquée à l'entraînement des troupes, à la formation des spécialités servant les engins de plus en plus nombreux et variés de la guerre moderne, à la production et au transport de munitions nécessitées par une consommation inconnue jusqu'alors, à la construction ou au rétablissement des communications, avait fait des Armées Britanniques un magnifique outil de guerre dès l'année 1917.

Mais il n'y a pas d'outil qui produise par lui-même. Il lui faudra toujours la main qui sache l'employer. Quand les dépêches se bornent là-dessus à nous dire qu'après la période de décision, que les Armées Allemandes épuisées, usées en 1914, 1915, 1916, 1917, allaient être battues en 1918, elles ne disent pas pourquoi l'usure a duré si longtemps, et la décision si peu, encore moins pourquoi elle s'est transformée en victoire des Alliés, menée au pas de charge pour aboutir à la capitulation de l'Armistice ; elles font sommairement connaître des effets sans en expliquer les causes, elles omettent la main qui mania l'outil. Qu'il nous soit permis de combler cette lacune dans laquelle disparaît l'action opérante au premier chef, du Commandement Britannique.

En fait, la période d'usure avait correspondu à l'impuissance pour les Alliés, résultat d'une incomplète préparation à la guerre de leur part. L'Entente n'avait amené sur les champs de bataille de 1914 qu'une Armée Anglaise de 6 divisions, et une Armée Française sans l'artillerie suffisante comme sans la quantité de munitions nécessaire pour la guerre moderne.

Avec ces moyens incomplets, nous avions bien arrêté l'invasion dès la première année, mais tant que les insuffisances de nos effectifs et de notre matériel n'étaient pas comblées, nous restions hors d'état d'entreprendre l'offensive étendue et soutenue seule capable de conduire à une décision par les armes, nous étions réduits à des actions partielles, momentanées. Au moins eût-il fallu pouvoir les coordonner dans l'espace et dans le temps.

De là, la faiblesse des résultats obtenus par l'Entente jusqu'en 1917. Heureusement pour elle, l'ennemi obligé dans ces années-là de tenir tête aux Armées Russes, puis aux Armées Roumaines d'Orient, n'avait appliqué en Occident qu'une insuffisante partie de ses forces pour y vaincre définitivement, ou qu'une conception étroite de l'attaque, comme à *Verdun*. Quoi qu'il en soit, les impuissances face à face risquaient de faire durer longtemps encore ce que l'on a appelé la guerre d'usure—cette lutte, sans avantage marqué et soutenu, qui use les deux armées sans profit pour l'une ou pour l'autre, c'est-à-dire la guerre sans issue. Il faudra bien toujours lui trouver une autre forme si l'on veut aboutir à la victoire. Dans cette course à la décision, toujours nécessaire cependant, l'Allemagne, dès l'année 1917, se débarrasse du front oriental par la Révolution russe comme par les Traités de *Brest-Litowsk* et de *Bucharest*, et quand elle tourne la masse de ses armées fortes de plus de 200 divisions et d'un matériel formidable contre le front d'occident, pour en faire sortir ses attaques violentes et au début victorieuses de mars 1918 sur la Somme, puis d'avril sur la Lys, de mai au Chemin des Dames, de juin sur l'Oise, enfin de juillet sur la Marne, qui pourrait y trouver les marques d'une usure décisive à son détriment et les préludes d'une victoire de l'Entente ? Qui oubliera les dangers de nouveaux progrès ennemis sur la Somme, à Amiens, coupant les Armées Britanniques des Armées Françaises, ou vers St.-Omer et Dunkerque, coupant les Armées Britanniques de la Grande-Bretagne ; ou vers Paris, cœur de la France, et nœud de communications indispensables à la Coalition ? Que devenait ce soi-disant avantage de l'usure des Armées Allemandes au cours des années précédentes ? La bataille des armées, même des meilleures, comme les Armées Britanniques, ne risquait-elle pas de se solder par un désastre, sans un Commandement capable de dominer la situation, de maîtriser les événements et de reprendre ses troupes en main pour les reconstituer, les mettre en position d'arrêter définitivement l'ennemi d'abord, de l'attaquer ensuite avec une violence, un aplomb, une répétition de coups, qui jamais ne furent dépassés ? A tous les degrés, ce Commandement et ces États-Majors se trouvaient à la hauteur de leur tâche. Par l'activité qu'ils allaient déployer après les attaques allemandes du printemps de 1918 et malgré les pertes éprouvées, plus de 60 divisions britanniques, 10 fois plus qu'en 1914, seront maintenues en état de combattre jusqu'à la fin de l'année. Elles auront un moral plus élevé que jamais. Les lignes de résistance se multiplient en avant d'Amiens, d'Arras, de Béthune, d'Hazebrouck, de St.-Omer, de Cassel ; les inondations se préparent également, car le terrain doit être disputé pied à pied, avec acharnement. Par dessus tout, un jeu puissant de réserves alliées est assuré ; il sera pratiqué avec la plus grande facilité entre toutes les armées, permettant ainsi de relever avec les troupes françaises la Vᵉ Armée Britannique au sud de la Somme au commencement d'avril ; de soutenir la IIᵉ Armée Britannique dans les Flandres avec 7 divisions françaises dans le même mois ; de renforcer la VIᵉ Armée Française avec 5 divisions britanniques au Chemin des Dames, puis la Vᵉ Armée Française dans la Forêt de Reims, avec 2 divisions britanniques, et la Xᵉ Armée Française à Villers-Cotterets, avec deux autres divisions qui prennent part à la contre-offensive du 18 juillet.

C'est ainsi que, grâce en particulier à l'activité du Commandement Britannique et à la compréhension des besoins, plus de 200 divisions allemandes étaient définitivement arrêtées dans leur offensive, par un nombre moindre de divisions alliées et que notre defensive s'était montrée victorieuse. Il en est de même, dans l'offensive, du concours prêté aux autres armées par les troupes britanniques.

Dans cette dernière période, il suffit, pour mesurer l'ardeur et l'endurance de ces troupes, de relever les dates et l'importance des principaux événements :

Bataille d'Amiens.—Du 8 au 13 août, dans laquelle la IVe Armée conquit 22,000 prisonniers et plus de 400 canons.

Bataille de Bapaume.—21 août au 1er septembre, IIIe Armée et gauche de la IVe ; 34,000 prisonniers, 270 canons.

Bataille de la Scarpe.—26 août au 3 septembre, de la I^e Armée ; 16,000 prisonniers, 200 canons.

Bataille d'Havrincourt et d'Epéhy.—12 au 18 septembre, des IVe et IIIe Armées ; 12,000 prisonniers, 100 canons.

Bataille de Cambrai et de la Ligne Hindenburg.—27 septembre au 5 octobre, IVe, IIIe, et I^e Armée, aboutissant à la rupture de la Ligne Hindenburg et à la prise de 35,000 prisonniers et de 380 canons.

Bataille des Flandres.—28 Septembre au 14 Octobre, de la IIe Armée.

Bataille du Cateau.—6 au 12 octobre, des IVe, IIIe et I^e Armées.

Bataille de la Selle.—17 au 25 octobre, des IVe et IIIe Armées ; 20,000 prisonniers, 475 canons.

Bataille de la Sambre.—1er au 11 novembre, des IVe, IIIe et I^e Armées ; 19,000 prisonniers, 450 canons.

Les effets de ces attaques britanniques, violentes et répétées, augmentaient grandement par leur concordance avec les actions des autres armées alliées française, américaine, belge pour finir, qui frappaient aussi puissamment dans un assaut convergent préparé de la Mer du Nord à la Moselle.

Jamais, à aucun moment de l'histoire, les Armées Britanniques n'avaient obtenu dans l'offensive de plus grands résultats que dans cette attaque continue de 116 jours, du 18 juillet au 11 novembre. C'était bien là une victoire complète obtenue grâce à la valeur des Commandants d'Armée et de grandes unités, grâce surtout au désintéressement, à l'intelligente, loyale et énergique volonté de leur Commandant en Chef qui avait facilité les plus grandes combinaisons et permis les plus vastes et les plus longs efforts. Nettement éclairé par l'expérience, n'était-il pas intervenu en effet, dès le 24 mars 1918, près de son Gouvernement, dès le 26 près des Gouvernements Alliés réunis à *Doullens,* pour que les Armées Française et Britannique de *France* et des *Flandres* soient immédiatement placées sous un commandement unique, dût sa situation personnelle s'en trouver réduite ? Et par la suite ne se montrait-il pas avant tout soucieux de marcher de l'avant et en parfait accord avec le plan général des Alliés tracé par ce nouveau Commandement Suprême.

Sur ce point, les Dépêches présentaient des lacunes qui ne permettaient pas au lecteur de tenir toutes les causes de notre victoire. Je devais à la vérité de les compléter.

F. Foch

INDEX

INDEX

ABLAINZEVELLE, 208, 212
Acheville, 286
Achiet-le-Petit, 266
Adjutant-General's Branch, 340, 341
Advance to Victory—State of the British armies, 245, 246; position of Allies, 246; enemy's position, 246; enemy's intentions, 247; policy of British armies, 247, 248; reorganisation, 248, 249; minor operations in May and June, 249, 250; operations in July—Hamel captured, 250, 251; operations on French front, 252; operations of IX. Corps in Aisne battle, 252-254; second battle of the Marne, 254, 255; operations by XXII. Corps, 255; situation at end of July, 256, 257; general scheme of British operations, 257, 258; battle of Amiens (Aug. 8-12), 258-264; battle of Bapaume, 264-273; battle of the Scarpe, 273-276; battle of Havrincourt and Epéhy, 276-279; battle of Cambrai and Hindenburg Line, 280-285; battle in Flanders, 285-287; second battle of Le Cateau, 287-291; battle of the Selle River, 291-293; battle of the Sambre, 293-296; return to Mons, 296, 297; the Armistice, 298; work of the Troops, 298-300; Infantry, 300; Artillery, 300; Cavalry, 301; Royal Air Force, 301, 302; Tanks, 302; Trench Mortars, 302; Machine Gun Corps, 303; Royal Engineers, 303; Gas Services, 304; Signal Services, 304; Transportation Services, 304, 305; Supply Services, 306; Forestry, 306; Omnibus Park, 306; Labour Corps, 306, 307; Medical Services, 307; Chaplains' Department, 307; Administrative Services and Departments, 308; Navy and Home Authorities, 308; our Allies, 308
See also Amiens, battle of; Bapaume, battle of; Cambrai and the Hindenburg Line, battle of; Flanders, battle in; Havrincourt and Epéhy, battle of; Le Cateau, battle of; Sambre, battle of the; Scarpe, battle of the; Selle River, battle of the.

Agricultural Production, Directorate of, 338
Air-burst ranging, 331 *n.*
Albert, 208, 266, 268
Alexander, Maj.-Gen. E. W., 353
Allenby, Gen. Sir E. H. H., 25, 87, 349
Ameral, 292
Amiens, 328, 329
Amiens, battle of (Aug. 8-12), xii, 361; plan of operations, 258-260; troops employed, 260; battle opened, 260, 261; advance continued, 262, 263; results, 263, 264
Ancre, operations on the—Enemy's position, 65; operations commenced, 65, 66; Beaumont Hamel Spur, 66; Grandcourt, 66, 67; advance against Serre, 67; advance towards Miraumont, 68; Miraumont and Serre evacuated, 69, 70; Le Barque and Gommecourt, 70; Irles, 70; the Loupart Line, 71; general withdrawal, 71, 72; Bapaume and Peronne, 72, 73; difficulty of communications, 73, 74; enemy resistance increasing, 74, 75; Hindenburg Line, 75; general review, 75-78
Andechy, 206, 262
Anderson, Maj.-Gen. W. H., 353
Angre, 94, 296, 297
Angreau, 296
Anneux, 156, 158, 281
Anthoine, Gen., 109
Anti-Aircraft and Searchlight Sections, 139
Antoing, 297
Argonne, 280
Arleux, 99
Armentières, 51, 224
Armistice, the, 298, 311, 312
Arras, battle of (April 9-June 7) —
Preparations, 85; enemy's defences, 86; final preparations—fight for aerial supremacy, 86, 87; the bombardment, 87; troops employed, 87, 88; method of attack, 88; general attack, 89-91; advance continued, 91, 92; Monchy-le-Preux, 92, 93; Hèninel, Wancourt and the Souchez River, 93; withdrawal of enemy, 94, 95; results of first attacks, 95, 96; subsidiary

365

Arras, battle of—*continued*
  operations, 96; attack resumed—Guémappe and Gavrelle, 97, 98; policy of subsequent operations, 98, 99; final attacks—Arleux, 99; Fresnoy, 99, 100; situation reviewed, 100, 101; activity maintained, 101; Bullecourt and Rœux, 102
Arras Line (April 9, 1917), *facing* 89
Arrow Head Copse, 30
Arsiero, 19 n.
Artillery, importance of, 332, 333
Arvillers, 210
Aschhoop, 131
Asiago, 19 n.
Asser, Lt.-Gen. Sir J. J., 354
Athies, 90
Athlone, Brig.-Gen. the Earl of, 356
Atkinson, Maj.-Gen. E. H. de V., 353
Attichy, 253
Aubercourt, 214
Aubigny, 196
Aulnoye, 291 n.
Aunelle river, 296
Austro-German attack on Isonzo front, 152 n.
Aveluy Wood, 208, 231, 250
Avesnes, 268, 297, 298
Ayette, 208

Babington, Maj.-Gen. J. M. (Sir), 27, 107 n.
Babœuf, 204
Bac St. Maur, 222
Bacon, Col. Robert, 356
Baillescourt Farm, 67
Bailleul, 94, 226, 228, 229, 273
Baillie, Col. H. F., 356
Bainbridge, Maj.-Gen. E. G. T., 20, 106 n., 192, 252
Baisieux, 297
Bancourt, 271
Bapaume, 46, 72
Bapaume, battle of (Aug. 21–Sept. 1), xii, 361; scheme of operations, 264, 265; opening attacks—Albert, 265, 266; main attack launched, 266–269; Bapaume taken, 269, 270; fight for Mont St. Quentin and capture of Peronne, 270, 271; results, 271, 272; withdrawal from Lys salient, 272, 273
Barastre, 73, 199
Barnes, Maj.-Gen. R. W. R., 67, 281
Barter, Maj.-Gen. Sir C. St. L., 20, 41 n.
Bassevillebeek, 121
Battle Wood, 107
Bavai, 296, 297
Bayonvillers, 210
Bazentin-le-Grand, 29

Bazentin-le-Petit, 23, 29, 30
Beaucoup, 281
Beaucourt-sur-Ancre, 49, 50, 65, 66, 203
Beaulencourt, 46, 271
Beaumetz, 74, 192, 197
Beaumont Hamel, 26, 47 n., 49, 50, 66
Beaurains, 73, 75
Beauregard Dovecot, 69
Beaurevoir, 284
Becelaere, 286
Behagnies, 269
Beho, 313
Belgians, H.M. the King of the, 290
Bell, Maj.-Gen. G., 262
Bellenglise, 282
Bellevue Spur, 131
Bellewaarde Ridge, 114
Bellicourt, 283
Benay, 189
Benson, Col. E., 355
Bernafay, 27
Bertincourt, 73, 199
Bethell, Maj.-Gen. H. K., 288
Bethencourt, 196, 201
Beugny, 197, 271
Beugny-Ytres line, 73
Biache St. Vaast, 289
Biddulph, Brig.-Gen. H., 351
Biefvillers, 268
Bihucourt, 202, 267
Birch, Maj.-Gen. Sir J. F. N. (Lt.-Gen.), 240, 351
Birdwood, Lt.-Gen. Sir W. R. (Gen.), 70, 96 n., 286
Bixschoote, 114, 230
Black Watch Corner, 122
Blackader, Maj.-Gen. C. G., 113 n.
Blacklock, Maj.-Gen. C. A., 233, 275
Blankaart Lake, 131
Blécourt, 284
Bluff, 5–7, 104
Bohain, 288
Boiry Becquerelle, 267
Bois du Sart, 274
Bois-en-Hache, 93
Bois Hugo, 117
Bois l'Abbaye, 295
Bois l'Evêque, 293
Bois Rasé, 117
Bols, Maj.-Gen. L. J., 107 n., 113 n., 352
Bombing raids into Germany, 138
Bonavis Ridge, 155, 165
Bonham-Carter, Brig.-Gen. C., 356
Bonn, 318
Bony, 283, 284
Boraston, Maj. J. H., 356
Bouchavesnes, 64, 198, 271
Bouchoir, 262
Bouleaux Wood, 38
Boulogne, hospital at, 338
Bourlon, 158–162, 168, 281

INDEX 367

Bousies Forest, 293
Boyce, Maj.-Gen. Sir W. G. B., 355
Boyd, Maj.-Gen. G. F., 282
Boyelles, 267
Braches, 260
Braithwaite, Maj.-Gen. W. P. (Lt.-Gen. Sir), 93, 155, 208, 255, 294
Brancourt, 288
Bray, Maj.-Gen. Sir C. A., 355
Bray-sur-Somme, 200, 262, 268
Bremen Redoubt, 122
Bridges, Maj.-Gen. G. T. M., 27, 65 n., 107 n.
Bridgford, Maj.-Gen. R. J., 197
Brie Bridge, 73, 76
Briqueterie, 26, 27
British Offensive, opening of final (Aug., 1918), *following* 262; second battle of Le Cateau (Oct. 8), *facing* 287
British Red Cross Society, 343
Broenbeek, 128
Broodseinde, 125, 333
Brouchy, 196
Brussilov's Galician offensive, 20 n.
Brutinel, Maj.-Gen., 260
Bry, 296
Buckland, Maj.-Gen. R. U. H., 352
Buckle, Maj.-Gen. C. R., 353
Bucquoy, 207, 211, 212, 215
Budworth, Maj.-Gen. C. E. D., 352
Bughas, Col. de Bellaigue de, 356
Buissy, 275
Bullecourt, 93, 99, 102, 157, 180, 269, 271
Burnett-Stuart, Maj.-Gen. J. T., 354
Burstall, Maj.-Gen. H. E. (Sir), 89 n., 273
Burtchaell, Lt.-Gen. C. H., 307, 354
Bus, 73, 199
Bussu, 73
Butler, Lt.-Gen. Sir R. H. K., 184, 260, 350
Buzancy, 256
Byng, Lt.-Gen. Sir J. H. G. (Gen. the Hon.), 44, 87, 152, 173, 184, 265, 271, 349

Cabaret Rouge, 5
Cachy, 231
Cagnicourt, 275
Caix, 261
Cambrai and the Hindenburg Line, battle of (Sept. 27–Oct. 5), xii, 361; battle opened, 280–282; Hindenburg Line broken, 282–284; Montbrehain and Beaurevoir, 284; results, 284, 285
Cambrai Line (Nov. 20, 1917), *facing* 154; (Nov. 30), *facing* 163; (Sept. 27, 1918), *facing* 280

Cambrai operations—General plan, 151–153; enemy's defences, 153, 154; the attack, 154–157; advance continued, 157, 158; position on Nov. 21, 158, 159; decision to go on, 159, 160; struggle for Bourlon Wood, 160–162; German attacks—early warnings, 162; our dispositions for defence, 163; battle re-opened, 164, 165; the northern attack, 166, 167; fighting at Gonnelieu and Masnières, 168, 169; withdrawal from Bourlon, 169, 170; results, 170; general review, 171–173
Cameron, Maj.-Gen. N. J. G., 226, 294
Campaigns of 1917—General Allied plan, 81–85; spring campaign, 85–102; summer campaign, 103–132; general review, 133–135; defensive fronts, 135; our troops, 136; Infantry, 136; Artillery, 136, 137; Royal Flying Corps, 137–139; Anti-Aircraft and Searchlight Sections, 139; Cavalry, 139; Special Services, 139; Tanks, 139; Trench Mortars, 139; Machine Gun Corps, 140; Royal Engineers, 140; Signal Services, 141; Gas Services, 141, 142; Field Survey Companies, 142; Meteorological Section, 142; Transportation Services, 142, 143; Forestry and Quarry Units, 143, 144; Army Service Corps, 144; Ordnance Corps, 144; Medical Services, 144, 145; Veterinary Corps, 145; Chaplains' Department, 145; Army Commanders, 145; Staff, 146; Army's acknowledgments—to the Navy, 146; to Home Authorities, 147; to our Allies, 147
See also Arras, battle of; Messines, battle of; Ypres, third battle of.
Campbell, Maj.-Gen. D. G. M., 25 n., 88 n., 187, 252
Campbell, Maj.-Gen. J., 251
Campbell, Col. R. B., 354
Canadian Army Medical Corps, 13
Canal de l'Escaut, 155, 156
Cantaing, 158, 160
Canteens, Expeditionary Force, 338
Capello, Col. C., 356
Capper, Maj.-Gen. J. E., 6, 93
Carey, Maj.-Gen. G. G. S., 205, 206, 210, 214, 286
Carrier Pigeon Service, 141, 334
Carter, Maj.-Gen. Sir E. E., 354
Carter-Campbell, Maj.-Gen. G. T. C., 189, 255
Cassel, Conference of Allied Armies at (Sept. 9, 1918), 285
Casualties, extent of, 323, 324

Caterpillar Wood, 27
Catillon, 295
Cator, Maj.-Gen. A. B. E., 131, 191
Cattigny Wood, 288
Caudry, 288
Cavalry Farm, 102
Cavalry in modern war, value of, 54, 327, 328
Cavan, F. R., Lt.-Gen. the Earl of, 41 n., 113
Cavendish, Brig.-Gen. F. W. L. S. H., 356
Cayley, Maj.-Gen. D. E., 226, 250
Cérisy, 209
Channel Train Ferry, 305
Chantilly, Conference of Allied Powers at (Nov., 1916), 81
Chapel Hill, 189
Chaplains, Army, 342
Chapperton Down Artillery School, 332
Charleroi, 313
Charles, Maj.-Gen. J. R. E., 288
Charteris, Brig.-Gen. J., 350
Château Thierry, 253
Chaulnes, 72
Chauny, 202, 275
Chemin de Fer du Nord, 77
Chemin des Dames, 100, 253
Chérisy, 100, 274
Chichester, Maj.-Gen. A. A., 353
Chipilly, 261
Chuignes, 267
Chuignolles, 267
Cité des Petits Bois, 98
Cité St. Auguste, 117
Cité St. Emile, 117
Cité St. Laurent, 117
Cité Ste. Elizabeth, 117
Clarence River, 226
Clarke, Lt.-Gen. Travers (Sir), 240, 351
Clary, 288
Cléry, 38, 199, 200, 270
Clive, Brig.-Gen. G. S., 350, 356
Coffin, Maj.-Gen. C., 285
Colincamps, 207
Cologne, 317, 318
Combe, Capt. E. P. (M.C., Brig. Major), 206
Combles, 39, 43, 199, 269
Comines, 286
Comines-Ypres Canal, 6
Commegnies, 296
Condé, 297
Conference at Cassel (Sept. 9, 1918), 285; at Chantilly (Nov., 1916), 81; at Paris (May 4, 5, 1917), 100 n.
Congreve, Lt.-Gen. W. N. (Sir), 25 n., 88, 184
Contalmaison, 27, 28
Contoire, 210

Cortemarck, 290
Coulaincourt, 194
Couper, Maj.-Gen. V. A., 5, 41 n., 88 n.
Courcelette, 42, 203, 268
Courcelles, 266
Cox, Brig.-Gen. E. W., 240, 350
Cox, Maj.-Gen. Sir H. V., 36 n.
Crest Farm, 132
Crèvecœur, 284
Croisilles, 190, 269
Croix du Bac, 222
Crookshanks, Maj.-Gen. S. D'A. (Brig.-Gen.), 240, 351
Crozat Canal, 189, 190, 195, 275
Cubitt, Maj.-Gen. T. A., 269
Cugny, 196, 201
Currie, Maj.-Gen. A. W. (Lt.-Gen. Sir), 20, 89, 117, 260, 273
Cuthbert, Maj.-Gen. C. J., 113 n.
Cutting-out parties or raids, 4
Czernovitz, 20 n.

Dadizeele, 286
Daly, Maj.-Gen. A. C., 187, 296
Damery, 263
Dam Strasse, 107
Davenscourt, 210
Davidson, M.P., Maj.-Gen. J. H. (Sir), 127 n., 240, 355
Davidson, Maj. T. (D.S.O.), 206
Davies, Maj.-Gen. H. R., 107 n., 282
Davies, Maj.-Gen. R. H., 5
Davy, Miss Lila, 355
Dawnay, Maj.-Gen. G. P., 240, 356
Dawson, Maj.-Gen. R., 48
Debeney, Gen., 259, 260
Delville Wood, 23, 30, 34, 35, 269
Demicourt, 189
Demuin, 214
Denain, 292
Dernancourt, 211
Despatch Rider Letter Service, 334, 335
Despatches, sources of information and methods of collection, v, vi
Destremont Farm, 45
Deverell, Maj.-Gen. C. J., 50, 66, 88 n., 157, 190, 266
Dill, Brig.-Gen. J. G., 355
Dixmude, 181
Dobbie, Lt.-Col. W. G. S., 356
Docks, Directorate of, 335
Doignies, 75, 188, 189
Dormans, 253
Douai, 291
Doulieu, 226
Douve valley, 223
Draaibank, 128
Dreyer, Col. J. T., 351
Drie Grachten, 118
Drocourt-Quéant Line, 86, 96, 274

INDEX 369

Du Cane, Lt.-Gen. Sir J. P., 220, 356
Dudgeon, Maj.-Gen. F. A., 119, 160, 211
Dumbarton Lakes, 122
Dummy tanks, 277 n.
Duncan, Maj. G. F. J., 294
Dury, 275

Eaucourt, 201
Eaucourt l'Abbaye, 45
Ecoust St. Mein, 188
Edmonds, Brig.-Gen. J. E., 351
Eleu dit Leauvette, 110
Elles, Maj.-Gen. H. J., 302, 353
Elliot, Lt.-Gen. Sir E. Locke, 354
Embury, Brig.-Gen. J. F. L., 354
Engineering Stores, Directorate of, 337
Epéhy, 75, 187, 192, 276, 277
Epéhy, battle of Havrincourt and (Sept. 12-18): see Havrincourt
Epinoy, 282
Equancourt, 194
Erches, 206
Ervillers, 202, 267
Esnes, 288
Estaires, 222, 223
Estrées, 284
Etaples, hospital at, 338
Eterpigny, 274
Eth, 296

Faillouel, 196
Falfemont Farm, 35, 37, 38
Fampoux Village, 90
Fanny's Farm, 107
Fanshawe, Lt.-Gen. Sir E. A., 184
Fanshawe, Maj.-Gen. H. D., 102 n.
Fanshawe, Maj.-Gen. R., 30, 73, 119
Farbus Wood, 90
Fargnier, 188
Favreuil, 269
Features of the War—A single great battle, 319-321; length of the War, 321-323; extent of our casualties, 323-325; why we attacked whenever possible, 325, 326; end of the War, 326, 327; value of cavalry in modern war, 327, 328; value of mechanical contrivances, 329; close and complete co-operation between all arms and services, 330-333; Signal Service, 334, 335; Rearward Services and Personnel — Transportation, 335 - 340; Replacement, Discipline and Welfare of Troops, 340-343; Training and Organisation, 343-346; our New Armies, 346-349
Feetham, Maj.-Gen. E., 121, 194
Feilding, Maj.-Gen. G. P. T., 41 n., 113 n., 162, 199, 269

Fergusson, Lt.-Gen. Sir C. (Bart.), 87, 184, 271, 318
Fesmy, 295
Festubert, 225, 230
Feuchy, 90
Feuillières, 270
Field Survey Companies, 56
Final Despatch—Advance into Germany — arrangements for the advance, 311, 312; re-adjustment of British forces, 312; advance to German frontier, 313, 314; supply difficulties, 314-316; further re-adjustment of troops, 316; advance into Germany, 317; British troops in Cologne, 317; occupation of Cologne bridgehead, 318; conduct of the troops, 318, 319; features of the War, 319-349; my thanks to Commanders and Staffs, 349-357 See also Features of the War.
Flanders, battle in (Sept. 28-Oct. 14), xii, 83, 84, 285, 361; withdrawal from Lens and Armentières, 286, 287
Flash spotting, 331 n.
Flers, 42, 269
Flesquières, 155, 157, 170, 188, 189, 192, 194, 281
Fletcher, Lt.-Col. A. F., 356
Fleurbaix, 222
Foch, Field-Marshal, Introduction by, ix-xiii, 358; Generalissimo, 208, 229, 254
Fontaine-les-Clercs, 193
Fontaine-lez-Croisilles, 94, 99, 102
Fontaine-notre-Dame, 158, 160-162, 168, 281, 282
Ford, Maj.-Gen. R., 354
Forenville, 288
Forestry Directorate, 143, 338
Foulkes, Brig.-Gen. C. H., 354
Four Winds Farm, 198
Fowke, Lt.-Gen. Sir G. H., 146, 240, 350
Fowler, Maj.-Gen. Sir J. S., 240, 351
Framerville, 209, 262
Franks, Maj.-Gen. G. McK., 130, 353
Fransart, 263
Frasnoy, 296
Frégicourt, 43, 271
Frélinghien, 290
Frémicourt, 271
French, Field-Marshal Viscount, 15
Fresnoy, 99, 100, 102, 262
Frezenberg, 114
Fricourt, 25-27
Friend, Maj.-Gen. the Rt. Hon. L. B., 355
Furze, Maj.-Gen. W. T., 29

Gapaard, 108
Garratt, Maj.-Gen. Sir F. S., 355
Gas shell, new forms of, 332; and liquid flame employed by British, 55
Gauche Wood, 168
Gavrelle, 97, 99, 274
Geddes, Maj.-Gen. Sir Eric, 77, 351
Geleide Creek, 111
Gellibrand, Maj.-Gen. J., 283
Gemeau, Commandant E. A., 356
German gas attacks at St. Eloi, 8, 9
German offensive, the great—General situation, 177; transition from offensive to defensive policy, 177; extension of British front, 178; man-power and training, 178, 179; preparations for defence, 179; arrangements for co-operation with French, 180; operations during the winter, 180, 181; indications of coming attack, 182; British dispositions to meet enemy's offensive, 182, 183; situation on eve of attack, 183, 184; enemy's dispositions, 184, 185; comparison of forces engaged, 185, 186; the second Somme battle, 186-218; situation on northern front, 218, 219; Lys battle opened, 220-222; crossing at Bac St. Maur, 222; struggle for Estaires, 223; attack at Messines, 223; withdrawal from Armentières, 224; fall of Merville, 224; withdrawal from Nieppe and Hill 63, 225; southern flank steady, 225, 226; thrust towards Hazebrouck, 226, 227; struggle for Neuve Eglise, 228; capture of Bailleul, 228; withdrawal at Passchendaele, 229; arrival of French troops, 229; first attacks on Kemmel, 229, 230; operations north of Bethune, 230, 231; attacks on Villers Bretonneux, 231, 232; capture of Kemmel Hill, 232, 233; enemy's advance stayed, 233, 234; task of British armies, 234, 235; our Troops, 235; Infantry, 236; Artillery, 236; Cavalry, 237; Royal Air Force, 237; Tank Corps, 237; Machine Guns and Trench Mortars, 238; Royal Engineers, 238; other Services, 239; Commanders and Staffs, 239, 240; Home Authorities and Royal Navy, 241; our Allies, 241
See also Somme, second battle.
Gheluvelt, 131
Gheluwe, 286
Gibb, Brig.-Gen. E., 355
Gillemont Farm, 283
Ginchy, 37, 38, 225, 230, 238

Girdwood, Maj.-Gen. E. S., 277
Givenchy-en-Gohelle, 94
Glasgow, Maj.-Gen. T. W., 267
Glencorse Wood, 115, 122
Glubb, Maj.-Gen. Sir F. M., 353
Godley, Lt.-Gen. Sir A. J., 106 n., 220, 255
Goligher, Brig.-Gen. H. G., 355
Gommecourt, 25, 26, 70
Gonnelieu, 165, 168, 172, 282, 284
Gordon, Lt.-Gen. Sir A. Hamilton, 220, 252, 254 n.
Gorringe, Maj.-Gen. Sir G. F., 45, 107 n., 166, 198, 268
Goudberg Spur, 132
Gough, Gen. Sir H. de la P., 27, 30, 35, 57, 58, 76, 88, 113, 184, 210, 349
Gouy, 284
Gouzeaucourt, 165, 280
Government Farm, 198
Graham, Maj.-Gen. Sir E. R. C., 354
Graincourt, 156, 170, 281
Grammont, 297
Grand Bois, 107, 233
Grandcourt, 26, 64, 66, 67
Grant, Maj.-Gen. P. G., 205, 352
Gravenstafel, 125, 127
Graves Registration and Enquiries, Commission of, 13, 342
Greenland Hill, 97, 98, 102, 110, 212, 274
Greenly, Maj.-Gen. W. H., 92, 163
Grévillers, 71, 202, 268
Gricourt, 277
Guémappe, 97, 98, 273
Gueudecourt, 43, 48
Guillemont, 35-38
Guiscard, 201, 204
Guise, 296
Gwynne, Rt. Rev. Bishop L. H., 307, 355

Haking, Lt.-Gen. Sir R. C. B., 220, 291
Haldane, Maj.-Gen. J. A. L. (Lt.-Gen. Sir), 6, 29, 87, 184, 265
Ham, 196, 201, 275
Hambro, Maj.-Gen. P. O., 352
Hamel, 215, 251, 267, 268
Hamilton-Gordon, Lt.-Gen. A., 107 n.
Hancourt, 73
Hangard, 215, 231
Hangest-en-Santerre, 210
Harbonnières, 209, 261
Hardecourt, 269
Hargicourt, 187
Harington, Maj.-Gen. C. H., 353
Harlebeke, 290
Harman, Maj.-Gen. A. E. W., 201, 262
Harp, 89
Harper, Maj.-Gen. G. M. (Lt.-Gen. Sir), 35, 89 n., 113 n., 155, 184, 265

INDEX 371

Harrison, Brig.-Gen. G. H., 355
Harvey, Brig.-Gen. R. N., 354
Haspres, 292
Hattencourt, 206
Haute Deule Canal, 291
Hautmont, 297
Hautrève, 295
Havrincourt, 75, 155, 170, 192
Havrincourt and Epéhy, battle of (Sept. 12–18), xii, 276, 361; development of Allied plan, 277; rôle of British armies, 278; the Hindenburg Line, 278, 279
Haynecourt, 282
Hazebrouck, 227
Heath, Maj.-Gen. G. M. (Sir), 240, 351, 353
Hébuterne, 213
Hendecourt, 269, 271
Heneker, Maj.-Gen. W. C. G., 75, 113 n., 201, 252
Henin, 199 n., 269
Héninel, 93, 94
Henin-sur-Cojeul, 73, 75, 269
Herbécourt, 206
Herbignies, 295
Herleville, 267
Hermies, 96, 192
Hervilly, 191, 192 n.
Heurtebise, 295
Hickie, Maj.-Gen. W. B., 37 n., 107 n., 157
Higginson, Maj.-Gen. H. W., 262
High Wood, 30, 34, 35, 37, 42
Hill 60, 104
Hill 63, 225, 273
Hill 70, 117
Hill 145, 89, 91, 92
Hill, Maj.-Gen. J., 269
Hindenburg Line, 278, 279; (Sept. 29, 1918), *facing* 282
Hindenburg Line, battle of: *see* Cambrai and the Hindenburg Line, battle of.
Hindenburg Line, retreat to the—Nature of operations, 63, 64; operations on the Ancre, 65–78; enemy's retreat, 71–75; general review, 75–78
See also Ancre, operations on the.
Hirings and Requisitions, Directorate of, 339
Hobbs, Maj.-Gen. J. J. T. (Sir), 102 n., 231, 283
Holland, Lt.-Gen. Sir Arthur, 88, 220, 297
Hollebeke, 115, 223
Holman, Maj.-Gen. H. C., 352
Holmes, Maj.-Gen. W., 75, 93, 106 n.
Holnon, 193, 276
Honnechy, 288
Honnelle river, 296, 297
Hooge, 20, 114, 137

Horne, Lt.-Gen. H. S. (Gen. Sir), 25 n., 41 n., 87, 198, 220, 275, 349
Houthulst Forest, 130, 286
Howell, Lt.-Col. G. L. H., 354
Hudson, Maj.-Gen. H., 25 n., 48
Huit Maisons, 222
Hull, Maj.-Gen. C. P. A. (Sir), 25 n., 41 n., 88 n., 269
Hunter-Weston, Lt.-Gen. Sir A. J., 25 n.
Hyderabad Redoubt, 90

Indian Army Corps, departure for the East, 12
Infantry Hill, 97, 110
Ingouville-Williams, Maj.-Gen. E. C., 25 n.
Inland Water Transport, 336
Inverness Copse, 115, 120, 122
Irles, 70, 71, 268
Iseghem, 290
Isonzo, 152 n.

Jack, Lt.-Col. E. M., 356
Jack, Major F. C. (M.C.), 226
Jackson, Maj.-Gen. H. C., 209, 252
Jacob, Lt.-Gen. C. W. (Sir), 44, 113, 220, 290
Jeancourt, 75
Jeffreys, Maj.-Gen. G. D., 189, 252
Jeudwine, Maj.-Gen. H. S. (Sir), 113 n., 164, 220, 286
Joffre, Gen., 19, 20, 81 n., 83 n.
Jolimetz, 295
Joncourt, 284
Jussy, 191, 195

Kavanagh, Lt.-Gen. Sir C. T. M'M., 87, 260
Keerselaarhoek, 129
Kemmel Hill, 230, 232, 273
Kennedy, Maj.-Gen. A. A., 165
Kenyon, Maj.-Gen. E. R., 353
Ker, Brig.-Gen. C. A., 356
Kiggell, Lt.-Gen. Sir L. E., 146, 350
Kippe, 131
Knockshoek, 131
Kortewilde, 286
Kruiseecke, 286

La Basse Ville, 115
La Becque, 225, 226, 251
La Boisselle, 26, 27
Labour, Controller of, 339
La Coulotte, 110
Lacouture, 222
La Crèche, 228
La Fère, 187
La Folie, 89, 295
Lagnicourt, 96, 187–189
La Groise, 295
Laguiche, Gen. de, 356

Lambert, Maj.-Gen. T. S., 267
Lambton, Maj.-Gen. Hon. W., 25 n., 48, 89 n.
La Montagne, 191
Landon, Maj.-Gen. H. J. S., 34
Landrecies, 295
Langemarck, 118
Laon, 289
La Potterie Farm, 108
Larken, Lt.-Col. E., 355
Lateau Wood, 155, 164
La Terrière, 284
Laurie, Maj.-Gen. C. E., 97, 203
La Vacquerie, 155, 164–166, 169, 181
Lawe River, 250
Lawford, Maj.-Gen. S. T. B. (Sir), 41 n., 107 n., 197, 285
Lawley, Col. the Hon. Sir Arthur, 355
Lawrence, Maj.-Gen. the Hon. Sir H. A. (Lt.-Gen.), 129 n., 240, 350
Lawrie, Maj.-Gen. C. E., 265
Le Barque, 70
Le Bucquière, 197
Le Cateau, second battle of (Oct. 6–12), xii, 287, 288, 361; withdrawal from Laon, 289; advance in Flanders resumed, 289, 290; evacuation of Lille, 290, 291
Le Catelet, 284
Lechelle, 199
Lecky, Maj.-Gen. R. St. C., 353
Ledeghem, 286
Lee, Maj.-Gen. R. P., 66, 100, 113 n., 189, 266, 352
Le Forest, 38
Lehaucourt, 283
Leipzig Salient, 26
Le Mesnil-en-Arrouaise, 199
Lempire, 75
L'Enfer Hill, 107
Lens, 117
Le Preseau, 297
Le Quesnel, 261
Le Quesnoy, 206, 294, 295
Le Sars, 45, 48
Les Bœufs, 43, 46, 48, 200
Les Rues des Vignes, 157
Les Tilleuls, 89
Lestrem, 223
Le Touret, 221
Le Transloy, 46, 48, 70
Le Transloy-Loupart Line, 65, 71
Le Triez, 269
Le Tronquoy, 283 n., 284
Le Tronquoy Tunnel, 283, 284
Leuze Wood, 37, 38
Levergies, 283 n., 284
Le Verguier, 187, 192, 193, 276
Le Verrier, 225
Lewis, Maj.-Gen. E. M., 283
Liancourt, 205
Libermont Canal, 205

Licourt, 205
Liddell, Maj.-Gen. W. A., 353
Liévin, 94
Ligny-Thilloy, 70, 202
Lihons, 262
Lille, 290, 291
Limerick Post, 165
Lipsett, Maj.-Gen. L. J., 20, 89 n., 273
Lisle, Maj.-Gen. H. de B. de (Lt.-Gen. Sir), 25 n., 95, 155, 211, 291
Locon, 226
Locquignol, 295
Locre, 233, 234, 250
Logeast Wood, 266
Lombartzyde attack, 111
London Gazette (May 26, 1916), 3 n.; (Dec. 29, 1916), 19 n.; (June 19, 1917), 63 n.; (Jan. 4, 1918), 81 n.; (Mar. 1, 1918), 151 n.; (Oct. 21, 1918), 177 n.; (Jan. 3, 1919), 245 n.; (April 8, 1919), 311 n.
Longatte, 188, 271
Longueval, 29, 30, 34, 35, 269
Loomis, Maj.-Gen. F. O. W., 281
Louage Wood, 38
Loupart, 71, 268
Louverval, 188
Louvignies, 295
Lovat, Brig.-Gen. Lord, 355
Lucas, Maj.-Gen. C. H. T. (Brig.-Gen.), 294, 354
Luck, Brig.-Gen. C. M., 355
Ludendorff's *Memoirs*, 75 n., 91 n., 126 n., 133 n., 199 n., 211 n., 263 n.
Luisenhof Farm, 69
Lukin, Maj.-Gen. T., 89 n.
Lutsk, 20 n.
Ly-Fontaine, 189
Lys, 272
Lys battle, 220–222
Lys Line (April 10, 1918), *facing* 220; (April 25), *facing* 232

Macandrew, Maj.-Gen. H. J. M., 74, 156
Macdonell, Maj.-Gen. A. C., 117, 281
Machine Gun Corps, 55
Mackenzie, Maj.-Gen. C. J., 72, 163, 194
Macpherson, Surg.-Gen. Sir W. G., 354
Macready, Lt.-Gen. Sir Nevil, 350
Magny la Fosse, 283
Maing, 293
Maissemy, 188, 276
Maistre, Gen., 254 n.
Malcolm, Maj.-Gen. N., 192, 352
Malincourt, 288
Maltz Horn Farm, 28
Mametz, 26–28

INDEX

Mangelare, 128
Marcelcave, 210
Marchélepot, 205
Marcoing, 155, 168, 282
Marden, Maj.-Gen. T. O. (Sir), 155, 188, 250
Maresches, 294
Marfaux, 255
Marindin, Maj.-Gen. A. H., 285
Marne, 255
Marquise Quarries, 143 n.
Marrières Wood, 199
Marshall, Maj.-Gen. F. J., 281
Martinpuich, 42, 268
Marvilles, 296
Masnières, 155–158, 172, 283
Matheson, Maj.-Gen. T. G., 75, 126, 211, 275, 281
Mathew, Maj.-Gen. Sir C. M., 354
Maubeuge, 297
Maxse, Maj.-Gen. F. I. (Lt.-Gen. Sir), 25 n., 65 n., 87, 184, 351
Maxwell, Lt.-Gen. Sir R. C., 146, 351
May, Maj.-Gen. R. S., 354
Maybury, Brig.-Gen. H. P., 355
McCracken, Maj.-Gen. F. W. N., 36 n., 41 n., 88 n.
Meault, 207
Meaurain, 296
Medical Services, 13, 57, 78; Director-General of, 342
Méharicourt, 262
Mennessis, 195
Mercatel, 75, 265, 266
Mercer, Maj.-Gen. H. F., 353
Merckem, 131
Méricourt, 286
Merris, 226, 230, 250–252
Merville, 224–226, 230, 250, 272
Messenger Dog Service, 334
Messines, 223, 225, 286, 332
Messines battle—Preparations for attack, 103; underground warfare, 103, 104; description of front, 105; German defences, 105; preparations completed, 106; the assault, 106–108; subsequent operations, 108, 109
Messines Line (June 7, 1917), *facing* 106
Messines-Wytschaete Ridge, 105
Messing and Economies, Inspectorate of, 337
Meteren, 228–231, 251
Metz-en-Couture, 75
Mezières, 214, 295
Military Prisons, Director of, 341
Miraumont, 68, 69, 268
Mœuvres, 158, 161, 280, 281
Moislains Wood, 72
Molenaarelsthoek, 125
Monash, Maj.-Gen. J. (Lt.-Gen. Sir), 106 n., 214, 251, 260

Monchy-le-Preux, 91, 92, 95, 139, 265, 273
Monro, Gen. Sir Charles, 349
Mons, 297
Montagne de Bligny, 253, 255
Montaubon, 25, 200
Montbrehain, 284
Montdidier, 210, 214, 262
Montgomery, Maj.-Gen. Sir A. A., 352
Mont St. Quentin, 73, 270, 271
Moore, Maj.-Gen. J., 355
Moorseele, 290
Morchain, 201
Morchies, 73
Morcourt, 209, 261, 262
Moreuil, 214
Morlancourt, 250
Morland, Lt.-Gen. Sir T. L. N., 25 n., 107 n., 295
Mormal, 24, 43, 45, 200, 271, 292–295
Mory, 195, 197, 199, 269
Mosselmarkt, 132
Mount Sorrel, 127
Mouquet Farm, 44
Moyenneville, 266
Mullens, Maj.-Gen. R. L., 92, 158 n., 192, 262
Murray, Brig.-Gen. V., 355

Namur, 313
Nash, Maj.-Gen. Sir F. A. M., 351
Nauroy, 283
Nesle, 73, 205, 206, 270
Neuf Berquin, 224
Neuf Wood, 155
Neuve Eglise, 228, 273
Neuville Vitasse, 89
Neuvilly, 292
Nicholson, Maj.-Gen. C. L., 36 n., 89 n., 190
Nieppe, 225
Niergnies, 288
Nieuwemolen, 129
19 Metre Hill, 126
Nivelle, Gen., 83 n., 100 n.
Nonne Boschen, 122
Noordemdhoek, 125
Noreuil, 73, 96, 188, 196
Noyelles, 156, 158, 282
Noyon, 204, 270
Nugent, Maj.-Gen. O. S. W., 25 n., 107 n., 155, 196
Nurlu, 73

Observation Ridge, 89, 90
Offoy, 196
O'Gowan, Maj.-Gen. R. Wanless, 25 n., 110
Oisy-le-Verger, 282
Ollezy, 196

Omignon River, 101
Oosttaverne, 105, 106, 108
Oppy, 110, 289
Orange Hill, 92, 265
Ordnance Corps, 56; Service, Directorate of, 337; Survey Department, 14
Orival Wood, 281
Ors, 295
Orsinval, 296
Orth, Lt.-Gen. A. L. E., 356
O'Ryan, Maj.-Gen. J. F., 283
Ostend, 290
Outtersteene, 226, 264
Ovillers, 26, 28, 30, 268

Pacaut, 226
Paget, Lt.-Col. C. W., 355
Palluel, 282
Pargny, 201
Paris, Conference at (May 4, 5, 1917), 100 n.
Partridge, Col. S. G., 355
Parvillers, 263
Passchendaele, 130, 132, 229
Peck, Maj.-Gen. A. W., 353
Peizière, 187
Pendant Copse, 26
Perceval, Maj.-Gen. E. M., 26 n., 129 n.
Percy, Maj.-Gen. J. S. J., 352, 353
Pereira, Maj.-Gen. C. E., 68, 69, 166, 198, 281
Peronne, 73, 195, 270, 275
Peruwelz, 297
Petain, Gen., 100 n., 198 n.
Petillon, 221
Petit Miraumont, 68
Petit Vimy, 94
Peyton, Maj.-Gen. Sir W. E., 291, 351
Phillips, Maj.-Gen. I., 27
Pierrepont, 261
Pilcher, Maj.-Gen. T. D., 6, 27
Pilckem, 114
Pill-boxes, 118
Pimple, 93
Pinney, Maj.-Gen. R. J. (Sir), 34, 102, 226, 250
Pithon, 196
Pitman, Maj.-Gen. T. T., 191, 262
Plessier, 261
Ploegsteert, 223, 225, 286
Plouvain, 274
Plumer, Gen. Sir Herbert, 101, 106, 119, 198, 220, 290, 312, 316, 349
Poelcappelle, 126, 129, 286
Pœuilly, 194
Point du Jour, 90
Polderhoek Château, 125, 126, 131, 180
Polygon Wood, 122, 124, 129
Pommereuil, 293

Pommern Redoubt, 114
Ponsonby, Maj.-Gen. J., 160, 197, 268
Pont-à-Vendin, 291
Pont d'Achelles, 225
Pont d'Aire, 288
Pont Riqueul, 222
Pont Tournant, 251
Pozières, 35, 268
Prémont, 288
Premy Chapel, 281
Preseau, 294
Preux-au-Bois, 295
Preux-au-Sart, 296
Price, Maj.-Gen. W., 355
Printing and Stationery Services, Directorate of, 341, 342
Prisches, 296
Prisoners of War Section, 342
Promotion by Merit, 347, 348
Proyart, 209, 262
Puisieux-au-Mont, 70
Pulteney, Lt.-Gen. Sir W. P., 25 n., 41 n.
Pys, 69, 268

Quadrilateral, 42
Quéant, 274, 275
Queen Alexandra's Imperial Military Nursing Service, 342
Queen Mary's Auxiliary Army Corps, 343
Quessy, 189, 191
Quiévrechain, 297

Radnor, Brig.-Gen. J., Earl of, 355
Railway Triangle, 89, 90
Ramicourt, 284
Ramillies, 288
Ramsay, Maj.-Gen. F. W., 269
Rancourt, 43, 199, 271
Ravebeek, 131
Ravelsberg Heights, 228, 229
Ravine Wood, 107
Rawlins, Col. S. W. H., 351
Rawlinson, Gen. Sir H. S. (Bart.), 26, 29, 31, 57, 58, 76, 88, 259, 261, 313, 349
Read, Gen. G. W., 282
Reed, Maj.-Gen. H. L., 211, 255
Regina Trench, 48
Remounts, Directorate of, 336
Renaix, 297
Renny, Brig.-Gen. L. F., 354
Retreat to Hindenburg Line: see Hindenburg Line; Ancre, operations on the.
Reumont, 288
Reutel, 120, 125, 129
Reutelbeek, 124
Rhonelle river, 294

INDEX

Riaumont Wood, 94
Ribécourt, 170, 281
Rice, Maj.-Gen. Sir S. R., 351
Ridge Wood, 250
Riencourt-les-Bapaume, 271
Riencourt-lez-Cagnicourt, 93, 269, 271
Riez du Vinage, 226, 228
Riquerval Wood, 288
Ritchie, Maj.-Gen. A. B., 66, 286
Roads, Directorate of, 336
Robertson, Maj.-Gen. P. R., 129, 188, 269
Roclincourt, 89
Rocquigny, 199, 271
Rœux, 93, 97, 100, 102, 212, 274
Rogers, Brig.-Gen. H. S., 354
Roisel, 192
Roisin, 296
Rombies, 296
Romer, Maj.-Gen. C. F., 124
Ronssoy, 75, 187, 188
Rosenthal, Maj.-Gen. C., 270
Rosières, 209
Ross, Maj.-Gen. C., 41 n.
Rossignol Wood, 215
Roubaix, 291
Rouge de Bout, 221
Roupy, 189
Route "A" Keep, 230
Rouvroy, 262
Roye, 64, 205, 270
Ruesnes, 293
Ruggles-Brise, Maj.-Gen. H. G., 351
Rumilly, 156, 284
Russell, Maj.-Gen. A. H. (Sir), 41 n., 106 n., 207, 268
Russian revolution on French operations, effect of, 84
Ruyaulcourt, 75
Rycroft, Maj.-Gen. W. H., 25 n., 65 n.

Saillisel, 199
Sailly, 282
Sailly-le-Sec, 208
Sailly-Saillisel, 46-48, 64, 271
Sailly-sur-la-Lys, 249 n.
Sains-lez-Marquion, 281, 282
St. Christ, 201
St. Eloi—Local operations, 3-15; Ypres Salient and the Bluff (Feb. 8-Mar. 2, 1916), 5-7; German gas attacks, 8, 9; troops engaged, 9-11; Royal Flying Corps, 12; Royal Engineers, 13; Tunnelling Companies, 13; Military Police, 13; Medical Services, 13; Canadian Army Medical Corps, 13; Graves Registration and Enquiries, Commission of, 13; Central Laboratory and Chemical Advisers, 14; Administrative Services, 14; Ordnance Survey Department, 14

St. Eloi, map *facing* 7
St. Hilaire, 288
St. Janshoek, 128, 131
St. Julien, 114-117
St. Laurent Blangy, 90
St. Leger, 73, 190, 193, 197, 269
St. Martin-sur-Cojeul, 90, 269
St. Mihiel, 277
St. Olle, 283
St. Pierre Divion, 25, 49
St. Pierre Vaast Wood, 48, 72
St. Pol, 259
St. Quentin, 165, 168, 193
St. Yves, 286
Ste. Emilie, 191
Salisbury Plain, Artillery school at, 332
Salmond, Gen. J. M. (Sir), 237, 353
Salvage, Controller of, 338
Sambre, battle of the (Nov. 1-11), xii, 293-296, 361
Sambre Line (Nov. 4, 1918), *facing* 294
Sambre et Oise Canal, 291, 292
Sancourt, 283
Sanctuary Wood, 6, 114
Sapignies, 202, 268, 269
Sargent, Maj.-Gen. H. N., 352
Sassoon, Maj.-Gen. Sir Philip, 356
Sauchy Cauchy, 282
Sauchy Lestrée, 280, 282
Savy, 74, 189
Scarpe, battle of the (Aug. 26-Sept. 3), xii, 361; retaking of Monchy-le-Preux, 273, 274; storming of Drocourt-Quéant Line, 274, 275; enemy in retreat, 275, 276
Schaap Baillie, 286
Scheldt, 297
Schwaben Redoubt, 44, 45
Scott, Maj.-Gen. A. B., 28, 88 n., 154
Scottish Wood, 250
Searchlight Sections, Anti-Aircraft and, 139
Sebourg, 296
Selency, 74, 75
Selle River, battle of the (Oct. 17-25), xii, 287, 303, 361; forcing of the river crossings, 291-293; enemy's position at end of October, 293
Septième Barn, 108
Sequehart, 284
Serain, 288
Seranvillers, 288
Serre, 26, 67, 69, 264
Sewell, Brig.-Gen. J. W. S., 355
Shea, Maj.-Gen. J. S. M., 25 n., 88 n.
Shoubridge, Maj.-Gen. T. H., 75, 102
Shrewsbury Forest, 114, 115
Shute, Maj.-Gen. C. D., 50, 67, 74, 111, 213, 295
Sillem, Maj.-Gen. A. F., 353
Simms, Rev. J. M., 307, 355

Sinclair-MacLagan, Maj.-Gen. E. G., 124, 207, 277
Skinner, Maj.-Gen. P. C. B., 285
Sloggett, Lt.-Gen. Sir A. T., 239, 354
Smith, Maj.-Gen. W. D., 37 n., 118, 155, 193
Smoke shell, use of, 332
Smyth, Maj.-Gen. N. M., 72, 100, 250, 291
Snow, Lt.-Gen. Sir T. D'O., 25 n., 87
Solesmes, 292
Solly-Flood, Maj.-Gen. A., 202, 268
Somme, first battle of the—Overrunning of German entrenched positions, 24; opening assault (July 1), 25, 26; attack continued, 26–28; attack of July 14, 28–30; results (July 17), 30, 31; struggle for the ridge, 31–34; German strength, 33 n.; attack and counter-attack, 34, 35; problem of Guillemont, 35, 36; minor operations, 36; Guillemont taken, 36, 37; barrier broken—Ginchy, 37, 38; results achieved, 38, 39; exploitation of success, 39–41; attack (Sept. 15), 41, 42; Combles, 43; Thiepval, 44; further successes, 44–46; the situation, 46; other minor operations, 47, 48; Beaumont Hamel, 49; the assault, 49, 50; our other armies, 50, 51
Somme, second battle of the—Attack opened, 186, 187; Ronssoy captured, 187; struggle for battle zone, 188–190; first withdrawals, 190, 191; second day of battle, 191; fight for Crozat Canal, 191; Le Verguier and Epéhy lost, 191–192; battle on Third Army front, 192, 193; break through at St. Quentin, 193, 194; withdrawal to the Somme, 194; decision to abandon the Peronne bridgehead, 195; Crozat Canal crossed, 195; crossing at Ham, 196; northern front firm, 197; retreat to the Tortille, 197, 198; extension of French front, 198; retreat across the Somme battlefield, 199, 200; fight for the Somme crossings, 200, 201; retreat from Chauny, 201, 202; the Ancre crossed, 202, 203; situation south of the Somme, 204; enemy in Noyon, 204; retreat from the Somme, 205; Carey's force, 205; attempt to sever Allied armies, 206; northern advance stopped, 207; withdrawal from Bray-sur-Somme, 207, 208; General Foch appointed Generalissimo, 208; enemy in Albert, 208; fight for Rosières line, 209; Amiens defences, 210; attack on Arras, 211, 212; end of first stage, 213; fighting in the Avre and Luce Valleys, 213–215; final effort, 215; reason for retirement on right of battle front, 216–218
Somme Line (July 1, 1916), *facing* 25; (July 14), *facing* 29; (Sept 15), *facing* 41; (Sept. 25, 26), *facing* 44; (Nov. 13), *facing* 49; (March 21, 1918), *facing* 186; (March 23–April 5), *facing* 196
Souchez River, 93
Sound ranging, 331 n.
Spanbroekmolen, 104, 231
Staff Colleges, 344
Steenbeek, 114, 116, 117
Steenwerck, 226
Stephens, Maj.-Gen. R. B., 34, 89 n., 251, 290
Stirling Castle, 114
Stockley, Brig.-Gen. A. F. U., 192
Strength of British armies on Western front (Jan.–July, 1916), 19 n.
Strickland, Maj.-Gen. E. P., 29, 111, 230, 283
Stroombeek, 126
Stuart, Maj.-Gen. Sir A. M., 355
Stuart-Wortley, Maj.-Gen. E. J. Montague, 25 n.
Stuff Redoubt, 44, 48
Supplies, Directorate of, 337
Suspension of Sentences Act, 341

Tadpole Copse, 160–162
Tandy, Brig.-Gen. E. Napper, 356
Tank Corps Mechanical School, 345
Tanks in action, 42, 55
Tara Hill, 267
Templeux-le-Guérard, 187, 276
Tergnier, 191, 195
Terhand, 286
Thélus, 90
Thiepval, 24, 26, 44, 49, 268
Thilloy, 70
Thomson, Maj.-Gen. J., 354
Thorigny, 283, 284
Thourout, 290
Thuillier, Maj.-Gen. H. F., 113 n.
Thun St. Martin, 289
Thwaites, Maj.-Gen. W., 110
Tilloy-lez-Mofflaines, 74
Tournai, 297, 298
Training, Inspectorate of, 346
Transport, Directorate of, 335, 337
Trench weapons, 345
Trenchard, Maj.-Gen. Sir H. M., 353
Trentino, Austrian attack in the, 19 n.
Trescault, 276

INDEX

Troisvilles, 288
Trônes Wood, 28, 29, 269
Trouville, hospital at, 338
Tudor, Maj.-Gen. H. H., 189, 251
Turcoing, 291
Turner, Col. E. V., 351
Turner, Maj.-Gen. R. E. W., 8, 42
22 Ravine, 165
Twining, Maj.-Gen. P. G., 353

Umfreville, Brig.-Gen. P., 355
Uniacke, Maj.-Gen. H. C. C., 352
Usna Hill, 267

Vaire Wood, 215
Valenciennes, 294
Vallières, Gen. des, 356
Van Straubenzee, Maj.-Gen. C. C., 352
Vaughan, Maj.-Gen. J., 92, 352, 355
Vaulx, 193, 197, 271
Veldhoek, 122, 128
Vélu, 73
Vendegies-sur-Ecaillon, 293
Venhuile, 162, 283
Verdun, moral and political importance of, 51, 52
Verlaines, 196
Verlorenhoek, 114
Vermelles, 9
Vesle, 253
Veterinary Services, Directorate of, 336
Vieille Chapelle, 222
Vierstraat, 233
Viesly, 288
Vieux Berquin, 227, 264
Villeret, 187
Villers Bretonneux, 231, 232, 251
Villers Bretonneux (April 25, 1918), *facing* 231
Villers Cotterets Forest, 253
Villers Faucon, 74, 192
Villers Guislain, 165, 168, 282, 284
Villers-les-Cagnicourt, 275
Villers Outréaux, 288
Villers Plouich, 192
Villeselve, 201
Ville-sur-Ancre, 250
Vimy Ridge, 20, 89, 90, 94
Vis-en-Artois, 274
Von Below, 199 n.
Voormezeele, 233, 234
Vraucourt, 193
Vrély, 210

Wace, Brig.-Gen. E. G., 355
Wagstaff, Brig.-Gen. C. M., 356
Walker, Maj.-Gen. H. B. (Sir), 35, 102 n., 227, 250

Wancourt, 93, 94, 273
Wardrop, Maj.-Gen. A. E., 353
Ware, Maj.-Gen. Fabian, 355
Warfusée-Abancourt, 210
Wargnies-le-Grand, 296
Wargnies-le-Petit, 296
Warlencourt-Eaucourt, 69
Warnave valley, 223
Warnbeke valley, 108
Waterlot Farm, 30, 34
Watson, Maj.-Gen. D. (Sir), 65 n., 89 n., 281
Watts, Maj.-Gen. H. E. (Lt.-Gen. Sir), 25 n., 66, 87, 184, 290
Wearing-out battle—Opening of—general situation towards end of May, 19, 20; preparations for the Somme battle, 21; enemy's position, 21–23; arrangement, 23, 24; the first Somme battle, 24–51; our other armies, 50, 51; our main objects achieved, 51–53; our troops, 53–57; Army Commanders and Staffs, 57, 58; our Allies, 58; future prospects, 58, 59.
See also Somme, first battle of the.
Wedgwood, Brig.-Gen. R. L., 355
Welsh Ridge, 155, 169, 181, 282
Wervicq, 286
Westhoek, 115, 117
Weston, Gen. Sir A. Hunter, 291
Whigham, Maj.-Gen. Sir R. D., 297
Whippet tanks, 207
White, Maj.-Gen. Sir C. B. B., 352
White Château, 107
Wigram, Brig.-Gen. K., 356
Wijdendrift, 118
Wilkinson, Maj.-Gen. P. S., 94
Willerval, 94
Williams, Maj.-Gen. H. B., 65 n., 88 n., 216, 268
Williams, Maj.-Gen. P. S., 41 n.
Williams, Maj.-Gen. W. de L., 113 n., 189, 286
Wonderwork, 41
Wood, Maj.-Gen. P. R., 124 n.
Woollecombe, Maj.-Gen. Sir C. L., 41
Works, Directorate of, 339
Wulverghem, 8
Wytschaete, 107, 223, 224, 228–230, 232, 286

Ypres, third battle of—Preliminary stages, 111, 112; Yser Canal crossed, 112; plan of first attack, 112, 113; battle opened, 113–115; results of first day, 115; effects of the weather, 116; hostile counter-attacks—St. Julien and Westhoek, 116, 117; Lens operations resumed—Hill 70,

Ypres, third battle of—*continued*
117; Langemarck, 118, 119; effects of hostile resistance—methods revised, 119, 120; minor operations, 120; preparations for third attack completed, 121; Menin Road Ridge, 121, 122; counter-attacks, 123; Polygon Wood and Zonnebeke, 123, 124; further counter-attacks, 124; further advance on main ridge—Broodseinde, 125, 126; results, 127; Houthulst Forest reached, 128, 129; progress continued, 129; plan of subsequent operations, 130;

Merckem peninsula, 130, 131; Passchendaele, 132
Ypres-Comines Canal, 6
Ypres Line (July 31, 1917), *facing* 113; (Sept. 20), *facing* 121; (Sept. 26), *facing* 123; (Oct. 4), *facing* 125
Yser Canal, 112

Zandvoorde, 286
Zevenkote, 122
Zillebeke Lake, 137
Zollern Redoubt, 44
Zonnebeke, 122, 124, 286

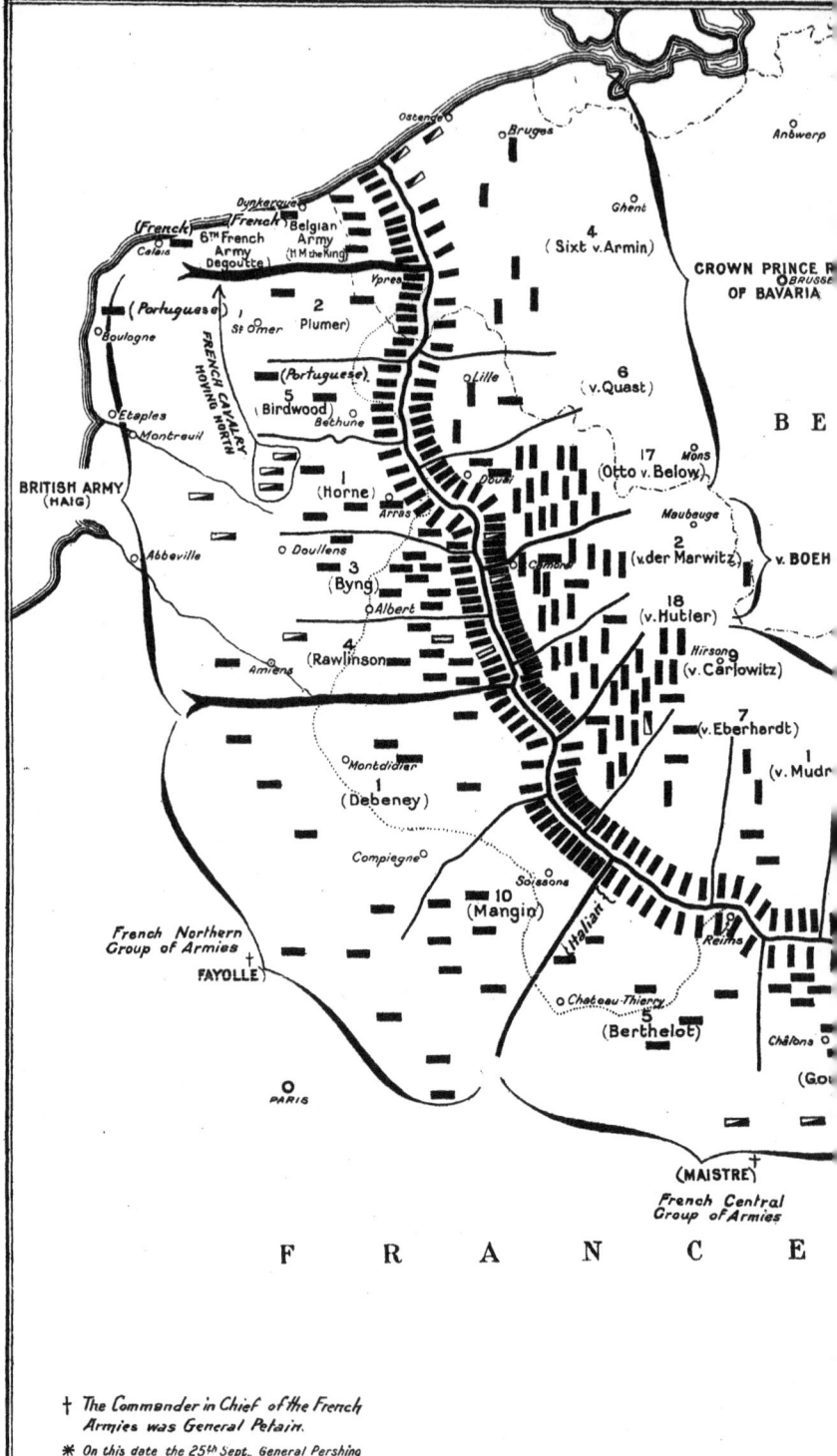

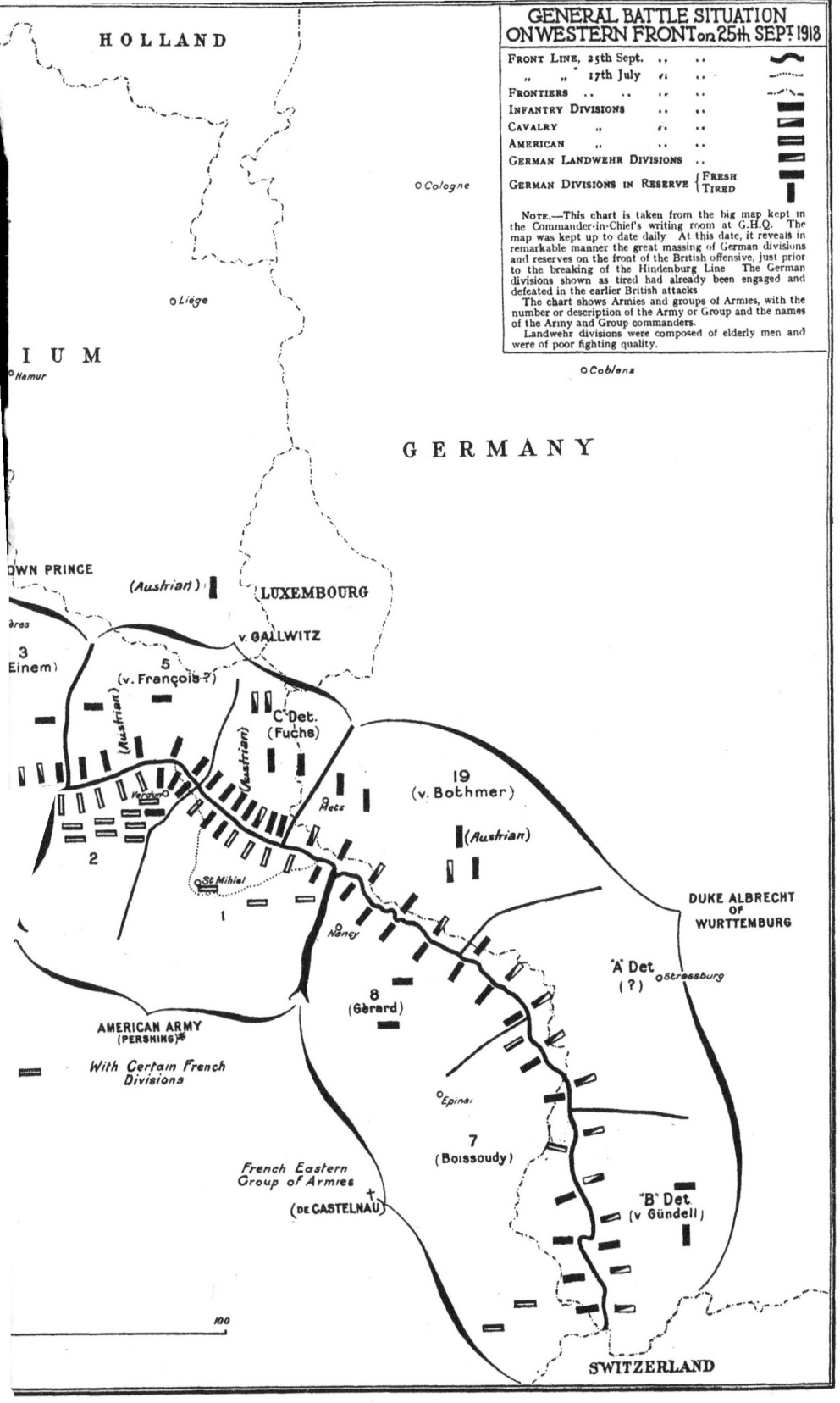

www.ingramcontent.com/pod-product-compliance
Lightning Source LLC
Chambersburg PA
CBHW071354300426
44114CB00016B/2065